Attention in Action

Attention in Action
Advances from Cognitive Neuroscience

Edited by
Glyn W. Humphreys and
M. Jane Riddoch

Psychology Press
Taylor & Francis Group
HOVE AND NEW YORK

First published 2005
by Psychology Press

27 Church Road, Hove, East Sussex BN3 2FA

Simultaneously published in the USA and Canada
by Psychology Press
270 Madison Avenue, New York, NY 10016

Psychology Press is a part of the Taylor & Francis Group

Copyright © 2005 Psychology Press

Typeset in Goudy by RefineCatch Limited, Bungay, Suffolk
Printed and bound in Great Britain by
TJ International, Padstow, Cornwall

British Library Cataloguing in Publication Data
A catalogue record for this book is available from the British Library

Library of Congress Cataloging-in-Publication Data
Attention in action : advances from cognitive neuroscience / edited by
Glyn Humphreys and Jane Riddoch.
    p. cm. – (Advances in behavioural brain science)
Includes bibliographical references and index.
  ISBN 1-84169-354-5 (hardcover)
   1. Attention.   2. Clinical neuropsychology.   3. Cognitive
therapy.   4. Psychology, Pathological.   I. Humphreys, Glyn W.
II. Riddoch, M. Jane.   III. Series.
RC455 4.A85A885 2004
616.8–dc22

                            2003021537

ISBN 1-84169-354-5

Contents

Contributors

Tamsin Astor-Jack, Institute of Cognitive Neurosciences, University College London, Alexandra House, 17 Queen Square, London WC1N 3AR, UK

Harold Bekkering, Department of Experimental Psychology, Nijmegen Institute for Cognition and Information (NICI), University of Nijmegen, PO Box 9104, 6500 HE Nijmegen, The Netherlands

Umberto Castiello, Department of Psychology, Royal Holloway and Bedford New College, University of London, Egham Hill, Egham, Surrey, UK

Heidi Chapman, Howard Florey Institute, Centre for Neuroscience, University of Melbourne, Melbourne 3010, Australia

Asher Cohen, Department of Psychology, The Hebrew University, Jerusalem 91905, Israel

Dylan F. Cooke, Department of Psychology, Princeton University, Princeton, NJ 08544, USA

Frans W. Cornelissen, Laboratory of Experimental Ophthalmology, School for Behavioral and Cognitive Neurosciences (BCN), University of Groningen, PO Box 30.001, 9700 RB Groningen, The Netherlands

Shai Danziger, Department of Psychology, Ben Gurion University of the Negev, 84105 Beer Sheva, Israel

Sarah de Maeght, Department of Cognition and Action, Max Planck Institute for Psychological Research, Amalienstrasse 33, 80799 Munich, Germany

Heiner Deubel, Department of Psychology, Ludwig-Maximilians-Universität, Leopoldstrasse 13, 80802 München, Germany

Martin G. Edwards, Behavioural Brain Sciences, School of Psychology, University of Birmingham, Edgbaston, Birmingham B15 2TT, UK

Gary Egan, Howard Florey Institute, Centre for Neuroscience, University of Melbourne, Melbourne 3010, Australia

Amanda Ellison, Department of Psychology, University of Durham, Stockton Campus, Stockton-on-Tees TS17 6BH, UK

Maria Gavrilescu, Howard Florey Institute, Centre for Neuroscience, University of Melbourne, Melbourne 3010, Australia

Michael S.A. Graziano, Department of Psychology, Princeton University, Princeton, NJ 08544, USA

Sarah Grison, Beckman Institute, University of Illinois at Urbana-Champaign, 405 North Mathews Avenue, Urbana, IL 61801, USA

Patrick Haggard, Institute of Cognitive Neurosciences, University College London, Alexandra House, 17 Queen Square, London WC1N 3AR, UK

Aave Hannus, Department of Experimental Psychology, Nijmegen Institute for Cognition and Information (NICI), University of Nijmegen, PO Box 9104, 6500 HE Nijmegen, The Netherlands

Glyn W. Humphreys, Behavioural Brain Sciences, School of Psychology, University of Birmingham, Edgbaston, Birmingham B15 2TT, UK

Masud Husain, Division of Neuroscience and Psychological Medicine, Imperial College, University of London, London W6 8RF, UK

Georgina M. Jackson, Institute of Neuroscience, School of Psychology, The University of Nottingham, University Park, Nottingham NG7 2RD, UK

Stephen R. Jackson, Institute of Neuroscience, School of Psychology, The University of Nottingham, University Park, Nottingham NG7 2RD, UK

Heather Jordan, Department of Experimental Psychology, Oxford University, South Parks Road, Oxford OX1 3UD, UK

Michael Kean, Howard Florey Institute, Centre for Neuroscience, University of Melbourne, Melbourne 3010, Australia

Klaus Kessler, Department of Neurology, University of Düsseldorf, D-40225 Düsseldorf, Germany

Lothar Knuf, Department of Cognition and Action, Max Planck Institute for Psychological Research, Amalienstrasse 33, 80799 Munich, Germany

Nilli Lavie, Department of Psychology, University College London, Gower Street, London WC1E 6BT, UK

Karina J. Linnell, Department of Psychology, Goldsmiths College, University of London, New Cross, London SE14 6NW, UK

Hagit Magen, Department of Psychology, The Hebrew University, Jerusalem 91905, Israel

Tirin Moore, Department of Psychology, Princeton University, Princeton, NJ 08544, USA

Dominic Mort, Division of Neuroscience and Psychological Medicine, Imperial College, University of London, London W6 8RF, UK

Sebastian F.W. Neggers, Helmholtz Research Institute, Utrecht University, Psychonomics Division, Heidelberglaan 2, 3584 CS Utrecht, The Netherlands

Roger Newport, Institute of Neuroscience, School of Psychology, The University of Nottingham, University Park, Nottingham NG7 2RD, UK

Richard E. Passingham, Department of Experimental Psychology, University of Oxford, South Parks Road, Oxford OX1 3UD, UK

Matthew A. Paul, Department of Psychology, University of Wales Bangor, Bangor, Gwynedd LL57 2PX, UK

Sally Pears, Institute of Neuroscience, School of Psychology, The University of Nottingham, University Park, Nottingham NG7 2RD, UK

Wolfgang Prinz, Department of Cognition and Action, Max Planck Institute for Psychological Research, Amalienstrasse 33, 80799 Munich, Germany

David J. Punt, Behavioural Brain Sciences, School of Psychology, University of Birmingham, Edgbaston, Birmingham B15 2TT, UK

M. Jane Riddoch, Behavioural Brain Sciences, School of Psychology, University of Birmingham, Edgbaston, Birmingham B15 2TT, UK

James B. Rowe, Wellcome Department of Imaging Neuroscience, Institute of Neurology, University College London, London WC1E 6BT, UK

Matthew F.S. Rushworth, Department of Experimental Psychology and Centre for Functional Magnetic Resonance Imaging of the Brain (FMRIB), University of Oxford, Oxford OX3 1UD, UK

Katz Sakai, Wellcome Department of Imaging Neuroscience, Institute of Neurology, University College London, London WC1E 6BT, UK

Werner X. Schneider, Department of Psychology, Ludwig-Maximilians-Universität, Leopoldstrasse 13, 80802 München, Germany

Rachel Swainson, Institute of Neuroscience, School of Psychology, The University of Nottingham, University Park, Nottingham NG7 2RD, UK

Charlotte S.R. Taylor, Department of Psychology, Princeton University, Princeton, NJ 08544, USA

Steven P. Tipper, Department of Psychology, University of Wales Bangor, Bangor, Gwynedd LL57 2PX, UK

Robert Ward, Centre for Cognitive Neuroscience, School of Psychology, University of Wales Bangor, Bangor, Gwynedd LL57 2PX, UK

Barbara Wilson, MRC Cognition and Brain Sciences Unit, Cambridge CB2 2QQ, UK

Alan M. Wing, Behavioural Brain Sciences, School of Psychology, University of Birmingham, Edgbaston, Birmingham B15 2TT, UK

Preface

The external world is a complex place, full of many objects, and we have only a limited number of effectors with which we can make actions. Because of these constraints, we must limit our processing of stimuli and our planning of actions, so that we behave efficiently to meet our behavioural goals. Some of the constraints on stimulus processing may be influenced directly by our actions, so that, for example, processing is enhanced at locations and for stimulus dimensions that are relevant to a given movement (see Chapters 1, 3 and 6). Similarly, some of the ways that perception is organized can influence the programming and selection of actions to objects (see Chapters 1 and 13). There may be independent processes concerned with selecting stimuli for action and selecting the appropriate actions to make to stimuli (see Chapters 2, 7 and 10), and between the processes leading to internally and externally driven actions (see Chapters 4 and 5). Furthermore, there may be interactions between different action systems, and direct coding of complex actions based on the goal of the action (see Chapter 9), which, in turn, can influence how we attend to stimuli (see Chapter 13). The processes involved in the selection of action to objects not only operate over the short term, determining momentary priorities of stimuli and actions, but also over the longer term, modulated by (among other things) long-term inhibition of episodic memories (see Chapter 8).

Traditionally, the study of attention has tended to emphasize the processes involved in selecting stimuli for action. In contrast, the processes and brain mechanisms involved in selecting the appropriate action to objects, and the interactions between selective perception and action, have been somewhat neglected. Recently, however, this has changed. This change comes partially through the development of new procedures for measuring actions accurately, and for measuring the relations between attention and action (three-dimensional kinematic analysis, saccadic contingent display changes). The change has also been facilitated by the use of new brain imaging procedures that enable us to assess the relations between activation in neural areas concerned with perception and action (see Chapters 11 and 12), and by intervention techniques that allow us to assess the consequences of directly altering neuronal activation (see Chapters 9 and 10). These new procedures both support and extend more traditional approaches to analysing the relations between brain function and behaviour, through neuropsychological analyses of patients. Nevertheless, such neuropsychological studies can often provide the starting place for convergent work, since they can indicate counterintuitive ways in which performance fractionates when attentional coupling between perception and action is disrupted (or, indeed, left intact, when other attentional functions are disturbed; see Chapters 1 and 14).

In this book, we have brought together contributions from leading researchers in the field that highlight the relations between attention and action (in both perceptual selection and action selection). The chapters are built around the first Behavioural Brain Sciences Symposium, held at the Behavioural Brain Sciences Centre, University of Birmingham, UK, in September 2002. We were delighted to host such a distinguished set of contributors and we hope both the meeting and the chapters that have emerged will help advance our understanding of the interactions between attention and action—a topic central to the psychology of both perception and action.

We have divided the 14 chapters according to whether they deal with the functional relations between attention and action or whether they deal with the underlying brain mechanisms. In the first chapter in Part I, Humphreys *et al.* use experimental studies with both normal and neuropsychological individuals to evaluate how action and attention interact. We summarize recent neuropsychological and experimental evidence indicating that there is a close coupling between action and attention. This coupling can be affected by the placement of objects in potent positions for action, with the positional relations between objects affecting both visual selection and action selection. In addition, new evidence is presented demonstrating that the effects of object-relations interact with the effects of action towards an object, and that action towards an object can modulate "object-based" selection—making a part represented as the target object for selection or emphasizing spatial selection at the expense of the selection of whole objects.

In Chapter 2, Cohen and Magen examine the proposal that there are two distinct attentional networks, one "executive" network dealing with action-related selection and another specialized for visual attention (dedicated to selection among input stimuli). They further propose that the systems are hierarchically related. The lower-level network (e.g. visual attention) operates to resolve online conflicts, at both the input and output ends of processing, with a limited set of selection cues (e.g. location or feature-enhancement). The higher-level network is recruited for selection primarily when these lower-level cues are not available.

Some of the experiments reported in the chapter by Humphreys et al. examine the effects of movement on the deployment of visual attention, showing a strong coupling between movement and attention. The paradigm used in these studies was invented by Deubel and Schneider and, in Chapter 3, they investigate covert selective attention in more complex movement situations, as when sequential eye and hand movements are directed to two targets, when we make reaching movements around an obstacle, when movements are delayed and when we grasp an object. Similar to the results reported in Humphreys et al., Deubel and Schneider find that visual attention is largely confined to the action-relevant parts of the object—that is, those parts that will be grasped. They argue for the existence of covert sensorimotor selection processes (influenced by both visual and motor stimuli), which occur before complex open movements are initiated.

In Chapter 4, Prinz et al. examine the relations between the effects of intending to make an action and the effects of perceptually cueing a so-called "ideomotor action", made in response to another action (e.g. yawning in response to someone else yawning). They develop a new paradigm in which participants see a ball going towards or away from a target. Participants can alter the trajectory of the ball's movement through a mouse, but only for a certain period of time (the instrumental period), after which their movements are not effective (the induction period). Movements made during the induction period can then be assessed to determine whether they are driven by the ball ("perceptual induction") or by the intended action ("intentional induction"). Prinz et al. report that intentional induction is weaker, and perceptual induction stronger, with other-generated than with self-generated actions. This work, then, begins to unpick the nature of ideomotor actions, to understand the extent to which they are induced by intention or simply by observing an event.

Astor-Jack and Haggard also focus on the interactions between internally generated actions and externally triggered actions in Chapter 5. They, too, use a novel experimental procedure (the "truncation procedure") in which participants have to prepare an intentional action but which can be truncated so that they make the same action but to a perceptual event. They find a substantial cost of truncation relative to when participants make the same response just to the perceptual event, and this is attributed to the need to switch from the control of action by an intentional system to control by a reactive response system. In this case, there are attentional constraints on selecting the same response through different "action control" systems.

In Chapter 6, Hannus and colleagues examine the effects of the intended response on the selection of perceptual events. They discuss evidence suggesting that the constraints of a task can sensitize visual selection to properties of the world relevant to the particular action (e.g. making a grasp response heightens our sensitivity to orientation information). They argue that the perception of specific object features and the planning of an action to interact with an object are to some extent tapping into the same mechanism. Again, action affects perceptual selection.

In Chapter 7, Lavie deals not just with how we select a particular target (and an action to that target), but also how we prevent responses to distractors. She argues that responses to distractors are prevented either through reduced distractor perception or through active inhibition of responses to irrelevant distractors, depending on factors such as the perceptual load of a task. The results from several new experiments are reported, which show reduced distractor perception under conditions of high perceptual load and also the involvement of active response inhibition when distractors are rejected under low load conditions. Here specific attentional processes may be recruited for the control of action.

In the last chapter in Part 1, Grison et al. discuss the role of inhibition of return (IOR) in the control of action. They review imaging and neuropsychological evidence distinguishing between IOR of spatial locations and IOR of objects, and they provide novel evidence for long-lasting object-based IOR, operating over at least 20 minutes. This new evidence suggests that there can be inhibition of episodic memory traces, affecting behaviour over the long term. This object-based IOR provides a flexible mechanism for selecting objects for action.

In Part II, the chapters deal more specifically with the neural underpinnings of attention in action. In Chapter 9, Graziano et al. discuss recent studies from their laboratory in which they examined motor responses elicited by prolonged stimulation of motor cortex and surrounding regions. In contrast to previous work, Graziano et al. demonstrate that complex, goal-directed movements can be evoked from stimulation. Stimulation of primary motor cortex generates actions in central space, where monkeys most often manipulate objects with their fingers. Stimulation in premotor cortex evoked a variety of other responses, including apparent defensive movements (e.g. to defend the head). These striking findings contradict the view that actions are constructed in a hierarchical fashion, suggesting instead that the motor cortex may include a topographic map of postures that are of behavioural relevance to individuals.

In the Chapter 10, Rushworth and Ellison differentiate between parietal areas concerned with attention to movement and those concerned with visuospatial attention. Thus lesions and transcranial magnetic stimulation (TMS) of posterior parietal cortex affect the redirecting of visuospatial attention from one location to another, while lesions and TMS of left anterior parietal cortex interfere with the redirecting of motor attention from one movement to another. Hence at a neural level, some distinction is possible between attentional circuits involved in the control of action and visuospatial attention, even if these processes interact at a functional level (see also Chapters 1 and 3).

In Chapter 11, Passingham et al. discuss fMRI studies for the learning of motor sequences. They demonstrate activity in the dorsal prefrontal cortex during initial learning, which subsequently reduces to baseline levels. However, the dorsal prefrontal cortex is reactivated when participants are asked to attend to their actions. They argue that, during attention to action, there are top-down interactions between the prefrontal and premotor areas, with the prefrontal cortex serving to integrate information about the external context and the individual's goals.

Chapman et al., in Chapter 12, attempt to identify the neural correlates underlying selective reaching and grasping when multiple objects are present. When targets appeared at predictable locations, activations in the left parieto-occipital sulcus and the right intraparietal sulcus were found; however, when the distractors were visible at all times, reducing the need for selection, only the right occipital cortex was found to be more activated when the distractors were present relative to when they were absent. Chapman et al. suggest that the left parieto-occipital sulcus and the right intraparietal sulcus specifically mediate the selection of objects for action.

In Chapter 13, Jackson et al. present neuropsychological evidence on action control and planning. They document data from two patients with optic ataxia (a deficit in misreaching to visual information) following damage to parietal cortex. Traditionally, optic ataxia has been conceptualized as a problem in integrating spatially congruent eye and hand movements, due to damage to parietal systems that code and transform visual information for action. Jackson et al., however, argue for a different interpretation, suggesting instead that there is a problem in representing simultaneously two "visuomotor objects", in different frames of reference, for different actions (hand and eye movements). The parietal lobe may be crucially important for maintaining these "visuomotor objects" for independent actions.

In the final chapter, Ward and Danziger discuss the role of a subcortical structure, the pulvinar, in relation to the control of action. They question theories that the pulvinar is critical for the spatial filtering of stimuli on the contralesional side of space, arguing instead that the pulvinar is involved in modulating the activation of responses to such stimuli, especially under conditions of response competition. They suggest that the pulvinar appears to be involved both in binding a stimulus representation to a response, and in binding visual features to coherent representations of visual objects.

Taken together, the work reported here helps to provide new constraints on our understanding of the relations between attention and action, paving the way for the development of detailed accounts of perceptuo-motor function. We very much look forward to these developments, not least because of the prospect of generating theoretically informed therapies for patients with perceptuo-motor dysfunction.

We are very grateful to several organizations and individuals who made both the conference and this book possible. We thank the Experimental Psychology Society, whose workshop fund supported the conference, together with the Medical Research Council, Wellcome Trust and Stroke Association (UK), who fund our research. The running of the meeting was helped by Marietta Remoundou and Eun Young Yoon, and most especially by Elaine Fox. Thanks to you all.

Glyn W. Humphreys
M. Jane Riddoch
June 2003

Part I
Functional processes

1 Attending to what you are doing

Neuropsychological and experimental evidence for interactions between perception and action

*Glyn W. Humphreys, M. Jane Riddoch,
Karina J. Linnell, David J. Punt,
Martin G. Edwards and Alan M. Wing*

Abstract

What are the relations between perceptual selection (e.g. for object identification) and action selection (the selection of an appropriate action to an object)? We discuss four pieces of novel neuropsychological and experimental evidence indicating that perception and action interact in determining human performance. First, we show that action relations between stimuli constrain the amount of visual extinction present in neuropsychological patients. There is less extinction when objects are in the correct co-locations for action. In addition, action relations between objects can lead to the coupling of movements to objects in patients who otherwise show uncoupled actions to separate objects (in Balint's syndrome and in a case of motor extinction). Thus action relations between stimuli affect both perceptual selection (in cases of extinction) and action selection (in Balint's syndrome and motor extinction). Subsequently, we note evidence indicating that (1) action relations between objects and (2) actions to objects combine multiplicatively in their effects on visual selection. Finally, we introduce evidence from normal observers showing that action to an object can change the nature of the processes mediating visual selection. Perception and action are coupled when there are action relations between objects in the environment and when actions are made towards stimuli.

Perceptual selection and selection for action

Over the last 10 years or so, a good deal of evidence has accumulated that perception and action can dissociate from one another (for reviews, see Milner & Goodale, 1995; Rossetti & Pisella, 2002). For example, damage to different brain regions can selectively disrupt either perception but not action to visual stimuli (e.g. after damage to ventral areas mediating visual processing), or action but not the perception of stimuli (e.g. after damage to more dorsal areas of cortex). Similarly, the effects of some visual illusions can be larger on perceptual judgements than on actions (Aglioti, DeSouza, & Goodale, 1995; Bridgeman, 2002; Haffenden & Goodale, 1998; for alternative views, see Franz et al., 2000; Pavani et al., 1999), while effects of temporal delay can be larger on action than on perceptual judgement tasks (Milner & Goodale, 1995). This contrast between perception and action may extend also to the processes involved in selecting between multiple stimuli for perception and in selecting the appropriate actions to a stimulus (selection for perception and selection for action). Neuroanatomical research indicates that selection for perception and selection for action to visual stimuli depend, respectively, on networks within anterior (frontal) and more posterior (parieto-occipital) regions (e.g. Posner & Petersen, 1990). Neuropsychological research indicates that patients with parietal damage can be impaired in the perceptual selection of stimuli on one side of space, rather than in acting to the affected side. For example, when required to cancel lines seen through a mirror, patients can have problems in orienting visual attention towards stimuli on the perceived contralesional side of space, even when an action to that stimulus would be made on the ipsilesional side. In contrast, they may orient appropriately to stimuli on the perceived ipsilesional side even when their actions are then made on the contralesional side (e.g. Ackroyd et al., 2002; Na, Adair, Williamson, Schwartz, Haws, & Heilman, 1998). This suggests a problem in perceptual selection rather than in acting towards the affected side. In contrast, patients with damage to, or disconnection of, more frontal brain regions can be impaired in selecting a task-appropriate action to a stimulus even though they select the appropriate stimulus to make an action to (e.g. Riddoch, Humphreys, & Edwards, 2000a, 2000b). In this case, action selection seems to be impaired while perceptual selection continues to operate. On this view, there are separate systems not only for object identification and the parameretization of actions to objects (e.g. Milner & Goodale, 1995), but also for selecting the objects to identify and the actions to make in the first place.

Dissociations between tasks are useful for highlighting structural constraints on information processing, since they indicate that the processing system must have an anatomical and functional organization such that one task can be affected more than another. However, this does not rule out the possibility that processes that are isolatable under some circumstances nevertheless interact to determine normal performance. Indeed, there is mounting evidence that perception can be affected by action. For example, our ability to identify briefly presented stimuli is tightly bound to where an action is made. Deubel, Schneider and colleagues (e.g. Deubel & Schneider, 1996, this volume; Deubel, Schneider, & Paprotta, 1998; Schneider & Deubel, 2002) have presented elegant evidence that identification is improved if we point to a location where a stimulus appears, relative to when we point to another location close by. This appears to be a necessary coupling, because the same result occurs even when the stimulus is presented at a constant location; if perceptual selection could normally be insulated from effects of action, then we ought to be able to set perceptual selection to the known stimulus location independent of where an action is directed to. In addition, perceptual judgements (such as whether stimuli are inverted or not) are affected by the position of the handle of the stimulus with respect to the effector used for the response and by compatibility between the particular response required (fine *vs* power-grip) and the response typically used with the object (Ellis & Tucker, 2000; Tucker & Ellis, 1998, 2001). This suggests that perception is influenced by action-related properties of objects (e.g. the degree to which an object "affords" a particular action; cf. Gibson, 1979; see Phillips & Ward, 2002, for an alternative account of some of these last results). Even in frontal-lobe patients showing dissociations between (impaired) action selection and (spared) perceptual selection, there can be incorrect selection of a stimulus for action if a distractor has the same perceptual attribute as that of a stimulus that was recently responded to and if the distractor carries a strong affordance (Boutsen & Humphreys, 2003). Here a temporary association between the perceptual attribute recently used for selection, the affordance of the stimulus and the response last made seems to increase the potency of that attribute for subsequent perceptual selection. Thus perception appears to be sensitive to action-related properties of stimuli, while perceptual selection is influenced by where an action is directed to and by temporary associations between perceptual attributes, object affordances for action and the recent response history. Perceptual selection and action selection may interact in determining both the object to which an action is directed and the action that is used.

In this chapter, we review recent neuropsychological and experimental evidence from our laboratory supporting the view that perceptual selection and action selection are interactive processes. The evidence is also relevant to the form of the interactions between the processes. For example, we suggest that action relations between objects in the environment play an important role in both perceptual selection and action selection, enhancing any effect of action towards an object. In addition, we propose that making an action to an object does not merely add to the processes that determine perceptual selection (e.g. increasing the activation of targets that are visually attended) but it changes the way they operate. We begin by first discussing the effects of action relations on perceptual selection and on action.

Action relations affect perceptual selection: evidence from visual extinction

There is a large amount of experimental and neuropsychological evidence that perceptual selection is influenced by factors that affect object recognition, such as whether visual elements group on the basis of a Gestalt property (e.g. continuation, collinearity, common motion), whether they form a known object, or whether separate objects are associatively related.

Particularly clear examples come from the neuropsychological syndrome of visual extinction, where patients (often with unilateral damage involving the parietal lobe) are good at selecting a single stimulus presented on the contralesional side of space but are unable to perceive the same item when another (independent) stimulus appears simultaneously on the ipsilesional side (e.g. Karnath, 1988). Extinction can decrease, however, if the contra- and ipsilesional stimuli group by continuation, collinearity, common enclosure, common shape and contrast polarity (e.g. Gilchrist, Humphreys, & Riddoch, 1996; Humphreys, 1998; Mattingley, Davis, & Driver, 1997; Ward, Goodrich, & Driver, 1994). Even when low-level Gestalt factors are unavailable to link stimuli, extinction can be reduced if stimuli are parts of a known object (e.g. if two letters form a word rather than a nonword; Kumada & Humphreys, 2001). It can also be reduced if two stimuli are associatively related to one another (e.g. with two associated words; see Coslett & Saffran, 1991). The factors that are influential here (Gestalt grouping, object unit formation and associative relations between stimuli) can all be conceptualized as operating within a system that jointly recognizes objects and selects between competing perceptual representations.

In addition, are the competitive processes underlying perceptual selection also sensitive to action relations between stimuli (e.g. whether or not two stimuli are in the appropriate locations to be used together)? Furthermore, are any effects of action relations dissociable from whether or not stimuli are associatively related or form a familiar unit for object recognition? Recently, we addressed these questions in studies of patients with visual extinction, where we assessed the effects of action relations between stimuli on perceptual selection (Riddoch, Humphreys, Edwards, Baker, & Willson, 2003). Five patients were tested, three with unilateral right parietal damage (JB, MB, MP), one with unilateral left parietal damage (RH) and one with bilateral parietal damage, more pronounced on the right than on the left (GK). All the patients showed spatial extinction, with items on the contralesional side of space being difficult to identify when another item appeared simultaneously on the ipsilesional side.[1] In a first experiment (Experiment 1), we assessed the identification of pairs of objects that were commonly used together and that were either placed in the correct spatial locations for actions (e.g. a corkscrew going into the top of a wine bottle) or placed in incorrect spatial locations for action (the corkscrew going into the bottom of the bottle; see Figure 1.1a). In both the correct and incorrect location conditions, the pairs were presented twice, with each object appearing once in each field. In addition, single-object trials were included in which each

---

1   For GK, we class his left side as contralesional and his right as ipsilesional, even though he has bilateral lesions, since the damage is more extensive within his right hemisphere and he shows left-side extinction.

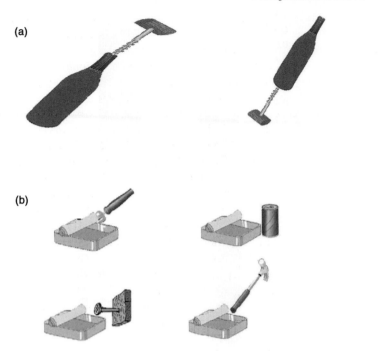

Figure 1.1 Example stimuli from studies examining the effects of action relations
between stimuli on visual extinction (after Riddoch et al., 2003). (a) The
stimuli used in Experiment 1 contrasting report when objects are in correct versus incorrect positions for action. (b) The stimuli employed in
Experiment 2 contrasting report with objects that are used jointly in action
versus objects that are verbally associated.

individual stimulus was exposed in the same location as it appeared in the
two-object trials. The task was to identify the objects presented on a trial,
and stimulus exposure times were adjusted for individual patients so that
they were able to identify about 80% of the contralesional objects on single-
item trials (Figure 1.2a). On two-object trials, performance was reliably better when the stimuli were placed in the correct positions for action relative
to when they fell in incorrect positions for action (Figure 1.2b). This held
across all the individual patients. This effect was not due to guessing. First,
the same objects were used in the correct and incorrect location conditions,
so the chances of guessing the identity of the contralesional item from the
ipsilesional one should have been equal. In addition, while some of the
patients reported that they could tell that "something" was present along
with the ipsilesional item on unsuccessful two-object trials, two patients
(MP and GK) made errors in which they reported that only an ipsilesional
item occurred, but they never made errors on single-item trials by guessing
the identity of a second object. Thus is appears that perceptual selection in

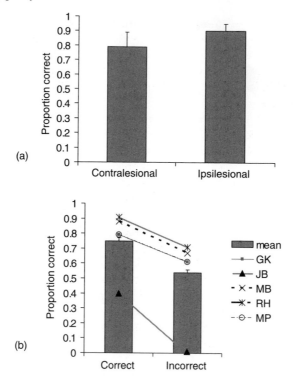

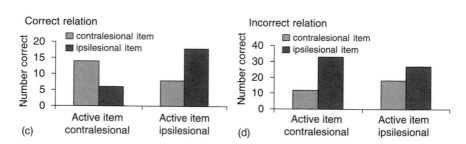

Figure 1.2 The results from Experiment 1. (a) Single-item reports. (b) Number of
correct reports of two objects. (c, d) Data from trials on which only one
object was reported (on two-item trials), as a function of whether the
objects were in the correct (c) or incorrect (d) positions for action (after
Riddoch et al., 2003).

the patients was better if two objects fell in the correct positions for action
relative to when they were in incorrect positions.

We also examined the performance of the patients when they only
reported one of the two objects present in a pair. We categorized each pair
according to whether an object was an "active" partner (that was moved
when the action was performed) or a "passive" partner (that was stationary

during the action). In the example in Figure 1a, the corkscrew was categorized as the active partner and the wine bottle as the passive partner. A clear difference emerged between the identification of the active and passive partners, on trials where only one was reported, in the correct and incorrect location conditions. In the correct location condition, the patients tended to identify the active member of a pair irrespective of whether it was in the contra- or ipsilesional field. However, when the objects fell in incorrect locations for action, the patients tended to report the ipsilesional item irrespective of whether it was the active or passive partner in the pair (see Figure 1.2c, d). This result is interesting, since it suggests that having the correct action relations between objects induces a bias in perceptual selection, where the active partner in an action tends to win any competition for selection. The effect of the action relationship here is implicit, and affects performance even when only one of the objects in a pair is identified.

It might be argued that the improved report on correct location trials in Experiment 1 was not due to the action relations between the stimuli but because we altered the visual familiarity of the object pair, when we varied their locations. Objects in the correct locations are more visually familiar as a pair than objects in incorrect locations, and hence only correct location objects may activate a higher-order recognition unit (e.g. for both objects, as a pair). We examined this possibility in a second experiment (Experiment 2) in which we contrasted the identification of objects that would be used together with objects that were associatively related but not directly used together in an action. Within each pair, one object was designated a target (e.g. a mallet) and it appeared along with either an action-related partner (e.g. a nail) or an associatively related partner (e.g. a hammer) (see Figure 1.1b). The associatively related items were determined on the basis of the Birkbeck College word association norms. The partner chosen as the associate to the target was given as the first verbal association to the target by over 32% of the sample in the norms. The object chosen as the action-related partner to the target was given as the first verbal association to the target by less than 3% of the sample. We also asked a group of independent participants to rate the visual familiarity of the objects, as a pair. There was no difference in the rated visual familiarity of the action-related pairs relative to the associatively related pairs. We tested three of the original patients (JB, RH and GK) and, for both the action-related and the associatively related items we generated control (unrelated) pairs in which we exchanged partners for different targets within the action or the association set.[2] All the stimuli appeared on both the contra- and ipsilesional sides, for each patient. There were also single-object

---

2   This meant that the same objects appeared in the action-related experimental condition and its control, and the same objects in the associatively related experimental condition and its control. Note that, because the partners were different in the two experimental conditions, direct comparisons cannot be made.

trials, adjusted so that patients identified about 80–90% of the contralesional objects.

    The results are presented in Figure 1.3. On single-object trials, there was a
small advantage for objects on the ipsilesional side (Figure 1.3a). On two-
object trials, performance was poorer due to spatial extinction; errors typically involved the ipsi- but not the contralesional object being identified.
Nevertheless, there were more object pairs correctly identified in the action-
related condition compared with its control. In contrast, there was no difference between the association condition and its control (Figure 1.3b, c). Given
that object pairs in the action-relation and the association conditions were
equally visually familiar, the relative improvement for action-related pairs
can be attributed to their being in the correct locations for action, and not to
their visual familiarity. Also note that, on a guessing account, we would
expect the association condition to be favoured, since objects in this condition were more likely to be generated as a verbal associate to the target
compared with the action condition. Instead, we suggest that objects placed
in correct locations for action tend to be perceptually selected together.
Perceptual selection is sensitive to action relations between objects.

Action relations affect action selection: evidence from Balint's syndrome and motor extinction

If action relations between stimuli affect perceptual selection, is there any
evidence that they might also affect the ability to select and effect actions? In
a third experiment, we evaluated this with GK, one of the original group of
patients used in Experiments 1 and 2. As we pointed out above, GK has
bilateral parietal lesions. Although he shows spatial extinction (favouring
right- over left-side items), he also demonstrates the cardinal symptoms of
Balint's syndrome (Balint, 1909), associated with bilateral parietal damage.
He often is able only to report a single stimulus at a time (requiring
abnormally long exposures before multiple items can be reported), and he
manifests optic ataxia (misreaching to visual targets; see Gilchrist *et al.*, 1996,
for a case description). Previously we have reported results from a study
examining GK's ability to make actions to visual stimuli (Edwards &
Humphreys, 2002). GK was presented with single stimuli (either on his left or
right) or he was presented bilaterally with two stimuli. He was asked to point
with either his left or right arm alone to the single left and single right targets,
or with both arms to the bilateral targets. Normally, bilateral pointing
movements are coordinated, so that actions start and finish at the same time
(e.g. Kelso, Southard, & Goodman, 1979). In contrast to this, we found that
GK's actions were completely uncoordinated, with one arm starting and
completing its movement before the other began. GK was unable to select
both pointing movements together, perhaps because of a severe limit in perceptually selecting the two stimuli in the first place. Interestingly, if there was
grouping between the stimuli to which GK had to move, then the kinematics

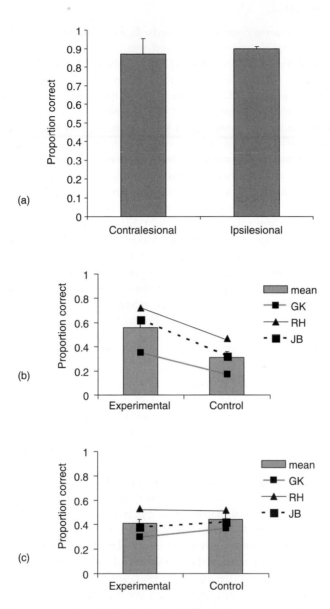

Figure 1.3 The results from Experiment 2. (a) Single-item reports. (b, c) Number of correct reports of two objects according to whether the objects were action-related (b) or associatively related (c) to one another (after Riddoch et al., 2003).

of his actions became coupled (Edwards & Humphreys, 2002). Grouping elements into a single object facilitated the programming of coordinated action. We have recently documented similar results in a patient with motor extinction rather than Balint's syndrome (Punt, Riddoch, & Humphreys, submitted). This patient, MM, had suffered right parietal and thalamic damage following a stroke. Nevertheless, she was able to make reasonable unilateral reach and grasp actions with her left as well as her right hand. In contrast, when she was asked to make bilateral reaches to two separate objects, her left hand movements were slow. Example results are depicted in Figure 1.4, where we illustrate the peak velocities reached by the right (dark line) and left hands (light line) when making unimanual and bimanual reaches (to separate objects). Note that the left hand reaches peak velocity a full second after the time taken by the right hand. We take this pattern, of impaired performance with the contralesional limb only under bimanual action conditions, to indicate a case of "motor extinction"—the contralesional limb seems to suffer competition when being activated for a motor response when there is simultaneous programming of a movement with the ipsilesional limb. In MM this was a modality-specific deficit and there was no indication of visual extinction. In a third condition conducted with MM, we linked the two objects by a connecting bar. Now the movements of MM's right and left hands became more closely coupled, with peak velocity being reached about the same time. This effect of coupling elements into a single object is particularly striking here because there was no evidence of perceptual extinction. Thus MM could perceive the two targets for action under all conditions, so that the effects of grouping cannot be attributed to improved perception; nevertheless, perceptual grouping still influenced motor programming. We elaborate further on why the effect might arise in the Conclusions section.

In one other study (Experiment 3), we asked whether these perceptual effects on action were determined not only by low-level relations between objects (e.g. the presence of a connecting bar between two elements), but also by associations between the stimuli and actions. In this experiment, we asked GK again to make either unimanual or bimanual pointing responses to stimuli (on single- and on two-item trials, respectively). However, we now introduced objects that were commonly used together, and placed them either in the correct positions for action (e.g. fork on the left, knife on the right) or in incorrect positions to be used directly together (fork on the right and knife on the left). At the start of each trial, either one or two objects were positioned directly in line with either his left or right hand, and a tone cued him to make the pointing action(s). Performance was videotaped so that the start of the actions could be seen but not the objects. Ten independent observers were then asked to decide whether, on bilateral trials, GK began his pointing responses simultaneously or sequentially. A movement was classed as simultaneous only if judged so by eight of the ten observers. There were 24 trials in each condition.

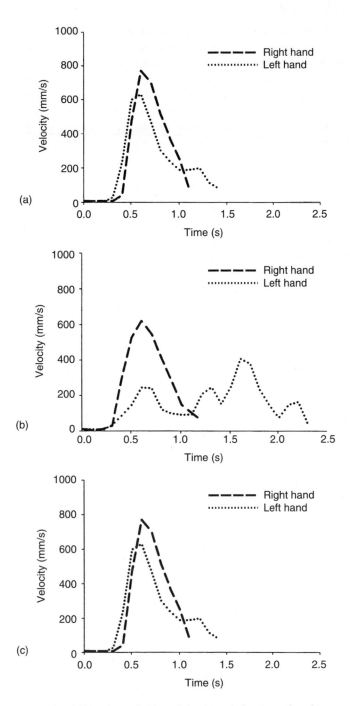

Figure 1.4 Examples of unimanual (a) and bimanual (b, c) reaches by patient MM (with motor extinction), with bimanual reaches either made to separate objects (b) or to parts of a single object (c).

Figure 1.5 gives the percentage of bilateral trials for which GK was classed as making simultaneous reaching movements. There was a clear advantage for objects positioned in the correct positions for action than for objects in the incorrect relative positions. Here the appropriate action relations between objects affected the ability to select and effect actions together. In GK's case, this might reflect an improvement on perceptual selection for the action-related stimuli (cf. Experiments 1 and 2); nevertheless, the net effect was that the initiation of actions became temporarily coupled.

The coupling of action to action relations: evidence from Balint's syndrome

Some of the clearest evidence for an interaction between perceptual selection and action comes from studies in which participants make actions to stimuli, when perceptual selection seems closely tied to the end location of the action (Deubel et al., 1998). In a further study with GK (Experiment 4), we examined how making an action towards a location combined with the effects of action relations between stimuli to influence perceptual selection. There were two parts to the study. First, to help overcome some of GK's problems in pointing to visual stimuli (see above), we trained him to point to four set locations: on his near left, far left, near right and far right (locations 1, 2, 3 and 4), respectively. GK was asked to make bimanual movement and was given either numbers 1 and 4 or 2 and 3 at the start of a training trial, and he then had to point to the locations (making bilaterally symmetric movements) as soon as he heard an auditory tone. Once he was trained to do this, we ran experimental trials in which objects were positioned at the locations (either at locations 1 and 4 or at locations 2 and 3). For these trials, GK wore PLATO

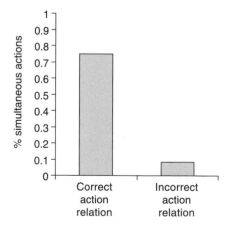

Figure 1.5 The percentage of trials on which GK was judged to initiate bimanual actions simultaneously as a function of whether the objects were in the correct or incorrect relative locations for action (Experiment 3).

spectacles that were opaque but cleared with millisecond timing to give him vision for a limited period (500 ms, starting from the onset of the tone at the start of each trial). On "pointing" trials, GK was given the numbers of the locations he was to point to, followed by a tone to make a bimanual reaching action. Simultaneously, the Plato spectacles cleared and then became opaque again as (typically) the reach was completed. At the end of each trial, he was asked whether he could identify any objects that were present. The objects were always presented in pairs and they could either be used together (fork and knife, toothpaste and toothbrush) or they were unrelated (fork and toothbrush, toothpaste and knife—the same objects as in the action-relation condition, but re-paired). The objects appeared in symmetrical locations (positions 1 and 4 or 2 and 3) and the pointing instruction was congruent with the locations of the objects on half the trials. In addition to "pointing" trials, we also included "cueing" trials, in which GK was simply told to pay attention (if he could) to the locations consistent with the numbers given at the start of each trial, but not to make a reaching movement. Cueing trials were otherwise identical to pointing trials (with action-related or unrelated objects being presented equally often, and the location cues being correct on 50% of the trials). GK took part in six sessions, with there being 10 trials of each type per session (action-related or unrelated, in a valid or an invalid location, randomly assigned), with the pointing and cueing trials presented in separate blocks in each session (order counterbalanced across sessions).

With the short exposures used here, GK never reported two items on a trial. However, as we observed in Experiment 1 (see Figure 1.2c, d), performance was affected by our manipulations even when he only reported one item on a trial. The results are shown in Figure 1.6. Overall, GK was more likely to identify one of the objects on a trial if it was part of an action-related pair than if it appeared in an unrelated pair. He was also more likely to identify one of the objects if it was a "pointing" trial than if it was a "cueing" trial, and if it was in a valid rather than an invalid location. Most importantly, movement (pointing *vs* cueing) interacted with location validity and type of pair (action related *vs* unrelated). The advantage for related over unrelated pairs was increased if GK was asked to make a pointing movement (relative to when he was cued to attend to the two locations), and if the pointing movement was made to valid locations (where the objects were positioned). The effect of making a movement was not due to generally increased arousal (which could have been increased when an action was required), since there was no advantage for pointing over cueing trials when objects appeared in invalid locations. Given that, at most, only one object per trial was identified, the difference between related and unrelated pairs also cannot be attributed to guessing from an ipsilesional stimulus. The results are, however, consistent with perceptual selection being improved when an action is made to the location where a target object is presented, and with this enhancing any implicit effect due to the objects present being action-related.

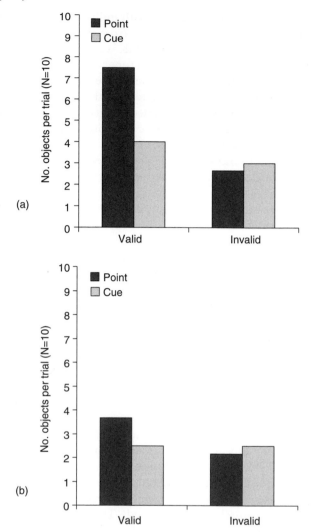

Figure 1.6 The number of correct reports by GK of one object for (a) objects used together in action and (b) unrelated objects, as a function of whether he was required to point or merely cued to object locations, and according to whether the pointing response or cue was valid or invalid (Experiment 4).

We have conducted further variations of this study in which GK made only a unimanual hand movement to a single location, again contrasting perceptual report for related and unrelated object pairs. Here we found no extra enhancement for related over unrelated pairs when GK made a valid unimanual right hand movement to a member of an action-related pair. Thus the extra advantage apparent in Figure 1.6 is contingent on a bimanual action being made, with GK's left hand moving to the location of the left side object. We also failed to find any difference between related and unrelated pairs when, on related trials, the stimuli were placed in incorrect spatial positions for direct action (knife and fork, toothbrush and toothpaste). Hence the effect does seem tied to the stimuli being in appropriate positions for action rather than their simply being associatively related to one another. It is noteworthy that this interaction between action and the effects of action relations between stimuli, apparent here, occurred even though GK never identified the left member of a pair (and, indeed, denied that there was a second object present). Again, the effects arise implicitly, independent of conscious perceptual report. It seems that, even if GK ended each trial by perceptually selecting only the ipsilesional (right side) object, there was enhanced processing of the contralesional item when (a) an action was made to it and (b) it was in a location where it could be used in relation to the ipsilesional stimulus.

The effect of action on object selection

This last study with GK indicates that action can enhance effects of a stimulus relationship on perceptual selection. We have also completed a recent series of studies with normal participants in which action apparently changed the nature of the processes taking place in perceptual selection (Linnell, Humphreys, McIntyre, Laitinen, & Wing, 2004). These experiments were closely modelled on the studies by Deubel et al. (1998), which demonstrated that perceptual report of stimuli was improved if a pointing action was made to location where the stimuli were presented. Though Deubel and colleagues' findings indicate that action can influence perceptual selection, they do not provide detailed information on the nature of this interaction (but see Deubel & Schneider, this volume; see also Schiegg, Deubel, & Schneider, 2003, for some relevant evidence). For example, is the interaction dependent on enhanced processing at the location common to action and perceptual selection (a location-base effect), or is it dependent on enhanced processing of the object to which the action is made (an object-based effect or an effect influenced by grouped locations)?

There are numerous results in the literature on perceptual selection showing that performance is modulated by whether elements belong to the same or to different perceptual objects[3] (e.g. Baylis & Driver, 1992, 1993; Duncan, 1984; Egly, Driver, & Rafal, 1994; Vecera & Farah, 1994). In particular,

---

3   We do not distinguish here between whether there is an object representation abstracted from the locations occupied by the elements or whether the "object" representation is derived from grouped locations. This distinction is orthogonal to our current concern, which is whether some form of object representation mediates selection, and whether this remains the case when an action is made to a part of the object.

perceptual report of the second of two stimuli is better if it belongs to the same object as the stimulus first reported (e.g. Duncan, 1984). Such results suggest that parts of an object are selected together. However, consider when we make an action to a part of an object (e.g. picking up a cup by its handle). Is the whole object then necessarily selected (the cup) or just the part (the handle)? Does the action to a part direct attention away from the whole to just the part?

To address this question, we used displays containing six circles presented at equal distances from each other and from a central fixation cross. The circles were grouped into three perceptual objects by having continuous line segments join two members of an adjacent pair, and by filling in the circles and their adjoining sections in the same colour (see Figure 1.7). Participants took part in two different studies. One (Experiment 5) examined perceptual identification alone. At the start of each trial, a line cue (in a central circle) indicated the circle where a target stimulus would fall (either an "n" or a "u"). Participants were asked to discriminate whether an "n" or a "u" appeared at the cued location, and they were then asked to decide whether an "E" or "reversed E" was presented in any of the other circles. These targets were presented simultaneously with a set of four distractor stimuli (2s and 5s), which fell within the other circles. We were interested in three critical conditions, according to the relative locations of the target first reported (the "n" or "u") and the item reported second. This second item could be: (1) one circle away from the first target, but in the same object ("1, within object"; Figure 1.7a); (2) one circle away from the first target but in a different object ("1, between object"; Figure 1.7b); or (3) two circles away from the first target and in a different object ("2, between object"; Figure 1.7c).[4] If there is "object-based" selection of each pair of grouped circles, then report of the second target should be better in the "1, within object" condition than when it occurs the same distance from the first target, but in a different object ("1, between object"). However, if there is merely an effect of spatial distance on selection, then the second target should be better reported when it is in a circle close to the first target ("1, within" and "1, between") than when it is in a more distant circle ("2, between").

In the second study (Experiment 6), we combined a perceptual identification task with a pointing task. Now, instead of having to discriminate the stimulus at the cued location, participants were instructed to make a rapid pointing movement to that location.[5] As well as making a pointing

---

4   There was also a further condition in which the second target appeared in the location opposite to the cue and the first target. However, as noted by Deubel et al. (1998), this "opposite location" condition can generate results that are difficult to interpret. For example, in our study it is unclear whether participants sometimes attended to the opposite rather than the cued location, due to the alignment of the arrow with the opposite location. This problem does not apply when the second target appears in the other positions.

5   The apparatus and procedure were very similar to those used by Deubel et al. (1998).

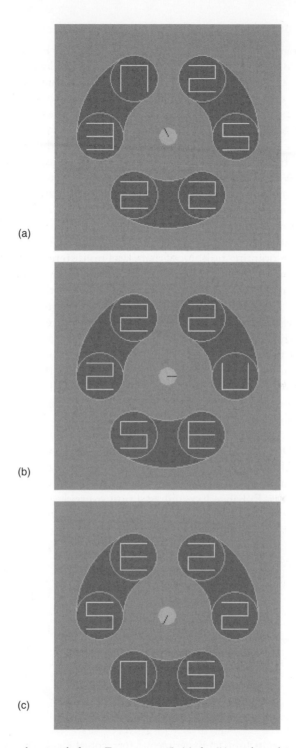

Figure 1.7 Example stimuli from Experiment 5: (a) the "1, within object" condition; (b) the "1, between object" condition; (c) the "2, between object" condition.

movement, participants had to identify whether an "E" or "reversed E" appeared at any of the locations (now including the cued location), which were equally likely to contain a target. The circles not containing the target had either a 2 or a 5 distractor. Does this pointing movement, to one of the grouped circles, alter any influence of object-based selection on perceptual report (e.g. an advantage for the "1, within" over the "1, between" condition)?

The results from the perceptual identification study are presented in Figure 1.8a, while those from the pointing + identification study are given in Figure 1.8b. When perceptual identification alone was required, there was a reliable advantage for reporting a second target when it appeared in the same "object" as the target first selected (in the "1, within" condition compared with the "1, between" condition). In contrast to this, we found no evidence on target identification for a "within object" advantage when participants carried out the pointing task. Now there was no difference between the "1, within" and the "1, between" conditions, though target identification was improved when it fell at the location that was cued and that a movement was made to (the "same location" condition, shown in Figure 1.8b). In neither experiment was there an effect of the spatial distance between the cued location and the location of the critical "E" or "reversed E" target.

The results from Experiment 5 (perceptual identification alone) are consistent with previous studies showing object-based effects on perceptual selection (Duncan, 1984; Egly et al., 1994). The novel finding is that this object-based benefit is eliminated when an action is directed to one of the grouped circles. This result again indicates that action has a direct impact on perceptual selection (cf. Deubel & Schneider, this volume; Deubel & Schneider, 1996; Deubel et al., 1998; Schneider & Deubel, 2002). We can view this result in several ways. One possibility is that action enhances a process of spatial selection that operates independently of an object-based selection process. Enhanced spatial selection overrides the effect of coding

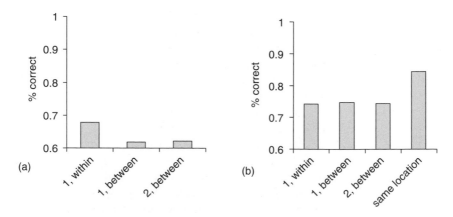

Figure 1.8 The results from (a) Experiment 5 (perceptual identification only) and (b) Experiment 6 (pointing + perceptual identification).

together multiple properties of an object. A further possibility is that action changes the nature of the representation(s) mediating perceptual selection. While parts of the same object are selected together when perceptual identification alone is required, the "reached-to" part may be represented as the "object" when an action is directed to it rather than to the whole stimulus.

Conclusions

The results reported here indicate that:

(1) Both perceptual selection and action selection are influenced by action relations between objects (Experiments 1–3)—objects are better reported, and actions made to the objects are more likely to be initiated together, if the stimuli are in the appropriate relative locations for action.
(2) Making actions to a pair of objects enhances the effect of action relations between objects on perceptual selection (Experiment 4).
(3) Making an action to an object can change the processes mediating perceptual selection (Experiments 5 and 6)—a tendency to select together parts belonging to a single object can be eliminated when a pointing action is directed towards one of the parts.

These results are consistent with the idea that perception and action are interactive rather than independent processes. For example, if action and perceptual selection do not interact, it is difficult to understand how the processes mediating perceptual selection could be modulated by action to a part (Experiment 6). Similarly, if the processes were independent, we would expect the effects of bilateral action to a pair of stimuli simply to increment any effects of the stimulus relations present; instead, we observe a form of multiplicative increase (Experiment 4; see Figure 1.6).

This interaction between action and perceptual selection is dependent not only on actions being made to objects (Experiments 4–6), but also on what we have termed the action relations present between stimuli (stimuli being in appropriate relative locations to be used together). The effects of action relations occur over and above any effects due to associative or visual familiarity (e.g. Experiment 2), indicating that they do not come about solely by associative learning of individual object pairings. One way to account for these effects is to suggest that perceptual selection is sensitive to whether objects can be used together, but this knowledge is abstracted from particular object pairs to reflect something more like the potential for action between known and even novel objects in the environment. This in itself may depend on factors like the positions of the objects with respect to the observer (including the distance from an effector; see Tipper, Howard, & Houghton, 1998; Tipper, Howard, & Jackson, 1997) and the task goals (Riddoch, Edwards, Humphreys, West, & Heafield, 1998). The tuning of perceptual selection to these action relations may itself be influenced by prior actions to the stimuli (see Boutsen & Humphreys, 2003), helping to "weight" for perceptual selection those factors common across different learning environments.

In addition to effects of action relations between stimuli, we have also observed that grouping relations modulate the programming and execution of bimanual actions (e.g. Punt et al., 2004). These effects can arise even in cases of motor extinction, where the patient does not appear to have a perceptual deficit. We propose that this effect of perceptual grouping on motor extinction reflects the close coupling of perception and action. For example, due to competition in programming bimanual motor actions, there may be a motor bias in such patients that favours the ipsilesional stimulus. This motor bias may, in turn, generate a bias in perception towards the ipsilesional target. The perceptual bias can be overridden, however, when the ipsi- and contralesional stimuli group together, and this, in turn, reduces the impact of any induced perceptual bias on the motor system.

Neural loci of perception–action interactions

The neuropsychological data discussed here indicate that, even after damage to the parietal lobe, patients can remain sensitive to action relations between stimuli (Experiments 1–3) and to whether actions are effected to stimuli (Experiment 4). One popular view, when discussing the relations between perception and action, is that "vision for action" is controlled by regions of dorsal visual cortex (e.g. Milner & Goodale, 1995), perhaps modulated by more frontal regions concerned with selecting the action in the first place. On this account, we might expect that damage to the parietal lobe would abolish the ability of a patient to respond either to action relations present between stimuli or to any modulatory effects of action on perception. This, however, is not the case. It may be, then, that effects of action relations between stimuli, and of action on perception, operate through undamaged (e.g. more ventral) areas of cortex in patients. Alternatively, it may be that patients remain able to respond on the basis of partial activation within a damaged parietal system sensitive to action relations between stimuli and to actions made to stimulus locations. This might be addressed through appropriate functional imaging studies with normal observers (see Grèzes & Decety, 2002; Phillips, Humphreys, Nopenney, & Price, 2002).

Implicit coding of action

Finally, we note that, in some of the neuropsychological evidence, the factors we have studied operate implicitly; for example, performance can be affected by action relations between object pairs or by bimanual actions even though only one of two stimuli is reported on a trial (Experiments 1 and 4). The effects of action on perceptual selection are not necessarily dependent on the prior conscious identification of stimuli.

Acknowledgements

This work was supported by grants from the Medical Research Council, the Stroke Association and the Wellcome Trust.

References

Ackroyd, K., Riddoch, M. J., Humphreys, G. W., & Townsend, S. (2002). When near becomes far and left becomes right: using a tool to extend extra personal visual space in a patient with severe neglect. *Neurocase*, 8, 1–12.

Aglioti, S., DeSouza, J. F. X., & Goodale, M. A. (1995). Size contrast illusions deceive the eye but not the hand. *Current Biology*, 5, 679–685.

Balint, R. (1909). Seelenlähmung des Schauens, optische Ataxie, räumliche Störung der Aufmerksamkeit. *Monatschrift für Psychiatrie und Neurologie*, 25, 51–81.

Baylis, G. C., & Driver, J. (1992). Visual parsing and response competition: the effects of grouping. *Perception and Psychophysics*, 51, 145–162.

Baylis, G. C., & Driver, J. (1993). Visual attention and objects: evidence for hierarchical coding of location. *Journal of Experimental Psychology: Human Perception and Performance*, 19, 451–470.

Boutsen, L., & Humphreys, G. W. (2003). On the interaction between perceptual and response selection: evidence from a patient with frontal lobe damage. *Neurocase*, 9, 239–250.

Bridgeman, B. (2002). Attention and visually guided behaviour in distinct systems. In W. Printz & B. Hommel (Eds.), *Attention and performance XIX. Common mechanisms in perception and action* (pp. 120–135). Oxford: Oxford University Press.

Coslett, H. B., & Saffran, E. (1991) Simultanagnosia: to see but not two see. *Brain*, 114, 1523–1545.

Deubel, H., & Schneider, W. X. (1996). Saccade target selection and object recognition: evidence for a common attentional mechanism. *Vision Research*, 36, 1827–1837.

Deubel, H., Schneider, W. X., & Paprotta, I. (1998). Selective dorsal and visual processing: evidence for a common attentional mechanism. *Visual Cognition*, 5, 1827–1837.

Duncan, J. (1984). Selective attention and the organization of visual information. *Journal of Experimental Psychology: General*, 113, 501–517.

Edwards, M. G., & Humphreys, G. W. (2002). Visual selection and action in Balint's syndrome. *Cognitive Neuropsychology*, 19, 445–462.

Egly, R., Driver, J., & Rafal, R. D. (1994). Shifting visual attention between objects and locations: evidence from normal and parietal lesion subjects. *Journal of Experimental Psychology: Human Perception and Performance*, 123, 161–177.

Ellis, R., & Tucker, M. (2000). Micro-affordance: the potentiation of components of action by seen objects. *British Journal of Psychology*, 91, 451–471.

Franz, V. H., Gegenfurtner, K. R., Bülthoff, H. H., & Fahle, M. (2000). Grasping visual illusions: no evidence for a dissociation between perception and action. *Psychological Science*, 11, 20–25.

Gibson, J. J. (1979). *The ecological approach to visual perception*. Boston, MA: Houghton Mifflin.

Gilchrist, I., Humphreys, G. W., & Riddoch, M. J. (1996). Grouping and extinction: evidence for low-level modulation of selection. *Cognitive Neuropsychology*, *13*, 1223–1256.

Grèzes, J., & Decety, J. (2002). Does visual perception of object afford action? Evidence from a neuroimaging study. *Neuropsychologia*, *40*, 212–222.

Haffenden, A. M., & Goodale, M. A. (1998). The effect of pictorial illusion on prehension and perception. *Journal of Cognitive Neuroscience*, *10*, 122–136.

Humphreys, G. W. (1998). Neural representation of objects in space: a dual coding account. *Philosophical Transactions of the Royal Society B*, *353*, 1341–1352.

Karnath, H.-O. (1988). Deficits of attention in acute and recovered visual hemi-neglect. *Neuropsychologia*, *26*, 27–43.

Kelso, J. A. S., Southard, D. L., & Goodman, D. (1979). On the coordination of two-handed movements. *Journal of Experimental Psychology: Human Perception and Performance*, *5*, 229–238.

Kumada, T., & Humphreys, G. W. (2001). Lexical recovery from extinction: interactions between visual form and stored knowledge modulate visual selection. *Cognitive Neuropsychology*, *18*, 465–478.

Linnell, K. J., Humphreys, G. W., McIntyre, D. B., Laitinen, S., & Wing, A. M. (in press). *Action modulates object-based selection*. *Vision Research*.

Mattingley, J. B., Davis, G., & Driver, J. (1997). Preattentive filling-in of visual surfaces in parietal extinction. *Science*, *275*, 671–674.

Milner, A. D., & Goodale, M. (1995). *The visual brain in action*. London: Academic Press.

Na, D. L., Adair, J. C., Williamson, D. J. G., Schwartz, R. L., Haws, B., & Heilman, K. M. (1998). Dissociation of sensory attentional from motor attentional spatial neglect. *Journal of Neurology, Neurosurgery and Psychiatry*, *64*, 331–338.

Pavani, F., Boscagli, I., Benvenuti, F., Ratbuffetti, M., & Farne, A. (1999). Are perception and action affected differently by the Titchener circle illusion? *Experimental Brain Research*, *127*, 95–101.

Phillips, J. A., Humphreys, G. W., Nopenney, U., & Price, C. J. (2002). The neural substrates of action retrieval: an examination of semantic and visual routes to action. *Visual Cognition*, *9*, 662–684.

Phillips, J. C., & Ward, R. (2002). S–R correspondence effects of irrelevant visual affordance: time course and specificity of response activation. *Visual Cognition*, *9*, 540–558.

Posner, M. I., & Petersen, S. E. (1990). The attention system of the human brain. *Annual Review of Neuroscience*, *13*, 25–42.

Punt, D., Riddoch, M. J., & Humphreys, G. W. (in press). *Perceptual grouping affects motor extinction*. *Cognitive Neuropsychology*.

Riddoch, M. J., Edwards, M. G., Humphreys, G. W., West, R., & Heafield, T. (1998). Visual affordances direct action: neuropsychological evidence from manual interference. *Cognitive Neuropsychology*, *15*, 645–684.

Riddoch, M. J., Humphreys, G. W., & Edwards, M. G. (2000a). Neuropsychological evidence distinguishing object selection from action (effector) selection. *Cognitive Neuropsychology*, *17*, 547–562.

Riddoch, M. J., Humphreys, G. W., & Edwards, M. G. (2000b). Visual affordances and object selection. In S. Monsell & J. Driver (Eds.), *Attention and performance XVIII* (pp. 603–626). Cambridge, MA: MIT Press.

Riddoch, M. J., Humphreys, G. W., Edwards, S., Baker, T., & Willson, K. (2003). Actions glue objects but associations glue words: neuropsychological evidence for multiple object selection. *Nature Neuroscience, 6,* 82–89.

Rossetti, Y., & Pisella, L. (2002). Several different "vision for action" systems: a guide to dissociating and integrating dorsal and ventral functions. In W. Printz & B. Hommel (Eds.), *Attention and performance XIX. Common mechanisms in perception and action* (pp. 62–119). Oxford: Oxford University Press.

Schneider, W. X., & Deubel, H. (2002). Selection-for-perception and selection-for-spatial-motor-action are coupled by visual attention: a review of recent findings and new evidence from stimulus-driven saccade control. In W. Printz & B. Hommel (Eds.), *Attention and performance XIX. Common mechanisms in perception and action* (pp. 609–627). Oxford: Oxford University Press.

Schiegg, A., Deubel, H., & Schneider, W. X. (2003). Attentional selection during preparation of prehension movements. *Visual Cognition, 10,* 409–432.

Tipper, S. P., Howard, L. A., & Houghton, G. (1998). Action based mechanisms of attention. *Philosophical Transactions of the Royal Society B, 353,* 1385–1393.

Tipper, S. P., Howard, L. A., & Jackson, S. R. (1997). Selective reaching to grasp: evidence for distractor interference effects. *Visual Cognition, 4,* 1–38.

Tucker, M., & Ellis, R. (1998). On the relations between seen objects and components of potential actions. *Journal of Experimental Psychology: Human Perception and Performance, 24,* 830–846.

Tucker, M., & Ellis, R. (2001). The potentiation of grasp types during visual object categorisation. *Visual Cognition, 8,* 769–800.

Vecera, S. P., & Farah, M. J. (1994). Does visual attention select objects or locations? *Journal of Experimental Psychology: General, 123,* 146–160.

Ward, R., Goodrich, S., & Driver, J. (1994). Grouping reduces visual extinction: neuropsychological evidence for weight-linkage in visual selection. *Visual Cognition, 1,* 101–130.

2 Hierarchical systems of attention and action

Asher Cohen and Hagit Magen

Abstract

We hypothesize that attention is divided into two separable but hierarchically organized networks in which both are involved in action-related processes. The higher-level system is in charge of setting up the task. The two networks share the duty of resolving online competition arising during task performance. The lower-level network (e.g. visual attention) can resolve online conflicts, at both the input and output ends of processing, with a limited set of selection cues. The higher-level network is recruited when these cues are not available. We review the literature and show that our hypothesis is compatible with the available findings. Our hypothesis has clear predictions when two tasks are performed concurrently, as in the psychological refractory period paradigm. We describe experiments, using this paradigm, that support these predictions, and discuss some of the outstanding questions.

Introduction

People are normally faced with a vast amount of information impinging on their senses and/or produced by their own cognitive system. It is well documented that the cognitive system, at least in most circumstances, cannot fully process all this information (for reviews, see Driver, 2001; Shiffrin, 1988). These inherent capacity limitations on response call for a selection mechanism (selective attention), whose role is to determine the priority of processing (e.g. Yantis & Johnson, 1990). The nature of the selective attention mechanism has been extensively investigated over the last half century (see Pashler, 1998, for a review).

The first attempts to characterize selective attention all assumed that it is a unitary mechanism; these characterizations differed with respect to the locus at which attention was thought to perform its selection. One dichotomy that emerged was between a perceptual locus of selection (e.g. Broadbent, 1958; Kahneman & Treisman, 1984) and an action locus (e.g. Allport, 1987; Duncan & Humphreys, 1989). This debate has continued for a long time and, to some extent, continues today because there seems to be good evidence for both a perceptual (e.g. Hillyard, 1985; Kahneman & Treisman, 1984) and an action (e.g. Duncan, 1980) locus of selection.

One way to account for the vast and conflicting literature in this domain is to assume that there are in fact two attentional systems, one dedicated for selection at the perceptual level and the other concerned with selection for action (e.g. Johnston, McCann, & Remington, 1995; Pashler, 1991; Posner & Petersen, 1990). Indeed, evidence from behavioural and cognitive neuroscience studies, reviewed shortly, supports this division into two attentional systems dealing separately with input and output selection. A higher-level system, called "executive functions" or "central attention", performs selection related to action. A lower-level system, possibly modality-specific, deals with perceptual selection. [Because we focus primarily on visual tasks, we shall refer to the latter system as "visual attention", but bear in mind that attention operates at other modalities as well, and that some of its operations may be cross-modal (e.g. Driver & Spence, 1999).] This distinction between input- and output-based attention systems has been echoed in recent studies (Maddox, 2001; Remington & Folk, 2001; Riddoch, Humphreys, & Edwards, 2000; Turatto, Benso, Galfano, & Umilta, 2002; Wong, 2002). By this division into two systems, we can neatly account for the conflicting studies about the locus of selection. Perceptual selection can be explained by the operation of the system dealing with input selection, and action selection can be caused by the second, output-based system.

As detailed below, we endorse the distinction between two attentional systems. However, we challenge the classification of the two systems as output-based and input-based, respectively, and propose an alternative classification. According to our hypothesis, the two attentional systems have a hierarchical relation in which both can perform selections on response-related processes, but we suggest that visual attention is limited in its selection because it can only use a small set of visual cues for this purpose. We describe evidence from our laboratory indicating that selection based on executive functions and on visual attention can operate simultaneously, showing at least some degree of separability. Importantly, our studies show that both types of selection can operate on action-related processes, with visual attention being constrained by the availability of the visual cues required for its operation.

The first half of this chapter reviews the literature on the two attentional systems. The second half introduces our hypothesis and the evidence we have accumulated for it to date. In finer detail, the structure of the chapter is as follows: We begin with a brief description of the main properties of the two attentional systems. We then review studies that bear more directly on whether the two systems are indeed separate. A variety of cognitive neuroscience and behavioural studies point to this separability. Many of the studies propose, either explicitly or implicitly, that the visual attention system deals with input selection, whereas the executive functions are concerned with action selection. Our review suggests, however, that this input–output distinction may not be justified. In particular, we propose that visual attention is also involved in selection for action. We then describe our hypothesis for the hierarchical relation between the two attentional systems. We describe experiments from our laboratory that test and support novel predictions of our hypothesis. Finally, many issues concerning the relation between the two attentional systems are still unresolved. We discuss some of these issues in the last part of the chapter.

Two attentional systems

The executive functions

Although there were several early hypotheses of the role of executive functions in task performance, the paper by Norman and Shallice (1986)[1] may have been the first modern cognitive study to focus specifically on these control processes. In this influential paper, Norman and Shallice (1986) referred to the executive functions as strategic and possibly conscious control processes dealing with action (as opposed to perception). They identified several roles for the executive functions. In general, the executive functions establish the task situation (which in their terminology means creating schemata; see Rogers & Monsell, 1995, for a discussion of the various components of a task set), determine the schedule for the execution of the various tasks, plan anything else that may be required for achieving the cognitive goal, deal with novel tasks, and address conflicts that may arise during the task performance. Norman and Shallice proposed that three entities are involved in these roles: the schemata, a system in charge of scheduling these schemata, and an attentional system that deals with novel events and tasks and resolves any conflicts that may arise during task performance.

A number of paradigms have been used extensively over the last decade to explore selective properties of executive functions (e.g. Allport, Styles, & Hsieh, 1994; Pashler, 1994; Rogers & Monsell, 1995). These studies uncovered some basic processes concerned with task switching and queuing two tasks. Nevertheless, the nature of executive functions is still not fully understood. It is not even agreed whether executive functions should be divided into smaller modular components (see, for example, Pashler, 1998) or be regarded as a single, distributed and adaptive system (e.g. Duncan, 2001). This is quite natural given the putative complexity of executive functions, and the relatively recent emergence of interest in them.

---

1 A central executive had been proposed earlier by Baddeley and Hitch (1974) for working memory.

As specifically emphasized by Norman and Shallice (1986) and others (e.g. Allport et al., 1994), operations such as the configuration of a task set are performed by functions that are also sensitive to instructions, which makes certain stimulus-to-response mappings more likely to be executed. In addition, environmental stimuli might also trigger some habitual actions. These ensembles of configurations are constructed so that there is sufficient control as to whether certain tasks will be executed or not, there is control on the queuing of executed tasks, and there are processes that enable switching between tasks.

Visual attention

Visual attention, as the label suggests, controls selection of visual stimuli. The study of visual attention is most closely associated with the spatial cueing paradigm (e.g. Eriksen & Hoffman, 1972; Posner, 1980), although many other paradigms have also addressed its properties (Ashby, Prinzmetal, Ivry, & Maddox, 1996; Cohen & Ivry, 1989, 1991; Theeuwes, 1992; Treisman & Gelade, 1980; Treisman & Schmidt; 1982; Wolfe, Cave, & Franzel, 1989; Yantis & Jonides, 1984). Many researchers have shown that cueing a particular location facilitates responses to targets at the cued location, and hinders performance for targets at other locations (e.g. Bashinski & Bacharach, 1980; Müller & Rabbitt, 1989; Posner, Snyder, & Davidson, 1980). The cost and benefit observed in the cueing paradigm are ascribed to the operation of visual attention, which presumably pre-selects the cued location, thereby leading to a performance benefit in that location and a performance cost in other locations.

A variety of issues that are unique to visual attention have been investigated. One debate, for example, is whether visual attention selects space (e.g. Posner et al., 1980; Tsal & Lavie, 1993), objects (e.g. Driver & Baylis, 1989; Duncan, 1984), or both (Behrmann & Tipper, 1999; Egly, Driver, & Rafal, 1994). Another major concern is the extent to which visual attention can be captured involuntarily (or exogenously) by visual distractors (e.g. Theeuwes & Godijn, 2001), and whether this exogenous attention is different in its operation from endogenous (voluntary) processes of visual attention (e.g. Briand & Klein, 1987) or not (e.g. Müller & Rabbitt, 1989).

The issues raised about the executive functions and visual attention, and the paradigms used to investigate them in the two domains, appear to be different. This raises the possibility that the two attentional mechanisms are distinct. We now review evidence for the separability of the two systems.

The two attentional systems: cognitive neuroscience studies

Several studies using different methods have suggested that visual attention and executive functions activate different anatomical areas. In one of the earliest imaging studies, Petersen, Fox, Posner, Mintun, and Raichle (1988;

see also Posner, Petersen, Fox, & Raichle, 1988) showed that processes that have to do with visual attention activate the posterior parietal lobe. Posner et al. (1988; see also Posner & Petersen, 1990) also considered findings from studies using single cell recordings and research with neurologically impaired patients, and proposed that the visual attention system consists of a distributed network that includes the posterior parietal region, the superior colliculus in the mid-brain and the lateral pulvinar nucleus in the thalamus.

Petersen et al. (1988) also showed that executive functions (e.g. the ability to make arbitrary responses in their study) activate the anterior cingulate gyrus. Posner and his colleagues (e.g. Posner & Dehaene, 1994; Posner & Petersen, 1990; Posner et al., 1988) proposed that two attentional systems exist: a posterior system that includes the posterior parietal, the pulvinar and the superior colliculus regions, and an anterior system that includes the anterior cingulate region.

Subsequent imaging studies generally supported the notion that the two attentional systems involve different anatomical regions, but extended the regions involved in each system. The executive functions activate bilateral dorsolateral prefrontal regions in addition to the anterior cingulate (e.g. Carter, Braver, Barch, Botvinick, Noll, & Cohen, 1998; Gehring & Knight, 2000; Milham et al., 2001). The role of prefrontal cortex in the executive functions is also evident in the deficits exhibited by patients suffering from frontal damage (e.g. Shallice & Burgess, 1993). In addition to the network mentioned above, visual attention activates the superior frontal regions, including the frontal eye field and the supplementary eye fields (e.g. Corbetta, Kincade, Ollinger, McAvoy, & Shulman, 2000; Nobre, Sebestyen, Gitelman, Mesulam, Frackowiak, & Frith, 1997).

Because the frontal regions involved in visual attention are associated with control of eye movements, which, in turn, are closely associated with visual input, the distinction between the posterior and anterior systems seems to hold (see, for example, Casey et al., 2000). Moreover, it is customary to relate the control of visual perception, to the posterior regions and the control of action to the anterior regions (e.g. Fuster, 1989). Indeed, Posner and colleagues (Posner et al., 1988; Posner & Petersen, 1990) equated the anterior system with "attention for action" and the posterior system with orienting to locations.

There are, however, at least two potential problems with the analogy between the posterior system and input selection. First, the frontal areas activated by visual attention may be involved in other motoric activities (e.g. Connolly, Goodale, Desouza, Menon, & Vilis, 2000; see also Corbetta & Shulman, 2002). Second, single cell recordings in the parietal lobe and neuropsychological studies with humans suggest that this region is also associated with action-related processes (Andersen, Snyder, Bradley, & Xing, 1997; Rizzolatti, Riggio, & Sheliga, 1994; see Andersen & Buneo, 2002, for a review). Thus, while the anatomical distinction between a visual attention network and a network of executive functions is supported, the relation of the two systems to input and output selection, respectively, on the basis of the cognitive neuroscience literature, is questionable.

The two attentional systems: behavioural studies

Few behavioural studies have examined explicitly the distinction between the two attentional systems. The pioneering study by Posner and Boies (1971) assumed a relation between selectivity to input (which is an aspect of visual attention) and capacity limitations as defined by interference from a secondary probe task (which is now considered part of executive functions). Posner and Boies found that input selection was not affected by capacity limitations and concluded that these are distinct components of attention (but see Posner, Inhoff, Friedrich, & Cohen, 1987).

Other studies have used the psychological refractory period (PRP) paradigm to examine the two attentional systems (Johnston et al., 1995; Pashler, 1991). We focus for now on the study by Pashler (1991; see also Pashler, 1989) because the method he used was similar to that used in our research. Later, we address the study by Johnston et al. (1995). Pashler (1991) used what is known as the locus-of-slack method with the PRP paradigm. We first describe this method, as well as the theoretical implications of findings produced by it, because they are relevant for our studies as well.

In the PRP paradigm, participants respond as quickly as possible to two tasks whose input is presented in succession, with the constraint that the response to the first task (T1) is performed before the response to the second task (T2). The main manipulation is the temporal gap—the stimulus onset asynchrony (SOA)—between the presentation of the inputs to T1 and T2. The typical findings in this paradigm are that, whereas reaction times for T1 are minimally affected by the SOA, those for T2 become progressively longer with shorter SOAs, with a slope approximating −1 (e.g. Fagot & Pashler, 1992; Van Selst & Jolicoeur, 1997; Welford, 1952; see Pashler, 1994, for a review). This pattern of results is known as the PRP effect. One dominant explanation of the PRP effect (e.g. Pashler, 1994), the response selection bottleneck (RSB) hypothesis, is related to the prevailing view (Sternberg, 1969) that any task is performed by a series of processing stages that includes perception, response selection and response execution. The main claim from the RSB hypothesis is that the central response selection stage can only be used by one task at a time and, therefore, the computation of response selection for T2 (in the short SOAs) "waits" until the response selection for T1 is completed (e.g. Pashler, 1994).

The main evidence for the RSB hypothesis comes from the "locus-of-slack" method. This method involves a selective manipulation of the difficulty of specific processing stages for T2 (see Figure 2.1). The hypothesis examined in the locus-of-slack method is that the PRP effect is caused by an inherent limitation in using one of these processing stages simultaneously for two tasks. If two tasks require this processing stage at the same time, as

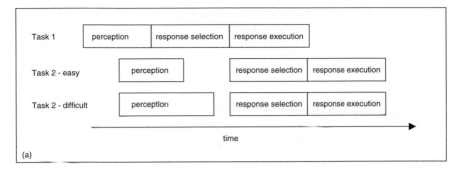

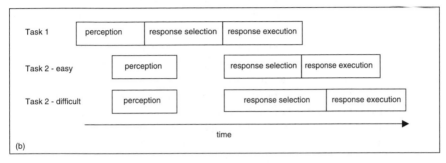

Figure 2.1 (a) An illustration of underadditivity in the PRP paradigm. (b) An illustration of additivity in the PRP paradigm.

might be the case in the short SOA conditions of the PRP task, one of them (T2 in the PRP paradigm) has to wait until the other task has undergone this processing stage. In this case, the processing of T2 is said to be "postponed", and the waiting period until the processing is resumed constitutes a form of "cognitive slack" (cf. Schweickert, 1980). Manipulating the difficulty of a distinct stage in T2 yields clear predictions (see Figure 2.1): If the manipulated stage occurs before the bottleneck stage, the difference between the easy and difficult conditions will be apparent in the long SOAs, but will be reduced and may even be eliminated in the short SOAs. The relation between SOA and the manipulation on T2 is then "underadditive" (see Figure 2.1a). If, however, the manipulation involves a stage at or beyond the bottleneck stage, the difference between the easy and difficult conditions will not be affected by SOA (i.e. the relation between the SOA and the T2 manipulation is "additive", see Figure 2.1b).

Many studies using this method have demonstrated an underadditive relation between the SOA and the difficulty of the perception stage of T2 (e.g. De Jong, 1993; Johnston et al., 1995; Pashler & Johnston, 1989). The locus-of-slack logic implies that perceptual processes can be performed concurrently for T1 and T2. In contrast, manipulating the response selection difficulty of T2 produces an additive effect with SOA (e.g. Fagot & Pashler,

1992; McCann & Johnston, 1992; Pashler & Johnston, 1989; Van Selst & Jolicoeur, 1997). These findings support the RSB hypothesis that the PRP effect is due to a bottleneck at the response selection stage. The RSB hypothesis is the cornerstone in the study of Pashler (1991) about the relation between visual attention and the executive functions, which we now consider.

Pashler (1991) used a variant of the locus-of-slack method to determine whether shifts of visual attention can be done for T2 concurrently with the performance of T1. The first task in his study was auditory and the second task involved responding to a target letter embedded in an array of distractors. The location of the target letter was not known in advance and was indicated by a cue. Several experiments showed that the efficiency of using the cue was minimally affected by the SOA between T1 and T2, indicating that individuals can shift their attention to a cued location for T2 concurrently with the performance of T1. Moreover, as mentioned earlier, shifts of visual attention can be done exogenously (by a cue appearing at or near the target's location) or endogenously (by a central cue that symbolizes the location of the target). Several researchers have suggested that different processes are used for exogenous and endogenous cueing (e.g. Briand & Klein, 1987). Pashler (1991) showed that shifts of visual attention could be made on the basis of either cue concurrently with T1. He concluded that visual attention and central attention are distinct. Furthermore, visual attention deals with selection among input stimuli, whereas central attention deals with action-related processes.

The underlying assumptions behind Pashler's (1991) conclusion are crucial and we now examine them carefully. Two of the assumptions are general and appear to be shared by all researchers in this domain (e.g. Logan & Gordon, 2001; Meyer & Kieras, 1997a; Pashler, 1991). One assumption is that a central attention system must play a role in the queuing of T1 and T2 (making sure that T1 is done first). A second, related assumption is that the queuing must be affected by the processing limitation at short SOAs. Presumably, the queuing by central attention must be done so that the factors causing the processing limitation be first allocated to T1, making sure that it is performed without regard to T2, as only then can these factors be released with the guidance of the central attention mechanism for T2. These two assumptions imply that processes that can be performed in the short SOAs for T2 are separated from the central attention mechanism. Pashler made a third, more specific assumption by adopting the RSB hypothesis, namely that the processing bottleneck is at the response selection stage. This assumption leads to the distinction between input and output processes. Essentially, it entails that processes that have to do with action (response selection and subsequent action-related programming) are the arena of central attention. Processes that are not part of this bottleneck are pre-action, or input-related. Because shifts of visual attention are not affected by the RSB, they must be dealing with input selection.

However, while there is evidence to support the RSB hypothesis, the results of some studies appear to contradict it. Hommel (1998; see also Logan & Gordon, 2001) showed that the response association of a T2 target, presented in close succession to the T1 input (i.e. in the short SOAs conditions), may affect the response for T1. This can only happen if the response association of the T2 target is retrieved while participants still perform T1, contradicting the assumption that no response selection is computed for T2 until the response selection of T1 is complete. The results of studies using the locus-of-slack method are also not always consistent with the RSB hypothesis. Some studies that have varied response selection difficulty for T2 have obtained underadditivity with such manipulations (e.g. Karlin & Kestenbaum, 1968, Schumacher et al., 1999). These studies led other researchers, most prominently Meyer and his colleagues (Meyer & Kieras, 1997a, 1997b, Schumacher et al., 1999; see also Logan & Gordon, 2001; Navon & Miller, 2002), to suggest that there is no structural limitation at the response selection stage. Meyer and his colleagues suggest instead that, due to strategic reasons, individuals postpone the processing of response selection for T2. This postponement is performed by executive functions (see Meyer & Kieras, 1997a, for details). Other researchers have also proposed, in contrast to the RSB hypothesis, that response selection processes are activated simultaneously for T1 and T2 (Hommel, 1998; Lien & Proctor, 2002; Magen & Cohen, 2004).

These alternative perspectives on the PRP studies raise the possibility that while the results of Pashler (1991) support the existence of two attentional systems, they do not necessarily imply the division of these two systems on the basis of input versus output. We now review studies that specifically support the role of visual attention in action-related selection.

Visual attention and the selection of action-related processes

Most studies of visual attention have examined its operation in circumstances in which there is a need for input selection (e.g. Pashler, 1991; Posner, 1980). As mentioned earlier, the processing level at which attention selects a target among distractors in such circumstances is controversial (see, for example, Driver, 2001). When Pashler (1991) reviewed the literature, he concluded that there was no behavioural evidence for the involvement of visual attention in action selection. Although there had been evidence for action-based selection (e.g. Allport, 1987; Duncan, 1980), this selection could have been attributed to the operation of central attention. As reviewed below, the situation has changed since then and there is now considerable behavioural evidence for the involvement of visual attention in selection for action.

In a pioneering study by Tipper, Lortie, and Baylis (1992), participants had to reach to a stimulus positioned in a three-dimensional setting and surrounded by distractors whose positions varied relative to the target. Tipper et al. (1992) examined the role of visual attention by looking at the positions in which distractors most affected this reaching task. A series of experiments showed that distractors influenced performance as a function of their spatial relationship to the target in a hand-centred frame of reference. Within this frame, attention operates much like it does in standard visual tasks. Distractors that are spatially close affect performance more than distant distractors, just as they do for input selection (e.g. Eriksen & Eriksen, 1974), and negative priming is observed in a similar manner to that observed for input selection (e.g. Tipper, Brehaut, & Driver, 1990). The similarities between the styles of selection for input and action suggest that the selection for input and for action may be performed by a single mechanism. Recent research with patients suffering from neglect has converged on this finding (Buxbaum & Permaul, 2001; Husain, Mattingley, Rorden, Kennard, & Driver, 2000; Rafal, Danziger, Grossi, Machado, & Ward, 2002). Neglect is a neurological syndrome that occurs most often following a lesion to regions of the posterior parietal lobe and the temporo-parietal junction (e.g. Rafal, 1994). Patients with neglect fail to act upon stimuli that appear on the side opposite to their lesion, and there is evidence that this impairment is due to a deficit of visual attention (e.g. Posner, Walker, Friedrich, & Rafal 1984). Buxbaum and Permaul (2001) and Husain et al. (2000) showed that neglect patients also suffer from hand-centred deficit during a reaching task. Rafal et al. (2002) also showed that neglect patients exhibit deficits at the action end of processing. These findings are consistent with the notion that the same visual attention mechanism is involved in both input and action selection (see also Humphreys et al., this volume).

A second line of evidence linking attention to both perception and action comes from studies showing that perception affects selection for action and that action affects selection for perception. The former was recently demonstrated by Anderson, Yamagishi, and Karavia (2002). These investigators found that the compatibility of responses to visual objects is a function of the participants' attention. For example, participants who judged scissors' orientations on the basis of the scissors' handles, showed response compatibility to the orientation determined by the handles. In contrast, participants' who judged the scissors' orientation according to their pointed end showed response compatibility to the location of the pointed end. The effect of action on input selection has also been demonstrated most clearly by Deubel, Schneider, and their colleagues (for a review, see Deubel & Schneider, this volume). Similarly, Craighero, Fadiga, Rizzolatti, and Umilta (1999) showed that preparing for a grasping movement facilitates a subsequent detection of visual stimuli compatible with the to-be-grasped movement even if the grasping movement is not in fact executed (see also Diedrichsen, Ivry, Cohen, & Danziger, 2000; Hommel & Schneider, 2002). The results of these studies suggest that the same visual attention is used to perceive input and to execute an action.

Some studies have directly shown the involvement of visual attention in selection among response decisions. Feintuch and Cohen (2002) showed that cueing attention to a specific region enhances the response to two redundant targets when responses to the two targets are defined by different dimensions (e.g. colour and shape), but not when the responses for the two targets are defined by one dimension (e.g. colour). These findings suggest that cueing attention in this context does not affect the perception of the targets. Rather, given the evidence that response selection can be performed separately in different dimensions (e.g. Cohen & Magen, 1999; Cohen & Shoup, 1997), the results of Feintuch and Cohen (2002) suggest that visual attention enhances selection among responses.

Perhaps the most direct evidence for the role of visual attention in response selection comes from studies using the flanker task (e.g. Cohen & Shoup, 1993; Eriksen & Eriksen, 1974). In this task, participants respond to a centrally presented target flanked by irrelevant stimuli, leading to three basic conditions. In the congruent and incongruent conditions, the target and flankers are associated with the same response (e.g. a red target flanked by red flankers) and with alternative responses (e.g. a red target flanked by green flankers), respectively. In the neutral condition, the flankers are not associated with any response (e.g. a red target flanked by blue flankers). Many studies have shown that response latencies are fastest for the congruent condition, slowest for the incongruent condition and intermediate for the neutral condition (e.g. Eriksen & Eriksen, 1974; Miller, 1991). Most relevant for the present review, there is convincing evidence that the flanker congruency effect is caused by response selection processes (e.g. Eriksen & Eriksen, 1979; see Cohen & Shoup, 1997, for a review). The results of a recent study by Diedrichsen et al. (2000) reinforce this conclusion. They showed that a flanker affects more strongly the response to a central target if it is positioned on the same side as the required response. This finding suggests that the flanker congruency effect is closely tied to the assigned responses.

The evidence from the flanker task suggests that, in the incongruent condition, the two alternative responses (stemming from the target and flankers) are simultaneously selected. In most of these cases, the correct response is eventually selected and executed, but how? Several studies have suggested that this selection among potential responses is performed by visual attention. For example, LaBerge, Brown, Carter, Bash, and Hartley (1991) showed that the size of the flanker congruency effect is determined by manipulation of visual attention. Gratton, Coles, and Donchin (1992) showed that the flanker congruency effect is contingent on the congruency situations in the preceding trials. A sequence of incongruent trials leads to a smaller effect because individuals expect incongruent trials and tighten their focus of attention. Indeed, existing models of the flanker task (Cohen & Shoup, 1997, 2000; Cohen, Servan-Schreiber, & McClelland, 1992; LaBerge, 1994; Servan-Schreiber, 1990) generally assume that visual attention is the mechanism responsible for resolving the response conflict in the flanker task.

In summary, the results of many behavioural and neuropsychological studies, using a variety of methods, suggest that visual attention performs at least some selection among actions, and that it is probably the very same mechanism that controls visual input selection. Studies with patients converge on these findings. In addition, the results of neurophysiological studies using single cell recordings are also consistent with this notion. Cells in the posterior parietal lobe appear to be selective for action (e.g. Andersen et al., 1997; Rizzolatti et al., 1994). This large body of evidence from a variety of approaches casts serious doubts on the notion that visual attention operates solely for input selection.

Importantly, although the evidence suggests that visual attention affects both input- and action-based processing, the manner by which it operates has not been specified. Does attention operate directly on representations at the response selection stage (i.e. at the locus where response competition takes place)? Does it exert its influence indirectly by affecting visual input representations, which, in turn, affect response-based processes (as would probably be the standard view)? As will be elaborated at length in the next section, we propose a third possibility. In brief, in line with the more standard view, we suggest that visual attention can affect response selection processes only indirectly, via visual representations. However, we suggest that attention can affect response competition via both input-based and output-based visual representations.

Hierarchy of attentional systems

Our review so far suggests the following: First, there is convincing evidence, both from cognitive neuroscience and from psychology, for the existence of two control systems, one involved with executive functions and one with visual attention (as an example of a modality-specific attention mechanism). Second, the attempt to divide the two networks on the basis of input–output processes is highly questionable. There is strong evidence that visual attention is involved in the control of at least some action-related processes. What, then, is the difference between the two control systems?

We propose that the executive functions and visual attention are organized hierarchically. As reviewed earlier, executive functions are responsible for establishing the set for a task (e.g. Rogers & Monsell, 1995). So, when participants are asked in a standard cognitive experiment to respond to one colour with one arbitrary response, and to respond to another colour with another arbitrary response, the task configuration is performed by the executive functions, which allow the participant to perform the task accurately. The same is true for the performance of any other task. When more than one task is required, as in the PRP paradigm, the executive functions arrange the configuration of the two tasks (e.g. when the two tasks involve an auditory tone discrimination and a colour discrimination, two task configurations are established: one linking the two tones to their required responses, and the other linking the colours to their required responses) as well as the scheduling of the two tasks (e.g. Norman & Shallice, 1986).

It is worth specifying what a task configuration entails. Consider, again, a colour task in which participants are required to respond with a left key to the colour "red" and with a right key to the colour "green". There are good reasons, dating back to the work of Sternberg (1969), to assume that by setting up the task, the perceptual representations of the colours (e.g. red) are linked to abstract response codes, which, in turn, are linked to commands for the performance of the required output (e.g. hit the left key). The abstract response codes are part of the response selection stage, where the mapping of stimuli to responses is made (see Sternberg, 1969, for a discussion of the response selection stage). Most discussions of the topic focus on the links between the response selection representations and the visual input representations. However, the output layout also has visual representations (e.g. the visual representations of the keys that participants have to push) and, as just described, those are also linked to the response selection representations. Recent work by Hommel and colleagues (e.g. Hommel, Müsseler, Aschersleben, & Prinz, 2001; Müsseler & Hommel, 1997) has demonstrated elegantly the importance of the links between the representations of the required output and representations of response selection.

In many tasks, the input display includes one or more targets and one or more distractors. Part of a successful task set is to arrange the system so that it selects the target(s) rather than the distractor(s). Consider, for example, the flanker task described earlier. In a typical flanker task, the participant views a central target and flanking distractors. The task has to be set so that the central target will be selected. We hypothesize that in many circumstances, this selection is accomplished by setting up the parameters of the lower-level modality-specific attention system (e.g. visual attention for visual tasks). In the example just described of the flanker task, visual attention has to be set to focus on the location of the central target, thereby leading to its eventual selection (e.g. LaBerge et al., 1991), and this can be arranged before the appearance of the input display. In this case, visual attention affects response competition via input representations. That is, visual attention increases the activation of specific input representations (e.g. the central location), leading to enhanced activation of the input at that location, which, in turn, enhances the activation of the abstract response code to which it is linked, leading eventually to the resolution of the response competition.

As has been known for some time, however, attention is quite limited in its selection capabilities (e.g. Broadbent, 1958; Treisman, 1969). In particular, visual attention can only use certain visual cues to select targets efficiently (von Wright, 1968, 1970, 1972). Adopting a partial report technique, von Wright used the classical iconic memory paradigm of Sperling (1960). Using this paradigm, participants see a display containing a matrix of stimuli for a brief time. A short while after the disappearance of the display, the participants receive a cue indicating which items from the display should be reported. As shown in a series of studies by von Wright (1968, 1970, 1972), participants can perform these tasks very well with certain cues, including location, colour, luminance and discriminable shapes. Thus, items that appear in a certain cued location (e.g. middle row of the matrix), have a certain cued colour (e.g. the blue items), have a certain cued luminance (e.g. high luminance) or are cued by distinct shapes (e.g. rounded versus angled items) can be selected. Visual attention cannot use other cues, however. For example, it cannot efficiently select letters among digits.[2]

As the preceding paragraph suggests, some tasks can be set to allow visual attention to efficiently select the target over the distractors. There are tasks, however, whose specification does not afford efficient selection by visual attention. Consider, for example, the well-known Stroop task (Stroop, 1935; see MacLeod, 1991, for a review). In a typical Stroop task, participants respond to the ink colour of a word whose content may also be a colour. As shown in many studies, relative to a baseline condition in which the word does not denote any colour, participants are slower in the incongruent condition in which the ink colour and the word content are different, and they are faster in the congruent condition in which the ink colour and the word content match. Note that visual attention may not be set to resolve the conflict that arises in the incongruent condition of the Stroop task. To resolve the conflict, participants have to figure out which of the two colour outputs came from the ink colour rather than the word content. In the terminology of Treisman (1969), one has to perform a selection between analysers. As Treisman noted at the time, selection between analysers is not efficient. In our terminology, it is not possible to pre-set visual attention to perform selection in this case because, unlike the example of the flanker task, the cues that visual attention can use do not differentiate between the target and distractors. We hypothesize that when a conflict arises in cases where visual attention cannot be used to resolve it (as in the incongruent condition of the Stroop task), other operations may be recruited by executive functions to achieve conflict resolution. Because executive functions are involved in these latter types of conflict resolution, their operation may also interrupt other executive operations. When these other operations are essential, conflict resolution may be postponed until these other operations are no longer required (as when additive effects are found in PRP procedures).

Crucially, we do not make any distinction between input and output selection. When visual attention can use a visual cue (e.g. location, colour) to resolve a conflict, it will do so whether the conflict is at the perceptual or at the response end of processing. Moreover, the visual cue could be part of the input specification, but it could also be part of the output specification. The

---

2   The assertion that categories cannot be used is, in fact, controversial (e.g. Duncan, 1983). It is widely agreed though that the set of visual cues is limited and this is the main point we make.

partial report task used by von Wright (e.g. 1970) is a good example of using a cue at the input end for selection at the input end. The flanker task is an example of using a cue at the input end to resolve a response-based conflict. Later, we provide examples where visual attention can use a visual cue that is part of the output specification to resolve a response-based conflict.

Some theorists (Duncan, 2001; Miller & Cohen, 2001) have emphasized the adaptive nature of executive functions. They focused, among other things, on the need to resolve online competitions (e.g. a conflict between a target and a distractor) that may arise during task performance. We believe that our hypothesis adds an interesting ingredient to this scheme. There is a division of labour between the two attentional systems with respect to the resolution of such conflicts. The resolution of some forms of competition may be relegated to the lower-level attentional system when the task set affords it. The executive functions step in when the task set conditions do not allow visual attention to be used efficiently.

To summarize, we propose that the executive functions are responsible for setting up task performance. Part of this task set is to define parameters for selection by visual attention when conditions for efficient operation of visual attention are available (i.e. when selection cues by location, colour, luminance or shape can be used). These cues can be present in conflicts that may arise at both the input and output ends of processing. In such cases, the lower-level control mechanism can perform its selection online without consulting the task set and without interrupting the online operations of the executive functions. When these cues are not part of the task set and a conflict arises, the executive functions are recruited to resolve the conflict. This can prevent other online processes performed by the executive functions.

Implications for the PRP paradigm

We now return to the PRP paradigm. Our hierarchical hypothesis has clear implications for this paradigm, and we have already tested many of them. We briefly outline these implications and then focus on the experiments we performed. As reviewed earlier, most manipulations of response processes for T2 have led to additivity with the SOA. The RSB hypothesis explains these findings by assuming that the response selection computation for T2 is postponed while it is being used for T1. Our hypothesis regarding the hierarchy of the attentional systems leads to an alternative explanation. We propose that, as a general rule, response selection is performed simultaneously for T1 and T2. In some cases, a conflict or competition between two or more alternative responses for T2 may arise. The key issue in such cases is whether this conflict is resolved concurrently with the performance of T1 (i.e. in the short SOAs). We propose that competition can be resolved concurrently with the performance of T1, leading to underadditivity, when visual cues are available and it is possible to use visual attention for conflict resolution. When the executive functions are required to resolve the competition, resolution may not occur concurrently with the performance of T1, presumably because the executive functions may be busy in the online queuing of the two tasks (cf. Pashler, 1991).

This analysis leads to the following predictions. When the response conflict in T2 can be resolved by using one of the visual cues available for visual attention (e.g. location, colour, luminance or discriminable shape), we should observe underadditivity. These cues could be part of the input or output specification. When these visual cues cannot be used to resolve the conflict, we should observe additivity. Previous studies in the literature generally conform to the latter case. Fagot and Pashler (1992), for example, obtained additivity of the Stroop task with the SOA. As discussed earlier, the conflict in the incongruent condition of the Stroop task cannot be resolved by visual attention. In general, however, our hypothesis has never been tested. We now review a series of studies, some of them still in progress, which attempt to systematically test our hypothesis.

The experiments

We used a similar PRP method in all of the experiments reported here. We first briefly describe this method (see Magen & Cohen, 2002, for more details). The main difference between the experiments was the nature of the second task (T2).

Method

Stimuli

The first stimulus in all the experiments was a tone, presented at 300 or 900 Hz, that lasted 150 ms. The second stimulus was visual and will be described with each experiment. Participants responded to the tone task manually. The responses to the visual task varied, being manual in some experiments and vocal in others.

Design

Each trial consisted of two tasks and began with the presentation, for 250 ms, of a central achromatic asterisk, serving as a fixation point. This was followed by a tone; participants had to decide if this tone was "high" or "low". The tone (S1) and the subsequent visual stimulus (S2) were separated by four different SOAs: 50, 150, 300 or 900 ms. Each of the four SOAs appeared on 25% of the trials. The participants were asked specifically to respond rapidly to the tone, to discourage them from grouping the two responses and responding to both as one unit (Pashler & Johnston, 1989).

The experiments consisted of two sessions. We will report the results of the second session; the results of the first session, while more variable, were qualitatively the same. A final remark concerns the responses for the tone discrimination task (T1). The sole purpose of T1 is to create the PRP effect by making sure that participants first respond to this task as fast as possible. In general, our participants conformed to this constraint. Therefore, we present the mean reaction times for T1, but do not discuss them any further.

Output interference paradigms

We shall first focus on experiments that used a variety of interference paradigms for T2 (for an extensive description of these paradigms see Kornblum, Hasbroucq, & Osman, 1990). As outlined by Kornblum et al. (1990), the various interference paradigms can be divided on the basis of different properties. We focused on one property not discussed by Kornblum et al. (1990); namely, whether the conflict that arises in these tasks can be resolved by a visual cue. Importantly, a common feature of the paradigms we use is that there is good evidence that the main interference associated with them is due to response selection processes. Thus, the involvement of visual attention in the resolution of the conflicts in these paradigms affects the output rather than the input end of processing.

Magen and Cohen (2002) compared a T2 using the Stroop paradigm with a T2 using the flanker paradigm. The stimuli and basic conditions for these two tasks are shown in Figure 2.2. As described earlier, the flanker conflict can be resolved by a visual cue (location), whereas the Stroop conflict cannot.

The mean reaction times for these tasks are shown in Figure 2.3. Figure 2.3a shows the results when T2 used a Stroop paradigm and Figure 2.3b shows the results when T2 used a flanker paradigm. As can be seen in Figure 2.3a the Stroop effect was found at all SOAs, and its magnitude was roughly similar at each. In other words, the Stroop effect was additive with the SOA. Similar results were reported by Fagot and Pashler (1992). The more interesting results are those for the flanker task. The flanker effect was observed in the long SOA. However, this effect essentially vanished for the short SOAs. In other words, the flanker effect was underadditive with the SOA.

These results are predicted by our hypothesis. As mentioned earlier, the flanker conflict can be resolved by visual attention; this is not the case for the Stroop task (see above).

One potential weakness of the flanker task is that the target is presented at a fixed location. Therefore, it may represent a unique case in which attention can simply be focused on the target location throughout the task. To generalize these findings further, we used a spatial Stroop task as T2. The main conditions for this task are shown in Figure 2.4. In this task, participants respond to the physical location of words, whose content also denote spatial locations. For example, a word can appear either on the right or left side of the screen, and the word itself is either "LEFT" or RIGHT". Participants

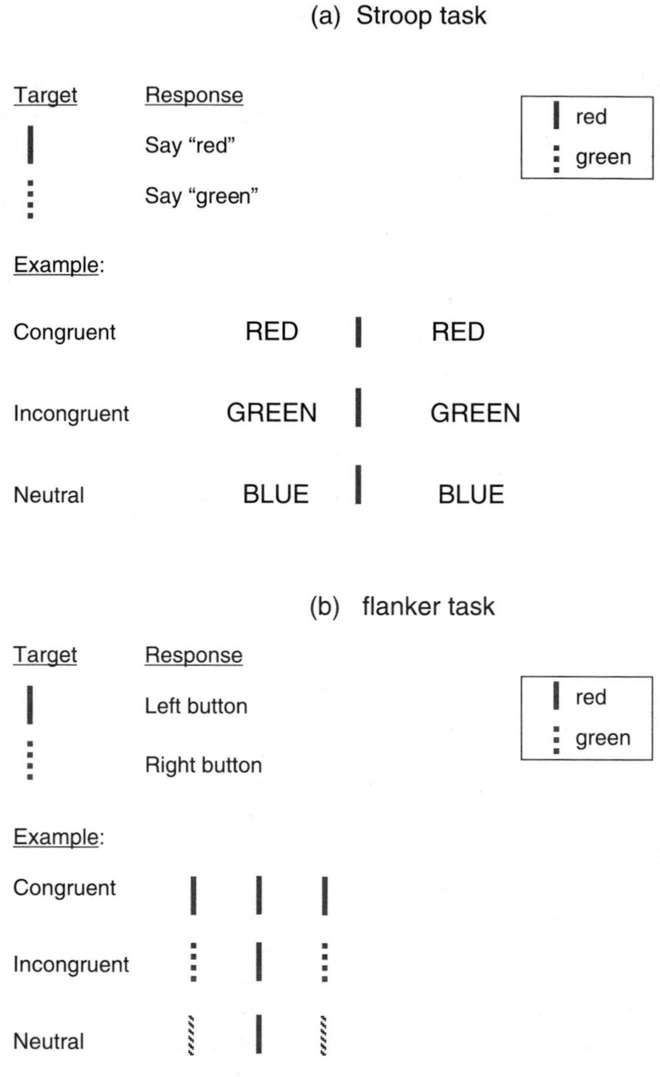

(a) Stroop task

Target	Response
|	Say "red"
⋮	Say "green"

|	red
⋮	green

Example:

Congruent   RED **|** RED

Incongruent   GREEN **|** GREEN

Neutral   BLUE **|** BLUE

(b) flanker task

Target	Response
|	Left button
⋮	Right button

|	red
⋮	green

Example:

Congruent   **| | |**

Incongruent   **⋮ | ⋮**

Neutral   **⦚ | ⦚**

Figure 2.2 (a) The stimulus-to-response mapping in the Stroop task and an example of the congruency conditions. (b) The stimulus-to-response mapping in the flanker task and an example of the congruency conditions.

responded vocally by saying (in Hebrew) the word "LEFT" for a left-side target and the word "RIGHT" for a right-side target. The words LEFT and RIGHT, appearing on the left and right side respectively, create congruent conditions because of the match between the physical location and the word's content. The words LEFT and RIGHT, appearing on the right and left side respectively, create incongruent conditions. Many studies have shown that mean reaction times are faster in the congruent than in the

(a) Stroop task

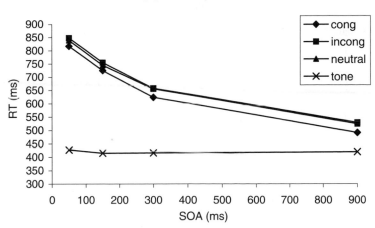

(b) flanker task

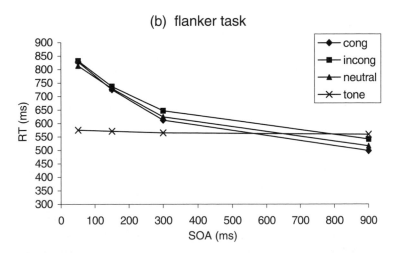

Figure 2.3 The reaction time (RT) results for the first and second task in the Stroop
task (a) and the flanker task (b). SOA = stimulus onset asynchrony (from
Magen & Cohen, 2002). Reprinted with permission of Springer-Verlag.
Copyright © 2002 Springer-Verlag.

incongruent condition (e.g. Seymour, 1973; for a review, see Lu & Proctor,
1995). There is also convincing evidence that the effect is due to response
selection processes (e.g. DeSoto, Fabiani, Geary, & Gratton, 2001; Lu &
Proctor, 1995).

Our hypothesis predicts underadditivity between the spatial Stroop effect
and the SOA for the following reason: the task set specifies the connection
between spatial positions and responses. Participants can enhance the connection between the target's location and its required response by focusing

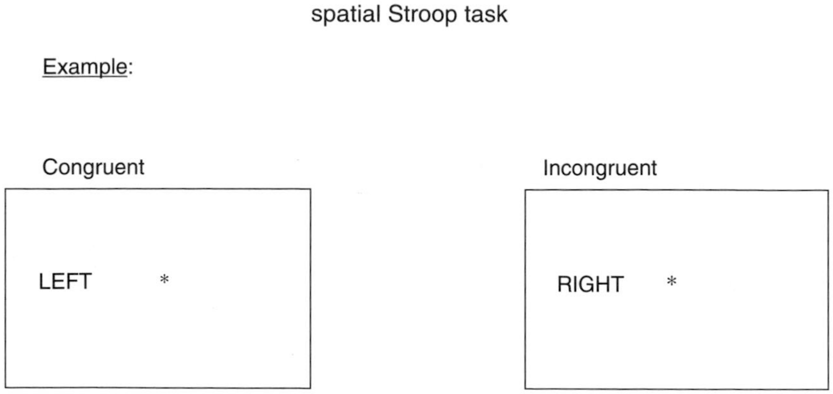

spatial Stroop task

Example:

Congruent		Incongruent
LEFT *		RIGHT *

Figure 2.4 Example of the congruent and incongruent conditions of the spatial
Stroop task.

their attention on the target's location. As in the flanker task discussed
earlier, the conflict aroused in the incongruent condition is resolved by shifting visual attention to the physical location of the target. Such a shift presumably increases the activation of that location as well as its connection to
the required response, eventually leading to its selection over its competitor.
Because shifts of visual attention for T2 can be done concurrently with the
performance of T1, our hypothesis predicts underadditivity of the spatial
Stroop congruency effect with the SOA.

There is, however, a potential complication. To resolve the conflict, visual
attention is required to focus on the physical location and ignore the spatial
location denoted by the word. As stated above, the additivity between the
colour Stroop interference and SOA suggests that visual attention cannot
select between analysers in the colour domain (cf. Treisman, 1969). Resolution of the spatial Stroop requires also selection between analysers, but in
the space domain. Can this be done before the central processing bottleneck?

The mean reaction times for T1 and T2 are shown in Figure 2.5. As before,
our main interest is in the results for T2. As can be seen in Figure 2.5, the
spatial Stroop effect interacted with the SOA in an underadditive fashion.
Apparently, the response competition arising in the spatial Stroop task for
T2 can be resolved while central attention is engaged with response selection
for the first task. Coupled with the evidence that the spatial Stroop effect is
caused by interference at the output end (e.g. DeSoto et al., 2001), our findings suggest that visual attention can resolve conflicts at the output end
concurrently with performance of other tasks as long as it can use a visual
cue to resolve the conflict.

These results are different from those obtained when the standard colour
Stroop is used for T2 (Fagot & Pashler, 1992; Magen & Cohen, 2002). Thus,

spatial Stroop task

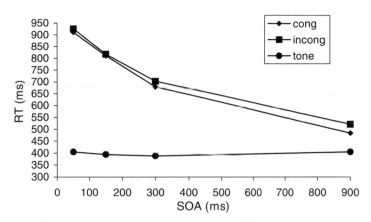

Figure 2.5 The reaction time (RT) results for the first and second task in the spatial Stroop task. SOA = stimulus onset asynchrony.

another implication of our findings is that the spatial dimension is different from the colour dimension. In the former attention can separate output of physical location from verbal output, whereas in the latter it cannot.

The findings with the spatial Stroop are compatible with those obtained when the flanker task is used for T2 (Magen & Cohen, 2002). In both cases, the conflict that arises in the incongruent condition can be resolved by focusing attention on a particular location in the input space. The spatial Stroop represents a step forward because the location of the target is not fixed and attention has to actively shift to its location.

Our hypothesis is that resolution of the flanker and the spatial Stroop conflicts is done by focusing attention on the location of the target input. The next experiment we describe aimed to expand the role of visual attention by looking at cases where focusing on the response location rather than input location could resolve response conflict. We use the Simon task for this purpose. In the standard spatial Simon task, participants discriminate between non-spatial visual properties (e.g. colours), which may appear in one of two spatial locations (e.g. the right and left sides of the screen), by pressing response buttons that are similarly organized in space (e.g. right and left). Even though the spatial organization of the targets and responses is not relevant for the discrimination task, participants are typically faster when the location of the required response matches the spatial location of the target than when it does not match (e.g. Craft & Simon, 1970).

As in the interference paradigms used in our previous experiments, there is clear evidence that the Simon effect is due to response selection processes (e.g. Hommel, 1995; Lu & Proctor, 1995). Two previous studies examined the Simon task for T2 (Lien & Proctor, 2000; McCann & Johnston, 1992), both of which reported underadditivity of the Simon effect with the SOA. There is evidence that the Simon effect dissipates with time and some investigators have suggested that this dissipation is due to a passive decay of the irrelevant location code (e.g. De Jong, Liang, & Lauber, 1994; Hommel, 1993). Based on this evidence, it has been suggested (McCann & Johnston, 1992; Pashler, 1994) that the underadditivity of this effect in the PRP paradigm is caused by the relatively long time that elapses in the short SOA between the presentation of the target stimulus and its response. That is, the reaction times for T2 in the short SOAs are particularly long (which is essentially the hallmark of the PRP effect), but it also means that a relatively long time elapses between the presentation of the stimulus for T2 and its response. The explanation is that, in these short SOA conditions, location information from the irrelevant location decays while T1 is being performed. By the time the response selection for T2 takes place, there is no activation of the response from the (already decayed) location of the T2 target, hence the lack of the Simon effect (but see Lien & Proctor, 2000).

Our hypothesis leads to an alternative explanation, which is best appreciated by considering the details of the spatial Simon task. The response configuration of this task maps the relevant stimulus (e.g. colour) to its response, which, in turn, activates the required response location. At the same time, and regardless of the task set, the irrelevant location of the target stimulus activates the alternative response. As reviewed earlier, visual attention is used to focus on the required motoric response (e.g. Craighero et al., 1999; Deubel & Schneider, this volume; see also Hommel & Schneider, 2002). In the Simon task, visual attention can follow the pathway created by the task configuration as described earlier (colour input to response location) and focus on the location of the required response, thereby resolving the conflict. In this sense, the spatial Simon is the output version of the flanker task and the spatial Stroop. In the latter tasks, the conflict is resolved by focusing on the input location, whereas in the Simon task it is resolved by focusing on the response location.

One way to differentiate between our hypothesis and the decay hypothesis is to examine non-spatial versions of the Simon task in which it is not possible to use visual attention for conflict resolution. To this end, we compared a T2 in which a spatial Simon task was used with a T2 in which a non-spatial Simon task was used. Our hypothesis predicts that, unlike the underadditivity of the spatial Simon task with the SOA, the non-spatial Simon effect would be additive.

The stimuli for the two versions of the Simon task are shown in Figure 2.6. Figure 2.6a shows the stimuli and main conditions for the spatial Simon task. The targets consisted of coloured lines, either red or green, that appeared on the left or right side of the screen. Participants responded by pressing two keys, arranged laterally on the keyboard, with their right hand. For half of the participants, the green line was assigned to the left button and the red line to the right button; for the other half of the participants, the mapping was

(a) spatial Simon task

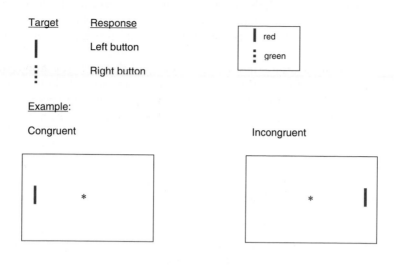

Target   Response

Left button

Right button

red

green

Example:

Congruent   Incongruent

(b) non-spatial Simon task

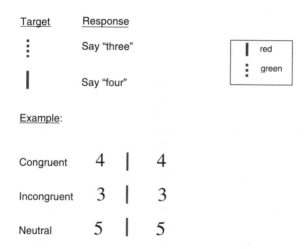

Target   Response

Say "three"

Say "four"

red

green

Example:

Congruent   4 | 4

Incongruent   3 | 3

Neutral   5 | 5

Figure 2.6 (a) The stimulus-to-response mapping in the spatial Simon task and an example of the congruency conditions. (b) The stimulus-to-response mapping in the non-spatial Simon task and an example of the congruency conditions.

reversed. This assignment resulted in two conditions. In the congruent condition, the target appeared on the same side as its assigned response button (e.g. for the group in which the green line was associated with the right key, it appeared on the right side). In the incongruent condition, the target appeared on the opposite side of the response button (e.g. the green line appeared on the left side).

Figure 2.6b shows the stimuli and main conditions for the non-spatial Simon task. As in the spatial Simon task, the targets consisted of coloured lines, but in the non-spatial version we asked the participants to respond to a centrally presented colour target flanked by digits. We created the non-spatial Simon conflict by requiring the participants to respond to the colour targets with digit names. When the participants saw a green line they had to say "three", and when they saw a red line they had to say "four". The flanking digits either matched the required response (e.g. a green target associated with the response "three" and flanked by the digit "3") or matched the alternative response (e.g. a red target flanked by the digit "3"). We also used a baseline neutral condition in which the target was flanked by the digit 5, which was not associated with any response. This task is considered a "Simon" task because the congruency is between an aspect of the required response and an irrelevant aspect of the stimulus array. That is, in the spatial Simon the conflict is between one aspect of the required response (the response's location) and an irrelevant aspect of the stimulus (its location). Similarly, in our task the conflict is between an aspect of the required response (the digit) and an irrelevant aspect of the stimulus array (the flanking digits). In both Simon tasks, the relevant feature of the target (its colour) is not in conflict with the response.

The results of the paradigms with the spatial and non-spatial versions of the tasks are shown in Figures 2.7a and 2.7b respectively. As can be seen in Figure 2.7a, there was a clear underadditivity for the spatial Simon task. The Simon effect is clear in the long SOA and essentially vanishes in the short SOAs. These results mirror those of McCann and Johnston (1992) and Lien and Proctor (2000). In contrast, as shown in Figure 2.7b, the non-spatial Simon effect was additive with the SOA. The magnitude of the effect was similar for all SOAs.

These results are problematic for the explanation given previously for the underadditivity observed with the spatial Simon task (e.g. McCann & Johnston, 1992); namely, that it is due to a decay of the response code that gave rise to the incongruent response. According to this explanation, there is no *a priori* reason to distinguish between spatial and non-spatial causes of Simon interference. On the other hand, the results fit well with our hypothesis. Visual attention can resolve the spatial Simon interference by using a spatial cue, the location of the response. In the non-spatial Simon task, it is not possible to resolve the response conflict with the aid of a visual cue. Instead, the resolution must be based on sorting out which of the analysers (the digits or the colours) activated competing responses.

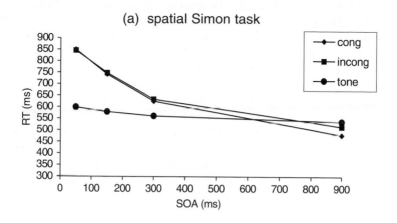

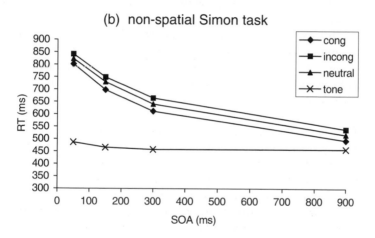

Figure 2.7 The reaction time (RT) results for the first and second task in the spatial (a) and non-spatial (b) Simon tasks. SOA = stimulus onset asynchrony.

There may be, however, an alternative interpretation of the extant results. The conflicts in all the experiments in which we obtained underadditivity (the flanker task, the spatial Stroop and the spatial Simon) were in the spatial domain. The conflicts in the interference paradigms in which additivity was obtained were in dimensions other than space. We have already seen that space may be special. Thus, an alternative explanation is that tasks in the spatial domain *per se* (rather than the operation of visual attention) create underadditivity.

To test this possibility, we used a spatial manipulation of stimulus–response compatibility (Fitts & Deininger, 1954) for T2. Participants had to discriminate between the positions of input stimuli. The response set for the task was also spatially organized. The spatial compatibility effect refers to the finding that performance is better when a stimulus is mapped to a spatially compatible response, rather than to a spatially incompatible response. For example, performance is better when responding with a left side button to a left side stimulus than when responding with a right side button to a left side stimulus. The spatial compatibility task is useful for our purpose because of two of its properties. First, it is a spatial task. If the underadditivity obtained with the flanker, spatial Stroop and spatial Simon tasks is due to their spatial nature *per se*, we should observe underadditivity in spatial stimulus–response compatibility as well. However, location is part of the stimulus–response configuration in the spatial stimulus–response compatibility task. The conflict is assumed to arise because stimuli in the spatial domain have an automatic set of spatial responses, namely the compatible responses. In the incompatible condition of this task, participants have to determine which of two mappings, each of which connects a relevant stimulus to a relevant response, is the required one. Thus, one cannot simply focus on the location of a particular stimulus or the location of a particular response to resolve the conflict. Instead, one has to establish which of the two stimulus-to-response mappings matches the instructions for the task. This type of resolution cannot be performed by visual attention and, consequently, has to be resolved by executive functions. Therefore, we predict that, in contrast to the previous spatial tasks, manipulation of spatial stimulus–response compatibility for T2 should produce additivity with the SOA.

There are some previous studies that used the stimulus–response compatibility manipulation for T2. McCann and Johnston (1992) and Lien and Proctor (2000) obtained additivity of this manipulation with the SOA. Schumacher et al. (1999) obtained additivity under some conditions (relatively low practice) and underadditivity under other conditions (after more practice). We manipulated spatial stimulus-to-response compatibility using exactly the same level of practice and the same instructions as in our previous experiments.

The stimuli and main conditions for our spatial compatibility task are shown in Figure 2.8. A single stimulus (a red or a green line, the colour being irrelevant for the task) appeared on the left or right side of the screen. Participants had to respond by pressing a left or a right response button. The compatibility manipulation was carried out between participants. In the compatible condition, participants pressed the right button when the stimulus appeared on the right side, and the left button when it appeared on the left side. In the incompatible condition, the mapping was reversed; participants pressed the right button when the stimulus appeared on the left side, and the left button when it appeared on the right side.

In this experiment, we also manipulated the type of response for T1. In one experiment, participants responded manually to the tone task (as in previous experiments); in the other, they responded vocally. This manipulation did not affect the main results and therefore we present the results,

The spatial compatibility task

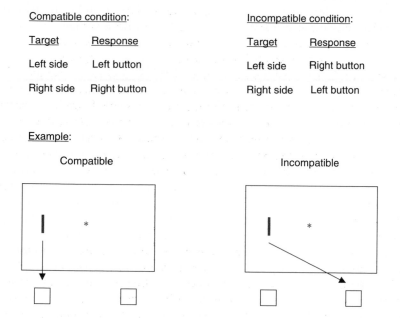

Compatible condition:

Target	Response
Left side	Left button
Right side	Right button

Incompatible condition:

Target	Response
Left side	Right button
Right side	Left button

Example:

Compatible

Incompatible

Figure 2.8 The stimulus-to-response mapping in the spatial compatibility task and an example of the compatibility conditions.

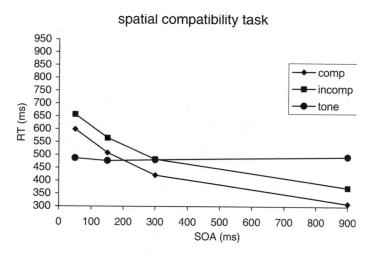

Figure 2.9 The reaction time (RT) results for the first and second task in the spatial compatibility task. SOA = stimulus onset asynchrony.

shown in Figure 2.9, collapsed across the two experiments. The results are quite straightforward. The compatibility effect was additive with SOA. These results clearly show that a spatial task is not sufficient to create underadditivity for interference paradigms in the PRP paradigm.

Concurrent response activation for overlapping tasks

An important claim of our attentional hierarchy hypothesis is that visual attention can be recruited to perform an action-related selection concurrently with executive functions operations when appropriate visual cues are available. The experiments reviewed so far have generally supported this claim. A crucial assumption, embedded in our interpretation of the results from these experiments, is that response activation can be carried out concurrently for two overlapping tasks. Consider, for example, the flanker task. The flanker effect vanished with the short SOAs (see Figure 2.3b). Our explanation is that presenting the target and flankers led to activation of their corresponding response codes concurrently with the performance of the first auditory task. The resultant conflict (in the incongruent conditions) is resolved by visual attention, hence the elimination of the flanker effect.

As reviewed earlier, the results of some research (e.g. Hommel, 1998) support this assumption of concurrent activation of response codes for overlapping tasks. However, it has never been tested directly with the locus-of-slack method. We now briefly describe two additional experiments (see Magen & Cohen, 2004) that aimed to show directly that response codes can be activated simultaneously for T1 and T2. Both experiments used the same PRP paradigm as in the previous experiments and, as detailed below, both employed response priming for T2.

The first experiment used a colour task in which we asked the participants to respond in T2 to one of four possible colour targets with one of two responses. Two colours (e.g. red and green) were mapped to one response, and the other two colours (e.g. blue and yellow) were mapped to the second response. In addition, a cue was presented for 100 ms before the target. The cue was a word denoting one of the colours. The colour target matched the cue on 70% of the trials. The other three colour targets that did not match the cue were presented with a frequency of 10% each. This design led to three conditions: the valid condition in which the target matched the cue (e.g. a red target following a RED cue); the invalid/same-response (SR) condition in which the cue and target were different colours, but both were associated with the same response (e.g. a green target following a RED cue); and the invalid/different-response (DR) condition in which the colour of the target differed from the cue colour and was associated with the alternative response (e.g. either a blue or a yellow target following a RED cue).

Previous studies adopting a similar design (Di Pace, Marangolo, & Pizzamiglio, 1997) showed that participants are fastest in the valid condition, intermediate in the SR condition and slowest in the DR condition. The facilitation of the valid condition over the SR condition can be explained by perceptual factors. The advantage of the SR over the DR condition, however, can only be explained by priming of response-related processes because the only possible reason for this advantage is membership in the response category. This design allowed us to examine whether response-related processes for T2 take place while participants perform T1.

In the long SOA, we expected to find the same pattern of results as in a single task (Di Pace et al., 1997). Because the advantage of the valid condition over the SR condition might be due to perceptual priming, underadditivity of this effect is expected. The critical comparison concerns the difference between the SR and DR conditions. This difference must be due to response-related priming. Our assumption, that response activation is done concurrently for the two tasks (augmented by the hierarchical attention assumption that attention can resolve conflicts), predicts underadditivity of this priming effect with the SOA as well.

The task and the main conditions for this experiment are shown in Figure 2.10. The reaction time results for T1 and T2 are shown in Figure 2.11. We present the results of the cueing effects separately. The perceptual priming effect was assessed by the difference in reaction time between the valid and the SR conditions. The response cueing effect was assessed by the difference in reaction time between the SR and DR conditions. As can be seen in Figure 2.11, there is a clear underadditivity of the two types of

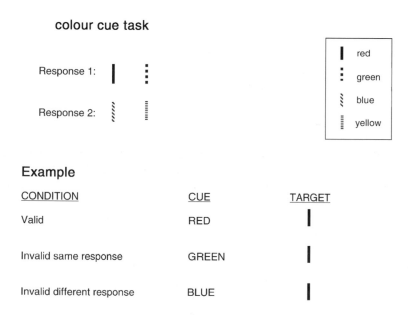

Figure 2.10 The stimulus-to-response mapping in the colour cue task and an example of the valid, invalid same response and invalid different response conditions.

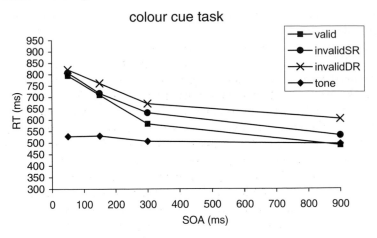

Figure 2.11 The reaction time (RT) results for the first and second task in the colour cue task. SOA = stimulus onset asynchrony.

priming with the SOA. Both effects were largely eliminated with the short SOA, presumably because visual attention could be shifted from the cued colour to the target colour. The substantial reduction in the difference between the SR and DR conditions, the response priming, strongly suggests that response activation took place for both T1 and T2 concurrently, and that most of the resultant response competition was eliminated by attention.

The final experiment reviewed here examined this issue from yet another perspective. Now, T2 consisted of a categorical judgement of digits versus letters. Participants made one response when one of three digits (3, 7 or 9) was presented, and made another response when one of three letters (p, s and z) was presented. A prime, either the word "DIGIT" or the word "LETTER", was presented 100 ms before the appearance of the stimulus. On 80% of the trials the prime was valid. For example, presentation of the prime DIGIT was followed on 80% of the trials by a target digit. In the remaining 20% of the trials (the invalid condition), the prime was followed by a letter target. The prime can be considered as a response priming because all the digits required one response and all the letters required another response.

The results of this experiment are shown in Figure 2.12. A clear under-additivity was obtained. As shown in Figure 2.12, there was a robust priming effect at the long SOA. This effect, however, almost disappeared with the short SOA. Once again, then, we see that response priming can be reduced, indeed almost eliminated, with the short SOAs, strongly suggesting that response activation does take place for the two tasks simultaneously. The conflict can be eliminated when visual attention can select the target as in our experiments.

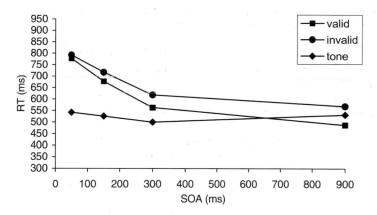

Figure 2.12 The reaction time (RT) results for the first and second task in the categorical cue task. SOA = stimulus onset asynchrony.

Summary and some further thoughts

The main hypothesis explored in this research project is that attentional control processes are organized hierarchically. We made a distinction between two levels of control processes. A high-level network, concerned with the control of "executive functions", is responsible for establishing the task set. During online performance of the task(s), competition that may arise between stimuli is resolved by either the executive functions or by a lower-level modality-specific attentional control (e.g. visual attention). The division of labour between the two systems is determined, at least to a considerable extent, by the limited capabilities of the lower-level system. Visual attention, the modal example of a modality-specific control mechanism, can only use certain visual cues to resolve competition. Nevertheless, it will often be responsible for resolving online conflicts when visual cues can be used to resolve competition. This is true whether the selection is at the input or output end. Where this is not the case, the executive functions may be required to resolve competition.

Our proposed hierarchical scheme has clear predictions for the PRP paradigm with the locus-of-slack method. Manipulations of response-related processes for T2 would be underadditive with the SOA when visual attention is used to resolve the conflict stemming from them. Manipulations that cannot be resolved by the lower-level network will be for the most part additive. The series of experiments described by us here support our hypothesis. One set of experiments, using interference paradigms that occur at the action end of processing, showed that conflicts arising in these tasks can be resolved concurrently with the performance of another task provided that efficient visual cues are available for visual attention. It is worth emphasizing again that in these experiments visual attention performs an action rather than an input selection. A second set of experiments supported an embedded assumption in the interpretation of our experiments, namely that response activation can take place for two tasks concurrently. We now briefly discuss several additional issues related to our hypothesis.

Setting up the online role of visual attention

Visual attention is used when visual cues can be exploited for the task goals (i.e. selection of the target). The use of visual attention is advantageous because it can be done simultaneously with other operations of the executive functions. This advantage is evident in the underadditivity observed when visual attention is used. Interestingly, our results clearly show that the use of visual attention is not just a function of the availability of visual cues. The pre-configuration of the task set also plays an important role in determining whether to use visual attention or not. This can be seen in one aspect of our experiments that we have not yet discussed. Consider the non-spatial Simon task (Figure 2.6b) in which we obtained additivity (Figure 2.7b). Note that the participants responded to a central colour target in the presence of flanking digits that could in some conditions be congruent and in some other conditions incongruent with the required response. As argued earlier, in general the conflict between the required response and the digit cannot be resolved by visual attention. However, because in our design the target always appeared in the centre and the distracting digits were always to its sides, the conflict could have been resolved by simply focusing visual attention on the location of the target (as is done in the standard flanker task, and as is done in the spatial Stroop by shifting attention to the target's location).

Similarly, in the standard Stroop task (Figure 2.2a), we used a Stroop task version for T2 in which the ink colour was spatially separated from the words. A coloured line appeared in the middle flanked by words that could be congruent or incongruent with it. In this case, too, the participants could take advantage of the consistent central location of the target and filter out the distractors by focusing on that location. However, as is evident in Figure 2.3a, the participants did not appear to use visual attention in these cases since the non-spatial Simon effect and the Stroop effect were additive with the SOA. Why is it that the participants did not take advantage of the location cue? We suggest that it has to do with the pre-configuration of the task set. In both cases, the appearance of the target in the centre of the display is not part of the task set. The instructions are to respond to the colour of a line. All other stimuli are different from the target (digits in the non-spatial Simon and words in the standard Stroop). Thus, participants do not have to rely on the target's location and they can pre-configure the task without emphasizing the location cue. As a result, visual attention is not pre-set to select by location and additivity is observed.

The dependency between the two attentional networks

The relation between the two attentional networks could vary from complete independence to strong dependence. Pashler (1991; see also Pashler, 1998) suggested that the two networks are completely independent. In contrast, Posner and his colleagues (Posner et al., 1987, Posner, Sandson, Dhawan, & Shulman, 1989) claimed that there is strong cross-talk between the two networks (but see Pashler, 1991, for counterarguments to these claims). The preceding paragraph about the role of the pre-configuration of the task set hints that there is some dependence between the two networks in that the details of the task set determine whether visual attention is used for selection. Nevertheless, it still leaves open the question of the dependence between the two networks once the task configuration is set. Our research shows that visual attention can operate simultaneously with the "executive" queuing operation. The tasks used in our study, however, are just a small sample of possible tasks. Whether visual attention can be independent in other situations is open to debate. For example, there are tasks in which one or more visual cues are available (e.g. both location and colour cues or just one of them). Can visual attention choose the selection cue independently of the executive functions in such instances? This and other possible concerns with the relation between the two networks require further research.

Visual attention for both input and output selection

As reviewed earlier, a large body of evidence suggests that visual attention operates on both input and output selection. Our hypothesis explains the findings by Pashler (1991) that were originally attributed to the input–output distinction without resorting to this distinction. Pashler relied on the RSB hypothesis to claim that visual attention operates on input processes. As we have shown here, however, our hypothesis can account for his findings without the RSB assumption.

There is one more study (Johnston et al., 1995) that appears to support the division of the two systems on the basis of input versus output selection. A closer look at the results of this study, however, suggests that it does not in fact provide any evidence whatsoever for this claim. Johnston et al. (1995) conducted two experiments. In the first, they used the locus-of-slack methodology by manipulating the difficulty of encoding letters for T2. They showed that this manipulation was underadditive with the SOA. Even if one accepts the RSB hypothesis, the results of this study simply suggest that letter encoding (presumably a perceptual process) is done before the bottleneck. As reviewed earlier, the results of other studies support the finding that manipulation of perceptual processes for T2 are underadditive with SOA. The second experiment conducted by Johnston et al. (1995) showed that manipulation of letter encoding and manipulation of visual attention (using the well-established cueing method mentioned earlier) are additive. The results of this experiment suggest, using Additive Factors logic (e.g. Sternberg, 1969), that visual attention and letter encoding processes are not operating on the same processing stage. Put differently, manipulation of visual attention does not affect the quality of encoding itself. Johnston et al. (1995) argued that the combined findings of the two experiments are compatible with a sequence of events in which visual attention first operates on perceptual processes before letter encoding, and that central attention operates on processes that take place after letter encoding and are response related. Hence, they concluded that visual attention is an input selection process and that central attention is operating on central processes (presumably response selection processes) and beyond.

There are two problems with the chain of reasoning proposed by Johnston et al. (1995). First, there is nothing that prevents visual attention from operating past the letter encoding stage and before the central attention stage (although Johnston et al. offered some arguments why this possibility does not account well for the data). Second, and more fundamentally, Johnston et al. assumed that attention is a processing stage, like perception, response selection, and so on. We believe that this assumption is not tenable. Several studies have suggested that visual attention may exert its effects on a number of distinct stages, and that contextual factors may determine where it operates (e.g. Lavie, 1995; Yantis & Johnston, 1990). Similarly, we reviewed earlier evidence that visual attention may affect both input and output selection. From this perspective, visual attention cannot be taken as a fixed stage in the chain of processes from input to output. Given this perspective, the fact that visual attention may in some experiments operate on input selection (and, again, the experiments by Johnston et al. are questionable in this regard too), has no bearing on whether visual attention can or cannot operate on output selection. We conclude that the literature is fully compatible with our hypothesis that visual attention can select at either the input or output side of processing.

References

Allport, D. A. (1987). Selection for action: some behavioral and neurophysiological considerations of attention and action. In H. Heuer & D. F. Saunders (Eds.), *Perspectives on perception and action* (pp. 395–419). Hillsdale, NJ: Lawrence Erlbaum Associates Inc.

Allport, D. A., Styles, E. A., & Hsieh, S. (1994). Shifting intentional set: exploring the dynamic control of tasks. In C. Umilta & M. Moscovitch (Eds), *Attention and performance XV. Conscious and nonconscious information processing* (pp. 421–452). Cambridge, MA: MIT Press.

Andersen, R. A., & Buneo, C. A. (2002). Intentional maps in posterior parietal cortex. *Annual Review of Neuroscience, 25,* 189–220.

Andersen, R. A., Snyder, L. H., Bradley, D. C., & Xing, J. (1997). Multimodal representation of space in the posterior parietal cortex and its use in planning movements. *Annual Review of Neuroscience, 20,* 303–330.

Anderson, S. J., Yamagishi, N., & Karavia, V. (2002). Attentional processes link perception and action. *Proceedings of the Royal Society of London, B, 269,* 1225–1232.

Ashby, F. G., Prinzmetal, W., Ivry, R., & Maddox, W. T. (1996). A formal theory of feature binding in object recognition. *Psychological Review, 103,* 165–192.

Baddeley, A., & Hitch, G. (1974). Working memory. In A. Collins, S. Gathercole, M. Conway, & P. Morris (Eds.), *Recent advances in learning and motivation* (Vol. 8, pp. 47 90). New York: Academic Press.

Bashinski, H. S., & Bacharach, B. R. (1980). Enhancement of perceptual sensitivity as the result of selective attending to spatial locations. *Perception and Psychophysics, 28,* 241–248.

Behrmann, M., & Tipper, S. P. (1999). Attention accesses multiple reference frames: evidence from visual neglect. *Journal of Experimental Psychology: Human Perception and Performance, 25,* 83–101.

Briand, K. A., & Klein, R. M. (1987). Is Posner's "beam" the same as Treisman's "glue": on the relation between visual orienting and feature integration theory. *Journal of Experimental Psychology: Human Perception and Performance, 13,* 228–241.

Broadbent, D. E. (1958). *Perception and communication.* London: Pergamon Press.

Buxbaum, L. J., & Permaul, P. (2001). Hand-centered attentional and motor asymmetries in unilateral neglect. *Neuropsychologia, 39,* 653–664.

Carter, C. S., Braver, T. S., Barch, D. M., Botvinick, M. M., Noll, D., & Cohen, J. D. (1998). Anterior cingulate cortex, error detection, and the online monitoring of performance. *Science, 280,* 747–749.

Casey, B. J., Thomas, K. M., Welsh, T. F., Badgaiyan, R. D., Eccard, C. H., Jennings, J. R. et al. (2000). Dissociation of response conflict, attentional selection, and expectancy with functional magnetic resonance imaging. *Proceedings of the National Academy of Sciences, 97,* 8728–8733.

Cohen, A., & Ivry, R. (1989). Illusory conjunctions inside and outside the focus of attention. *Journal of Experimental Psychology: Human Perception and Performance, 15,* 650–663.

Cohen, A., & Ivry, R. (1991). Density effects in conjunction search: evidence for a coarse location mechanism of feature integration. *Journal of Experimental Psychology: Human Perception and Performance, 17,* 891–901.

Cohen, A., & Magen, H. (1999). Intra- and cross-dimensional visual search for single feature targets. *Perception and Psychophysics, 61,* 291–307.

Cohen, A., & Shoup, R. (1993). Orientation asymmetry in the flanker task. *Perception and Psychophysics, 53,* 693–703.

Cohen, A., & Shoup, R. (1997). Perceptual dimensional constraints on response selection processes. *Cognitive Psychology, 32,* 128–181.

Cohen, A., & Shoup, R. (2000). Response selection processes for conjunctive targets. *Journal of Experimental Psychology: Human Perception and Performance, 26,* 391–411.

Cohen, J. D., Servan-Schreiber, D., & McClelland, J. L. (1992). A parallel distributed processing approach to automaticity. *American Journal of Psychology, 105,* 239–269.

Connolly, J. D., Goodale, M. A., Desouza, J. F. X., Menon, R. S., & Vilis, T. (2000). A comparison of frontoparietal fMRI activation during anti-saccades and anti-pointing. *Journal of Neurophysiology, 84,* 1645–1655.

Corbetta, M., Kincade, J. M., Ollinger, J. M., McAvoy, M. P., & Shulman, G. L.

(2000). Voluntary orienting is dissociated from target detection in human posterior parietal cortex. *Nature Neuroscience, 3,* 292–297.

Corbetta, M., & Shulman, G. L. (2002). Control of goal-directed and stimulus-driven attention in the brain. *Nature Reviews Neuroscience, 3,* 201–215.

Craft, J. L., & Simon, J. R. (1970). Processing symbolic information from a visual display: interference from an irrelevant directional cue. *Journal of Experimental Psychology, 83,* 415–420.

Craighero, L., Fadiga, L., Rizzolatti, G., & Umilta, C. (1999). Action for perception: a motor–visual attentional effect. *Journal of Experimental Psychology: Human Perception and Performance, 25,* 1673–1692.

De Jong, R. (1993). Multiple bottlenecks in overlapping task performance. *Journal of Experimental Psychology: Human Perception and Performance, 19,* 965–980.

De Jong, R., Liang, C. C., & Lauber, E. (1994). Conditional and unconditional automaticity: a dual-process model of the effects of spatial stimulus–response correspondence. *Journal of Experimental Psychology: Human Perception and Performance, 20,* 731–750.

DeSoto, M. C., Fabiani, M., Geary, D. C., & Gratton, G. (2001). When in doubt, do it both ways: brain evidence of the simultaneous activation of conflicting motor responses in a spatial Stroop task. *Journal of Cognitive Neuroscience, 13,* 523–536.

Diedrichsen, J., Ivry, R. B., Cohen, A., & Danziger, S. (2000). Asymmetries in a unilateral flanker task depend on the direction of the response: the role of attentional shift and perceptual grouping. *Journal of Experimental Psychology: Human Perception and Performance, 26,* 113–126.

Di Pace E., Marangolo, P., & Pizzamiglio, L. (1997). Response bias in colour priming. *Acta Psychologica, 95,* 3–14.

Driver, J. (2001). A selective review of selective attention research from the past century. *Journal of the British Psychological Society, 92,* 53–78.

Driver, J., & Baylis, G. C. (1989). Movement and visual attention: the spotlight metaphor breaks down. *Journal of Experimental Psychology: Human Perception and Performance, 15,* 448–456.

Driver, J., & Spence, C. (1999). Cross-modal links in spatial attention. In G. W. Humphreys, J. Duncan, & A. Treisman (Eds.), *Attention, space, and action: studies in cognitive neuroscience* (pp. 130–149). Oxford: Oxford University Press.

Duncan, J. (1980). The locus of interference in the perception of simultaneous stimuli. *Psychological Review, 87,* 272–300.

Duncan, J. (1983). Perceptual selection based on alphanumeric class: evidence from partial reports. *Perception and Psychophysics, 33,* 533–547.

Duncan, J. (1984). Selective attention and the organization of visual information. *Journal of Experimental Psychology: General, 113,* 501–517.

Duncan, J. (2001). An adaptive coding model of neural function in prefrontal cortex. *Nature Reviews Neuroscience, 2,* 820–829.

Duncan, J., & Humphreys, G. W. (1989). Visual search and stimulus similarity. *Psychological Review, 96,* 433–458.

Egly, R., Driver, J., & Rafal, R. D. (1994). Shifting visual attention between objects and locations: evidence from normal and parietal lesion subjects. *Journal of Experimental Psychology: General, 123,* 161–177.

Eriksen, B. A., & Eriksen, C. W. (1974). Effects of noise letters upon the identification of a target letter in a nonsearch task. *Perception and Psychophysics, 16,* 143–149.

Eriksen, C. W., & Eriksen, B. A. (1979). Target redundancy in visual search: do repetitions of the target within the display impair processing? *Perception and Psychophysics, 26*, 195–205.

Eriksen, C. W., & Hoffman, J. E. (1972). Temporal and spatial characteristics of selective encoding from visual displays. *Perception and Psychophysics, 12*, 201–204.

Fagot, C., & Pashler, H. (1992). Making two responses to a single object: implications for the central attentional bottleneck. *Journal of Experimental Psychology: Human Perception and Performance, 18*, 1058–1079.

Feintuch, U., & Cohen, A. (2002). Visual attention and co-activation of response decisions for features from different dimensions. *Psychological Science, 13*, 362–370.

Fitts, P. M., & Deininger, R. L. (1954). S–R compatibility: correspondence among paired elements within stimulus and response codes. *Journal of Experimental Psychology, 48*, 483–492.

Fuster, J. M. (1989). *The prefrontal cortex: anatomy, physiology, and neuropsychology of the frontal lobe*. New York: Raven.

Gehring, W. J., & Knight, R. T. (2000). Prefrontal–cingulate interactions in action monitoring. *Nature Neuroscience, 3*, 516–520.

Gratton, G., Coles, M. G. H., & Donchin, E. (1992). Optimizing the use of information—strategic control of activation of responses. *Journal of Experimental Psychology: General, 121*, 480–506.

Hillyard, S. A. (1985). Electrophysiology of human selective attention. *Trends in Neurosciences, 8*, 400–405.

Hommel, B. (1993). The relationship between stimulus processing and response selection in the Simon task: evidence for a temporal overlap. *Psychological Research, 55*, 280–290.

Hommel, B. (1995). Stimulus–response compatibility and the Simon effect: toward an empirical clarification. *Journal of Experimental Psychology: Human Perception and Performance, 21*, 764–775.

Hommel, B. (1998). Automatic stimulus–response translation in dual-task performance. *Journal of Experimental Psychology: Human Perception and Performance, 24*, 1368–1384.

Hommel, B., Müsseler, J., Aschersleben, G., & Prinz, W. (2001). The Theory of Event Coding (TEC): a framework for perception and action planning. *Behavioral and Brain Sciences, 24*, 849–878.

Hommel, B., & Schneider, W. X. (2002). Visual attention and manual response selection: distinct mechanisms operating on the same codes. *Visual Cognition, 9*, 392–420.

Husain, M., Mattingley, J. B., Rorden, C., Kennard, C., & Driver, J. (2000). Distinguishing sensory and motor biases in parietal and frontal neglect. *Brain, 123*, 1643–1659.

Johnston, J. C., McCann, R. S., & Remington, R. W. (1995). Chronometric evidence for two types of attention. *Psychological Science, 6*, 365–369.

Kahneman, D. & Treisman, A. (1984). Changing views of attention and automaticity. In R. Parasuraman & D. R. Davies (Eds.) *Varieties of attention* (pp. 29–62). New York: Academic Press.

Karlin, L., & Kestenbaum, R. (1968). Effects of number of alternatives on the psychological refractory period. *Quarterly Journal of Experimental Psychology, 20*, 167–178.

Kornblum, S., Hasbroucq, T., & Osman, A. (1990). Dimensional overlap: cognitive bias for stimulus–response compatibility—a model and taxonomy. *Psychological Review, 97*, 253–270.

LaBerge, D. (1994). Quantitative models of attention and response processes in shape identification tasks. *Journal of Mathematical Psychology, 38*, 198–243.

LaBerge, D., Brown, V., Carter, M., Bash, D., & Hartley, A. (1991). Reducing the effects of adjacent distractors by narrowing attention. *Journal of Experimental Psychology: Human Perception and Performance, 17*, 65–76.

Lavie, N. (1995). Perceptual load as a necessary condition for selective attention. *Journal of Experimental Psychology: Human Perception and Performance, 21*, 451–468.

Lien, M. -C., & Proctor, R. W. (2000). Multiple spatial correspondence effects on dual-task performance. *Journal of Experimental Psychology: Human Perception and Performance, 26*, 1260–1280.

Lien, M.-C., & Proctor, R. W. (2002). Stimulus–response compatibility and psychological refractory period effects: implications for response selection. *Psychonomic Bulletin and Review, 9*, 212–238.

Logan, G. D., & Gordon, R. D. (2001). Executive control of visual attention in dual-task situations. *Psychological Review, 108*, 393–434.

Lu, C.-H., & Proctor, R. W. (1995). The influence of irrelevant location information on performance: a review of the Simon and spatial Stroop effect. *Psychonomic Bulletin and Review, 2*, 174–207.

MacLeod, C. M. (1991). Half a century of research on the Stroop effect: an integrative review. *Psychological Bulletin, 109*, 163–203.

Maddox, W. T. (2001). Separating perceptual processes from decisional processes in identification and categorization. *Perception and Psychophysics, 63*, 1183–1200.

Magen, H., & Cohen, A. (2002). Action-based and vision-based selection of input: two sources of control. *Psychological Research, 66*, 247–259.

Magen, H., & Cohen, A. (2004). *Concurrent response activation in overlapping tasks.* Manuscript submitted for publication.

McCann, R. S., & Johnston, J. C. (1992). Locus of the single-channel bottleneck in dual task interference. *Journal of Experimental Psychology: Human Perception and Performance, 18*, 471–484.

Meyer, D. E., & Kieras, D. E. (1997a). A computational theory of human multiple-task performance: the EPIC information-processing architecture and strategic response deferment model. *Psychological Review, 104*, 1–65.

Meyer, D. E., & Kieras, D. E. (1997b). A computational theory of human multiple-task performance: Part 2. Accounts of psychological refractory phenomena. *Psychological Review, 107*, 749–791.

Milham, M. P., Banich, M. T., Webb, A., Barad, V., Cohen, N. J., Wszalek, T. et al. (2001). The relative involvement of anterior cingulate and prefrontal cortex in attentional control depends on nature of conflict. *Cognitive Brain Research, 12*, 467–473.

Miller, E. K., & Cohen, J. D. (2001). An integrative theory of prefrontal cortex function. *Annual Review of Neuroscience, 24*, 167–202.

Miller, J. (1991). The flanker compatibility effect as a function of visual angle, attentional focus, visual transients, and perceptual load: a search for boundary conditions. *Perception and Psychophysics, 49*, 270–288.

Müller, H. J., & Rabbitt, P. M. A. (1989). Reflexive and voluntary orienting of visual attention—time course of activation and resistance to interruption. *Journal of Experimental Psychology: Human Perception and Performance, 15,* 315–330.

Müsseler, J., & Hommel, B. (1997). Blindness to response-compatible stimuli. *Journal of Experimental Psychology: Human Perception and Performance, 23,* 861–872.

Navon, D., & Miller, J. (2002). Queuing or sharing? A critical evaluation of the single-bottleneck notion. *Cognitive Psychology, 44,* 193–251.

Nobre, A. C., Sebestyen, G. N., Gitelman, D. R., Mesulam, M. M., Frackowiak, R. S. J., & Frith, C. D. (1997). Functional localization of the system for visuospatial attention using positron emission tomography. *Brain, 120,* 515–533.

Norman, D. A., & Shallice, T. (1986). Attention to action: willed and automatic control of behavior. In R. J. Davidson, G. E. Schwartz, & D. Shapiro (Eds.), *Consciousness and self-regulation* (Vol. 4, pp. 1–18). New York: Plenum Press.

Pashler, H. (1989). Dissociations and dependencies between speed and accuracy: evidence for a two component theory of divided attention in simple tasks. *Cognitive Psychology, 21,* 469–514.

Pashler, H. (1991). Shifting visual attention and selecting motor responses: distinct attentional mechanisms. *Journal of Experimental Psychology: Human Perception and Performance, 17,* 1023–1040.

Pashler, H. (1994). Dual task interference in simple tasks: data and theory. *Psychological Bulletin, 116,* 220–244.

Pashler, H. (1998). *The psychology of attention.* Cambridge, MA: MIT Press.

Pashler, H., & Johnston, J. C. (1989). Chronometric evidence for central postponement in temporally overlapping tasks. *Quarterly Journal of Experimental Psychology, 41A,* 19–45.

Petersen, S. E., Fox, P. T., Posner, M. I., Mintun, M., & Raichle, M. E. (1988). Positron emission tomographic studies of the cortical anatomy of single-word processing. *Nature, 331(6157),* 585–589.

Posner, M. I. (1980). Orienting of attention. *Quarterly Journal of Experimental Psychology, 32,* 3–25.

Posner, M. I., & Boies, S. J. (1971). Components of attention. *Psychological Review, 78,* 391–408.

Posner, M. I., & Dehaene, S. (1994). Attentional networks. *Trends in Neuroscience, 17,* 75–79.

Posner, M. I., Inhoff, A. W., Friedrich, F. J., & Cohen, A. (1987). Isolating attentional systems: a cognitive-anatomical analysis. *Psychobiology, 15,* 107–121.

Posner, M. I., & Petersen, S. E. (1990). The attention system of the human brain. *Annual Review of Neuroscience, 13,* 25–42.

Posner, M. I., Petersen, S. E., Fox, P. T., & Raichle, M. E. (1988). Localization of cognitive operations in the human brain. *Science, 240,* 1627–1631.

Posner, M. I., Sandson, J., Dhawan, M., & Shulman, G. L. (1989). Is word recognition automatic? A cognitive-anatomical approach. *Journal of Cognitive Neuroscience, 1,* 50–60.

Posner, M. I., Snyder, C. R. R., & Davidson, B. J. (1980). Attention and the detection of signals. *Journal of Experimental Psychology: General, 109,* 160–174.

Posner, M. I., Walker, J. A., Friedrich, F. J., & Rafal, R. (1984). Effects of parietal injury on covert orienting of attention. *Journal of Neuroscience, 4,* 1863–1874.

Rafal, R. (1994). Neglect. *Current Opinions in Neurobiology, 4,* 231–236.

Rafal, R., Danziger, S., Grossi, G., Machado, L., & Ward, R. (2002). Visual detection is gated by attending for action: evidence from hemispatial neglect. *Proceedings of the National Academy of Sciences USA, 99,* 16371–16375.

Remington, R. W., & Folk, C. L. (2001). A dissociation between attention and selection. *Psychological Science, 12,* 511–515.

Riddoch, M. J., Humphreys, G. W., & Edwards, M. G. (2000). Neuropsychological evidence distinguishing object selection from action (effector) selection. *Cognitive Neuropsychology, 17,* 547–562.

Rizzolatti, G., Riggio, L., & Sheliga, M. (1994). Space and selective attention. In C. Umilta & M. Moscovitch (Eds.), *Attention and performance XV* (pp. 231–266). Cambridge, MA: MIT Press.

Rogers, R. D., & Monsell, S. (1995). Costs of a predictable switch between simple cognitive tasks. *Journal of Experimental Psychology: General, 124,* 207–231.

Schumacher, E. H., Lauber, E. J., Glass, J. M., Zurbriggen, E. L., Gmeindl, L., Kieras, D. E. et al. (1999). Concurrent response–selection processes in dual-task performance: evidence for adaptive executive control of task scheduling. *Journal of Experimental Psychology: Human Perception and Performance, 25,* 791–814.

Schweickert, R. (1980). Critical-path scheduling of mental processes in a dual task. *Science, 209,* 704–706.

Servan-Schreiber, D. (1990). *From physiology to behavior: computational models of catecholamine modulation of information processing.* Doctoral dissertation, Carnegie Mellon University, Pittsburgh, PA.

Seymour, P. H. (1973). Stroop interference in naming and verifying spatial locations. *Perception and Psychophysics, 14,* 95–100.

Shallice T., & Burgess, P. (1993). Supervisory control of action and thought selection. In A. Baddeley & L. Weiskrantz (Eds.), *Attention: selection, awareness, and control* (pp. 171–187). Oxford: Oxford University Press.

Shiffrin, R. M. (1988). Attention. In R. C. Atkinson, R. J. Herrnstein, G. Lindzay, & R. D. Luce (Eds.), *Steven's handbook of experimental psychology: Vol. 2. Learning and cognition* (pp. 739–811). New York: Wiley.

Sperling, G. (1960). The information available in brief visual presentation. *Psychological Monographs, 74(11, Whole No. 498),* 29.

Sternberg, S. (1969). The discovery of processing stages: extensions of Donders' method. In W. G. Koster (Ed.), *Attention and performance II* (pp. 276–315). Amsterdam: North-Holland.

Stroop, J. R. (1935). Studies of interference in serial verbal reactions. *Journal of Experimental Psychology, 18,* 643–662.

Theeuwes, J. (1992). Perceptual selectivity for colour and form. *Perception and Psychophysics, 51,* 599–606.

Theeuwes, J., & Godijn, R. (2001). Attentional and oculomotor capture. In C. L. Folk B. S. Gibson (Eds.), *Attraction, distraction and action: multiple perspectives on attentional capture.* (pp. 121–149). (Advances in Psychology, Vol. 133.) New York: Elsevier.

Tipper, S. P., Brehaut, J. C., & Driver, J. (1990). Selection of moving and static objects for the control of spatially directed action. *Journal of Experimental Psychology: Human Perception and Performance, 16,* 492–504.

Tipper, S. P., Lortie, C., & Baylis, G. C. (1992). Selective reaching: evidence for action-centered attention. *Journal of Experimental Psychology: Human Perception and Performance, 18,* 891–905.

Treisman, A. (1969). Strategies and models of selective attention. *Psychological Review, 76,* 282–299.

Treisman, A., & Gelade, G. (1980). A feature integration theory of attention. *Cognitive Psychology, 12,* 97–136.

Treisman, A., & Schmidt, H. (1982). Illusory conjunctions in the perception of objects. *Cognitive Psychology, 14,* 107–141.

Tsal, Y., & Lavie, N. (1993). Location dominance in attending to color and shape. *Journal of Experimental Psychology: Human Perception and Performance, 19,* 131–139.

Turatto, M., Benso, F., Galfano, G., & Umilta, C. (2002). Nonspatial attentional shifts between audition and vision. *Journal of Experimental Psychology: Human Perception and Performance, 28,* 628–639.

Van Selst, M., & Jolicoeur, P. (1997). Decision and response in dual-task interference. *Cognitive Psychology, 33,* 266–307.

von Wright, J.M. (1968). Selection in visual immediate memory. *Quarterly Journal of Experimental Psychology, 20,* 62–68.

von Wright, J. M. (1970). On selection in visual immediate memory. *Acta Psychologica, 33,* 280–292.

von Wright, J. M. (1972). On the problem of selection in iconic memory. *Scandinavian Journal of Psychology, 13,* 159–170.

Welford, A. T. (1952). The "psychological refractory period" and the timing of high-speed performance: a review and a theory. *British Journal of Psychology, 43,* 2–19.

Wolfe, J. M., Cave, K. R., & Franzel, S. L. (1989). Guided search: an alternative to the feature integration model for visual search. *Journal of Experimental Psychology: Human Perception and Performance, 15,* 419–433.

Wong, K. F. E. (2002). The relationship between attentional blink and psychological refractory period. *Journal of Experimental Psychology: Human Perception and Performance, 28,* 54–71.

Yantis, Y., & Johnson, D. N. (1990). Mechanisms of attentional priority. *Journal of Experimental Psychology: Human Perception and Performance, 16,* 812–825.

Yantis, Y., & Johnston, J. C. (1990). On the locus of visual selection: evidence from focused attention tasks. *Journal of Experimental Psychology: Human Perception and Performance, 16,* 135–149.

Yantis, S., & Jonides, J. (1984). Abrupt visual onsets and selective attention: evidence from visual search. *Journal of Experimental Psychology: Human Perception and Performance, 10,* 601–621.

3 Attentional selection in sequential manual movements, movements around an obstacle and in grasping

Heiner Deubel and Werner X. Schneider

Abstract

A number of previous studies have shown that during the preparation of a goal-directed movement, perceptual selection (i.e. visual attention) and action selection (the selection of the movement target) are closely related. In four experiments, we studied attentional selection in movement situations in which more than just a single movement target had to be considered. In all four experiments, a dual-task paradigm was used that combined a perceptual discrimination task with movement preparation (Deubel & Schneider, 1996). In Experiment 1, we studied attentional deployment in a task that required the participant to perform a sequence of two subsequent movements to two targets. The results suggest that visual attention is not only allocated to the first but also to the second movement target even before the onset of the initial movement. The results of Experiment 2 demonstrated that not just the movement goal but also an obstacle is selectively processed when it is part of the movement plan. In Experiments 3 and 4, participants had to grasp a cross-like object with thumb and index finger. The experimental results reveal that visual attention is largely confined to the action-relevant parts of the object—that is, those parts that will be grasped. Together the findings demonstrate that attention is basic to sensorimotor processing and that our dual-task paradigm is well suited for unveiling covert sensorimotor selection processes that occur before complex open movements.

Introduction

Selective attention is traditionally a major research area in cognitive psychology. Visual attention, more specifically, has long been thought to play a central role in visual perception. Attention facilitates detection (e.g. Posner, 1980), helps locate targets in an environment of distractors (e.g. Treisman, 1988), integrates features from different visual modules into "object files" (Treisman & Gelade, 1980), helps recognize objects (e.g. Schneider, 1995) and regulates entry into visual short-term memory (Duncan & Humphreys,

1989). In contrast to this classical view of visual attention as a mechanism that supports perception, the potential role of visual attention in the control of action had received considerably less attention in basic psychological research. It was at the end of the 1980s that Alan Allport (1987) and Odmar Neumann (1987) suggested that spatiomotor actions also imply a selection process. Goal-directed actions such as grasping an object are normally directed to a single target. In natural environments, normally many instead of just one object are present in the visual field. Therefore, a selective mechanism is required that provides the relevant spatial parameters of the movement target to the motor system, excluding the effects of action-irrelevant distractors. This selective process has been termed "selection-for-action" (Allport, 1987) and "parameter specification" (Neumann, 1987). Because the required spatial information is provided by the visual system, these authors have suggested that visual attention is central to the underlying selective processing. Unfortunately, these suggestions did not trigger much experimental work.

Our knowledge of the *physiological* basis of visual attention, on the other hand, advanced together with our knowledge of the architecture of the visual system. It is now commonly believed that visual processing occurs in parallel and interacting streams at different, quasi-hierarchical levels (see, for example, DeYoe & Van Essen, 1988; Milner & Goodale, 1995). Mishkin, Ungerleider, and Macko (1983) claimed that the visual system consists of two main pathways: the ventral "what"-pathway, whose function is to recognize objects based on their visual appearance, and the dorsal "where"-pathway, which computes spatial position information about objects. At the cortical level, the segregation of both pathways can be tracked back to the primary visual cortex, from where the "what"-pathway leads ventrally to the inferior temporal lobe, while the "where"-pathway runs dorsally into the posterior parietal lobe. Since this proposal, a large body of research has supported the distinction between the two cortical pathways (see, however, Zeki, 1993). The labelling of the ventral and dorsal pathway as "what"- and "where"-pathways, respectively, was later criticized by Goodale and Milner (1992; Milner & Goodale, 1995). These authors believed that we should continue to ascribe the computation of "what"-aspects—that is, the identification of objects—to the ventral pathway. However, they offered a different view of the presumed function of the dorsal pathway, suggesting a shift in emphasis from spatial perception to spatial information for action. Milner and Goodale (1995) argued that the main task of dorsal processing is the computation of spatial information for motor actions such as a saccade or a reach towards an object. Their view is supported by many human neuro-psychological studies and neurophysiological work in macaques, especially by single cell recordings (see Milner & Goodale, 1995). A related distinction was suggested by Jeannerod (1994), who differentiated a "semantic mode" of processing, located in the temporal lobe (ventral stream), and a "pragmatic mode", located in the parietal cortex (dorsal stream). Taken together, the reviewed data indicate that the idea of a single representation of external space is probably wrong, and that instead several spatiomotor representations—sometimes also called processing streams—exist in parallel for different kinds of motor actions (see, for example, Graziano & Gross, 1994; Rizzolatti, Riggio, & Sheliga, 1994; Stein, 1992). For instance, information about the parameters of goal-directed saccadic eye movements is presumably coded in the lateral intraparietal area, while endpoints for grasping movements are computed in area 7b—both are parts of the parietal lobe. These findings suggest that the brain codes spatial information for different effectors in different parts of the brain (see also Rushworth & Ellison, this volume).

Given that the primate visual system can be divided into a ventral stream for perception and a dorsal stream for action control, and granting that selective processing occurs in both streams, then what is the relationship between "selection-for-perception" and "selection-for-action"? Our empirical work, which will be presented later, grew out of a recently developed comprehensive model that comprises both aspects of selection, the visual attention model (VAM, Schneider, 1995). This model postulates that both selection functions are performed by a single, common visual attention mechanism that selects one object at a time for processing with high priority. More precisely, VAM makes the following assumptions: (1) "Selection-for-perception" is carried out within the ventral pathway of the visual brain. (2) "Selection-for-action" is assumed to occur in the dorsal pathway of the visual brain originating in V1 and ending in the posterior parietal cortex. The brain areas in this pathway compute spatial information required for motor action, including the location of, and size information for, the object that should be grasped. As a consequence of the selection of an object, spatial information for action is provided for the setting up of "motor programs" towards the selected object. These motor programs can refer to a grasp, to a pointing movement or a goal-directed eye movement. The model assumes that they do not imply overt execution. Rather, a separate control ("go") signal is postulated for that purpose (e.g. Bullock & Grossberg, 1988; Rizzolatti, Riggio, Dascola, & Umiltà, 1987). (3) A common visual attention mechanism is assumed for both selection functions, which gives a higher processing priority to the low-level visual representations (e.g. area V1) of the selected object. As a consequence, the neural activation flow representing the selected object (and its location) is processed with highest priority and projects to the higher-level ventral and dorsal areas. Within the ventral areas, the selected object is therefore recognized fastest and made available to conscious visual perception. Simultaneously, within the dorsal pathway, motor programs for a grasping, pointing or a saccadic eye movement towards the selected object are established with the highest priority.

VAM's assumption of a common selection mechanism for ventral and dorsal selection predicts, at the behavioural level, that the preparation of a spatial–motor action should bind the perceptual processing system to the movement target and its location. This means that the perceptual representation of the external world during the preparation of a movement should be best for the movement target, allowing for efficient recognition of the target object. In contrast, the intention to attend to a certain object for perceptual analysis should automatically lead to the implementation of (covert) motor programs towards this object.

Motivated by the predictions of VAM we began to study the coupling of visual attention and motor control for the case of saccadic eye movements (Deubel & Schneider, 1996). In this study, participants performed a dual-task experiment that required perceptual discrimination (discriminating the letter "E" from a reversed "E") while preparing a saccadic eye movement. The spatial relationship between the saccade target (ST) and the discrimination target (DT) was systematically varied. The discrimination target disappeared before the actual eye movement started, so that perceptual performance was measured during the saccade preparation phase only. If visual attention for perception and saccade target selection can be controlled independently, discrimination performance should not depend on the location of the saccade target. On the other hand, if both selection processes are coupled via a common selection mechanism, then discrimination performance should be best when both the saccade and discrimination targets refer to the same object. The results showed that there was indeed a high degree of spatially selective coupling between the ST position and DT position. Discrimination performance was good when both the saccade and discrimination targets referred to the same object. Performance for an object that appeared only 1° of visual angle away from the ST location, however, was close to chance level. A second experiment in this study revealed that the coupling between perceptual processing and the selection of the saccade target is obligatory; it is not possible to attend to one location in space while preparing a saccade to another (Deubel & Schneider, 1996; Schneider & Deubel, 2002). The claim that saccade programming and selective perception are related is not unique and has found support in other experimental studies (e.g. Hoffman & Subramaniam, 1995; Kowler, Anderson, Dosher, & Blaser, 1995; Shepherd, Findlay, & Hockey, 1986).

In addition to saccadic eye movements, the visual attention model postulates that *any* spatiomotor action towards an object—for instance, a pointing or a grasping movement—should bind the attentional mechanism in visual perception to the movement target. We tested this prediction in various dual-task paradigms in which participants had to make a fast manual pointing movement to a centrally cued item (the movement target) while trying to discriminate the letter "E" from a reversed "E" (the discrimination target) at that or at a different location. In one type of paradigm, the movement target and the discrimination target appeared within a linear string of distractors (Deubel, Schneider, & Paprotta, 1998). In a more recent version of the task (Paprotta, Deubel, & Schneider, 1999), they appeared within a ring of distractors placed on a circular array around the central fixation (cf. Figure 3.1). In both cases, the participants had to maintain strict ocular fixation at the centre of the screen. For goal-directed pointing, it seems less obvious than for saccades why the preparation of a goal-directed movement should also influence perception. Nevertheless, the results were again very clear-cut, showing that perceptual performance depended strongly on the position of the movement target; discrimination performance was best when both the movement and discrimination targets referred to the same location and considerably worse in the case of spatial non-congruency (see also Humphreys et al., this volume).

Evidence for the relevance of a visual selection process in manual movement programming comes from several studies that analysed the effect of task-related distractors on the preparation of manual movements. Tipper, Lortie, and Baylis (1992) examined the effect of a distractor on a reaching movement towards a target. Presentation of the distractor affected movement latency, however, only when the distractor appeared between the starting position of the hand and the target location. Distractors beyond the target location did not influence the response latency. Therefore, competition between target and distractor for movement control depended on their spatial relationship. In a study by Castiello (1996), participants had to grasp an object while counting the number of times a distractor object was illuminated by a spotlight. The results showed that the type of distractor influenced the amplitude of the peak grip aperture to the target—that is, the manipulation component of the movement. When the distractor was smaller/bigger than the target, the peak aperture

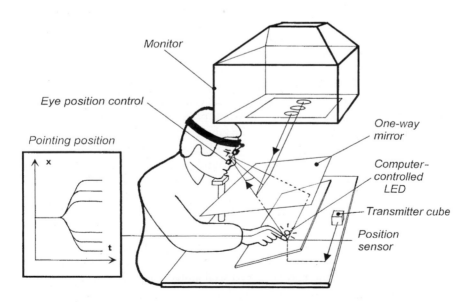

Figure 3.1 Experimental set-up.

was also smaller/bigger than in trials without a distractor. Craighero, Fadiga, Rizzolatti, and Umiltà (1998) investigated whether a non-relevant prime picture influenced the latency of the following grasping movement. They found a reduction of grasping latency when the prime picture depicted the to-be-grasped object compared with when the prime depicted a different object. So, visual perception of an object, here the prime, influenced the programming of a movement that immediately followed the perception.

Attention-related effects can also influence the transport and the manipulation components of a grasping movement differently. Bonfiglioli and Castiello (1998) had participants grasp an object while they had to attend to a moving distractor of the same size either overtly or covertly. Interference effects on the transport component were found for the case of covert attention. No effects were found for the manipulation component of the movement, supposedly because target and distractor involved programming the same parameters for their manipulation components. This view is supported by the results of Kritikos, Bennett, Dunai, and Castiello (2000), who varied distractor size and found that only distractors whose size was different from that of the target caused interference effects.

All of the research described above was characterized by the movements being directed to a single location in space, a single target object. Accordingly, the main task for the sensorimotor system is to selectively process the movement goal. However, many types of goal-directed movements in natural environments are more complex in the sense that their preparation requires us to consider more than just a single item or location. When we intend to open a bottle of wine, we first prepare and perform a grasp to the opener and only then move on to the bottle. The question arises as to whether in such sequential movements the selective processing is also purely sequential, which would mean that processing the second target would occur only after the first movement. Alternatively, the selection of the second movement target may already have begun before the onset of the first movement segment. A similar problem occurs when, in order to move to an object, the hand has to avoid an obstacle. At some point in time during movement preparation, the spatial location of an obstacle and possibly other properties, such as size and orientation, have to be computed to program a trajectory that leads the hand effectively around it. Finally, when we grasp an object with index finger and thumb, the two separate spatial locations where the fingers touch the object are both of some relevance for the grasp, while other parts of the object are of less importance for the prehension movement.

In this chapter, we present some of our recent work on attentional selection during these more complex movements. The results demonstrate that our discrimination paradigm is indeed well suited to study covert selection processes before the movements take place.

Experiment 1: attentional selection in sequential pointing movements

Several studies have shown that when participants have to begin a sequence of movements to several targets, the latency of even the first movement increases with the number of movements to execute; this holds for manual movements (e.g. Henry & Rogers, 1960; Sternberg, Monsell, Knoll, & Wright, 1978) as well as for sequences of saccades (Zingale & Kowler, 1987). This seems to suggest that when a sequence of two goal-directed movements is programmed, some aspects of the second movement target are processed before the onset of the movement to the first target. However, to our knowledge, there is no direct experimental evidence for this. If the assumed obligatory coupling between selection-for-perception and selection-for-action also holds in the case of sequential movements, this would imply that the second movement target should be perceptually selected for some time before the onset of the initial movement. We therefore studied the selective perceptual processing of the first and the second movement target at various times before movement onset with our dual-task paradigm.

The experimental set-up for this and the following experiments is outlined in Figure 3.1 (see also Deubel et al., 1998). The stimuli were presented on a 21-inch colour monitor with a resolution of 1024×768 pixels; the frame rate was 100 Hz. Visual information was presented via a half-translucent mirror at an effective viewing distance of 60 cm. By using this set-up it was possible to present movement targets and discrimination stimuli on the working plane in front of the participant without seeing the hand movement or having the hand obstructing the discrimination targets during the movement. Eye fixation was controlled by an SMI-Eyelink Infrared Eye Monitoring system. Manual movements were recorded with a Polhemus Fastrak electromagnetic position and orientation measuring system. This system provides the spatial position of a small position sensor that was mounted on the tip of the participant's index finger. The overall accuracy of the system was better than 2 mm. A small red light-emitting diode (LED) was attached to the sensor, which allowed visual feedback to be provided about the spatial position of the fingertip at the beginning of each trial.

The sequence of stimuli and the experimental task are illustrated in Figure 3.2. The participant was asked to maintain fixation at the centre of the screen throughout the experiment. A circular array of 12 masking letters was initially displayed at an eccentricity of 7.2°. At the beginning of each trial, the participant put her finger on the small cross in the centre of the screen. After a random delay, a central arrow cue appeared indicating the first movement target. The participant was instructed to perform a pointing movement to this target, as fast and as precisely as possible, and to move on from there to the target "two hours" further in the clockwise direction. After a variable stimulus onset asynchrony (SOA), 11 of the masking letters changed into distractors (resembling "2" or "5"). At one position, however,

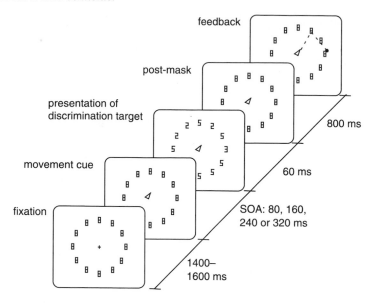

Figure 3.2 The sequence of stimuli in Experiment 1.

the critical discrimination target was presented. The discrimination target consisted of either an "E" or a reversed "E", which was presented for 60 ms. Then, the discrimination target and the distractors changed back to the masking letters. Since the typical movement onset latency in this experiment was around 350 ms, it is obvious from the timing of the stimulus sequence that the critical discrimination stimulus appears and disappears in most cases before the onset of the movement. At the end of each trial, the participant received feedback about movement accuracy by means of a red dot displayed at the landing position of the second movements. In the experiments presented here, the position of the discrimination target was held constant within blocks of 48 trials, while the location of the movement target was selected randomly from 6 of the 12 clock hour-hand positions. In addition to the experimental condition with sequential pointing, the participants also performed a control block with a single pointing movement to the indicated target.

Figure 3.3 provides perceptual performance (given as percent correct) as a function of the relative spatial distance, D, between the position of the discrimination target and the movement target. The data are averages for six participants. They are shown separately for the different SOA values. A distance D of 0 indicates that the discrimination target appeared at the location of the first movement target, a distance of +2 indicates that the discrimination target was presented two positions further in the clockwise direction, which is at the second movement target location. The other values of D present performance at the other relative locations which were irrelevant for the action. The results from the control block (single

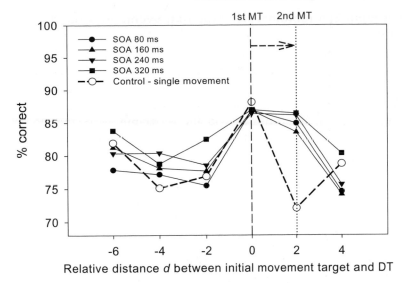

Figure 3.3 Perceptual discrimination performance as a function of the relative spatial
distance between the position of the movement target and the discrimination target (DT). Dashed curve: results from the "single movement" control block. Solid curves: results from the experimental conditions with
sequential pointing. The results are shown separately for the different
SOA values. A distance of 0 indicates that DT appeared at the location of
the first movement target (MT); a distance of +2 indicates that DT was
presented at the second movement target location.

movements) are depicted by the dashed curve. As expected from our previous work, the results for the single-movement condition reveal that
discrimination performance is best at the movement target location (i.e. at D
$= 0$), and drops steeply for the neighbouring locations. For the experimental
condition (solid curves), performance was again numerically best at the
location of the initial movement goal. However, the results also reveal that
performance at position 2, which is the location of the second movement
target, is now no longer statistically different from performance at position
0. Performance at both movement target positions is, however, significantly
better than performance at all the other, task-irrelevant positions.

The results indicate that when a sequence of two movements is prepared,
selective perceptual processing of the second movement target begins before
the onset of the first movement. We interpret this finding as evidence that,
during the preparation of the movement sequence, visual attention has
already moved to the second target, allowing for selective processing and
integration of the target location into the movement program. Somewhat
unexpectedly, the data analysis reveals that there is no significant effect of
SOA on perceptual performance. This seems to suggests that the first and the
second movement target are selected temporally in parallel.

Experiment 2: attentional selection in movements around an obstacle

Experiment 1 demonstrated that when two stimuli are sequentially accessed by goal-directed movements, both are selected and processed even before the onset of the first movement. However, what happens when only one of two stimuli is the goal of the movement, while the other has to be avoided but nevertheless has to be considered in the programming of the movement trajectory? To address this question, we examined covert selective processing of an object that constitutes an obstacle for a goal-directed manual movement.

Six individuals participated in this experiment, the layout of which is shown in Figure 3.4a. Throughout the experiment, the participants had to maintain fixation on a small fixation cross in the middle of the screen. The stimulus display consisted of three masking characters located at equal

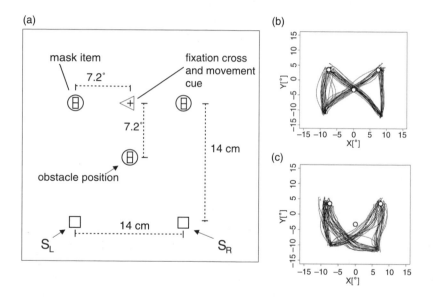

Figure 3.4 (a) Stimulus layout in Experiment 2. The participant had to maintain fixation on the small fixation cross in the middle of the screen. The display consisted of three masking characters located at equal distances from the fixation. In the "with obstacle" condition, a wooden cylinder was present at the location of the lower character. S_R and S_L indicate the starting positions for the right and left index finger, respectively. The arrow indicated the movement target and served as the "go" -signal for the reaching movement. After an SOA of 0, 100 or 200 ms, two of the masking items changed into distractors, and at one position into the critical discrimination stimulus ("E" or reversed "E"). (b, c) Typical movement trajectories for the "no obstacle" and "with obstacle" conditions.

distances from the fixation. Two basic experimental conditions were run in different blocks. In the "with obstacle" condition, a wooden cylinder (height 8 cm, diameter 1.7 cm) was placed at the location of the lower character. In the "no obstacle" condition, no obstacle was present. On each trial, the participants initially placed the index finger of their right hand on the starting position indicated by S_R in Figure 3.4a, and the index finger of their left hand on S_L. After a short delay, the finger with which the reach had to be performed was indicated by flashing either the right (S_R) or left (S_L) starting position. After a further delay of 500 ms, an arrow (also shown in Figure 3.4a) appeared at the fixation point, which indicated to the left or to the right and thus the target for the reach. The arrow also served as the "go" cue for the reaching movement. The participants were instructed to perform the reach as fast and as precisely as possible with the hand indicated. After a SOA of 0, 100 or 200 ms, two of the masking items changed into distractors, and at one position into the critical discrimination stimulus ("E" or reversed "E"). These stimuli were displayed for 120 ms and then replaced by the masking items. Figures 3.4b and 3.4c provide typical movement trajectories for the different conditions. It can be seen that the presence of the wooden cylinder was effective in forcing the participants to adjust their movement trajectories to avoid the obstacle (Figure 3.4c).

Perceptual performance at the obstacle location is shown in Figure 3.5 as a function of SOA. Figure 3.5a displays the data for vertical movements, and Figure 3.5b those for oblique movements. The open squares in each plot indicate the data for the conditions without the obstacle, the solid circles those with the obstacle present. It can be seen that for vertical movements, discrimination performance was generally low and independent of obstacle presence and SOA. This suggests that the obstacle location was not specifically processed. For oblique movements, however, perceptual performance turned out to be significantly better for the condition with the obstacle than in the no obstacle condition.

The results indicate preferential processing at the location of the obstacle for the diagonal movements, which require participants to adjust their movement trajectory to avoid the obstacle, given the obstacle is present. This implies that the obstacle is selected during movement preparation, but only if it is of relevance for the movement (i.e. for diagonal movements with obstacle present). The findings show that our paradigm demonstrates attention-related selective processing not just for movement goals, but also for other, action-relevant locations, such as an obstacle.

Experiment 3: attentional selection in grasping

When the task is to grasp an object with thumb and index finger, it is not just necessary for the visual system to compute the object's location in order to prepare the initial aiming phase of the movement, but also to compute the positions where finger and thumb will touch the object. The question arises

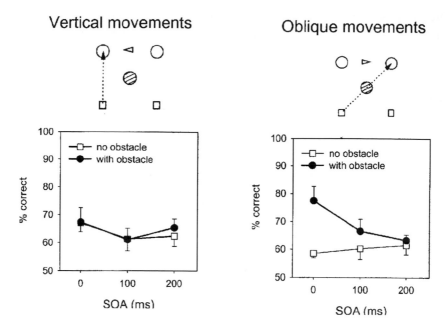

Figure 3.5 Discrimination performance at the obstacle location as a function of SOA in Experiment 2: (a) results for vertical movements, (b) results for oblique movements. Vertical bars indicate standard errors. The open squares in each plot depict movements without the obstacle, the solid circles those with the obstacle present.

whether these positions receive prioritized processing with respect to other, grasp-irrelevant locations. The aim of Experiment 3, therefore, was to study the spatial and temporal properties of attentional deployment in a task in which an X-shaped object had to be grasped with thumb and index finger. A more detailed account of the methodology and further, related experiments is provided by Schiegg, Deubel, and Schneider (2003).

Six right-handed individuals participated in this experiment. Their task was to grasp a wooden X-shaped object (see Figure 3.6a) that was mounted in the centre of the working plane in front. The display consisted of the outline of the object and the visual stimuli used for measuring discrimination performance. The participants had to grasp the object with either the left or right thumb and index finger. They had to grasp the top left branch end with the index finger and the bottom right branch end with their thumb when using the left hand. When using their right hand, they had to grasp the top right branch end with the index finger and the bottom left branch end with the thumb.

The basic stimulus layout is depicted in Figure 3.6b. In the centre of the screen there was a small fixation cross surrounded by the outline of the X-shaped object to be grasped, which was 6.3° of visual angle in diameter.

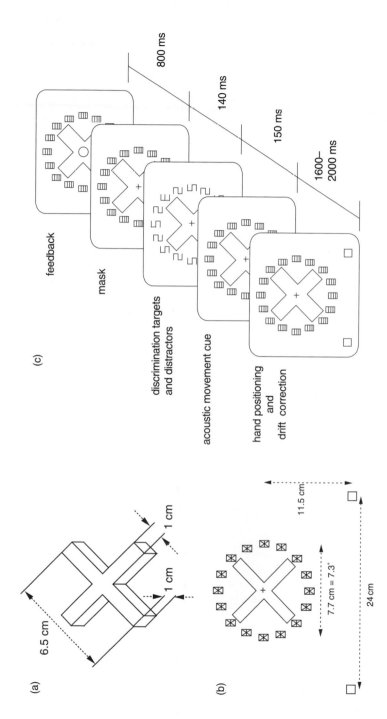

Figure 3.6 (a) Wooden cross-like object to be grasped in Experiment 3. (b) Spatial layout of display. The display consisted of the outline of the object and the visual stimuli used to measure discrimination performance. Sixteen mask elements (0.86 × 0.57° in size) were spaced equally at 3.35° eccentricity on a virtual circle around the object's centre. (c) Temporal stimulus sequence.

Sixteen mask elements (0.86 × 0.57° in size) were spaced equally at 3.35° eccentricity on a virtual circle around the object's centre, with one element being located at the end of each branch of the X and three between neighbouring branches. At the bottom of the display there were two small rectangles visible during the hand positioning phase before each trial. They served as markers for the starting position of the participant's hands.

The temporal stimulus sequence is shown in Figure 3.6c. The participants were told that the experiment consisted of two simultaneous tasks, grasping and discrimination, of which the former had priority. They were instructed to fixate the cross in the centre of the display and to place their hands on the grasping plane at the starting positions marked by the rectangles. After a delay, the pitch of an acoustic cue indicated the hand to grasp with. This tone also served as the movement "go" signal. Then, 150 ms after the "go" signal, all mask elements changed, displaying an "E" or a reversed "E" at exactly one of the four branch ends as the discrimination target, while "2" and "5" were displayed at all other positions as distractors. After a target presentation interval of 140 ms, targets and distractors were again replaced by the mask items. As in the previous experiments, the participants had to indicate by a keypress whether they had perceived an "E" or a reversed "E" in the stimulus. In addition to the experimental blocks, the participants also performed two control blocks: one "discrimination only, no grasping" block and one "grasping only, no discrimination" block.

The results are plotted in Figure 3.7, which shows discrimination performance as percent correct, at the grasped and at the non-grasped locations. Figure 3.7 also presents perceptual performance from the "discrimination only, no grasping" control block (horizontal dashed line). For analysing

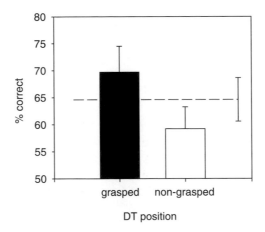

Figure 3.7 Discrimination performance in Experiment 3 at the grasped and at the non-grasped locations. Perceptual performance from the "discrimination only, no grasping" control block is indicated by the horizontal dashed line. DT = discrimination target.

percent correct discrimination, right and left hand data were pooled. The data show that perceptual performance is better at the grasped than at the non-grasped location (for details, see Schiegg et al., 2003). Thus, the results of Experiment 3 show that attention determined by measuring percent correct discrimination is increased for locations to be grasped compared to locations not to be grasped of the same object during preparation of prehension movements. A further experiment not reported here demonstrated that a similar conclusion holds even when participants know in advance where the critical discrimination stimulus will appear (Schiegg et al., 2003). This indicates that the coupling is obligatory in the sense that it is difficult to attend to a specific part of the object while preparing a grasp involving other object parts (see also Humphreys et al., this volume).

Experiment 4: attentional selection in grasping—location- or object-based?

The results for Experiment 3 provide evidence for selective perceptual processing when there is one object to be grasped, selecting relevant over irrelevant "parts" of the visual field, which in this case belong to the same object. However, the detailed nature of the selection process still remains unclear from this experiment. In particular, is selection specific to spatial locations, directing the focus of attention to the spots that would be the targets for thumb and index finger, or is it object-specific, as for example the visual attention model of Schneider (1995) would propose? While the results of previous studies (e.g. Downing & Pinker, 1985; Posner, 1980) supported the then dominant spotlight model, there has been growing evidence that objects can be the units of attention (e.g. Baylis & Driver, 1993; Duncan, 1984; Egly, Driver, & Rafal, 1994). The fact that in our paradigm the discrimination targets were very close to the object's locations relevant for the prehension task (its four branch ends), would at first glance argue in favour of the spotlight model to be the underlying selection mechanism, with the centre of attention being at one of the branch ends to be grasped. The problem with this interpretation is that one would have to assume sequential processing of the two target locations, or a split spotlight. These alternatives cannot be ruled out by our results, but they appear to be unlikely given the experimental data (for further discussion, see Schiegg et al., 2003).

As an alternative possibility, it might be that the whole object area between the spots where thumb and index finger touch is selected. In other words, attentional selection may be object-specific in the sense that a task-relevant sub-object—in the case of the cross, the bar extending between thumb and index finger—is selectively processed. We tested this hypothesis in Experiment 4 using the stimuli shown in Figure 3.8a. Now, the mask and the discrimination target always appeared in the centre of the cross. The object contour was modified such that it implied two bars, one above the other. Thus, visually, the discrimination target seemed to belong to the upper bar.

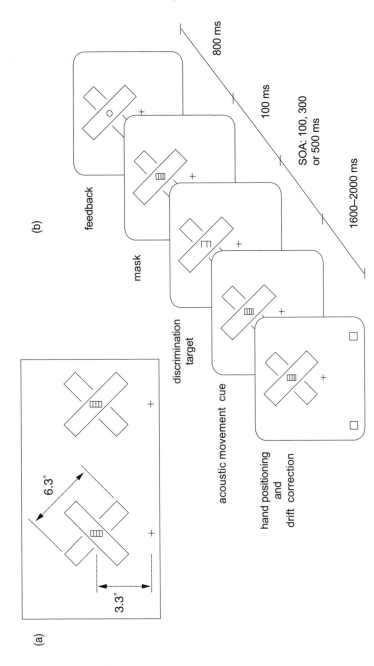

Figure 3.8 (a) Outlines of the stimuli used in Experiment 4. The mask and the discrimination target always appeared in the centre of the cross. The object contour was displayed such that it implied two bars, one above the other. Therefore, visually, the discrimination target seemed to belong to the upper bar. (b) Stimulus sequence.

The stimulus sequence is displayed in Figure 3.8b. The pitch of an acoustical cue determined whether the participant had to grasp with the left or the right hand; the tone also served as a "go" signal.

Figure 3.9 displays perceptual performance as a function of SOA. The discrimination data are shown separately for the cases where the grasped object was the upper or lower bar, respectively ("congruent grasping", solid circles versus "incongruent grasping", open squares). We found that perceptual performance was significantly superior for the cases where the discrimination target belonged to the grasped sub-object—that is, for the cases where the upper bar was grasped. Since the discrimination target appeared at exactly the same spatial location in all cases, this result strongly argues for object-specific selection in the sense that the to-be-grasped bar as a whole is selectively processed by the perceptual system during movement preparation.

Discussion

The aim of the four experiments reported here was to extend the results of saccade and reaching tasks suggesting an obligatory coupling between (dorsal) selection for action and (ventral) selection for perception (Deubel & Schneider 1996; Deubel et al., 1998) to more complex reaching and prehension tasks. In contrast to these earlier investigations in which one small, unstructured (with respect to motor parameter computation) object served as the movement target, the experiments reported here involved a more complex computation of motor parameters before the movement in which more than just a single object has to be considered in movement preparation. In particular, the first of the four experiments used a paradigm in which

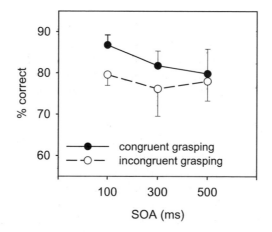

Figure 3.9 Perceptual performance as a function of SOA. The discrimination results are shown separately for the cases where the grasped object was the upper or the lower bar, respectively (solid circles *vs* open squares).

participants were required to perform a sequential movement to two pre-determined targets. The discrimination data reveal that perceptual perform-ance is significantly better both at the position of the first and of the second movement target with respect to the other possible discrimination target positions, suggesting that the second target position is selected before the first movement and processed with higher priority than task-irrelevant loca-tions. It is somewhat puzzling that this pattern is independent of SOA, which seems to suggest that both the first and the second movement locations are processed in parallel. This may pose a problem to models of visual attention, such as VAM proposed by Schneider (1995). VAM states that a common selection mechanism exists for dorsal and ventral processing, which is sug-gested to select *one object at a time* in the "early" stages of the visual system, resulting in an increased activation of the visual representations of this object in higher-level ventral and dorsal visual areas. This increased acti-vation then allows the selective perceptual analysis of the selected object to the level of recognition, and the selective computation of its spatial param-eters, such that a saccade, a reach or a grasp can be performed (as soon as an according "go" signal is provided). So, VAM suggests a strict one-object-at-a-time rule: Whenever a goal-directed action towards an object is prepared, only this movement target can be perceptually processed in higher-level ven-tral areas. On the other hand, whenever visual attention focuses on an item for the purpose of object recognition, no other object can be selected for goal-directed actions. According to VAM, dissociations can only occur by a serial process, implying that the visual recognition of an object should considerably delay a motor response towards a different, spatially separate target. It should be also emphasized that the selection is assumed to be object-specific; this is in contrast to other considerations that assume a purely spatial organization of attentional selection (e.g. Hughes & Zimba, 1987; Rizzolatti et al., 1987). If our interpretation of the experimental find-ings of Experiment 1 is correct, VAM needs to be modified, allowing the selection of more than one movement target at a time. Theories of visual attention such as Bundesen's TVA (1990) would be possible candidates for creating a parallel processing version of VAM. The TVA assumes a parallel, but capacity-limited, processing of the items presented in the visual field.

The finding that the second target is processed even before the onset of the first movement is in line with the results of Ricker, Elliot, Lyons, Gauldie, Chua, and Byblow (1999). These authors measured the latency of the first reaching movement in a sequence of two directed to two targets. They found that the latency of the initial movement was longer when a second movement was required. Blanking of the second movement target during the first movement resulted in longer latencies of the second movement segment. Ricker et al. suggested that the preparation of the second movement is com-pleted before the first movement is terminated, and that visual processing before movement onset can be used to formulate a movement plan to both targets in the sequence.

In the second experiment, we studied attentional selection when participants had to adjust their movement trajectory to avoid an obstacle in a reaching task. Although the obstacle was not the goal of the movement, its spatial properties had to be integrated into the movement preparation. As a consequence, we expected the obstacle location to be selectively processed at some time before the onset of the open movement. The experimental data (Figure 3.5) confirmed this expectation, showing that perceptual performance at the obstacle location is indeed superior to the other conditions, but only if (1) the movement is such that the obstacle has to be considered and (2) the obstacle is present. Thus it seems that in an early part of movement programming, the obstacle position is selected by visual attention, allowing the integration of its spatial location in the programming movement trajectory.

Probably the most interesting results, however, are those from Experiments 3 and 4 in which participants had to grasp a cross-like object with either the right or the left hand. As in the first experiment, there were two relevant "movement targets" for every single prehension movement, because the thumb and the index finger had to be directed to their final target locations on the object. Second, with respect to processing the to-be-grasped physical object itself, prehension tasks should cause some parts of the object (the to-be-grasped branch ends) to be more relevant to programming the motor parameters than other parts. Therefore, these experiments addressed two main questions: First, whether the coupling between selection-for-action and selection-for-perception observed for simple reaching tasks could also be found for the more complex prehension tasks. And, second, how a physical object would be processed when only parts of it were relevant for programming the motor task.

As to the first question, the results of Experiments 3 show that there is indeed a coupling between dorsal and ventral processing for both of the relevant parts (landing position of both the index finger and thumbs). Target discrimination, which served as a measure for visual attention during the preparation of the movement, was always best when during movement preparation the target appeared at a location that would be grasped—that is, next to a branch end that would be touched by either index finger or thumb.

Regarding the second question, we evaluated how attention is allocated to an object when only parts of it are relevant to the motor task. We have previously shown that there is selection of one relevant object from among other irrelevant objects during preparation of goal-directed pointing movements (e.g. Deubel et al., 1998). The results of Experiment 4 demonstrate that a similar selection process is at work when there is only one object, again selecting relevant over irrelevant "parts" of the visual field, which in this case belong to the same object. The results suggest that there is "attentional decomposition" (e.g., Schneider, 1995): the object (represented by its outline) is decomposed into movement-relevant and movement-irrelevant parts. Since both parts are superimposed in space, our result can be best explained by assuming object-specific attentional selection as the underlying mechanism. This is in line with experimental work on attention suggesting that attentional selection can be object- rather than space-based (e.g. Duncan, 1984; Egly et al., 1994). We therefore propose that when a more complex object has to be grasped, it is eventually decomposed into two or more sub-objects, one of which is relevant for the action. This sub-object is then selected as a whole by an object-based attentional mechanism.

Object-based selection is compatible with the visual attention model of Schneider (1995), which states that only one low-level object at a time can be selected. Two further attentional theories explicitly include selection in the dorsal stream, namely the "premotor theory" of Rizzolatti et al. (1987, 1994) and the "integrated competition hypothesis" of Duncan (1996) (for a comparison of these alternative attention models, see Schneider & Deubel, 2002). The central claim of premotor theory is that the control of "spatial attention" originates in the dorsal spatiomotor areas. Duncan (1996) also proposed a framework for attentional processes in the primate brain that incorporates dorsal spatiomotor processes. According to his integrated competition hypothesis, attention is considered to be an emerging state in which visual representations of one object win the competition against representations of other objects. The biasing of competition towards one object is assumed to be controlled by the current task instruction and to originate in brain areas where the task-relevant attributes are computed. Therefore, analogous to the visual attention model, the integrated competition hypothesis predicts an object-specific coupling between the ventral and dorsal streams.

In summary, our findings provide further evidence for an obligatory coupling of dorsal and ventral processing as proposed by the attention models of Rizzolatti et al. (1994), Schneider (1995) and Duncan (1996). They demonstrate that specific locations, objects and even parts of objects are selectively processed during the preparation of more complex reaching and grasping tasks, once they become relevant for the planned goal-directed action. Furthermore, our results demonstrate that our dual-task paradigm, which combines a letter discrimination task with the preparation of a goal-directed movement, is able to serve as a probe into otherwise covert, selective sensorimotor processing.

Acknowledgement

This research was supported by the Deutsche Forschungsgemeinschaft (SFB 462/B4 and De 336/2).

References

Allport, D. A. (1987). Selection for action: some behavioral and neurophysiological considerations of attention and action. In H. Heuer & A. F. Sanders (Eds.),

Perspectives on perception and action (pp. 395–419). Hillsdale, NJ: Lawrence Erlbaum Associates Inc.

Baylis, G., & Driver, J. (1993). Visual attention and objects: evidence for a hierarchical coding of location. *Journal of Experimental Psychology: Human Perception and Performance, 20*, 208–212.

Bonfiglioli, C., & Castiello, U. (1998). Dissociation of covert and overt spatial attention during prehension movements: selective interference effects. *Perception and Psychophysics, 60*, 1426–1440.

Bullock, D., & Grossberg, S. (1988). Neural dynamics of planned arm movements: emergent invariants and speed–accuracy properties during trajectory formation. *Psychological Review, 95*, 49–90.

Bundesen, C. (1990). A theory of visual attention. *Psychological Review, 97*, 523–547.

Castiello, U. (1996). Grasping a fruit: selection for action. *Journal of Experimental Psychology: Human Perception and Performance, 22*, 582–603.

Craighero, L., Fadiga, L., Rizzolatti, G., & Umiltà, C. (1998). Visuomotor priming. *Visual Cognition, 5*, 109–125.

Deubel, H., & Schneider, W. X. (1996). Saccade target selection and object recognition: evidence for a common attentional mechanism. *Vision Research, 36*, 1827–1837.

Deubel, H., Schneider, W. X., & Paprotta, I. (1998). Selective dorsal and ventral processing: evidence for a common attentional mechanism in reaching and perception. *Visual Cognition, 5*, 81–107.

DeYoe, E. A., & Van Essen, D. C. (1988). Concurrent processing streams in monkey visual cortex. *Trends in Neurosciences, 11*, 219–226.

Downing, C. J., & Pinker, S. (1985). The spatial structure of visual attention. In M. I. Posner & O. S. Marin (Eds.), *Attention and performance XI* (pp. 171–187). Hillsdale, NJ: Lawrence Erlbaum Associates Inc.

Duncan, J. (1984). Selective attention and the organization of visual information. *Journal of Experimental Psychology: General, 113*, 501–517.

Duncan, J. (1996). Coordinated brain systems in selective perception and action. In T. Inui & J. L. McClelland (Eds.), *Attention and performance XVI* (pp. 549–578). Cambridge, MA: MIT Press.

Duncan, J., & Humphreys, G. W. (1989). Visual-search and stimulus similarity. *Psychological Review, 96*, 433–458.

Egly, R., Driver, J., & Rafal, R. (1994). Shifting visual attention between objects and locations: evidence for normal and parietal lesion subjects. *Journal of Experimental Psychology: General, 123*, 161–177.

Goodale, M. A., & Milner, A. D. (1992). Separate visual pathways for perception and action. *Trends in Neurosciences, 15*, 20–25.

Graziano, M. S. A., & Gross, C. G. (1994). Mapping space with neurons. *Current Directions in Psychological Science, 3*, 164–167.

Henry, F. M., & Rogers, D. E. (1960). Increased response latency for complicated movements and a "memory drum" theory of neuromotor action. *Research Quarterly, 31*, 448–458.

Hoffman, J. E., & Subramaniam, B. (1995). The role of visual attention in saccadic eye movements. *Perception and Psychophysics, 57*, 787–795.

Hughes, H. C., & Zimba, L. D. (1987). Natural boundaries for the spatial spread of directed visual-attention. *Neuropsychologia, 25*, 5–18.

Jeannerod, M. (1994). The representing brain: neural correlates of motor intention and imagery. *Behavioral and Brain Sciences, 17*, 187–245.

Kowler, E., Anderson, E., Dosher, B., & Blaser, E. (1995). The role of attention in the programming of saccades. *Vision Research, 35,* 1897–1916.

Kritikos, A., Bennett, K. M. B., Dunai, J., & Castiello, U. (2000). Interference from distractors in reach-to-grasp movements. *Quarterly Journal of Experimental Psychology, 53A,* 131–151.

Milner, A. D., & Goodale, M. A. (1995). *The visual brain in action.* New York: Oxford University Press.

Mishkin, M., Ungerleider, L. G., & Macko, K. A. (1983). Object vision and spatial vision: two cortical pathways. *Trends in Neurosciences, 6,* 414–417.

Neumann, O. (1987). Beyond capacity: a functional view of attention. In H. Heuer & A. F. Sanders (Eds.), *Perspectives on perception and action* (pp. 361–394). Hillsdale, NJ: Lawrence Erlbaum Associates Inc.

Paprotta, I., Deubel, H., & Schneider, W. X. (1999). Object recognition and goal-directed eye or hand movements are coupled by visual attention. In W. Becker, H. Deubel, & T. Mergner (Eds.), *Current oculomotor research: physiological and psychological aspects* (pp. 241–248). New York: Plenum Press.

Posner, M. I. (1980). Orienting of attention. *Quarterly Journal of Experimental Psychology, 32,* 3–25.

Ricker, K. L., Elliot, D., Lyons, J., Gauldie, D., Chua, R., & Byblow, W. (1999). The utilization of visual information in the control of rapid sequential aiming movements. *Acta Psychologica, 103,* 103–123.

Rizzolatti, G., Riggio, L., Dascola, I., & Umiltà, C. (1987). Reorienting attention across the horizontal and vertical meridians: evidence in favour of a premotor theory of attention. *Neuropsychologia, 25,* 31–40.

Rizzolatti, G., Riggio, L., & Sheliga, B. M. (1994). Space and selective attention. In C. Umiltà & M. Moscovitch (Eds.), *Attention and performance XV. Conscious and nonconscious information processing* (pp. 231–265). Cambridge, MA: MIT Press.

Schiegg, A., Deubel, H., & Schneider, W. X. (2003). Attentional selection during preparation of prehension movements. *Visual Cognition, 10,* 409–431.

Schneider, W. X. (1995). VAM: a neuro-cognitive model for attention control of segmentation, object recognition and space-based motor action. *Visual Cognition, 2,* 331–374.

Schneider, W. X., & Deubel, H. (2002). Selection-for-perception and selection-for-spatial-motor-action are coupled by visual attention: a review of recent findings and new evidence from stimulus-driven saccade control. In W. Prinz & B. Hommel (Eds.), *Attention and performance XIX. Common mechanisms in perception and action* (pp. 609–627). Oxford: Oxford University Press.

Shepherd, M., Findlay, J. F., & Hockey, R. J. (1986). The relationship between eye movements and spatial attention. *Quarterly Journal of Experimental Psychology, 38A,* 475–491.

Stein, J. F. (1992). The representation of egocentric space in the posterior parietal cortex. *Behavioral and Brain Sciences, 15,* 691–700.

Sternberg, S., Monsell, S., Knoll, R., & Wright, C. (1978). The latency and duration of rapid movement sequences: comparison of speech and type writing. In G. E. Stelmach (Ed.), *Information processing in motor control and learning* (pp. 117–152). New York: Academic Press.

Tipper, S. P., Lortie, C., & Baylis, G. C. (1992). Selective reaching: evidence for action-centered attention. *Journal of Experimental Psychology: Human Perception and Performance, 18,* 891–905.

Treisman, A. (1988). Features and objects: the fourteenth Bartlett memorial lecture. *Quarterly Journal of Experimental Psychology, 40*, 201–237.

Treisman, A. M., & Gelade, G. (1980). A feature-integration theory of attention. *Cognitive Psychology, 12*, 97–136.

Zeki, S. M. (1993). *A vision of the brain*. Oxford: Blackwell Scientific.

Zingale, C. M., & Kowler, E. (1987). Planning sequences of saccades. *Vision Research, 27*, 1327–1341.

4 Intention in action

*Wolfgang Prinz, Sara de Maeght and
Lothar Knuf*

Abstract

Ideomotor movements may arise in observers (involuntarily or even counter-voluntarily) while they watch goal-directed actions or events. We developed a paradigm that allows us to assess how the movements induced in observers are related to the actions or events inducing them. We found that ideomotor movements were governed by two principles: perceptual induction (i.e. people move in accordance with what they see) and intentional induction (i.e. people move in accordance with what they would like to see). We review a series of experiments in which observers watch the outcomes of their own preceding actions, of somebody else's actions, or of actions generated by a computer. In our experiments, a complex pattern of action induction was observed in both hand and head movements. The results suggest that people tend to perform, in their own actions, what they see being performed in the actions they observe. Action induction can pertain to both the physical surface and the intentional subtext of the observed action. Though perceptual induction appears to be ubiquitous, it may become suspended for the sake of intentional action control.

Introduction

The working of *intention in action* is closely related to the working of *attention in action*. Intentions can be considered a specific brand of attentional states. A person is said to entertain a particular intention when her attention is focused on the goals of the particular action she is planning to perform. Thus, intentions are attentional states that refer to action goals. These states may play an important role in the planning of voluntary action.

The working of intention in action can be studied in two domains, action perception and action production. In the domain of perception, the issue is how intention follows from action—that is, how perceivers come to understand the intentional subtext underlying the pattern of physical action they are exposed to. Conversely, in the domain of production, the issue is how action follows from intention—that is, how agents come to realize the intentions they entertain through the actions they perform.

In this chapter, we will not discuss these two issues as such, but rather focus on the analysis of ideomotor actions. We believe that the study of ideomotor actions can help us understand important aspects of the workings of intentions in both action perception and action production and, at the same time, shed light on the common functional grounding of perception and production.

Ideomotor actions

Ideomotor actions may arise in observers while they watch other people perform certain actions. Hence, they imply both the perception of other people's actions and the production of one's own related actions. Typically, ideomotor movements occur involuntarily, sometimes even countervoluntarily. For instance, while watching a soccer match on TV, many individuals cannot help but move around in their armchairs, particularly when watching dramatic scenes, such as when their home team is facing a serious threat. The same applies to situations in which individuals watch the consequences of certain actions rather than the actions themselves. For instance, while sitting in the passenger seat of a car, many people cannot help but push phantom brakes when the driver approaches, say, a bend too quickly.

Ideomotor movements are commonplace and most people are familiar with them. Given this fact and the appeal arising from their non-rational character, it is perhaps not surprising that they have for long attracted the attention of philosophers, psychologists and other scientists concerned with the human mind—long before the advent of scientific psychology. For instance, eighteenth-century textbooks of empirical psychology would typically contain chapters on how we understand other individuals' actions or feelings. As an example we may refer to Ferdinand Überwasser's *Anweisungen zum regelmäßigen Studium der empirischen Psychologie* (1787), where we read, for example:

> Wenn wir einen Menschen in schnellem Laufe daher rennen sehen, so fühlen wir in den Füßen und andern Theilen unsers Körpers eine gewisse Behendigkeit, oder Hurtigkeit, es entstehen einige Anwandlungen zu ähnlichen Kraftäusserungen, die manches Mal, wenn die Seele sich ihnen überläßt, in merkliche Reizungen hervorgehen.[1]

(p. 240)

> Der Anblick eines Tanzenden, eines Seiltänzers, stimmt öfters den Körper des Zuschauers unwillkührlich zu ähnlichen Bewegungen. Wie oft fährt man nicht zusammen, zieht den Fuß, oder Arm zurück, wenn

---

1 "When we see a person, who is running fast, we feel in our feet and in other parts of our body some kind of nimbleness, or quickness; some indications of similar forces arise, which at times, . . . when our soul succumbs to them, lead to noticeable excitations".

der Fuß, oder Arm eines Andern, in unserer Gegenwart von einem Stoße, oder Schlage getroffen zu werden Gefahr hat?[2]

(p. 266).

A century later, when scientific psychology was in the making, ideomotor action entered the stage once more. It was William B. Carpenter who coined the term "ideomotor action" in his *Principles of Mental Physiology* (1874). Ironically, however, it was this very author who, from the outset, brought the term into discredit. This was for two reasons. One was that Carpenter used it in two ways, in a broad and in a narrow sense (cf. Knuf, Aschersleben, & Prinz, 1987; Prinz, 2000). In the broad sense, the term referred to any kind of automatic action performed under the control of what he called a *dominant idea*. In the narrow sense, it referred to actions that are performed *in accordance with the idea* that underlies and guides them—that is, to the special case in which bodily actions *bear some similarity* with the mental ideas guiding them. For instance, in the magic-pendulum demonstration, where a pendulum is suspended on a person's stretched forefinger and begins to swing despite the instruction to keep finger and pendulum absolutely immobile, Carpenter believed that the mere idea of the pendulum moving in a particular way caused the unintentional (or even counter-intentional) movement in accordance with that idea (Carpenter, 1874, p. 286).

Lack of clarity was one reason why the concept met distrust from the start. More important was the second reason that followed from Carpenter's preoccupation with all sorts of esoteric phenomena like pendulum swinging, table turning, mind-reading, or St. Vitus' Dance. For Carpenter, the ideomotor principle was the *deus ex machina* to account for all these phenomena: Whenever one encounters a strange form of human action, one can readily explain it by invoking in the agent certain strong and irresistible ideas that refer to these strange actions and eventually cause their execution. Carpenter was not aware of the circularity in this explanation, which actually rendered the explanation no less magic than the phenomena to be explained. This point was taken up by Thorndike's (1913) angry attack on the ideomotor principle, who ended up concluding that the principle entailed magic thinking: "Our belief that an idea tends to produce the act which it is like, or represents, or 'is an idea of', or 'has as its object', is kith and kin with our forebears' belief that dressing to look like a bear will give you his strength" (p. 105). Thorndike's attack was at that time part of the never-ending battle between contiguity and similarity as chief principles of association. Thorndike was of course on the side of contiguity (and reinforcement)

---

2 "The sight of someone dancing, of a rope-dancer, often involuntarily inspires the spectator's body to perform similar movements. So often are we startled, and so often do we withdraw our foot or our arm, when, in our presence, the foot or the arm of somebody else is about to be struck or hit."

and, as we know today, the *Zeitgeist* was with him. As a result, ideomotor phenomena were shelved as somewhat weird esoteric phenomena and the ideomotor principle fell into oblivion.

Notably, this occurred despite the fact that the ideomotor principle had in the meantime been ennobled by William James. James, after objecting to ideomotor action being relegated to the curiosities of mental life, introduced the ideomotor principle as a key concept to account for voluntary action: "We may [. . .] lay it down for certain that every representation of a movement awakens in some degree the actual movement which is its object" (James, 1890, Vol. II, p. 526). In other words, representing certain movements (e.g. perceiving them, thinking of them) makes the individual ready, or prone, to perform these movements. At first glance, the ideomotor principle serves to bridge the gap between mental ideas and bodily movements in general. However, in his discussion of the principle, James focused on cases in which action is induced by internally generated ideas, and he kept away from examples where action is induced by externally generated ideas—that is, perception—perhaps because such examples might have carried the *haut-goût* of esoteric dubiousness and scientific unseriousness.

We now turn from history to some, as we believe, innocent examples of these allegedly dubious and unserious phenomena. We shall consider situations in which people perceive the outcomes of their own or somebody else's actions, and we study to what extent and in which ways the mere observation of such action outcomes induces related action tendencies on the observer's part. In view of the long-standing debate about ideomotor induction, it may be surprising that the very nature of the relationship between the inducing events that are perceived and the induced actions that are performed has never been studied in any detail.

We address three major questions. First, under which conditions does ideomotor induction occur at all? Second, how is the pattern of induced movements related to the pattern of perceived movements? Third, what role is being played by similarity in that relationship?

For classical authorities like Lotze (1852), Carpenter (1874) and James (1890), it was natural to believe that the bridge between the action perceived (in the other) and the action performed (by oneself) is formed by similarity. On this view, ideomotor action is a special form of imitation. Observers tend to repeat, in their own actions, what they observe the others perform in theirs. We refer to this view as "perceptual induction" (Knuf et al., 2001), according to which observers tend to perform the same actions that *they see happening*. However, in a number of examples, evidence from introspection seems to suggest otherwise. Suppose you push a bowling ball and follow its course. As long as you cannot anticipate its final course with absolute certainty, you will often find yourself twisting your hand or bending your trunk, *as if* to give the ball the momentum it needs to move into the intended direction. In a situation like this, people seem to act in an *as-if mode*—that is, as if they could affect the course of the ongoing events in a desired direction. In this view, ideomotor actions are idle-running intentional actions: Observers tend to perform actions that, were they effective, would lead to the desired outcome. We refer to this view as *intentional induction* (Knuf et al., 2001), according to which observers tend to perform actions *they would like to see happen*.

As we noticed only recently, the distinction between these two principles is in fact already inherent in Chevreul's discussion of the mechanisms underlying the magic pendulum. Chevreul's (1833) "Lettre à M. Ampère" is a true classic on ideomotor action. Not only does it pre-empt James's ideomotor principle by stating that "il y a donc une liaison intime établie entre l'exécution de certains mouvements et l'acte de la pensée qui y est relative" (p. 260),[3] but it also suggests a distinction between two basic forms of action induction through perception:

> La tendance au mouvement déterminée en nous par la vue d'un corps en mouvement, se retrouve dans plusieurs cas, par exemple: lorsque l'attention étant entièrement fixée sur un oiseau qui vole . . ., *le corps du spectateur se dirige . . . vers la ligne du mouvement*; lorsqu'un joueur de boule ou de billard suivant de l'œil le mobile auquel il a imprimé le mouvement, *porte son corps dans la direction qu'il désire voir suivre à ce mobile.*[4]
>
> (p. 262; emphasis added)

Hence, there are two principles here, perceptual induction and intentional induction. Both address the impact of perception on action, but the second principle addresses the impact of intention on action as well.

Action induction through perception

We devised an experimental paradigm to allow us to study the relative contributions of perceptual and intentional induction to ideomotor action (Knuf, 1998; Knuf et al., 2001). Originally, the task had been designed for the study of ideomotor movements induced by watching self-generated actions. We then modified it such that it can also be used for the study of action induced by watching other-generated actions.

3 "Thus there exists a close relationship between the execution of certain movements and the act of thought, which refers to them."
4 "The tendency to move arising in us when watching a moving body can be found in several cases, such as: While the attention is fully focused on a bird flying . . ., *the body of the spectator is directed towards the line of movement*; while a player of bowling or billiards follows with his eyes the rolling ball to which he has given the impetus, *moves his body into the direction he wishes to see the ball roll*" (emphasis added).

Watching self-generated action

One of the standard examples given in the old literature to explain the nature of ideomotor action had always been taken from bowling. Following the lead of this tradition with modern means, we devised a computerized version of a simple bowling game, in which participants watched a ball on a screen moving towards a target, either hitting or missing it. At the beginning of a trial, the ball was shown at its starting position at the bottom of the screen, while the target position was shown at the top. Initial ball and target positions were always chosen such that, to hit the target, the ball had either to travel in a north-westerly or in a north-easterly direction (i.e. leftward *vs* rightward). On each trial, the computer selected a straight-line trajectory for the ball's travel. Computer-selected trajectories were chosen such that they would always lead the ball close to the target, but never yield a hit. At the beginning of a trial, participants triggered the ball's travel and then observed its course (see Figure 4.1).

The ball's travel was divided into two periods, instrumental and induction. During the instrumental period (about 1 s), participants were given the chance to influence the course of events by manipulating either the ball's or the target's horizontal position through corresponding joystick movements. In the ball condition, horizontal joystick movements acted to shift the ball to the left or the right (after which it continued travelling in the same direction as before). In the target condition, the same horizontal joystick movements would act to shift the target to the left or the right. Since initial motion directions were always chosen such that hits would never occur by themselves, these shifts were required for any chance of hitting the target (see Figure 4.2). The instrumental period was followed by the induction period (which lasted about 2 s). During the induction period, joystick movements

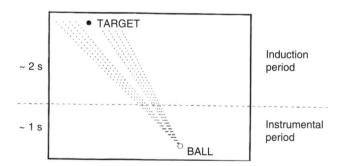

Figure 4.1 Basic paradigm used in the experiments. On a given trial, the ball left one of two possible starting positions at the bottom of the screen and travelled towards one of three possible target positions at the top. Dotted lines indicate eight pre-programmed trajectories, one of which was randomly chosen for a particular trial. Note that the ball would always miss the target if no correction was performed.

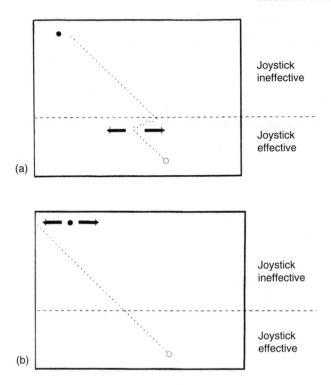

Figure 4.2 Illustration of possible corrections performed in the ball condition (a) and in the target condition (b). Note that the joystick was only effective during the initial instrumental period, but not during the induction period. (The dashed horizontal line was not visible on the screen.)

were ineffective, and participants were fully aware of this. The goal of our experiments was to study spontaneously occurring joystick movements arising during that period—that is, at a time when they were completely ineffective.

Would induced joystick movements still occur, and how would they be related to the events on the screen? Figure 4.3 illustrates the logic for inferring the operation of the two induction principles from experimental observations. *Perceptual induction* predicts the same pattern of joystick movements for both conditions: With perceptual induction, the joystick should always move in the same direction as the ball travels (leftward *vs* rightward). *Intentional induction* predicts a more complex pattern. First, intentionally guided joystick movements should only be observed on trials with upcoming misses, not with upcoming hits. On upcoming hits—that is, when participants can anticipate that the ball will hit the target—there is no point in instigating any further intentionally guided activity to reach the goal. However, on upcoming misses, when participants can anticipate that the

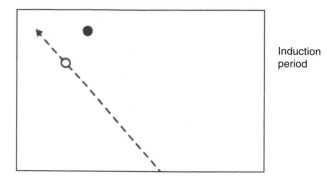

Figure 4.3 Example of a particular ball–target configuration arising in the induction period (ball travels leftward and is going to miss the target on its left side, i.e. left miss). For this particular configuration, perceptual induction predicts leftward movements (based on the ball's travel direction) irrespective of condition. Intentional induction predicts induced movements, too (based on the upcoming miss). In this case, opposite predictions apply to the two conditions. For the target condition, intentional induction predicts leftward movements (based on the intention to shift the target towards the ball). Conversely, for the ball condition, intentional induction predicts rightward movements (based on the intention to shift the ball towards the target).

ball will miss the target, intentional induction predicts movements performed in a (futile) attempt to influence the further course of events. The details of these attempts should depend on two factors: the object that had been under instrumental control immediately before (ball *vs* target) and the side on which the ball is anticipated to miss the target (left *vs* right misses). In the ball condition (where the ball had been under control before), joystick movements should act to push the *ball towards the target* (i.e. rightward in the case of a left miss and leftward in the case of a right miss). Conversely, in the target condition (where the target had been under control before), joystick movements should act to push *the target towards the ball* (leftward in the case of a left miss and rightward in the case of a right miss).

The results of our experiment showed that participants indeed generated a substantial body of unintentional joystick movements in the induction period of trials. Moreover, these movements were exclusively guided by intentional induction: Induced movements were absent in cases of upcoming hits, whereas in cases of upcoming misses they were dependent on task condition (ball *vs* target) and side of target miss (left *vs* right), the latter exactly in line with the pattern predicted by intentional induction. Somewhat surprisingly, the results did not show the slightest indication of perceptual induction. In summary, it seems that, at least under these conditions, goal-based movement induction plays a much stronger role than induction based on the movements that lead to those goals. For the time being, we may conclude that intention-in-action is strong in both senses: in perceiving the intentions behind the observed events and in generating actions that realize those intentions.

Still, perceptual induction was not completely absent. In our experiments, we also studied movements that were induced in non-instrumental effectors—that is, effectors that were not at all instrumentally involved in the control of the events on the screen (e.g. unintentional head and foot movements).[5] In unintentional effectors, we observed both perceptual and intentional induction. Perceptual induction was inferred from movements whose direction accorded with the ball's travel direction (left- *vs* rightward). Intentional induction was again inferred from the pattern of hits and left versus right misses in the two experimental conditions. Remarkably, however, the pattern of intentional induction that emerged for (non-instrumental) head and foot movements differed from that for (instrumental) hand/joystick movements: For non-instrumental effectors, intentional induction was always ball-related—that is, participants always acted as if to push the ball towards the target. This was true not only for the ball condition but for the target condition as well. These findings suggest that in non-instrumental effectors, induced movements are solely determined by the travel of the ball, but not by the demands of the task (i.e. ball *vs* target condition). It seems that the underlying induction mechanism relied on assessing the ball's movement in terms of both the direction into which it travels (perceptual induction: left- *vs* rightward) and the side on which it misses the target (intentional induction: on the left *vs* on the right), with additive contributions from these two factors.

In summary, the picture was quite different for instrumental and non-instrumental effectors. Effectors involved in instrumental action showed evidence of task-specific intentional induction—that is, related to the ball in the ball condition and to the target in the target condition. There was no indication of perceptual induction. Conversely, effectors not involved in instrumental action showed evidence of task-independent induction that was always related to the ball, with additive contributions from intentional and perceptual induction.

One may speculate about what this difference between actions with instrumental and non-instrumental effectors implies. There are two questions here. The first is why the ball plays such a prominent role for head and

---

5   Hand and foot movements were registered with an optical motion-measurement system: OPTOTRAK 3D, Northern Digital Inc. This non-contact motion-measurement system tracks small infrared markers attached to the participant. The precision of position measurement was about 0.15 mm and the sampling rate was 250 Hz. Like hand movements, head and foot movements were classified as left- *vs* rightward on each trial. On this basis, they could be related to the current stimulus pattern in exactly the same way as hand movements.

foot movements; the second is why no such prominence can be seen in hand movements. An answer to the first question is provided by an obvious difference between the two objects: the ball is dynamic and travels, whereas the target is more or less stationary. Accordingly, the ball is much more salient than the target and should therefore be more likely to capture attention than the target. Assuming that the power to attract attention goes along with the power to induce action, it may not be too surprising that the travelling ball is by itself a much stronger action inducer than the stationary target (in both the perceptual and the intentional sense).

If so, why is the same pattern not obtained for hands as well? This question has again two facets: to account for target-related intentional induction in the target condition, and for the lack of perceptual induction throughout. Both effects can be explained if one assumes that instrumental effectors exhibit some kind of intentional inertia—that is, an after-effect of the goal-directed instrumental activity performed right before. Such intentional inertia should exhibit two major features that are characteristic of any form of voluntarily guided activity (cf. Bayer, Ferguson, & Gollwitzer, 2003; Heckhausen, 1991, ch. 6; Kuhl, 1983). Just like any goal-directed action, it requires two things: strengthening of internal, goal-related intentions and weakening of external distractors that might attract attention and, hence, distract from the goal in focus. In a way, then, the hand behaves like an agent committed to a particular goal—both focusing on that internal goal, while sheltering itself from any external distractor. This is different for non-instrumental heads and feet. They are not committed that way and are, hence, more prone to be affected by distractions arising from the perceptual and intentional aspects of the events on the screen.

Watching other-generated action

As described so far, the bowling task allows us to study action induced by watching the outcomes of one's own previous actions. We extended this task so as to allow us to study action induced by watching the outcomes of someone else's actions (De Maeght, 2001; De Maeght & Prinz, 2004). For this we created a situation in which participants observed on a screen events that were generated by somebody else. On the stimulus side we used exactly the same events as in the previous study—that is, the travelling ball and the various patterns of hits and misses as they emerge under the various conditions of the bowling task. However, while watching the bowling game, participants were now also required to perform a simple tracking task on the response side. This task served as a means for recording movements induced by watching the bowling game.

The tracking task required participants to track the vertical position of the travelling ball. To do this, participants held a joystick in their right hand and controlled the vertical position of a marker visible on the right margin of the screen. The task was to track the travelling ball with the marker such that the marker's vertical position always matched the ball's vertical position. Accordingly, the instructions for this task emphasize the vertical dimension. However, in analyzing the results we were not interested in performance on the (relevant) vertical dimension. Instead, we focused on the (irrelevant) horizontal dimension: If action induction is also obtained by watching other-generated action, it should exhibit itself in spontaneously induced joystick movements to the left or the right.

The first question we wished to address was how the pattern of induced action varied for self- versus other-generated action. However, in comparing these situations we must not forget that the tracking task (which the other-generated action data rely on) differs from the bowling task (which the self-generated action data rely on) in two major respects. First, since the tracking task required participants to monitor somebody else's performance, we should expect that any induced movements would be free from short-term intentional inertia—that is, the after-effects of any intentional action performed immediately before. Therefore, to the extent these after-effects contributed to the pattern of induced action observed in the bowling task, we should anticipate that the corresponding pattern in the tracking task would exhibit weaker contributions of intentional induction. Second, since the tracking task required participants to track the vertical position of the travelling ball, it forced them to focus visual attention on the ball throughout. This differs from the bowling task, in which the attentional focus can be on the ball in the ball condition and on the target in the target condition. As a result, conflicting attentional demands may arise in the target condition of the tracking task. In this condition, the observed person's bowling required a focus on the target, whereas the observer's tracking required a focus on the ball. No such conflict is entailed in the ball condition, in which both bowling and tracking involved focusing on the ball. As a consequence, we should anticipate that the ball will act as a much stronger movement-inducing agent than the target. This may support both perceptual induction (based on the ball's manifest travel) and ball-related intentional induction (based on the ball's implied goal).

Our basic experiment had two parts. In the first part, participants were required to play the bowling game themselves (*player mode*); in the second part, they tracked the visible outcome of another alleged individual's performance on that game (*observer mode*). This allowed us to assess the pattern of induced action in both the bowling and the tracking task. Actually, the first part of the task was an exact replication of one of the basic experiments with self-generated actions. This was true not only in terms of design and conditions but results as well: The pattern of results of this part of the experiment (player mode/bowling task) mirrored completely the picture described in the previous section.

A different picture emerged in the second part, however (observer mode/ tracking task). Here, perceptual induction proved to be strong and reliable throughout (in both hand and head movements), whereas intentional induction was weaker. Remarkably, intentional induction was ball-related throughout—that is, observers acted as if to push the ball towards the target. This was true not only for the ball condition (where intentional induction was highly reliable for both hand and head movements), but also for the target condition (where it was only marginally significant for both effectors).

This pattern of findings is in line with the tentative conclusions drawn in the previous section. In the observer mode, intentional inertia can no longer be effective. Therefore, the hand and the head should behave like non-instrumental effectors. Both should exhibit (ball-induced) perceptual induction as well as (ball-related) intentional induction. As anticipated, it was now the ball's travel that attracted nearly all of the attention and induced nearly all of the action. Again, the pattern of induced movement seemed to be completely determined by what happened to the rolling ball (in terms of both travel direction and side of target miss).

In this experiment, participants were players first (i.e. watching self-generated action) before they became observers (i.e. watching other-generated action). Hence, though it may be true that short-term intentional inertia can play no role in the tracking task, some kind of long-term inertia may still be functional, due to participants' having been involved as active players of the bowling game before. Therefore, in a further experiment, we studied participants in what may be called a pure observer mode. In this experiment, they never played the bowling game themselves, but rather studied the rules of the game in the beginning and then started performing the tracking task right away, observing on the screen some other alleged individual's performance.

The results indicated that perceptual induction was as strong as in the previous experiments (for hand as well as head movements), whereas intentional induction was much weaker. Indeed, a reliable effect of intentional induction was only obtained for the ball condition (hand movements only), not for the target condition.

With respect to the working of intention in action, these observations suggest two conclusions. On the one hand, intentional induction in the observer mode seems to be more pronounced when the observer was an active player of the game before (compared with conditions without such active experience). On the other hand, prior active experience does not seem to be a prerequisite for intentional induction to occur. At least some aspects of the intentional structure of the events on the screen remain effective in the pure observer mode (e.g. ball-related intentional induction in hand movements).

Watching computer-generated action

In two further experiments, we studied ideomotor action induced by watching computer-generated action on the screen. In these experiments, we created a somewhat ambiguous situation. On the one hand, we first let participants play the bowling game themselves, providing them with a full grasp of what it is like to play the game. On the other hand, when they were then transferred from the player mode to the observer mode, we told them a cover story to make them believe that the hits and misses they would now observe were generated by a computer.[6] Would action induction still occur under these conditions? Perceptual induction should be basically unaltered, assuming that it mainly relies on the spatial configuration of the events on the screen. Similarly, assuming that intentional induction relies on an intentional interpretation of that configuration, one should anticipate that this induction component becomes weaker when observers believe they are watching the output of a non-intentional machine rather than the outcome of an intentional action.

We ran two experiments. The first experiment was equivalent to the basic experiment mentioned in the previous section. The only difference was in terms of instructions for the observer mode. In the former study, we made participants believe in an invisible partner playing the game, whereas in the present experiment we made them believe in a computer playing the game. We were surprised to find that these two instructions did not make much difference. For both hand and foot movements, the pattern of action-induction effects was very similar. Once more, perceptual induction was reliable throughout, whereas reliable intentional induction was only obtained in the ball condition. It seems that the cover story does not really matter, at least under conditions in which participants play the game first, before they are then exposed to exactly the same types of configurations they had been generating in their previous play.

In the second experiment, we made a serious (and eventually successful) attempt at fully suspending the working of intention in action induction. Again, we first had participants play the game themselves before we told them the story about a computer generating the events presented for the tracking task. This time, however, the computer-generated configurations differed from participants' self-generated configurations in one crucial detail: initial correction movements (of ball or target) were now completely lacking in the observed configurations—that is, the pattern on the screen was always a ball rolling *on a straight line* towards a target *at a fixed position*, sometimes hitting and sometimes missing it.

---

6 Of course, this was the true story about the happenings on the screen throughout (whereas the story about watching another individual's live performance was in fact a cover story).

The results showed that, in this condition, there was no longer any indication of intentional induction. However, perceptual induction was still preserved (albeit weakly). From these findings we may conclude that the mere belief in a non-intentional machine behind the events on the screen is not enough to extinguish intentional induction, as long as that machine generates an output that cannot be distinguished from the outcome of intentional action. In contrast, as soon as the machine's output is sufficiently different from an intentional agent's action, the intentional interpretation of that output breaks down—as does intentional induction, which is based on that interpretation.

Conclusions

What can we conclude from these findings about the workings of intention in action? Conclusions can be drawn about both perceptual and intentional induction. Perceptual induction refers to movements induced in accordance with external events. In our experiments, perceptual induction was observed throughout—that is, with self-, other- and computer-generated action. There was, however, one conspicuous exception: it was absent in participants' hand movements while they watched the outcome of self-generated action. These observations suggest two major conclusions. The first is that the travelling ball is a potent inducer of related action—that is, of body movements in accordance with the ball's travel. In principle, this can be seen in both hand and head movements. The second conclusion is that instrumentally active effectors may, for a while, be sheltered from perceptual induction. It is as if perceptual induction is temporarily suspended to allow for an effective operation of intentional control.

Intentional induction refers to movements in accordance with internal intentions. In our experiments, intentional induction was also observed throughout—that is, with self-, other- and computer-generated action. With self-generated action, intentional induction was task-dependent for instrumental effectors, but not for non-instrumental effectors. Once more this seems to reflect a difference in after-effects of preceding instrumental action. With other- and computer-generated action, intentional induction was only obtained in the ball condition. Once again this seems to reflect the fact that the travelling ball is a stronger attention capturer (and, hence, intention inducer) than the stationary target.

In summary, people tend to perform in their own actions what they see being performed by others. Action induction can pertain to both physical surface and intentional subtext. Though perceptual induction appears to be ubiquitous, it may become suspended (both locally and temporarily) for the sake of intentional action control.

References

Bayer, U., Ferguson, M., & Gollwitzer, P. M. (2003). Voluntary action from the perspective of social-personality psychology. In S. Maasen, W. Prinz, & G. Roth (Eds.), *Voluntary action* (pp. 86–107). Oxford: Oxford University Press.

Carpenter, W. B. (1874). *Principles of mental physiology*. London: John Churchill.

Chevreul, M. E. (1833). Lettre à M. Ampère sur une classe particulière de mouvements musculaires. *Revue des Deux Mondes, série II*, 258–266.

De Maeght, S. (2001). *New insights in ideomotor action: investigating the influence of perception, motor, and intention representations*. Dissertation, University of Munich, Germany.

De Maeght, S., & Prinz, W. (2004). Action induction through action observation. On the role of effects for the control of voluntary actions. *Psychological Research* (special issue), 68(2/3), 97–114.

Heckhausen, H. (1991). *Motivation and action* (2nd edn.). Berlin: Springer-Verlag.

James, W. (1890). *The principles of psychology (2 Vols.)*. New York: Holt.

Knuf, L. (1998). *Ideomotorische Phänomene: Neue Fakten für ein altes Problem. Entwicklung eines Paradigmas zur kinematischen Analyse induzierter Mitbewegungen. [Ideomotor phenomena: New facts about an old problem. Development of a paradigm for the kinematic analysis of induced ideomotor movements.]* Aachen: Shaker.

Knuf, L., Aschersleben, G., & Prinz, W. (2001). An analysis of ideomotor action. *Journal of Experimental Psychology: General, 130*, 779–798.

Kuhl, J. (1983). *Motivation, Konflikt und Handlungskontrolle [Motivation, conflict and action control]*. Berlin: Springer-Verlag.

Lotze, R. H. (1852). *Medicinische Psychologie oder Physiologie der Seele*. Leipzig: Weidmann'sche Buchhandlung.

Prinz, W. (1987). Ideomotor action. In H. Heuer & A. F. Sanders (Eds.), *Perspectives on perception and action* (pp. 47–76). Hillsdale, NJ: Lawrence Erlbaum Associates Inc.

Thorndike, E. L. (1913). Ideomotor action. *Psychological Review, 20*, 91–106.

Überwasser, F. (1787). *Anweisungen zum regelmäßigen Studium der Empirischen Psychologie für die Candidaten der Philosophie zu Münster: Erste Abtheilung [Instructions about the orderly study of empirical psychology for candidates of Philosophy at Münster-University]*. Münster: Theißing.

5   Intention and reactivity

Tamsin Astor-Jack and Patrick Haggard

Abstract

The evolution of the human brain, including the ability to make intentional actions, has resulted in our motor system being activated either via our own intentions or external stimuli. It is important that a balance is maintained between these internal and external drives. It is proposed that humans have an internally generated and an externally triggered motor system. Five ways that these motor systems might be related are posited. The relationship between these two systems was investigated using a novel experimental paradigm, called truncation. This requires participants to prepare an intentional action, which is randomly truncated with a stimulus to which they must react with the same action as they had prepared to make intentionally. Experiment 1 utilized pupil dilation as a physiological measure of the cognitive processes involved in the truncation condition and in control conditions where either internally generated or externally triggered actions occurred alone. Three of the proposed relationships were discounted and alternative objections, such as slower perceptual processing and foreperiod differences, were addressed. Experiment 2 recorded auditory-evoked potentials. This experiment suggested that the reaction time cost incurred in the truncation condition is mainly due to the deactivation of the preparation for impending intentional action, rather than the activation of the reactive response. Experiment 3 evaluated the locus of the interference between the two tasks. The results suggested that there was an incompatibility between intentional and reactive preparation for a single action. We conclude that: (1) The large and positive reaction time cost of truncation, which was consistently found when comparing a truncation condition with a simple reaction time condition, is due to switch costs between the hypothetical internally generated and externally triggered motor systems. (2) These two systems are not normally simultaneously active. The findings are discussed within the context of executive function.

Introduction

Most people recognize the feeling of trying to get on with something they want to do, yet being constantly distracted by other pressing demands. This feeling is one aspect of the constant balance between internally generated and externally triggered action. Indeed, an animal's survival depends on reconciling longer-term goals with short-term needs that cannot wait, such as avoiding predators.

Interestingly, neuroanatomical and neurophysiological studies have suggested that the brain's systems for internally generated and externally triggered actions are rather separate. Internally generated actions primarily involve a network centred on the basal ganglia and frontal lobes, notably the supplementary motor area. Externally triggered actions involve a different system, centred on the parietal and premotor cortices, and the cerebellum. Both the premotor cortex and supplementary motor area project to the primary motor cortex, which provides a final common path to the muscles for movement. However, several classes of evidence suggest these two routes to action are largely separate until convergence in the primary motor cortex.

First, ablation of the supplementary motor area causes deficits in internally generated action, but not in externally triggered actions, while the converse pattern is found after ablations of the premotor cortex (Passingham, 1987). Second, many cells in the supplementary motor area fire preferentially before performance of a skilled sequence of movements learned from memory, but not when the same sequence is visually triggered (Tanji & Shima, 1994). Cells in the premotor cortex, in contrast, appear to bind visual stimuli to a choice response, once the animal has learned the arbitrary association between them. Accordingly, they are often active during the delay period between a precue that specifies the response and an imperative stimulus instructing the animal to make the response (Kurata, 1998; Wise & Mauritz, 1985).

This segregation of internally generated and externally triggered action is found not only in the cortex, but persists in the subcortical loops that drive the supplementary motor area and premotor cortex. For example, the pathways from the cerebellum and from the basal ganglia to the frontal cortex relay in different ventrolateral thalamic areas. Specifically, the pathways from the cerebellum connect to the frontal areas via VPLo, VLc and area X and the pathways from the basal ganglia connect to the frontal areas via VLo (Kandel, Schwartz, & Jessell, 2000).

Everyday experience tells us that these two motor systems must cooperate to ensure that both internally generated and externally triggered actions can be successfully performed without interference. However, very little work has focused on how the two routes interact in normal action. One of the few insights in this connection comes from anarchic or alien hand syndrome. In the case reported by Della Sala, Marchetti, and Spinnler (1991), the right (anarchic) hand reacted appropriately and involuntarily to stimuli in the patient's immediate environment. More interestingly, the anarchic hand was not subject to the normal voluntary inhibition of such reactions. The authors reported an instance when the patient announced she would not drink a cup of tea immediately, as it was too hot. The anarchic hand nevertheless moved towards the cup, and the patient restrained it with the unaffected, left hand. This observation illustrates a direct conflict between the patient's intention and the reactive movement. The patient displayed dual lesions, in the anterior part of the callosum and of the frontal cortex bilaterally.

The interaction between intention and reactivity is a useful way to consider the concept of "attention to action". The situations described above involve a conflict between an intentional action and a reaction. When both routes converge on the motor output at the same time, the brain must have either a hard-wired or a strategic way of regulating the interaction between them. There are five possible ways the brain could achieve this. These could be conceptualized as five possible architectures for the interaction of brain areas within the two routes, such as the premotor cortex and supplementary motor area.

A key concept in discussing how different action systems might have access to motor output is Sherrington's "final common path" (Sherrington, 1906). Sherrington was perhaps the first to observe the strong convergence at the central levels of motor representation. Although there may be several reasons for making an action, and several ways that the action may be planned and programmed, all motor commands must eventually converge on the motor neurons. These provide the only way for neural commands to address the muscles, and control behaviour. In this context, intention and reactivity become two different high-level neural circuits, both converging on a single motor execution system. The final common path for voluntary action begins at the primary motor cortex. The intentional circuit based on the basal ganglia and frontal lobes, and the reactive circuit based on the premotor and parietal cortices and cerebellum, come together in the primary motor cortex.

We now turn to the functional, as opposed to the neuroanatomical, arrangement of the intentional and reactive motor systems. There are five possible ways in which the two systems might be arranged, schematized in Figure 5.1.

First, the two systems might be completely independent (a). The second possibility is a limiting case of the first: the two systems might effectively be unitary, sharing a single common repertoire or "lexicon" of actions. Intention and reactivity would then differ only in how the common lexicon is accessed, and not in the central representations of the actions themselves (b). The third possibility involves the systems being facilitatory, so that intending to produce a specific action might facilitate production of the same action (c). Fourth, the systems might be reactively mutually inhibitory systems. In this architecture, intending to produce an action produces an inhibition of the same action within the reactive representation (d). Fifth, the systems might be independent, but compete for exclusive use of a common resource, such as access to motor output (e).

Distinguishing between these various possibilities requires a behavioural task in which intentional and reactive motor systems operate simultaneously.

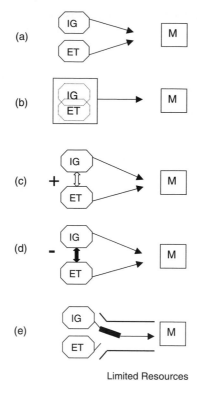

Figure 5.1 Schematic representation of the five possible ways in which the internally
generated and externally triggered motor systems might be related. IG =
internally generated system; ET = externally triggered system. M = motor
execution.

This task would differ profoundly from those used in previous studies of the
motor system, which typically involve *either* intention *or* reactivity, but not
both. To this end, we have developed a "truncation paradigm". The crucial
conditions of this paradigm are shown in Figure 5.2. Preparation for intentional action is represented as a ramp-like increase in activation in the motor
system (a). In externally triggered reactions (b), this preparation is absent,
particularly if the participant does not know when to expect the stimulus.
The truncation condition (c) is clearly a combination of the two previous
conditions. There is pre-movement preparation, as the participant prepares
the intentional action. This preparation is then *truncated* by the presentation
of the stimulus, resulting in the participant reacting.

Following the pattern of Figure 5.2, the participant is asked to prepare,
and make an intentional action at a time of his or her own choosing. The
process of intentional preparation is interrupted, or truncated, by a stimulus. The participant has been instructed to respond to the stimulus with the
simple manual response that they were preparing to make intentionally. The

(a) INTENTIONAL ACTION

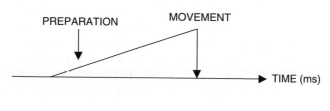

(b) REACTION

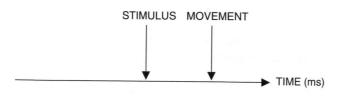

(c) TRUNCATION

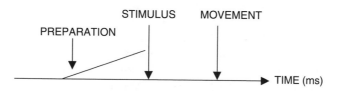

Figure 5.2 A schematic representation of the truncation paradigm.

participant's intention is assumed to be a random process, producing an action within a nominal time window given by instructions. The imperative stimulus to which the participant reacts is controlled to occur at a random time within the same time window. Critically, the process of intending and preparing the action may be interrupted by an imperative stimulus. Thus, on some trials in the truncation condition, the participant will make an intentional action. On other trials in the truncation condition, the participant will receive the imperative stimulus before making any intentional action, and will react to the stimulus, using the same movement that they were instructed to prepare intentionally. These reactive trials can be compared with a blocked control condition in which only reactions occur, and the participant does not make any intentional actions.

In essence, truncation involves a combination of activity in both internally generated and externally triggered motor systems, converging on a single motor output. The interaction between the two routes can be studied by comparing behavioural and physiological measures with control conditions in which only intentional actions, or only reactions, are performed. The simplest behavioural measure of performance involves comparing the reaction times to the imperative stimulus in those trials in the truncation condition where the stimulus truncated the participant's intentional preparation with reaction times in the simple reaction control condition. The five possible architectures for combining intention and reactivity differ according to whether they predict a reaction time (RT) benefit for the truncation trials due to preceding preparation (b, c in Figure 5.1), an RT cost (d, e) or no effect (a).

Experiment 1: examining the pre-movement processes in truncation using pupil dilation

Methods

Twelve right-handed individuals (age: M = 26.8 years, SD = 3.1 years) participated. There were three blocked conditions. In the intentional action condition, the participants were instructed to make a voluntary action at a time of their own free choice. The participants were asked to make the keypress with their right index finger, within a time window of 2–10 s after the experimenter verbally signalled the start of the trial. In the reaction condition, an ambient auditory tone (1 kHz, 100 ms) occurred at random during the same time window. The participants were instructed to respond as quickly as possible on hearing the tone. The response was a keypress identical to that made in the intentional action condition. In the truncation condition, the participants were instructed to make voluntary actions as before, but if they heard the tone, to react to it by pressing the response key as quickly as possible. Making a voluntary action prevented the tone from occurring, and advanced to the next trial. The participants first performed five practice trials in each condition in the order given above. They then performed four blocks of 20 trials each: one intentional action block, one reaction block and two truncation blocks. Each participant performed the actions in a different counterbalanced order.

The analysis of the truncation trials was performed by dividing the trials *post hoc* into reactive and intentional trials. Intentional trials were defined as those in which the participant pressed the response key before the auditory stimulus was due. Reactive trials were defined as those with reaction times between 150 and 1000 ms. Trials with longer reaction times were rejected. The reaction time to the auditory stimulus was recorded in the reaction blocks and for reactive trials in the truncation blocks. Mean reaction times were preferred to medians for comparability with averaging of physiological traces (see below).

In addition to reaction times, the diameter of the pupil was measured continuously at approximately 20 Hz using a custom-built infrared pupil-lometry system. Pupil diameter was used as a physiological measure of instantaneous processing load associated with generating the actions (Richer & Beatty, 1985). The human pupillary response provides a widely accepted measure of cognitive effort (Beatty, 1982; Kahneman, 1973). Individual pupil traces were inspected, blink artefacts were removed, and the traces were averaged across trials locked either to the stimulus or to the action. The traces were then baseline corrected and smoothed; and the key parameters—the peak dilation (in mm), the latency of the peak dila-tion (in ms) and the pre-movement mean dilation (in mm)—were calculated.

Results and discussion

Mean reaction time in the reaction blocks was 320 ms (SD = 82 ms), and in the reactive trials from the truncation blocks 379 ms (SD = 156 ms). This difference was statistically reliable (t_{11} = 2.51, p = .03). The RT cost of inten-tion is defined as the difference between the truncation RT and the simple RT. This implies an RT cost of intention of 379 − 320 = 59 ms.

Grand averaged movement-locked pupil traces are shown in Figure 5.3. The traces for the intentional action condition show a pattern of activity similar to that reported previously (Richer & Beatty, 1985), and reminiscent of an EEG readiness potential (Libet, Gleason, Wright, & Pearl, 1983). Briefly, the pupil begins to dilate at least 1 s before movement onset. Peak dilation is reached slightly after movement. This probably reflects the slug-gish response of the human pupil, which has a time-constant of around 1 s in most cognitive tasks (Kahneman, 1973).

In the reactive condition, no preparatory pupil dilation is seen, reflecting the fact that the imperative stimulus occurred at a random time. A single, clear peak is associated with the reactive response. Pupil traces for the trun-cation condition were averaged separately for intentional and reactive trials. In both cases, peak dilations were higher than in control conditions, pre-sumably reflecting the additional processing demands of the truncation condition.

Crucially, pupil traces provided clear evidence of dilation before move-ment in the truncation trials that resulted in reaction to the imperative stimu-lus. This pre-movement dilation was absent in the control reactive trials (mean dilations: M = 0.03 mm, SD = 0.02 mm for truncation reactions; M = −0.02 mm, SD = 0.05 mm for reactive control trials; t_{11} = 3.86, p = .003). This pre-movement dilation is essentially a smeared version of the ramp-like increase seen in the intentional action condition. It provides physiological evidence that the participants were indeed preparing an intentional action in

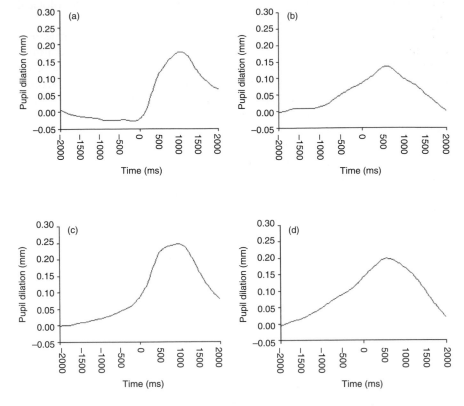

Figure 5.3 The movement-locked grand average pupil traces: (a) simple reaction time condition; (b) intentional action condition; (c) truncated reaction time trials; (d) truncated intentional action trials.

the truncation condition. This prepared but truncated intentional action could be responsible for the observed 59 ms RT cost of intention.

The significant RT cost of intention observed in Experiment 1 rules out independent, unitary or facilitatory architectures for the intentional and reactive motor systems. Those hypotheses predicted equal or faster reaction times for the truncation condition, whereas the opposite was observed. Mutually inhibitory or competitive systems provide the two plausible alternatives for modelling the interaction between the two systems. However, a number of additional objections could remain.

First, the RT cost of intention could result from slower perceptual processing of the imperative stimulus in truncation than in control reaction conditions. Participants might divide their attention between intentions and the imperative stimulus. This possibility is discussed in detail in Experiment 2. However, analysis of latency of peak stimulus-locked pupil dilation can provide an initial answer to this question. This showed that pupil latency was in fact non-significantly earlier in the truncation than in reaction conditions

(M = 1187 ms post-stimulus, SD = 202 ms for truncation; M = 1218 ms, SD = 196 ms for control reactions).

Moreover, in a control experiment (Control Experiment 1), we instructed 30 new participants either to attend very carefully to their intentional actions, responding to the imperative stimulus when they could, or, in a separate counterbalanced block, to listen out carefully for the stimulus and prioritize reacting to it, making their voluntary actions without thinking too much about them. These instructions were designed to divert the participants' attention to the intentional action at the expense of reactivity in the former condition, and to reaction at the expense of intention in the latter condition. The success of these instructional manipulations was demonstrated by the relatively high proportion of intentional relative to reactive trials in the truncation condition when participants focused on intention (68% *vs* 32%). This proportionality reversed in the truncation condition when participants were asked to focus on the imperative stimulus (48% intentional trials, 52% reactive). Control intentional and reactive conditions were also measured, and an RT cost of intention was calculated as in Experiment 1. Unsurprisingly, the RT cost of intention was greatest (122 ms) when participants focused on their intentions, but a significant (54 ms, p = .002) RT cost of intention remained when they focused on the imperative stimulus. Although task attention may contribute to the effect studied here, it seems unable to explain it entirely.

Second, the RT cost of intention could reflect a slight difference in the foreperiods for reactions in the truncation and control conditions. This was assessed in a control experiment, in which 16 new participants performed the truncation condition first, and then a control reactive block in which the foreperiods obtained in the preceding truncation block were replayed in random order. The mean reaction times were 347 ms (SD = 112 ms) for truncated reactions and 298 ms (SD = 63 ms) in the matched RT condition. A significant RT cost was again found (t_{15} = 4.25, p < .001).

Third, the RT cost of intention might arise because the motor system is initially inhibited during intentional action. Intentional action might involve a "withhold" process, prior to the "go" process. We know of no physiological evidence consistent with this withhold process, and many studies that reported a converse effect of motor facilitation before voluntary action (e.g. Chen, Yaseen, Cohen, & Hallett, 1998). Within our own data, a stronger evaluation of this view comes from dividing trials into those with imperative stimuli occurring earlier or later in the foreperiod. Although the time-course of the intentional process is not independently known, we can say with confidence that the "withhold" phase must necessarily precede the "go" phase.

Therefore, an imperative stimulus occurring unusually early is more likely to occur in the withhold phase than an unusually late stimulus. This view therefore, predicts that the RT costs of intention would decline as the foreperiod of the imperative stimulus increases. We therefore calculated reaction times separately for each participant's pre-median and post-median foreperiods in the truncation reaction and control reaction conditions. Significant effects of foreperiod were found ($F_{1,10} = 8.41$, $p = .016$), but there was no significant interaction with condition ($F_{1,10} = 2.41$, $p = .15$). The foreperiod effects in the truncation condition are comparable to those for simple reaction time. Therefore, we found no evidence for an inhibition of intentional actions preceding the intentional action itself.

Fourth, and most interestingly, the RT cost of intention might be dismissed as an instance of "dual-task performance". In the truncation condition, the participant both generates an intentional action while potentially reacting to the imperative stimulus. In this sense, the RT cost of intention is indeed an example of a dual-task decrement. However, it is a dual-task in a quite different sense to those seen in previous studies, in which the tasks involved have been clearly separable in terms of their behavioural outputs (Allport, Antonis, & Reynolds, 1972; Shallice, McLeod, & Lewis, 1985). In truncation, both intention and reactivity have the aim of producing the same motor output, yet they seem to be incompatible. Since there is only a single motor output, the dual-task cost must arise because of incompatibility between the inputs to the intentional and reactive action systems. Whatever initiates the intentional action (presumably volition) appears to be incompatible with initiating a reaction. Put this way, the dual-task objection appears no different from either the inhibitory or competitive architectures for combining intention and reactivity, and seems more like a finding than like a methodological objection.

Indeed, interpreting the RT cost of intention as a dual-task effect highlights two general points in the psychology of action (Haggard, 2001). These have a wider relevance beyond the paradigm studied here. First, actions are normally performed serially, and one at a time. Recent developments in visual neuroscience (DeYoe & van Essen, 1988) have emphasized the parallelism of perceptual processing, and serial models have generally fallen from favour. However, in the case of discrete, voluntary actions, we suggest the serial, limited-capacity model is broadly correct (Broadbent, 1982). Second, a dual-task interpretation reminds us of the importance of distinguishing between actions and movements. The two tasks studied here produce a single motor output, yet must clearly be different actions if they are to interfere. In general, the truncation paradigm shows that psychological representations of action are distinguishable in terms of the *source* of the action, not in terms of its motor *effect*.

Experiment 2: investigating the processing of the imperative stimulus using auditory-evoked potentials

In Experiment 2, we wished to examine the processing of the imperative stimulus more closely. Pupil dilation is not the ideal measure for investigating small latency differences because of the long time-constant of the pupillary response.

Methods

In Experiment 2, therefore, we repeated the design of Experiment 1 measuring the auditory-evoked potential elicited by the imperative stimulus. Evoked potentials in 12 new right-handed healthy individuals (age: $M = 23.8$ years, $SD = 3.0$ years) were recorded at 208.3 Hz (bandpass 0.03–40 Hz) from the vertex, relative to a reference electrode on the nose. Electroocculography (EOG) was recorded with bipolar electrodes placed diagonally across the right eye. Trials with rectified EEG in excess of 100 µV were rejected. Stimulus-locked averages were created from 100 ms before to 400 ms after the auditory tone, with baseline correction performed using the period −100 to 0 ms.

Intentional action, reaction and truncation conditions were similar to those in Experiment 1. Experiment 2 contained three additional conditions. In the *listen* condition, participants simply listened to and ignored the auditory stimulus. In the *intend–ignore* condition, participants prepared an intentional action and ignored the auditory stimulus if it occurred during action generation. In the *intend–stop*, condition, participants again prepared an intentional action, but withheld it if their preparation was interrupted by the imperative stimulus. The order of conditions was randomized for each participant. There were 40 trials in the listen, intentional action, intend–ignore and reaction conditions, and 80 in the truncation and intend–stop conditions. Other details of the analysis were as for Experiment 1.

Results and discussion

Mean reaction time was 354 ms ($SD = 101$ ms) in the reaction condition and 417 ms ($SD = 144$ ms) for the reactive trials in the truncation condition. These values were significantly different: $t_{11} = 3.45$, $p = .0062$. The RT cost of intention was, therefore, $417 − 354 = 63$ ms.

Inspection of the EEG signals showed an auditory-evoked potential similar to those reported previously (Schröger & Eimer, 1997). The main components were a P80, a N150 and a P300 wave. The P80 component was fairly similar across conditions. The N150 component was small when the auditory stimulus was irrelevant (e.g. *listen*, *intend–ignore*) but larger when the stimulus demanded either generation or withholding of a response (e.g. truncation, *intend–stop*). The P300 component was larger when the stimulus required a paradoxical or evaluative behaviour (e.g. not responding in *intend–ignore* or *intend–stop*) (Figure 5.4).

For our purposes, however, the key comparison is between the reactive control condition and the reactive truncation trials (Figure 5.4). The peak amplitude and peak latency were calculated in the windows 0–100, 100–250 and 250–400 ms to approximate the P80, N150 and P300 components, respectively. The P80 was visibly but non-significantly larger in the P80 window in the truncation trials than in the control trials. The truncation

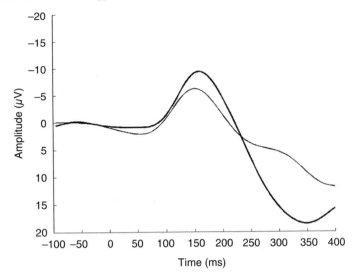

Figure 5.4 Stimulus-locked grand averages for simple reaction time (bold trace) and truncated reaction time (thin trace) auditory-evoked potentials measured at Cz.

trials also showed larger (p = .03) N150s than control reactions. Truncation N150s were also very slightly later (mean difference 8 ms, p = .01). P300s were also larger in the truncation condition (p = .001).

The increased amplitude in the key N150 time window suggests that the processing of the auditory stimulus is enhanced, rather than diminished, in the truncation trials. While the latency of this peak is slightly delayed, this delay is much too small to explain the delay in reaction time. The P300 enhancement can be attributed to the fact that the stimulus requires a more complex response in truncation than in purely reactive trials. In truncation, the stimulus requires that the participant stop preparation and respond; in reaction, the stimulus requires only a response.

Interestingly, both the N150 and P300 enhancements were seen in the *intend–stop* condition, as well as in the truncation condition (Figure 5.5). Therefore, the explanation for the enhanced neural response to the imperative stimulus lies in the way the stimulus shuts off the intentional action, rather than the way that it triggers the reaction. Figure 5.5 shows a strong similarity between the truncated reaction times and the *intend–stop* trials in which the occurrence of the stimulus resulted in the participant stopping the intentional preparation. Swapping intention for reactivity may be physiologically similar to just stopping preparation for an intentional action. This finding suggests that the RT cost of intention occurs due to the need to deactivate the intentional action before making an identical movement reactively. That is, most of the RT cost of intention is due to the deactivation of the intentional action, rather than the generation of the reactive action.

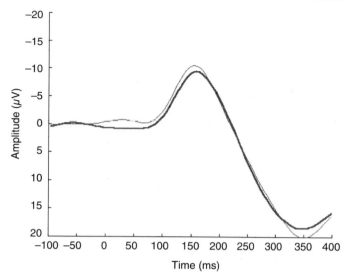

Figure 5.5 Stimulus-locked grand averages for truncated reaction time (bold trace) and *intend–stop* (thin trace) auditory-evoked potentials measured at Cz.

Finally, these effects were not simply due to differences in baseline. The auditory-evoked potential in the truncation condition presumably combines with a readiness potential associated with preparing the voluntary action. Our amplifier settings were deliberately chosen to attenuate slow potentials of this kind, allowing the faster stimulus-locked potentials to emerge. Moreover, both negative and positive peaks of the auditory-evoked potential are increased in the truncation condition. No simple interaction with a motor preparation potential can explain this finding. As a final confirmation, we additionally calculated movement-locked potentials for reaction controls and truncation reactions, using the period 1000 to 800 ms before movement as a baseline. These show no substantive difference in background levels of EEG and, indeed, a greater pre-movement deflection for truncation reactions than for control reactions (Figure 5.6).

Experiment 2 replicated the RT cost of intention seen previously. It failed to provide convincing evidence that the processing of the imperative stimulus is attenuated due to divided attention in the truncation condition. Instead, the RT cost of intention seems to arise because an intentional action must be stopped and deactivated before the same motor output can be made reactively. Intentional action temporarily locks motor outputs to prevent them occurring reactively. Two aspects of this finding are noteworthy.

First, the result confirms that intention and reactivity are dissociable representations of action at the central level. Second, the result fits with two important concepts of frontal lobe function. The frontal lobes play a key

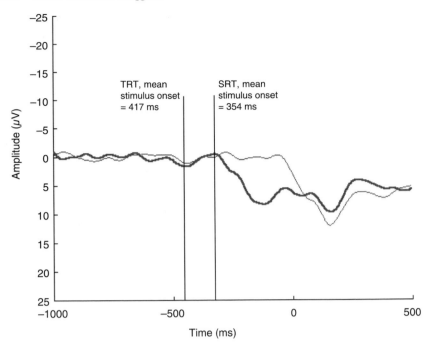

Figure 5.6 Movement-locked auditory-evoked potentials for simple reaction time (SRT, thin trace) and truncated reaction time (TRT, bold trace) measured at Cz. 0 = movement onset.

role in stopping and inhibiting behaviour, and their operation is characteristically slow (Shallice, 1988). In this sense, the truncation task appears to provide a good example of executive control of motor tasks. In keeping with the suggestion of supervisory systems, the truncation task seems to involve an executive process modulating the normal access of stimuli to motor output, thus allowing willed actions to occur.

Experiment 3: examining the locus of interference between intention and reactivity

The above experiments demonstrate a reliable interference between intention and reactivity. They also suggest this is not due to attenuation of the imperative stimulus. However, they do not otherwise reveal which elements of these two tasks interfere. To assess this, we compared the amount of interference between intention and two different RT tasks, the simple RT task studied previously and a two-alternative forced-choice RT task. These two tasks were chosen because they differ in a well-understood way: in simple reaction time, only one response is ever required. Therefore, the response can be prepared in advance, and is simply unleashed when the imperative stimulus occurs. In choice reaction time, two possible stimuli occur, each of which demands a different response. Thus, the response cannot be prepared in advance, and an additional information-processing stage is required to link the stimulus identity to the required response identity (Frith & Done, 1986).

Methods

Sixteen right-handed individuals (age: $M = 24.3$ years, $SD = 3.3$ years) participated in the experiment. In all conditions, participants prepared and made intentional keypress responses at a time of their own choice using the index finger of the right hand. The conditions differed only in the nature of the RT task that interfered with this intentional action. These RT tasks were structured according to a 2×2 factorial design with two within-participants factors. The first factor was the type of RT task (simple or choice). This factor was blocked. The second factor was the hand making the RT response (left or right). In the case of simple reaction time, participants responded with either the left or right hand in separate blocks. In the case of choice reaction time, the identity of the stimulus determined whether the participants responded with the left or right hand, and the factor was therefore randomized. Each RT task was performed in a truncation condition, in which participants always made intentional right keypresses unless interrupted by the truncating stimulus, and in a control condition where no intentional actions occurred. Thus, a RT cost of intention could be calculated for each cell of the factorial arrangement of interrupting task (simple or choice) and responding hand (left or right).

We aimed to measure 15 trials in each cell of this design. Therefore, control simple reaction time (SRT) conditions, without intentional actions, comprised 15 trials. Control choice reaction time (CRT) conditions comprised 30 trials, 15 requiring left hand responses and 15 requiring right hand responses. For truncated conditions including intentional actions, we assumed that the interaction between the participant's random time of action and the randomized time of the imperative stimulus would produce a 50/50 split between intentional actions and truncated reaction times, and therefore doubled the number of trials in each condition. Conditions were tested in separate blocks. However, conditions requiring more than 15 trials were split into a number of sub-blocks of 15 trials. Each participant received a different random order of blocks, with the proviso that no more than two identical blocks could occur in succession.

The experimental design was largely as in Experiment 1, so only key differences will be reported. There were response keys for the left and right index finger. The trial began with an ambient auditory warning tone. The imperative stimulus was visual rather than auditory, and the participants viewed a monitor at a comfortable distance. For the SRT trials, the imperative stimulus was "| |". For the CRT trials, it was either "=" or "+", requiring a left or right hand response, respectively. All stimuli were in 72-point Times font, presented centrally on the monitor.

Results and discussion

Only reactive trials were analysed. Altogether, 6.15% of trials were discarded as anticipations, as being too slow or incorrect reactions.

Choice reaction times were longer than simple reaction times, as previously found (Frith & Done, 1986) (Table 5.1). Our analyses, however, focus on the RT cost of intention, again defined as the difference between the reactive and truncation reaction times. The results for the right SRT condition essentially replicate those of Experiment 1. A significant RT cost of intention is again present (mean 51 ms; t_{15} = 2.70, p = .02). The results for the left SRT show a larger RT cost, which is again significant (t_{15} = 7.15, p < .0001). This cost comprises two elements: an RT cost of intention and an added RT cost attributable to the need to switch spatial attention from the right hand generating the intentional action to the left hand, which responds to the intentional stimulus. In the right CRT condition, no RT cost of intention is seen, and in fact a small RT benefit is found. A 19-ms RT cost of intention is seen in the left CRT condition, but this was not significant (t_{15} = 1.62, p = .13). The RT costs of intention are shown in Figure 5.7.

We also analysed error data for the CRT conditions only. In the truncation paradigm, the definition and interpretation of errors requires special care, because of the interaction with intentional actions. For example, if a participant presses the right response key 10 ms after a visual stimulus requiring a left keypress, this is probably an intentional action, rather than a CRT error. Because the intentional action always involves the right hand, the proportion of "right should have been left" and "left should have been right" errors is expected to differ, and this difference may interact with reaction time. An arbitrary assumption must be made about the minimum latency dividing true reactions from "left over" intentional actions, which merely happen to occur close in time to the stimulus. For the purposes of RT analysis (above), a cut-off of 150 ms was used, but for exploratory error analyses, more liberal

Table 5.1 Mean (SD) reaction time results

Condition	Reactive (ms)	Truncation (ms)
Right SRT	304 (73)	355 (120)
Left SRT	324 (86)	433 (91)
Right CRT	481 (123)	475 (140)
Left CRT	500 (111)	519 (116)

Abbreviations: SRT = simple reaction time, CRT = choice reaction time.

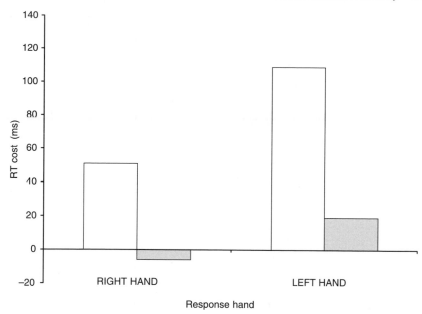

Figure 5.7 Reaction/time (RT) cost of intention for each truncating task and for each responding hand. Note that the participants prepared intentional actions of the right hand. □ simple reaction time; ▧ choice reaction time.

cut-offs of 200 and 250 ms were also applied. The resulting error rates are shown in Table 5.2.

Two features of the error data are particularly noteworthy. First, some errors in the truncated CRT task are clearly not true errors, but intentional actions masquerading as very fast reactions. When the minimum RT cut-off is taken as 250 ms, the number of such leftover intentional actions is much lower than with a cut-off of 150 ms. The error rates in truncation conditions are not universally higher than in normal choice reaction time.

Second, if 250 ms is taken as an appropriate cut-off for identifying true reactions, the truncation task produces an increased rate (10.14%) of "left should have been right" errors, but a slightly lower rate (3.97%) of "right should have been left" errors, compared with normal choice reaction time. The former effect suggests that preparing an intentional right keypress somehow biases participants against right reactive responses and in favour of left reactive responses. This is inconsistent with facilitation between intentional and reactive motor systems.

The most important result of Experiment 3 is the clear demonstration that the cost of intention is confined to simple reaction time, and is effectively absent in choice reaction time. Simple reaction time is assumed to involve advance preparation of responses, whereas choice reaction time does

Table 5.2 Percentage of "left should have been right" and "right should have been left" errors at three limits of reaction time (RT) acceptability for truncation and reactive movements

Condition	Stimulus	Participant's response	Type of error	Lower limit of RT acceptability (%)		
				150 ms	200 ms	250 ms
CRT	Right	Left	Left should have been right	1.54	1.54	1.54
CRT	Left	Right	Right should have been left	4.96	4.96	4.96
Truncated CRT	Right	Left	Left should have been right	10.14	10.14	10.14
Truncated CRT	Left	Right	Right should have been left	7.68	5.45	3.97

Abbreviation: CRT = choice reaction time.

not (Frith & Done, 1986). Therefore, our result clearly suggests that the reason for the basic RT cost of intention is an incompatibility between intentional and reactive *preparation* of an action. A given action, such as a right keypress, can be prepared reactively, or it can be prepared intentionally, but the two kinds of preparation are not the same and are to some extent exclusive.

The RT cost of intention in truncation trials would arise because the response preparation that normally occurs in simple reaction time is prevented by intentional preparation. The intentional preparation must be stopped before the reactive response can occur. Since this process occurs for simple but not for choice reaction time, the RT cost of intention must be considered as a switch between two mutually exclusive forms of preparation, rather than as a general intentional inhibition of all reactivity.

General discussion

Across a series of many experiments, we reliably observed that the preparation of an intentional action delays making the same action reactively. The average RT cost of intention was consistently around 50 ms. This delay does not appear to be due to a perceptual attenuation of the imperative stimulus.

We would like to discuss several aspects of this result. First, our results are not compatible with a unitary concept of the motor system. Instead, intentional and reactive motor systems appear to involve separate computational streams. Moreover, these streams are exclusive, in that they cannot be simultaneously active: making a movement intentionally seems to prevent making the same movement reactively. The source of an action seems more relevant than the physical effector that it causes to move; and it would appear that the information processing associated with the action should be considered as a central process rather than a peripheral one.

Second, our results clarify the possible relations between intentional and reactive motor systems, originally introduced in Figure 5.1. Facilitatory or independent action systems are ruled out by the RT cost of intention. An inhibitory link between intention and reactivity cannot explain why intention interferes with simple but not choice reaction time in Experiment 3. Moreover, inhibition cannot explain why the process of just stopping an intention seems so similar to the process of replacing it with a reaction. Instead, we postulate a switching process, between intentional actions and reactions, allowing just one of these exclusive access to motor execution. Since this exclusivity occurs for simple but not for choice reaction time, we conclude that it is the *preparation* of intentional and reactive actions which both demand exclusive access to motor output. The preparation associated with intentional action must be stopped and "dismantled" before a reactive response can be prepared in its place. This process has clear similarities with some accounts of selective attention. It also seems to be a fundamental process underlying the majority of executive functions.

We suggest that the essential features of conflict between intention and reactivity are seen in a number of dysexecutive syndromes. For example, Zanini, Rumiati, and Shallice (2002) studied the ability to produce a sequence of actions in frontal patients. They suggested that sequencing errors were attributable to a failure to suppress immediate responses, rather than a deficit in temporal organization of complex actions. The multiple errands test (Burgess & Shallice, 1991) provides a more ecological illustration of the same problem. Here, frontal patients were given a shopping list and asked to buy items in various neighbourhood shops. Frontal patients typically revisited a single location a number of times and failed to visit other shops. The results were interpreted as a difficulty in activating a specific intention in the presence of stimuli suggesting alternative actions. Interestingly, the same interpretation could be made of anarchic or alien hand syndrome, even though this is classically considered as a motor rather than executive disturbance.

In an important model of cognitive function (Shallice, 1988), the supervisory attentional system was held to play an important, though rather undefined, role in willed action. In particular, the supervisory attentional system inhibits routine processing during willed actions, by overriding the normal process of contention scheduling. Our results are compatible with this suggestion and, indeed, offer the first behavioural evidence for it. Intention appears to *reduce* reactivity by securing preferential and exclusive access for the intention to the motor output system. Our voluntary actions typically require our full attention, and we perform them only one at a time. Previous work has focused on how voluntary actions relate to goals. Our research shows that they are quite different from reactions and have profound implications for reactivity. We suggest this balance between intention and reactivity is, in large part, what is meant by attention in (voluntary) action.

Acknowledgement

We are grateful to Minako Kaeda for help with testing the subjects in Control Experiment 1.

References

Allport, D. A., Antonis, B., & Reynolds, P. (1972). On the division of attention: a disproof of single channel hypothesis. *Quarterly Journal of Experimental Psychology*, 24, 225–235.

Beatty, J. (1982). Task-evoked pupillary responses, processing load, and structure of processing resources. *Psychological Bulletin*, 91, 276–292.

Broadbent, D. E. (1982). Task combination and selective intake of information. *Acta Psychologica*, 50, 253–290.

Burgess, P., & Shallice, T. (1991). Higher-order cognitive impairments and frontal lobe lesions in man. In H. S. Levin, H. M. Eisenberg, & A. L. Benton (Eds.), *Frontal lobe function and dysfunction* (pp. 125–138). London: Oxford University Press.

Chen, R., Yaseen, Z., Cohen, L. G., & Hallett, M. (1998). Time course of corticospinal excitability in reaction time and self-paced movements. *Annals of Neurology, 44,* 317–325.

Della Sala, S., Marchetti, C., & Spinnler, H. (1991). Right-sided anarchic (alien) hand: a longitudinal study. *Neuropsychologia, 29,* 1113–1127.

DeYoe, E. A., & van Essen, D. C. (1988). Concurrent processing streams in monkey visual cortex. *Trends in Neuroscience, 11,* 219–226.

Frith, C., & Done, D. J. (1986). Routes to action in reaction time tasks. *Psychological Research, 48,* 169–177.

Haggard, P. (2001). The psychology of action. *British Journal of Psychology, 92,* 113–128.

Kandel, E. R., Schwartz, J. H., & Jessell, T. M. (2000). *Principles of neural science* (4th edn). St Louis, MO: McGraw-Hill.

Kahneman, D. (1973). *Attention and effort.* Englewood Cliffs, NJ: Prentice-Hall.

Kurata, K. (1998). Information processing for motor control in primate premotor cortex. *Behavioural Brain Research, 61,* 135–142.

Libet, B., Gleason, C. A., Wright, E. W., & Pearl, D. K. (1983). Time of conscious intention to act in relation to onset of cerebral activity (readiness-potential): the unconscious initiation of a freely voluntary act. *Brain, 106,* 623–642.

Passingham, R. (1987). *Two cortical systems for directing movement: motor areas of the cerebral cortex.* Ciba Foundation Symposium No. 132. Chichester: Wiley.

Richer, F., & Beatty, J. (1985). Pupillary dilations in movement preparation and execution. *Psychophysiology, 22,* 204–207.

Schröger, E., & Eimer, M. (1997). Endogenous covert spatial orienting in audition: "cost–benefit" analyses of reaction times and event-related potentials. *Quarterly Journal of Experimental Psychology, 50,* 457–474.

Shallice, T. (1988). *From neuropsychology to mental structure.* Cambridge: Cambridge University Press.

Shallice, T., McLeod, P., & Lewis, K. (1985). Isolating cognitive modules with the dual task paradigm: are speech perception and production separate processes? *Quarterly Journal of Experimental Psychology: Human Experience and Perception, 37A,* 507–532.

Sherrington, C. S. (1906). *The integrative action of the nervous system.* London: Archibald Constable & Co.

Tanji, J., & Shima, K. (1994). Role for supplementary motor area cells in planning several movements ahead. *Nature, 371,* 413–416.

Wise, K. H., & Mauritz, S. P. (1985). Set-related neuronal activity in the premotor cortex of rhesus monkeys: effects of changes in motor set. *Proceedings of the Royal Society of London B, 223,* 331–354.

Zanini, S., Rumiati, R. I., & Shallice, T. (2002). Action sequencing deficit following frontal lobe lesion. *Neurocase, 8,* 88–99.

6 Selective attention for action

New evidence from visual search studies

Aave Hannus, Sebastian F. W. Neggers, Frans W. Cornelissen and Harold Bekkering

Abstract

At any given time, only a small portion of information available in the visual environment can be selected and identified for conscious processing. Optimally, this selection should be based on the information necessary for control of current and planned behaviour and is most often described as selective attention. In this chapter, we discuss the models accounting for the selectivity of visual input from the perspective of functional connection between perception and action. This conception reflects the general idea that perceived events and planned actions share a common realm and view the attentional processes as selection-for-action. Some recent experimental evidence in line with such a selection-for-action view will be presented and some speculations about the underlying neural network will be made.

Stimulus-driven and user-driven control of visual attention

It is widely assumed that two types of processing guide visual attention. First, some objects attract our attention instantaneously, in a bottom-up manner. Such stimulus-driven control occurs when some internal attributes of the stimulus attract the attentional system and the attention is captured reflexively because a particular stimulus is salient in a given context. In contrast, in top-down or cognitively driven processing, the attention is guided voluntarily, based on the behavioural goals of the person. In this chapter, we focus on top-down modulation of the attentional system. For instance, Yantis and Jonides (1990) demonstrated elegantly the power of voluntary processes over reflexive attentional capture. They showed that if participants know with certainty the location of a target and have sufficient time to focus attention on that target, the distractors are at least temporarily unable to capture the attention. Furthermore, Folk, Remington, and Johnston (1992) claim that attentional capture does not occur due to the properties of the stimulus or distractors *per se*, but is determined by the relationship between distractor properties and target-finding properties. They suggest that the involuntary attentional capture is subject to top-down control and occurs if, and only if, distractors have a property that the participant is using to find the target. A comprehensive overview of the complex interplay between bottom-up and top-down processes is provided by Pashler, Johnston, and Ruthruff (2001).

Visual search

One research paradigm that has been developed to study the characteristics of selective visual processes is known as visual search. A visual search task typically requires participants to search for a target stimulus among a number of distractor stimuli. A typical visual search task starts with visual input and ends with output, usually in the form of some behavioural response indicating that the target (or its absence) was detected. As stated previously, attention is selective. The following question arises: At what level of processing does this selectivity start to operate? According to early selection models, the role of attention is to filter out some information at a very early stage and enable only attended information to reach cognitive processing, whereas unattended information undergoes only rudimentary processing. Early selection is thought to operate through two systems. In preattentive parallel processing, simple physical characteristics of stimuli are extracted (e.g. their colour). The attentive system, characterized by limited processing capacity (i.e. the entire visual scene cannot be processed at once, but rather piece by piece), processes only stimuli passed from the first, preattentive analysis; the categorical identity of stimuli should be processed at this later stage of processing. A typical example of the early selection approach is Broadbent's (1958) filter theory. In contrast, late selection models propose that unattended stimuli are not rejected from full processing, but only from entry into memory processes or into the control of voluntary responses (Duncan, 1980). It is assumed that already on the first, parallel level of processing, a full analysis and extraction of semantic categorization of the stimuli is performed, and this information is used as the basis for selection for the system with limited processing capacity. However, Allport (1987, 1990) notes that often in the literature there appears to be no systematic differentiation between selective cueing and selective processing. He claims that typically, early selection echoes the selective cueing or specifying of task-relevant information and that late selection characterizes further processing of both relevant and irrelevant information.

Another dichotomy in the visual search literature is the distinction between serial and parallel processing. The cognitive processing is termed "parallel" if all elements are processed at the same time, assuming that processing of all entities starts simultaneously over the entire visual field. Alternatively, with "serial" processing the elements are processed one by one, with the processing of one element being completed before starting the processing of another (Townsend, 1971). Originally, Treisman and Gelade (1980) suggested that visual search for targets defined by unique salient features could be performed in parallel: the target is effortlessly located on the basis of preattentive visual processing over the visual scene, which means that it pops out from the visual array and can be found almost immediately (the reaction time does not depend on the number of distractors). Conversely, searching for a specific conjunction of features leads to a less efficient serial search. However, as suggested by Wolfe (1996a), the parallel and serial search patterns only represent the two extremes of a continuum of search results rather than indicating the existence of a strict dichotomy. The search efficiency can be explained by stimulus similarity rather than by distinctive parallel and serial processing (Duncan & Humphreys, 1989). Pashler (1987) suggests a molar serial self-terminating search over clumps of stimuli, while within these clumps a capacity-limited parallel search takes place; the size of clumps appears to be around eight items.

Modulation of visual attention

What are the determinants that decide which kind of information should be selected to enter conscious cognitive processing? Here, we present four dominant theories accounting for selection processes in visual search.

Feature integration theory

Feature integration theory (Treisman, 1977, 1991; Treisman & Gelade, 1980; Treisman & Sato, 1990) proposes the existence of two separate search mechanisms. Research on visual attention has shown that searching for targets defined by individual features is much less effortful than searching for targets defined by conjunctions of features (Treisman & Gelade, 1980). Effort is measured as the dependence of reaction time on the number of distractors, or the number of errors per set-size. According to feature integration theory, targets defined by single features can be detected without fully identifying distractors. The preattentive parallel search accounts for detection of single features; single-feature targets are detected via activity in independent feature maps tuned to discrete single features, which produces spatially parallel search functions. The function for reaction time in relation to the number of distractors is flat or almost flat; the display size effects are around 6 ms per item or less (Treisman & Souther, 1985). Alternatively, the detection of targets defined by feature conjunctions involves the much slower process of serial scanning of all the items in the array. The detection of a feature conjunction requires focused attention, which is serially directed and permits accurate localization and conjunction of several features. This occurs by serial conjoining of features at particular locations in different feature maps. According to the feature integration theory, different results emerge in the search for a target defined by a combination of features or feature conjunctions; search for a feature conjunction should be serial, precipitating linear increases in reaction time as a function of the number of distractors. Feature integration theory suggests that the identity of items in a visual scene ("what") and their location ("where") are unified by a serial scan of spatial locations using a window of attention. In this way, the features and properties of the visual scene are bound and then compared with stored representations of objects for recognition (Treisman, 1996; Treisman & Gelade, 1980; Treisman & Gormican, 1988). In general, this theory suggests that visual search differs qualitatively for targets defined by a single feature and by feature conjunction differences in relation to distractors. Attention serves to bind together the presumably separately represented features belonging to a particular object. In the case of feature search, attention is not devoted to separate spatial locations one at a time. However, during conjunction search, attention needs to be allocated to one location at a time to bind the features at that particular location and to make an overall decision about the representation of this stimulus—for example is it likely to be the target stimulus I want to foveate for further inspection.

Feature integration theory has received extensive experimental support. There is evidence of parallel search for targets containing a unique distinguishing feature in relation to distractors and such single features can yield texture segregation. For example, this is the case with the colour green in contrast with some other colour (Dehaene, 1989). The features leading to such a "pop-out" effect are colour, size, shape, orientation and curvature (e.g. Treisman & Gelade, 1980). Similarity among distractors determines the strength of perceptual grouping, while similarity between target and distractors determines the ease of segregating the target from distractors (Duncan & Humphreys, 1989; Humphreys & Müller, 1993).

Guided search model

Although influenced by feature integration theory, the guided search model (Wolfe, Cave, & Franzel, 1989) posits that the search for a single feature and for a feature conjunction is not processed differently. Parallel processes guide attention to probable targets but do not distinguish whether an item is a target or not, they just divide the set of stimuli into distractors and candidate targets. Then a serial process is used to search through the probable targets until the correct target is detected. Thus, the spotlight of attention is guided by information from parallel processes. Moreover, in triple conjunction search tasks, the search is even easier (the effect of set size on reaction time is weaker) because the ongoing parallel processes provide more information to the serial process (Wolfe et al., 1989). More recently, Wolfe has refined his model to account for visual search processes in real-world tasks (Wolfe, 1996b). Here, attention acts to allow only the features of one object at a time to reach the higher visual processing. Consequently, the activation map guides attention—the weighted sum of activity in the preattentive feature maps, working by a winner-takes-all principle that determines further processing.

Biased competition model

Desimone and Duncan (1995) proposed a further model to account for visual search processes, the biased competition model. Their explanation is based on the interplay between both bottom-up and top-down sources of attention. Features of an attended object are processed concurrently, but the limited ability to deal simultaneously with several sources of visual information determines the number of separate objects that can be seen. Due to these limitations in cognitive processing capacity, a selective attentional system should operate to restrict the huge amount of potential inputs and withhold information irrelevant to the current behaviour. Thus, competition for representation, analysis and control of behaviour among visual objects takes place. The preactivated target units have an advantage in this competition (Duncan, 1996). More specifically, within brain systems receiving visual input, a gain in activation for one object entails a loss to activation for other objects. For instance, Duncan (1984) indicated that two attributes of a single object (e.g. brightness and orientation) could be identified simultaneously without mutual interference, while attributes of two different objects could not, even if the objects overlapped spatially. The object-based theory suggests that focal attention is guided by parallel, preattentive processes representing discrete objects (Duncan, 1984). One plausible cause for this competition might be the structure of cortical areas in both the ventral and dorsal visual stream. As the complexity of visual processing increases in every consecutive area, receptive field sizes of individual neurons increase. When more objects are added to the receptive field, the information about any given individual object must decline. Desimone and Duncan (1995) propose competition between objects represented by the same receptive field. Here, importance in terms of behaviour plays a role: the competition is biased towards information relevant to the current behaviour. The information in a visual scene determines the spatial distribution and feature attributes of objects. During the search in this information, a target may "pop out" due to a bottom-up bias that directs attention towards local inhomogeneities (Sagi & Julesz, 1984). On the other hand, selectivity is implemented to bias the competition towards behaviourally relevant information by means of top-down control.

Selection-for-action

Allport (1987, 1990) proposed another model for visual processing with a somewhat different emphasis. In his 1990 article, Allport pointed out that since the 1950s the majority of research in the area of visual attention had considered the limited information-processing capacity of the brain as the fundamental constraint underlying all operations of attention. Thus, according to this view, the selection function of attention arises from the limited capacity of the information-processing system. Diverging from the general idea that attention operates as a mechanism for coping with central limited capacities of cognitive processing, Allport emphasizes the constraints on the preparation and control of action. The idea behind the selection-for-action perspective is that integrated actions require the selection of particular aspects or attributes from the environment that are relevant to the action at hand. At the same time, the information irrelevant to the action should be ignored. Thus, the attentional processes are viewed as the selection of action-relevant events or stimuli relying on particular action plans. The basis of this approach can be linked to the work of Lotze (1852), who proposed in his ideomotor principle that actions are selected and planned in terms of their sensory consequences. In other words, perception can be linked directly to upcoming action intentions, since both are represented in the brain in sensory terms. Thus, the attentional processing can reflect the need to select information relevant to the task at hand.

Support for this argument emerges from the observation that selecting a stimulus as a target for a saccade occurs before foveation. In addition, the phenomenon of covert attention suggests that foveation is neither a necessary nor a sufficient condition for selection (see Allport, 1987). During the perception of an object, information about different attributes of that object should be bound together to allow the purposeful use of the object according to intended action. If the intention is to take a yellow dictionary from the bookshelf, the information eventually about colour, size and orientation should be combined for an accurate grasping movement.

To summarize, the development of theories about visual selection seems to reflect a gradual shift from pure perceptual considerations towards a stronger emphasis on the interaction between perceptual processing and behavioural actions in visual search. In the next section, we first briefly present recent work by others that is in line with the selection-for-action notion of visual attention. We then present in more detail recent work by ourselves.

Selection-for-action: effects of action intention on visual perception

To extend the validity of attentional studies, Tipper, Lortie, and Baylis (1992) conducted an experiment in a more complex setting, requiring a direct manual contact with three-dimensional buttons. Evidence from front–back interference, negative priming asymmetries and left–right inference asymmetries suggested that visual attention accesses an action-centred representation of stimuli. The spatial characteristics of distractor inference in reaching tasks cannot be accounted for by visual biases to the locations of distractors only (Meegan & Tipper, 1999). That is, two distractors at the same location can cause different degrees of inference, depending on their visuomotor characteristics. For example, distractors were found to be specifically interfering in a hand-centred frame of reference—that is, when located between the starting position of the hand and the final target location to be reached to. In addition, the amount of interference depended on the nature of the task: when verbal responses instead of manual responses were required, the spatial interference effects did not appear.

Recently, Humphreys and Riddoch (2001) showed that visual search could be guided by intended actions. They studied patients with neglect symptoms and found that a lesion in the fronto-temporo-parietal region allowed one patient to find the targets defined by action faster and more accurately than targets defined by name, although he was able to name the objects and colours. Thus, the action templates helped him in visual search and selection independently of perceptual representations of targets. Two other neglect patients in the same study showed better performance in visual search when the target was defined by name. Humphreys and Riddoch suggested that these results reflect the impaired use of perceptual templates by the first patient, probably due to impaired functioning of the ventral visual stream, in contrast to two other patients with less damaged temporal lobes. In one experiment, Humphreys and Riddoch manipulated the orientation of the objects to be searched for. Consequently, the handle, the feature typically used to grasp the object, was oriented either near or far away from the patient's point of view. Interestingly, the action instruction "find the object you could drink from" only enhanced search performance when the handle was oriented near to the patient. The authors concluded from this that memory templates about actions are activated by critical affordances of objects.

Selection-for-action: new evidence from the classical visual search paradigm

Inspired by these action-related results of visual processing, we began a series of experiments employing a classical visual search paradigm, while explicitly manipulating the action instruction between blocks of trials. The aim of these studies was to determine whether visual selective processes are modulated by the action intentions of the actor. In particular, we examined whether the processing of task-relevant visual information is more enhanced than that of task-irrelevant visual information, and whether this is observed at an early feature level of search performance. Therefore, we designed two test conditions. In the first, participants were asked to saccade-and-point to a target object as quickly and accurately as possible; in the other condition, they were asked to saccade-and-grasp the predefined target object. Orientation but not colour is known to influence the way an object is grasped. In contrast, pointing to a target is likely to be insensitive for both object orientation (Smeets & Brenner, 1999) and colour, since humans typically point to the centre of the object anyway. If task-critical features are processed in a more efficient way, less orientation but equal colour errors are expected in the saccade-and-grasp than in the saccade-and-point condition.

In Experiment 1, eight individuals participated in a conjunction search task. The target had a unique combination of colour and orientation. At the beginning of each trial, the fixation point lit up; the system then waited until stable ocular fixation of the fixation light-emitting diode (LED) was reached before proceeding. Then a 2000 or 1000 Hz tone (fading away with a negative amplitude modulation) with a duration of 1000 ms instructed the participant whether a 45° or −45° had to be searched for. Simultaneously with the onset of the tone, the fixation point turned from red to green or orange to instruct the colour of the future target. Then, 1500 ms after the tone was given, the object set including a target and distracting objects lit up. Participants were instructed in one block of trials to make a *saccade-and-pointing* movement to the target object, and in another block of trials to make a *saccade-and-grasping* movement to the target object, as soon as they thought they located the target in their peripheral field of view. They were explicitly told not to make an eye movement before they thought they had identified the target's position.

The target was chosen randomly from one of eight objects (coloured black in Figure 6.1), of which four were oriented at 45° and four at −45°. Each target was chosen equally often in a session (eight times). Four of these eight objects were located at the same distance from the fixation point (see Figure 6.1, objects surrounded by squares). Only trials with a target picked from one of these four equidistant positions were analysed; the other four positions were included to prevent memorization of the target location. In

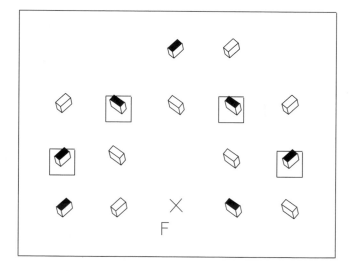

Figure 6.1 Object set. A schematic overview of the objects used in the first two experiments. Sixteen plexiglass bars were mounted on a table, at a distance of 100 mm from each other. Half the bars were oriented at 45° and half at −45°. The bars coloured black could be the target object.

the analysis of reaction time of correct saccades, trials with a target picked from all eight possible target positions were analysed, since sufficient data were available for trial types with higher distractor numbers.

Four display sizes were used, one containing the target object only and the others containing three, six or nine distracting objects and a target. Display sizes were randomized throughout a session; each display size was used equally often (16 times in a session). Distractors could differ from the target with respect to orientation (45° or −45°) and colour (green or orange). The positions of the distractors were randomly chosen from the remaining non-target objects (and the seven remaining possible target positions coloured black in Figure 6.1 from trial to trial, but according to the following rule: one-third of the distracting objects had the same colour as the target but a different orientation; one-third had the same orientation as the target but a different colour; and one-third differed from the target with respect to both orientation and colour. The positions, orientations and colours of the target and distractors were written into a file automatically for off-line analysis. An entire experiment consisted of four blocks of 64 trials (8 target positions × 4 display sizes × 2 target colours). Importantly, performance was defined as the accuracy of the first saccadic eye movement only. Since it is well known that saccades are initiated before the starting of the hand movements, it can only reflect the action intention and not the ongoing action demands during execution of the action.

The most interesting result was that participants were more likely to fixate an object with the wrong orientation when the saccade was executed in a saccade-and-pointing sequence than in a saccade-and-grasping sequence, although this effect was not significant on trials in which only three distractors were present. Saccades making a colour error or a double error, however, were statistically as frequent in the saccade-grasping condition as in the saccade-pointing condition. Hence, the improvement in saccadic target selection in the saccade-and-grasping condition compared with the saccade-and-pointing condition is not a general improvement, but is specific for orientation discrimination (see Plate 6.1).

Importantly, no significant differences in reaction time of saccadic eye movements were found between these two conditions. Thus, apparently, preparation for a grasping movement improved the selection of a target from a rich display for the accompanying saccade, as compared with preparing for a pointing movement. The improvement has to be caused by the intentional preparatory processes and not the executive processes belonging to a grasping movement, since the saccades were initiated based on visual information originating from before the hand started to move. The improvement was seen for the selection of the correct orientation only; no improvement was seen for the selection of the correct colour (see Figure 6.2). The improvement did not appear to cost any additional time per object present in the display (similar reaction time slopes for both conditions). It is likely that the early visual processing of orientation information was performed with a

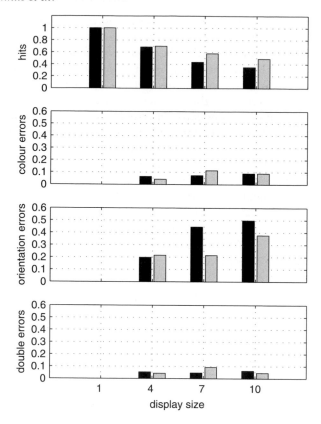

Figure 6.2 Saccadic error distributions in Experiment 1. The probabilities of occurrence of correct saccades to the target, an orientation error, a colour error or a double error are plotted as a function of display size, averaged over all participants. Black bars denote error rates in the pointing condition, grey bars in the grasping conditions. Saccadic orientation errors occur significantly less often when participants grasp the target object than when saccades accompany a pointing movement. The data are pooled for the four targets positioned at the same distance from the fixation point (see Figure 6.1).

higher accuracy when a grasping movement was planned (see also Bekkering & Neggers, 2002).

It has been assumed that a grasping movement can be subdivided into a transport and a grasping component (preshaping the hand to match the target object's orientation and size), which are individually controlled (Jeannerod, 1981), although that view has been challenged (Smeets & Brenner, 1999). In Experiment 2, therefore, we wished to determine whether the enhancement of orientation perception in Experiment 1 could be specifically attributed to the influence of the grasping component. In this second experiment, we examined what effect transporting the arm to the target region had on object orientation and colour perception. Participants had to point and saccade to the top surface target item in one condition, and only saccade to the target item in the control condition. The displays were identical to those used in Experiment 1. The only difference between the two conditions in Experiment 2 was the transporting of the hand to the target region. Any influence of (preparation for) transport of the hand on feature detection would become visible in the saccadic errors. We hypothesized that no such difference would be found, since for the pointing task to the top surface of the bar, neither colour nor the orientation of the side-surfaces of the bar plays an important role.

As can be seen in Figure 6.3, this was indeed what was observed. Interestingly, in this experiment participants were as likely to fixate an object with the wrong orientation when the saccade was executed in a saccade-and-pointing sequence, compared with a saccade-only sequence. Also, saccades making a colour error or a double error also were statistically as frequent in the saccade-pointing condition as in the saccade-only condition.

In a new series of experiments, we used two- instead of three-dimensional objects for the following three reasons. First, one could argue that special emphasis was placed on feature orientation in Experiments 1 and 2 because of the indirect cueing (by a tone). Consequently, any cognitive action modulation was reflected only in this feature processing. Second, although we performed a pilot study to obtain approximately equal colour and orientation errors in feature search tasks, the conjunction search task performed in the experiment clearly showed that there were more orientation errors.[1] The LED method used previously made it hard to manipulate the colour contrast between target and distractor objects. Therefore, we now used a computer and LCD beamer that allows manipulation of colour contrast to a much higher extent (256 intensity steps per colour) so that colour and orientation performance could be better matched. Third, we could only use the errors made on four possible target positions on our LED board, since all other positions were not equidistant from the fixation point. In the experiment with two-dimensional objects reported here, the search display contained seven stimuli that were presented in a circle with a diameter of 20°; one of them was always the target. The target (a tilted rectangle 0.5° × 2° in size) could have one of four possible combinations of colour and orientation: green 20°, red 20°, green 70° and red 70°. Targets and distractors were isoluminant (luminance 15 cd/m²) on a grey background (40% contrast). The viewing distance was 45 cm. In a trial, a white fixation cross of 1° was presented in the centre of the screen for 500 ms, followed by the target item in

---

1   Although an approximately equal number of colour and orientation errors were found in the pilot study, the colour discrimination accuracy was higher and the orientation discrimination accuracy was lower in the conjunction search. A similar gain reduction effect has been reported by Nothdurft (2000).

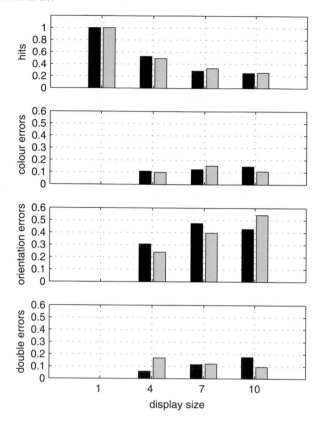

Figure 6.3 Saccadic error distributions in Experiment 2. The probabilities of occurrence of correct saccades to the target, an orientation error, a colour error or a double error are plotted as a function of display size, averaged over all participants. Black bars denote error rates in the saccade-only condition, grey bars in the pointing conditions. Saccadic orientation errors occur equally often when participants grasp the target object and saccades accompany a pointing movement, unlike in Experiment 1. The data are pooled for the four targets positioned at the same distance from the fixation point (see Figure 6.1).

the centre of the screen for 1000 ms. After the disappearance of the target, the search display was presented immediately for 1500 ms. Participants responded by making a saccade to the presumed target, while simultaneously making a pointing or grasping movement with their hand. The adapted paradigm is depicted in Plate 6.2.

As in Experiments 1 and 2, participants were instructed in one block of trials to make a *saccade-and-pointing* movement to the target object, and in another block of trials to make a *saccade-and-grasping* movement to the target object, as soon as they thought they had located the target in their peripheral field of view. Clearly, the results replicated the findings with three-dimensional stimuli. Again, participants were more likely to fixate an object with the wrong orientation when the saccade was executed in a saccade-and-point sequence than when it was executed in a saccade-and-grasp sequence. Saccades making a colour error or a double error, however, were statistically present as often in the saccade-and-grasp condition as in the saccade-and-point condition. Hence, the improvement in saccadic target selection when a grasping rather than a pointing movement followed is not a general improvement, but is specific for orientation discrimination (see also Figure 6.4). Again, no significant change in the latency of saccades was found between the two task conditions. Interestingly, although we again performed a pilot study in which we balanced colour and orientation search difficulty in feature search, clearly many more orientation than colour errors were made in the conjunction search. At the moment, we are investigating this interaction in more detail.

Neural substrate for visual selection

In 1969, Gerald Schneider postulated an anatomical separation between the visual coding of the location of a stimulus and the identification of that stimulus. The coding of the location of a stimulus was assigned to the

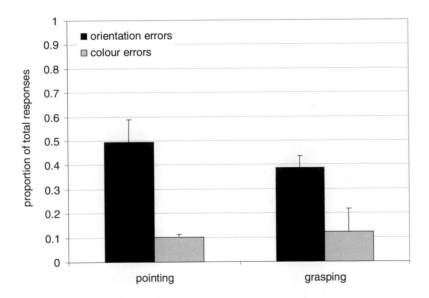

Figure 6.4 Saccadic error distributions in Experiment 3: the probabilities of occurrence of an orientation error in the saccade-and-pointing and saccade-and-grasping conditions. Saccadic orientation errors occur significantly less often when participants grasp the target object than when saccades accompany a pointing movement.

retinotectal pathway, whereas the identification of the stimulus was attributed to the geniculostriate pathway.

Another milestone in the study of visual information processing was passed in 1982 by Ungerleider and Mishkin. They proposed a distinction between processing of different kinds of visual information in the inferior temporal and superior parietal cortex, accounting for appreciation of an object's qualities ("what") and of its spatial location ("where"), respectively. Thus, the dorsal pathway mediates the location of visual objects and the ventral pathway is responsible for recognition and identification of those objects. The two visual systems have connections at several levels. Intermingled projection cells have been found in V4 and at the bottom of the anterior superior temporal sulcus (Baizer, Ungerleider, & Desimone, 1991). However, in behavioural terms the ventral and dorsal visual streams appear to have different functions (e.g. Ungerleider & Haxby, 1994). According to the "what" and "where" distinction, object-based information processing is the function of the ventral visual system, while visuospatial information is processed by the dorsal visual system. Differentiation between the visual streams is largely based on evidence derived from lesion studies that indicated that inferotemporal lesions impair the identification of visual objects, while lesions in the posterior parietal areas cause visuospatial deficits.

In 1991, Goodale, Milner, Jakobson, and Carey described the patient DF, who had damage to the lateral occipital and parasagittal occipitoparietal regions. This damage leads to visual agnosia, manifested by a severe deficit in the perception of size, shape and orientation of visual objects. However, when DF was asked to perform reaching movements and orient her hand or to pick up a block placed at different orientations in front of her, her aiming and prehension performance was correct. Thus, DF could use information about visual orientation accurately for visuomotor action, but was unable to use this kind of information for perceptual purposes.

Conversely, optic ataxia induces visuomotor deficits in reaching and grasping for objects, while recognition and matching of objects is not affected. Perenin and Vighetto (1988) have described 10 patients with optic ataxia resulting from unilateral lesions of mostly posterior parietal areas. Specifically, damage in parietal cortex can lead to deficits in positioning of the fingers and adjustment of the hand during reaching movements. Although the visual discrimination of form is unaffected, the ability to adjust the fingers to the circumferences of irregularly shaped objects is impaired (Goodale, Meenan, Bulthoff, Nicolle, Murphy, & Racicot, 1994). At the same time, verbal description of objects' orientation is not affected. Thus, optic ataxia reflects impairment in using visual inputs from the contralateral side of the lesion for preparation for appropriate action (Allport, 1987).

Unilateral lesions in the parietal cortex may cause a hemispatial neglect typically characterized by a deficit in awareness of stimuli that are presented contralateral to the lesion, while elementary sensory and motor functions are intact (Heilman, Watson, & Valenstein, 1997). As suggested by Rafal

(1997a), neglect represents a deficit in disengaging attention from the ipsilateral visual field.

Bilateral lesions in the area of the parietal–occipital junction can lead to an even more severe impairment of visual processing, the Balint syndrome, manifested as an inability to perceive more than one object at a time (or simultanagnosia) spatial disorientation, disturbance of oculomotor behaviour, poor visuomotor coordination in the form of optic ataxia, and deficits in depth perception (Rafal, 1997b). These manifestations reflect both a constriction of visual attention and impaired access to a spatial representation of the visual environment.

Based on their observations, Goodale et al. (1991) suggest the existence of two separate processing systems not for different subsets of visual information, but for different uses of this information. On their explanation, the focus is shifted from differences of visual information used by these two systems to differences in the way this information is transformed for the behavioural output. Thus, Goodale and his colleagues classify the ventral pathway as dealing with the "what" and the dorsal pathway as dealing with the "how" of visual input. The model proposed by Milner and Goodale (1995) emphasizes the behavioural goal of the observer. They distinguish between one system for conscious visual experience or perception and another system subserving visuomotor transformation or action. Although the information about visual stimuli and spatial locations used by these separate systems is the same, the way this information is transformed depends on the different functions of the two systems. In general, the specific visual analysis that enables the identification of visual objects may be distinct from the analysis underlying control of reaching and grasping movements while manipulating these objects (Milner & Goodale, 1993; though see Humphreys et al., this volume).

Neural substrate for selection-for-action

Recently, signals analogous to presumed top-down signals have been elegantly demonstrated, in as early as V2 and V4 (Luck, Chelazzi, Hillyard, & Desimone, 1997; McAdams & Maunsell, 1999, 2000). The tuning curves of visual cortex neurons (change of firing rate of neurons coding a certain feature with respect to a change in that feature) are enhanced when a feature becomes "attended" by giving it a certain behavioural relevance, such as being the target in a future detection task. This kind of extrastriatal involvement in selective attention seems to contrast with a rather rigid distinction between the "what" and "how", or "ventral" and "dorsal", accounts for motor-selective attention.

Other neurophysiological research supports the idea that processes underlying visual search are modulated by action plans. Snyder, Batista, and Andersen (1997) found that, before movement execution, the activity of most neurons in posterior parietal cortex of monkeys depends on the type of planned movement. They suggest that neurons in the lateral intraparietal area and posterior reach region are inhibited by nonpreferred motor plans. In addition, neurons in the lateral intraparietal area of the monkey's posterior parietal cortex code the intention to saccade specific locations independently of the actual appearance of a gaze shift (Bracewell, Mazzoni, Barash, & Andersen, 1996). There is reasonable support that both the lateral intraparietal area and posterior reach region contribute to the visual processing underlying motor planning (Snyder, Batista, & Andersen, 1998). Battaglia-Mayer et al. (2000) investigated single cell activity in monkey's dorsal parieto-occipital cortex during saccading without hand movement, reaching after saccading the peripheral stimulus, reaching to a peripheral stimulus while fixating a central stimulus, and delayed reaching tasks. They found enhanced neural activity when the fixation point and the position of the hand coincided, when compared with a condition in which the hand was stationary in the periphery of the visual field. The results indicated that the activity of posterior parietal neurons was related to the particular combination of signals rather than to specific visual, oculomotor or hand motor variables. Interestingly, approximately 50% of the neurons related to saccades were activated only during eye movement to the location indicating the target for subsequent hand movement, but not during classical saccades. In general, most neurons in the parieto-occipital area were influenced by reaching-related signals; very few responded exclusively to individual retinal, eye movement or hand movement signals. Rather, the responses of most neurons were influenced by all these signals or by different associations between them. Another interesting finding is that in the anterior intraparietal area of monkeys, a large population of neurons related to hand manipulation responds also to visual stimulation (Murata, Gallese, Luppino, Kaseda, & Sakata, 2000; Sakata, Taira, Murata, & Mine, 1995).

Conclusions

The results of the visual search studies reported here indicate that early visual selection might indeed be based on the information necessary for the control of current and planned behaviour. At least two cognitive theories can explain such a mechanism. In terms of the biased competition model, it is possible and probably even inevitable that the action intention plays the role of the agent that produces biasing towards particular aspects of the visual environment. A stricter version of such a selection mechanism is offered by the selection-for-action approach, which emphasizes that, primarily, the constraints in information processing are due to limits in the preparation and control of action. Consequently, integrated actions require the selection of particular aspects or attributes from the environment that are relevant to this action at hand and, at the same time, the information irrelevant to the action should be ignored. Recent neurophysiological studies in monkeys have shown action-related visual selection activity in the visual and parietal lobes. At the moment, we are initiating fMRI experiments using an adapted version of the presented paradigm. These and further behavioural experiments should shine some new light on how, in the brain, a specific action intention can select relevant visual information at the earliest possible level.

References

Allport, A. (1987). Selection for action: some behavioral and neurophysiological considerations of attention and action. In H. Heuer & A. F. Sanders (Eds.), *Perspectives on perception and action* (pp. 395–419). Hillsdale, NJ: Lawrence Erlbaum Associations Inc.

Allport, A. (1990). Visual attention. In M. I. Posner (Ed.), *Foundations of cognitive science* (pp. 631–682). Cambridge, MA: MIT Press.

Baizer, J. S., Ungerleider, L. G., & Desimone, R. (1991). Organization of visual inputs to the inferior temporal and posterior parietal cortex in macaques. *Journal of Neuroscience, 11*, 168–190.

Battaglia-Mayer, A., Ferraina, S., Mitsuda, T., Marconi, B., Genovesio, A., Onorati, P. et al. (2000). Early coding of reaching in the parietooccipital cortex. *Journal of Neurophysiology, 83*, 2374–2391.

Bekkering, H., & Neggers, S. F. W. (2002). Visual search is modulated by action intentions. *Psychological Science, 13*, 370–374.

Bracewell, R. M., Mazzoni, P., Barash, S., & Andersen, R. A. (1996). Motor intention activity in the macaque's lateral intraparietal area. II. Changes of motor plan. *Journal of Neurophysiology, 76*, 1457–1464.

Broadbent, D. E. (1958). *Perception and communication*. Oxford: Pergamon Press.

Dehaene, S. (1989). Discriminability and dimensionality effects in visual search for featural conjunctions: a functional pop-out. *Perception and Psychophysics, 46*, 72–80.

Desimone, R., & Duncan, J. (1995). Neural mechanisms of selective visual attention. *Annual Review of Neuroscience, 18*, 193–222.

Duncan, J. (1980). The locus of interference in the perception of simultaneous stimuli. *Psychological Review, 87*, 272–300.

Duncan, J. (1984). Selective attention and the organization of visual information. *Journal of Experimental Psychology: General, 113*, 501–517.

Duncan, J. (1996). Cooperating brain systems in selective perception and action. In T. Inui & J. L. McClelland (Eds.), *Attention and performance XVI. Information integration in perception and communication* (pp. 549–578). Cambridge: MIT Press.

Duncan, J., & Humphreys, G. W. (1989). Visual search and stimulus similarity. *Psychological Review, 96*, 433–458.

Folk, C. L., Remington, R. W., & Johnston, J. C. (1992). Involuntary covert orienting is contingent on attentional control settings. *Journal of Experimental Psychology: Human Perception and Performance, 18*, 1030–1044.

Goodale, M. A., Meenan, J. P., Bulthoff, H. H., Nicolle, D. A., Murphy, K. J., & Racicot, C. I. (1994). Separate neural pathways for the visual analysis of object shape in perception and prehension. *Current Biology, 4*, 604–610.

Goodale, M. A., Milner, A. D., Jakobson, L. S., & Carey, D. P. (1991). A neurological dissociation between perceiving objects and grasping them. *Nature, 349*, 154–156.

Heilman, K. M., Watson, R. T., & Valenstein, E. (1997). Neglect: clinical and anatomic aspects. In T. E. Feinberg & M. J. Farah (Eds.), *Behavioral neurology and neuropsychology* (pp. 309–319). New York: McGraw-Hill.

Humphreys, G. W., & Müller, H. J. (1993). Search via recursive rejection (SERR): a connectionist model of visual search. *Cognitive Psychology, 25*, 43–110.

Humphreys, G. W., & Riddoch, M. J. (2001). Detection by action: neuropsychological evidence for action-defined templates in search. *Nature Neuroscience, 4*, 84–88.

Jeannerod, M. (1981). Intersegmental coordination during reaching at natural visual objects. In J. Long & A. Baddeley (Eds.), *Attention and performance IX* (pp. 153–169). Hillsdale, NJ: Lawrence Erlbaum Associates Inc.

Lotze, R. H. (1852). *Medizinische Psychologie oder Physiologie der Seele*. Leipzig: Weidmenn'sche Buchhandlung.

Luck, S. J., Chelazzi, L., Hillyard, S. A., & Desimone, R. (1997). Neural mechanisms of spatial selective attention in areas V1, V2, and V4 of macaque visual cortex. *Journal of Neurophysiology, 77*, 24–42.

McAdams, C. J., & Maunsell, J. H. (1999). Effects of attention on orientation-tuning functions of single neurons in macaque cortical area V4. *Journal of Neuroscience, 19*, 431–441.

McAdams, C. J., & Maunsell, J. H. (2000). Attention to both space and feature modulates neuronal responses in macaque area V4. *Journal of Neurophysiology, 83*, 1751–1755.

Meegan, D. V., & Tipper, S. P. (1999). Visual search and target-directed action. *Journal of Experimental Psychology: Human Perception and Performance, 25*, 1347–1362.

Milner, A. D., & Goodale, M. A. (1993). Visual pathways to perception and action. In T. P. Hicks, S. Molotchnikoff, & T. Ono (Eds.), *Progress in brain research* (Vol. 95, pp. 317–337). Amsterdam: Elsevier.

Milner, A. D., & Goodale, M. A. (1995). *The visual brain in action*. Oxford: Oxford University Press.

Murata, A., Gallese, V., Luppino, G., Kaseda, M., & Sakata, H. (2000). Selectivity for the shape, size, and orientation of objects for grasping in neurons of monkey parietal area AIP. *Journal of Neurophysiology, 83*, 2580–2601.

Nothdurft, H.-C. (2000). Salience from feature contrast: additivity across dimensions. *Vision Research, 40*, 1183–1201.

Pashler, H. (1987). Detecting conjunctions of color and form: reassessing the serial search hypothesis. *Perception and Psychophysics, 41*, 191–201.

Pashler, H., Johnston, J. C., & Ruthruff, E. (2001). Attention and performance. *Annual Review of Psychology, 52*, 629–651.

Perenin, M. T., & Vighetto, A. (1988). Optic ataxia: a specific disruption in visuomotor mechanisms. I. Different aspects of the deficit in reaching for objects. *Brain, 111*, 643–674.

Rafal, R. D. (1997a). Hemispatial neglect: cognitive neuropsychological aspects. In T. E. Feinberg & M. J. Farah (Eds.), *Behavioral neurology and neuropsychology* (pp. 319–335). New York: McGraw-Hill.

Rafal, R. D. (1997b). Balint syndrome. In T. E. Feinberg & M. J. Farah (Eds.), *Behavioral neurology and neuropsychology* (pp. 337–356). New York: McGraw-Hill.

Sagi, D., & Julesz, B. (1984). Detection versus discrimination of visual orientation. *Perception, 13*, 619–628.

Sakata, H., Taira, M., Murata, A., & Mine, S. (1995). Neural mechanisms of visual guidance of hand action in the parietal cortex of the monkey. *Cerebral Cortex, 5*, 429–438.

Schneider, G. E. (1969). Two visual systems: brain mechanisms for localization and discrimination are dissociated by tectal and cortical lesions. *Science, 163*, 895–902.

Smeets, J. B., & Brenner, E. (1999). A new view on grasping. *Motor control, 3*, 237–271.

Snyder, L. H., Batista, A. P., & Andersen, R. A. (1997). Coding of intention in the posterior parietal cortex. *Nature, 386*, 167–170.

Snyder, L. H., Batista, A. P., & Andersen, R. A. (1998). Change in motor plan, without a change in the spatial locus of attention, modulates activity in posterior parietal cortex. *Journal of Neurophysiology, 79*, 2814–2819.

Tipper, S. P., Lortie, C., & Baylis, G. C. (1992). Selective reaching: evidence for action-centred attention. *Journal of Experimental Psychology, Human Perception and Performance, 18*, 891–905.

Townsend, J.T. (1971). A note on the identifiability of parallel and serial processes. *Perception and Psychophysics, 10*, 161–163.

Treisman, A. (1977). Focused attention in the perception and retrieval of multidimensional stimuli. *Perception and Psychophysics, 22*, 1–11.

Treisman, A. (1991). Search, similarity, and integration of features between and within dimensions. *Journal of Experimental Psychology: Human Perception and Performance, 17*, 652–676.

Treisman, A. (1996). The binding problem. *Current Opinion in Neurobiology, 6*, 171–178.

Treisman, A., & Gelade, G. A. (1980). A feature integration theory of attention. *Cognitive Psychology, 12*, 97–136.

Treisman, A., & Gormican, S. (1988). Feature analysis in early vision: evidence from search asymmetries. *Psychological Review, 95*, 15–48.

Treisman, A., & Sato, S. (1990). Conjunction search revisited. *Journal of Experimental Psychology: Human Perception and Performance, 16*, 459–478.

Treisman, A., & Souther, J. (1985). The search asymmetry: a diagnostic for preattentive processing of separable features. *Journal of Experimental Psychology: General, 114*, 285–310.

Ungerleider, L. G., & Haxby, J. V. (1994). "What" and "where" in the human brain. *Current Opinion in Neurobiology, 4*, 157–165.

Ungerleider, L. G., & Mishkin, M. (1982). Two cortical visual systems. In D. J. Ingle, M. A. Goodale, & R. J. W. Mansfield (Eds.), *Analysis of visual behavior* (pp. 549–586). Cambridge, MA: MIT Press.

Wolfe, J. M. (1996a). Visual search: a review. In H. Pashler (Ed.), *Attention* (pp. 13–74). London: University College London Press.

Wolfe, J. M. (1996b). Guided Search 3.0: a model of visual search catches up with Jay Enoch 40 years later. In V. Lakshminarayanan (Ed.), *Basic and clinical applications of vision science* (pp. 189–192). Dordrecht: Kluwer Academic.

Wolfe, J. M., Cave, K. R., & Franzel, S. L. (1989). Guided search: an alternative to the feature integration model for visual search. *Journal of Experimental Psychology: Human Perception and Performance, 15*, 419–433.

Yantis, S., & Jonides, J. (1990). Abrupt visual onsets and selective attention: voluntary versus automatic allocation. *Journal of Experimental Psychology: Human Perception and Performance, 16*, 121–134.

7 Attention and inaction

Mechanisms for preventing distractor responses

Nilli Lavie

Abstract

Attentional control of action involves rejection of responses towards goal-irrelevant distractors. In this chapter, I suggest that prevention of distractor responses is achieved either through reduced distractor perception or through active inhibition of responses to irrelevant distractors. I further argue that the level of perceptual load in a current task determines whether prevention of distractor responses is achieved by reducing distractor perception, or by active inhibition of responses to irrelevant distractors. Evidence for this claim is obtained in studies that show reduced distractor perception under high perceptual load, as well as in studies that suggest active response inhibition is involved in distractor rejection under low perceptual load.

Introduction

Attention is needed for control of action by goal-relevant stimuli rather than goal-irrelevant distractors. In this chapter, I make a distinction between two forms of such attentional control. The first is a rather passive form of control in which prevention of distractor responses is achieved through reduced perceptual processing of the distractor stimuli. The second is a more active process that serves to inhibit responses to irrelevant distractors that were nonetheless perceived. I argue that the level of perceptual load in a current task determines whether goal-relevant control of action is achieved by reducing perception of goal-irrelevant distractors, or by active inhibition of responses to goal-irrelevant distractors.

I start by discussing evidence for the claim that the level of perceptual load in a relevant task determines whether irrelevant distractors are perceived. The evidence discussed suggests that although perception of irrelevant distractors can be reduced when there is a high perceptual load, irrelevant distractors are clearly perceived when there is a low perceptual load. I then proceed to discuss recent evidence for the hypothesis that preventing responses to irrelevant distractors that were nonetheless perceived (in low perceptual load) involves active response inhibition.

Preventing distractor perception: the role of perceptual load

The extent to which prevention of distractor responses by attention involves some active means (e.g. inhibition of distractor responses) or may be achieved in a more passive manner (e.g. through reduced perception of distractor stimuli) has been debated for several decades between "early selection" and "late selection" views of attention. On early selection views, focusing attention on goal-relevant stimuli results in reduced perception of distractor stimuli, and the distractor stimuli that have not been perceived simply do not trigger any response. Thus, on early selection views, preventing distractor responses need not involve any active means (such as response inhibition), as distractor responses have simply never been initiated (Neisser, 1976). On late selection views, selective attention does not affect perceptual processing of distractors' attention; however, attention ensures correct response selection in these views through processes such as active suppression of the distractor responses (e.g. Tipper, 1985).

The debate between the early and late selection views on the extent to which irrelevant stimuli are perceived has stimulated much psychological research in the last few decades. This research has provided numerous demonstrations of successful exclusion of distractors from perception, thus supporting an early selection view of attention (e.g. Treisman, 1969; Yantis & Johnston, 1990). However, reports of various failures to reject distractors from perception have also accumulated (e.g. Driver & Tipper, 1989; Shiffrin & Schneider, 1977) apparently supporting the rival late selection view.

I have recently proposed that the extent to which *irrelevant* distractors can be excluded from perception depends on the load that is incurred while processing *relevant* stimuli. Situations of high load in relevant processing will exhaust perceptual capacity, leaving none of this capacity available for distractor processing, and so inevitably excluding them from perception. However, in situations of low load, any spare capacity left over from the less demanding relevant processing will "spill over" to the processing of irrelevant distractors, resulting in their perception. Thus, on this model, early selection is predicted for situations of high perceptual load, while late selection is predicted for situations of low perceptual load. Maintaining appropriate control of action in situations of low perceptual load, whereby goal-irrelevant distractors were perceived and thus compete with goal-relevant stimuli for control of action, will therefore require active inhibition of the distractor responses.

Evidence for this perceptual load model was obtained in a series of experiments that manipulated perceptual load in the relevant task and assessed the effects of load on the extent to which irrelevant distractors are perceived by using the response-competition paradigm (Eriksen & Eriksen, 1974). In a typical experiment of this series, task-relevant stimuli (targets) appear at the centre of the display while task-irrelevant stimuli (distractors) are presented at peripheral positions. The participant's task is to discriminate as quickly as possible between two alternative targets, for example the letters "X" and "N", while ignoring any distractors. The extent to which distractors are processed can be assessed through indirect effects on target reaction times. The distractors are either incompatible with the correct target response (e.g. distractor "X" with target "N"), compatible with the correct response (e.g. distractor "X" with target "X") or neutral with respect to the correct response (e.g. distractor "S" with target "X"). If target responses are significantly slower in the presence of incompatible distractors than in the presence of either compatible or neutral distractors, then this indicates that the distractors were perceived and competed with target response.

Perceptual load was manipulated either by varying the number of target stimuli (i.e. set size) or by altering the processing requirements in the relevant task (e.g. discriminating either a target feature or a conjunction of target features). In one such experiment, participants searched several letters near the centre of the display for one of two target letters, while ignoring irrelevant distractors in the periphery of the display (Lavie & Cox, 1997). Search load was manipulated by varying the similarity between the targets and non-targets in the centre. For example, participants searched for "X" or "N" targets among similar non-targets (e.g. "V", "Z" or "H") in the high-load condition, and among dissimilar non-targets (e.g. "O") in the low-load condition. In another experiment of this kind, search load was manipulated by varying the number of non-target letters. We consistently found that efficient searches (i.e. with flat search slopes) led to inefficient rejection of the peripheral distractor (i.e. response times depended on the nature of the distractor), presumably because the perceptual load was low and additional capacity remained available. By contrast, inefficient searches (i.e. with steep search slopes) led to efficient rejection of distractors (i.e. response times were independent of the distractor), as long as they involved more than four non-targets so that capacity was exhausted.

A concern in the interpretation of these studies is that high- and low-load conditions differed with respect to the physical display (i.e. in the shape or number of non-targets) and this might have led to differences in perceptual processing. However, similar results were obtained when high- and low-load conditions were created by varying processing requirements for identical displays (Lavie, 1995). Figure 7.1 illustrates the task used in this study. Participants discriminated a central target letter as quickly as possible while attempting to ignore a peripheral distractor. However, the task now involved an additional go/no-go component, which depended on the shape (circle or line) of another central stimulus adjacent to the target letter. In the low-load condition, participants responded to the target when the adjacent shape was present and withheld the response when it was absent. In the high-load condition, the decision as to whether or not to respond to the target depended on the exact size of the line or the exact position of the circle. A line of normal length or circle of normal position meant that the participant was to

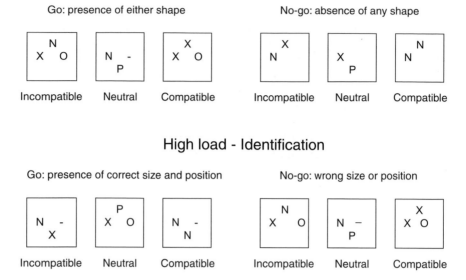

Figure 7.1 Example displays for a response competition experiment with high and low perceptual load (After Lavie, 1995). Copyright © 2001 Massachusetts Institute of Technology.

go ahead with the target response, whereas a slightly longer line or slightly displaced circle meant that the participant was to withhold a response.

The analysis of the results focused on the go trials, in which the displays for high- and low-load conditions were exactly the same (Figure 7.1). Once again the outcome was as expected from a perceptual load model: response competition from distractors was observed under low-load conditions (i.e. reaction times were longer with incompatible than with compatible or neutral distractors), but not under high-load conditions. Similar results were obtained when the go/no-go decision required the processing of either a simple feature (low load) or of a conjunction of features (high load).

Preventing distractor perception: effects of sensory limits versus capacity limits

Several experiments were carried out to dissociate the effects of perceptual load from the general effects of processing speed (Lavie & DeFockert, 2003). In this context, it is important to distinguish perceptual load, which is defined in terms of the demand on attentional capacity, from other types of task difficulty, which affect processing speed but do not place additional demands on attention. For example, a type of task difficulty that is unrelated to attentional demand concerns the quality of sensory information provided by a stimulus (i.e. signal-to-noise ratio), and can be manipulated by reducing stimulus contrast, superimposing noise or reducing presentation time.

Although degrading sensory information will increase task difficulty, it is important to realize that this will not necessarily increase the demand on attentional capacity. For example, if a target stimulus is degraded so severely that it becomes invisible, further allocation of attention will not improve its perception. This insight is behind the distinction between different kinds of processing limitations first suggested by Norman and Bobrow (1975): "data limits" in the quality of sensory information and "resource limits" in the processing of that information. They further suggested that "data limits" cannot be compensated by applying additional resources, and that "resource limits" cannot be compensated by improving sensory information. Thus, degrading sensory information should increase task difficulty and slow processing speed, but without increasing demands on attentional capacity.

As a further test of the perceptual load model, we may therefore compare the effects on distractor processing of manipulations that increase attentional demand and manipulations that degrade sensory information. To assess distractor processing under these conditions, we once again employed a variant of the response competition paradigm. Participants made a speeded choice between two central targets while ignoring an irrelevant distractor in the periphery, which was either compatible or incompatible with the correct response (i.e. the general design and display was similar to Figure 7.1). Attentional demand was manipulated by increasing the number of relevant targets near the centre of the display (see Lavie & Cox, 1997). That is, targets were presented either alone (low load) or accompanied by five non-targets (high load). Sensory information was degraded by reducing target size, by decreasing target contrast and presentation time, or by increasing the target's retinal eccentricity.

Representative results from one experiment of this series are presented in Figure 7.2. As shown in this figure, reaction times and error rates were increased similarly by high attentional load and by target degradation. However, response competition effects, which served to index distractor processing, were quite different. Response competition was weak under conditions of high load, but remained comparably high under both conditions of low load (i.e. with either an intact or degraded target) despite their substantial difference in task difficulty. The same pattern of results was obtained consistently in all experiments of the series. It is perhaps worth noting that the tendency for somewhat stronger response competition under low load/ degraded target (compared with low load/intact target) may be due to an increased frequency of distractor intrusions when the task is more difficult and target processing is slow. The important point is that under high load/ intact target, target processing was also more difficult and slower than in the low-load condition, yet distractor intrusions were significantly reduced in that condition.

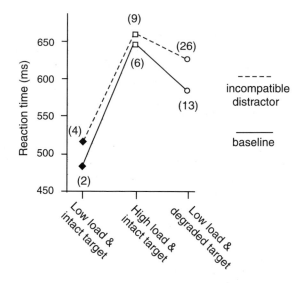

Figure 7.2 The effects on response competition of increasing attentional load versus degrading sensory information (After Lavie & DeFockert, 2003). Copyright © 2001 Massachusetts Institute of Technology.

Thus, these experiments provided support for my claim that distractors can only be excluded from perception under conditions of high attentional load that exhaust perceptual capacity limits in relevant processing. This conclusion has some interesting implications for neural activity in response to distractors, which are discussed in the next section.

Preventing distractor perception: effects of perceptual load on neural responses to distractors

Our perceptual load hypothesis raises some interesting predictions for the brain activity that should be produced by distractors. The theory predicts that the neural response of sensory systems to *irrelevant* distractors should depend on the perceptual load involved in a *relevant* task. Specifically, we claim that brain activity for entirely irrelevant distractors should be found despite participants' attempts to ignore them, provided the relevant task load is low. Activity to irrelevant distractors should only be reduced by higher load in the relevant task.

Moreover, we reasoned that if attentional load is the crucial factor in determining distractor processing, then processing of distractors should strongly depend on relevant processing load even when the relevant and irrelevant stimuli are processed in entirely different brain areas. We recently tested these predictions using fMRI to assess the neural responses to moving distractors (Rees, Frith, & Lavie, 1997). The task we used to test these predictions is illustrated in Figure 7.3. A stream of words was presented at fixation

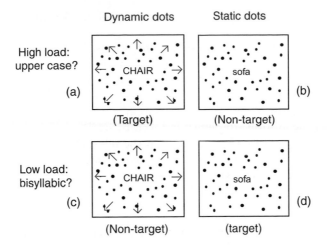

Figure 7.3 Example displays from the low-load (a, b) and high-load (c, d) conditions
with moving (a, c) or static (b, d) dot distractors from the functional
imaging study of Rees et al. (1997). The stimuli were the same for low- and
high-load conditions; only the task performed on the central stream
of words was different. Comparing the fMRI response for moving
versus static dot distractors allowed a measure of processing for irrelevant
background motion. Copyright © 2001 Massachusetts Institute of
Technology.

at a rate of one word per second, and was surrounded by a full field of dots
in the periphery. These dots were either static (Figure 7.3b, d) or moving
(Figure 7.3a, c) to induce a flow field; the participants were requested to focus
on the words and ignore the dots under all task conditions. In the low-load
condition, participants discriminated between lower- and upper-case letters
in the word stream, and in the high-load condition they discriminated
between bisyllabic versus mono- or trisyllabic words for the same stream.
Note that the stimuli themselves did not differ between high- and low-load
conditions.

Our main concern was regarding the extent of brain activity produced by
moving-dot distractors as a function of the relevant task load. The results
confirmed our predictions exactly: motion-related activity in cortical area
V5/MT varied as a function of load in the word task. Activity in V5/MT for
moving (versus static) dots was apparent in conditions of low load, and was
only eliminated in conditions of high relevant load. This interaction between
load and the neural responses to background motion was also found in
additional areas, such as the V1/V2 border and in the superior colliculus,
both of which respond to moving stimuli (Shipp & Zeki, 1985; Ungerleider,
Desimone, Galkin, & Mishkin, 1984). In sum, we found that a whole network of sensorimotor areas that are likely to be involved in motion perception were active in the presence of irrelevant moving distractors provided
that the relevant task involved only low load, but that this distractor-induced

activity was then significantly reduced as the load in relevant processing was increased.

In a further psychophysical experiment, we used the same task and displays as those used in our scanning experiment, while assessing irrelevant motion perception via the duration of the motion after-effect it induced (see Chaudhuri, 1990). The motion after-effect is known to be related to motion perception and also to involve activity in area MT/V5. We found that the duration of the motion after-effect induced by irrelevant moving distractors was significantly reduced by high load in the relevant word task. Thus, this behavioural experiment provided converging evidence in accord with our brain imaging experiment, to show that load in a word task can decrease perception of irrelevant moving distractors.

Active inhibition of distractor responses: evidence from negative priming

The studies discussed so far provide substantial evidence for our claim that distractor perception is prevented when the relevant task involves high perceptual load. However, all these studies have also clearly demonstrated that distractors were perceived in cases of low perceptual load. With low perceptual load, distractor letters produced significant response competition effects on targets responses, suggesting that these letters were identified and their response association was recognized; moving distractors (compared with static ones) produced a significant increase of activity in motion selective cortices (e.g. V5). Control of responses by goal-relevant stimuli in conditions of low perceptual load therefore requires some active means for suppressing the responses to the goal-irrelevant distractors that were nonetheless perceived.

Thus, we hypothesized that evidence for distractor inhibition should be found in conditions of low but not high perceptual load. To test this hypothesis, I ran a collaborative study with Elaine Fox in which we assessed negative priming (Tipper, 1985) effects from irrelevant distractors in conditions of low and high perceptual load (Lavie & Fox, 2000). Negative priming effects are typically found when the target stimulus on a "probe" trial was presented as the distractor stimulus on a previous "prime" trial (ignored repetition condition). Reaction times are slower to such targets (compared with an unrepeated target stimulus, control condition). This effect of slowing suggests that responses to the prime distractors were inhibited, so that a subsequent response to the same stimulus requires recovery from inhibition and is therefore delayed. We predicted that negative priming effects from prime distractors will depend on the level of load in the relevant task in the prime. Negative priming was expected from distractors in conditions of low perceptual load (thus indicating active inhibition of distractor responses); however, negative priming effects should be reduced or eliminated in conditions of high perceptual load, as this was expected to reduce distractor perception, thus obviating the need for active suppression of distractor responses.

Figure 7.4 shows the procedure used in these experiments. Participants were presented with pairs of prime and probe displays, and were asked to search for a target letter ("x", "n" or "s") in one of six positions in the centre of the display and indicate which target letter was present by a speeded keypress. An irrelevant peripheral distractor was also presented and the participants were asked to ignore it. This distractor was always incongruent with the prime target. The extent to which the irrelevant distractor was actively inhibited was assessed by comparing responses under ignored repetition and

(a) Low prime load

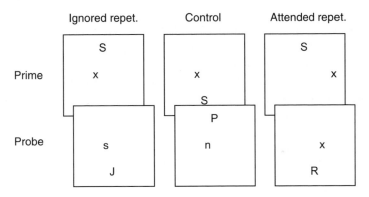

(b) High prime load

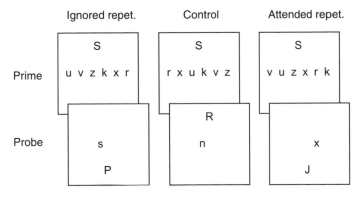

Figure 7.4 Example displays from the low-load (a) and high-load (b) conditions in Experiment 1 of Lavie and Fox (2000). A prime display and the immediately following probe display are shown for each condition. The attended repetition condition, in which prime target and probe target are the same letter, is less relevant in this context. Copyright © 2001 Massachusetts Institute of Technology.

under control conditions as a function of perceptual load in the processing of prime targets. Perceptual load was manipulated by increasing the number of non-target letters in the prime from one to six. The results were exactly as predicted by the perceptual load model. In several experiments, we always found negative priming (i.e. evidence for active inhibition) under low-load conditions, but this was consistently eliminated under high-load conditions (Lavie & Fox, 2000).

Several experiments allowed us to rule out alternative accounts for this load effect on negative priming. For example, the effect of load in our first experiment might be attributed to the greater similarity between prime and probe displays in the low-load versus the high-load conditions (as they both involved the same number of items, with a relevant set size of 1; see Figure 7.1). However, this was reversed in Experiment 2 in which prime and probe similarity was greater in the high-load than in the low-load prime conditions, as all the probes in Experiment 2 involved a relevant set size of 6. The same result was found in both experiments, namely less negative priming for conditions with a high perceptual load in the prime display. The two experiments taken together thus rule out any account for the results in terms of retrieval of episodic memory for the distractor, which can depend on the similarity between the prime and probe displays (see Fox & DeFockert, 1998; Neill, 1997).

In addition, these experiments demonstrated that negative priming crucially depends on the level of perceptual load in the relevant processing for the *prime* displays, rather than on some general task difficulty, as the same effect of this prime load on negative priming was obtained regardless of the level of load in the probes. Finally, negative priming did not depend on overall reaction times (and the associated variability in responses) in our experiments, as it was obtained in all the conditions of low prime-load even when the overall probe reaction times were just as slow as those in our high prime-loads (as was the case for our second experiment, which had a high load in its probes). We conclude that under high-load conditions, irrelevant distractors do not interfere because they are simply not perceived. However, under low perceptual load, distractors are perceived and goal-relevant control of responses involves inhibition of the distractor responses.

Active inhibition of distractor responses in low perceptual load: new line of evidence

Despite the extensive use of the negative priming method to assess processes of distractor inhibition, alternative accounts for negative priming that implicate processes other than inhibition have also been raised. The most prominent alternative account suggests that negative priming effects may depend on the extent to which the distractor identity and its role (as irrelevant in the prime trial) are retrieved during the probe processing (for recent discussions of this issue, see Fox, 1995; May, Kane, & Hasher, 1995; Neill & Valdes,

1996; Tipper & Milliken, 1996). On this account, the slowing of probe reaction times may not indicate that responses to the prime distractors were inhibited, but instead may be due to a conflict between the role of the probe target and the prime distractor that arises due to retrieval of the prime trial during encoding of the probe target of the same identity as the prime distractor.

Together with Guy Mizon, I sought a new method to examine the claim that prevention of responses to irrelevant distractors that were nonetheless perceived (in cases of low perceptual load) involves active inhibition (Mizon & Lavie, 2004). Although inhibition of distractor responses has only been assessed with negative priming to date, there are other measures available to assess general processes of response inhibition (i.e. which are not tied in specifically to distractor responses). For example, the stop-signal paradigm is conventionally used to assess inhibition of speeded responses to targets. In this paradigm, participants are instructed to make a speeded response to a target stimulus unless a "stop" signal is presented (e.g. a tone), in which case they have to stop their target response. Successful stopping of the target responses is thought to depend on active inhibition, as there are various indications that target responses have been prepared and then actively suppressed on stopped trials (e.g. De Jong, Coles, & Logan, 1995; Jennings, Van der Molen, Brock, & Somsen, 1992; McGarry & Franks, 1997).

We reasoned that we could determine whether distractor rejection involves active response inhibition by preceding a selective attention task (i.e. with irrelevant distractors that need not be responded to) with a general response inhibition task (such as the stop-signal task) on each trial. The availability of active inhibition for the selective attention task could then be manipulated by varying the demand for inhibition in the response inhibition task.

If rejection of responses to irrelevant distractors in the selective attention task involves active inhibition, then reducing the availability of inhibition for the selective attention task (through engaging inhibition in another task) should result in a reduced ability to inhibit distractor responses. Thus, we predicted greater distractor effects on responses in the selective attention task with greater engagement of inhibition in the preceding task. To assess distractor effects on responses in the selective attention task, we used the response competition paradigm described previously. In different experiments we used different paradigms to engage inhibition in the first task on each trial.

Active inhibition of distractor responses: effects of performance in a stop-signal task

In our first series of experiments, we used the stop-signal paradigm for the first task (Task 1) on each trial (Figure 7.5). In the stop-signal task, participants were required to perform a simple reaction time task, pressing the

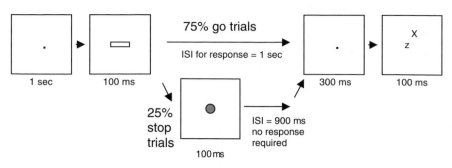

Figure 7.5 Stimulus sequence and presentation times for Experiment 1 in Mizon and
Lavie (2004). Note, to obtain a high probability of successful inhibition in
"stop" trials, a single, short stop-signal delay was used. ISI = inter-stimulus
interval.

same specified key upon appearance of a shape (a white rectangle). On 25%
of trials, however, the simple reaction time target was followed by a stop
signal (a red circle) instructing participants to withhold their response.

On each trial, the stop-signal task was followed by a selective attention task
similar to the response competition tasks described earlier. Response competition effects from the irrelevant distractor were examined as a function of
the type of trial in the stop-signal task. Our main interest was whether distractor effects in the selective attention task differed following successful
stop trials and following go trials. We predicted that if distractor rejection
involves active inhibition, then distractor rejection would be less efficient
following successful performance on stop trials than following go trials in
Task 1, as successful stopping of responses should engage inhibition, thus
reducing the capacity for inhibition of distractor responses in the immediately following selective attention task. The results supported these predictions. Response competition effects from the irrelevant distractors in the
selective attention task were greater following successful stop trials (mean
compatibility effect 81 ms) than following go trials (mean compatibility
effects 49 ms), as we predicted.

This finding was also replicated in another experiment in which the ratio
of stop to go trials was reversed (i.e. go trials were presented on 25% of the
trials; stop trials were presented on 75% of the trials). Distractor effects
in the selective attention task were again greater following successfully
stopped responses than following go responses. These findings allow us to
rule out accounts in terms of probability of each trial type. Clearly, distractor effects are not simply greater on less frequent trials; they are also
greater following stopped trials even when these are presented on the
majority of trials.

The possibility that distractor effects in the selective attention task are
always greater following no response than following a response in Task 1,

regardless of whether inhibition was involved, was ruled out in another experiment. In this experiment, we compared performance in the selective attention task between blocks in which Task 1 always required a response (i.e. stop signals were never presented) and blocks in which a stimulus for Task 1 was presented but a response to it was never required (in other words, Task 1 involved just passive viewing). As a response was never required in Task 1 of the no-response blocks, making no response in those blocks should not have involved any response inhibition. Moreover, to further discourage any response tendencies in the no-response blocks (as these would need to be suppressed to make no responses), the stimulus for Task 1 (a rectangle; see Figure 7.5) had a different colour in the response blocks (white) and the no-response blocks (red). Distractor effects in the selective attention task of this experiment showed no difference between the response blocks (mean compatibility effects 39 ms) and the no-response blocks (mean compatibility effects 36 ms). Taken together with the results of the stop-signal experiments, these results suggest that distractor effects in the selective attention task are only greater when the selective attention task follows an inhibited response.

The results of these experiments provide initial support for the hypothesis that efficient distractor rejection in a selective attention task requires active inhibition, as it depends on the extent to which a previous task engaged inhibition or left the capacity to inhibit responses available for the following selective attention task.

Active inhibition of distractor responses: effects of performance in a spatial stimulus–response mapping task

Convergent evidence for this hypothesis was provided in another series of experiments that used a different inhibition task for Task 1. Figure 7.6

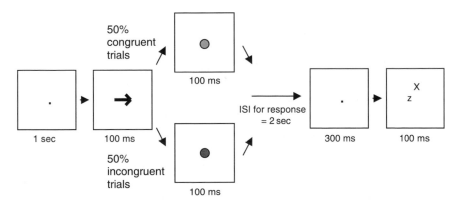

Figure 7.6 Stimulus sequence and presentation times for Experiment 4 in Mizon and Lavie (2004). ISI = inter-stimulus interval.

prescents the trial sequence in these experiments. For Task 1 in these experiments, we used a spatial mapping task. Participants were required to press a left or a right key according to the direction of a left- or a right-pointing arrow. The arrow was followed by a signal (a circle that could either be red or green) dictating whether the arrow response should be spatially congruent or incongruent with the direction pointed by the arrow. A green signal (presented on 50% of the trials) indicated a spatially congruent response (e.g. left key for a left-pointing arrow). A red signal (presented on the other trials) indicated a spatially incongruent response (e.g. right key for a left-pointing arrow). We reasoned that the incongruent mapping condition should involve inhibition of the spatially congruent response, and thus reduce the availability of inhibition for rejecting distractor responses in the following selective attention task. The results supported this prediction: distractor effects in the selective attention task were greater following incongruent (mean compatibility effect 85 ms) than congruent responses (mean compatibility effect 35 ms) in the spatial mapping task.

Other experiments in this series examined the time course of the effects of spatial mapping congruency on distractor rejection in the selective attention task. These experiments found that the effects lasted over a 6 second interval between the response to Task 1 and the onset of the selective attention task. Interestingly, similar durations have been estimated for response inhibition within the negative priming paradigm.

It important to note that, as in this series of experiments both the inhibition and the non-inhibition trials involved execution of a response, these experiments further clarify that the effects of inhibition on distractor rejection do not depend on whether the selective attention task follows an executed response or not (as in the stop-signal paradigm). What matters is whether response inhibition was involved (as when an incongruent response is made in the spatial congruency paradigm).

Active inhibition of distractor responses: effects of performance in a Stroop colour–word task

In another series of experiments, we sought convergent evidence for the role of inhibition in distractor rejection by examining whether the results can generalize across a different inhibition task. In these experiments, we used a manual Stroop colour–word task for Task 1. Participants were asked to indicate the colour of a word by a keypress (e.g. press one key for blue, another for red) while ignoring the word's identity. The word's identity could either be congruent with its colour (e.g. the word "blue" presented in a blue colour) or incongruent with its colour (e.g. the word "blue" presented in a red colour). Making a correct response to the colour of the word in the incongruent condition is typically thought to involve suppression of the

Table 7.1 Mean flanker task reaction times (RT) and error rates across participants (n = 12) as a function of flanker compatibility and colour–word (C–W) congruency

| | Flanker compatibility | | | | Effect size | |
| | Incongruent | | Congruent | | I – C | |
C–W congruency	RT (ms)	Errors (%)	RT (ms)	Errors (%)	RT (ms)	Errors (%)
Incongruent	782	9	670	5	112	4
Congruent	726	11	660	6	66	5

reading response to the incongruent word.[1] In such conditions, the dominant word reading response needs to be suppressed to make the less dominant response to the colour. We thus predicted that distractor effects in the selective attention task should be greater following incongruent colour words than congruent colour words. The results supported these predictions (see Table 7.1).

As can be seen in Table 7.1, there were also general slowing effects of Stroop congruency. Not only were colour-naming responses in the Stroop task slower in the incongruent than congruent condition, the overall reaction times in the selective attention task (pooled across conditions of distractor compatibility) were slower following incongruent than congruent trials. However, the greater distractor effects in the selective attention task following incongruent versus congruent trials are unlikely to be attributed to scaling due to slower reaction times in the incongruent trials, as the difference in distractor effects remained significant when the effect was calculated as the proportion of the overall reaction time for each individual in each condition. The distractor interference effect was 18% of the mean overall reaction time after incongruent trials and 11% of the mean overall reaction time after congruent trials, with this difference in proportional interference effects being significant.

To further ensure that general difficulty of performance in Task 1 cannot

---

1   We used a manual key press response instead of a verbal reading response in the Stroop task to avoid a switch in response modality between our first (Stroop) and second (flanker) task. Although congruency effects from words on responses to colours are typically stronger in vocal tasks than in manual tasks (e.g. Henik, Ro, Merrill, Rafal, & Safadi, 1999; Logan & Zbrodoff, 1998), congruency effects from words on responses to colour have also been established in previous manual Stroop studies (e.g. Besner, Stolz, & Boutilier, 1997; Pritchatt, 1968; Sugg & McDonald, 1994). Moreover, to confirm that responses to the word were dominant over responses to the colour in our manual task, we ran another condition of our manual Stroop task, in which participants responded to the word while ignoring the colour. Congruency effects in this condition were significantly smaller than in the word reading conditions, thus demonstrating the dominance of word responses in our manual Stroop task.

account for the greater distractor effect in the following selective attention task, we ran a control experiment in which the selective attention task was preceded by a colour discrimination task in which the visual difficulty was varied. Participants were either required to discriminate colour brightness for dark and light colours (easy discrimination condition) or for light and slightly lighter colours (hard discrimination condition). Although visual discrimination difficulty slowed reaction times both in Task 1 and in the selective attention task, it had no effects on distractor processing in the selective attention task. Thus, general difficulty cannot provide an alternative account for the effects of Stroop colour–word congruency on distractor processing in an immediately following selective attention task.

Perceptual load and active inhibition

In a final series of experiments, we tested the claim that evidence for active inhibition of distractor responses in the selective attention task should only be found in conditions of low perceptual load, not in of high perceptual load. Conditions of high perceptual load should allow for earlier exclusion of distractors from perception, and responses to distractors that were not perceived do not require inhibition—they are simply not initiated.

For Task 1 in this series of experiments, we used either the spatial mapping task or the Stroop colour–word task. The critical difference from the previous experiment was in manipulating perceptual load in the selective attention task. The relevant search set size in the selective attention task was either 1 (low perceptual load) or 6 (high perceptual load). Our main prediction was that distractor effects in the selective attention task would depend on the extent to which Task 1 engages inhibition in low perceptual load but not in high perceptual load (where they should be diminished overall).

As can be seen in Table 7.2, not only were distractor effects significantly

Table 7.2 Mean flanker task reaction times (RT) and error rates across participants (n = 14) as a function of distractor compatibility and trial type

	Distractor compatibility				Effect size	
	Incongruent		Congruent		I – C	
Trial type	RT (ms)	Errors (%)	RT (ms)	Errors (%)	RT (ms)	Errors (%)
Low load						
IM	799	7	716	2	83	5
CM	769	5	722	4	47	1
High load						
IM	891	13	892	9	−1	4
CM	896	11	883	10	13	1

Note: I = incompatible; C = compatible; IM = incongruent mapping; CM = congruent mapping.

reduced by high perceptual load, there was also a three-way interaction between distractor conditions, inhibition condition and load. Whereas in conditions of low perceptual load distractor effects were greater following inhibition trials (incongruent spatial mapping conditions) than non-inhibition trials in Task 1 (congruent spatial mapping), Task 1's inhibition conditions had no effect on distractor processing in conditions of high perceptual load.

The same pattern of findings was found when Stroop colour word congruency was used to manipulate the demand on inhibition in Task 1. These findings provide support for our hypothesis that rejection of irrelevant distractors involves active inhibition of distractor responses in conditions of low perceptual load but not conditions of high perceptual load, where distractors are simply not perceived.

Conclusion

I have discussed evidence for two means of attention control of action by goal-relevant stimuli rather than goal-irrelevant distractors. The results of several experiments converged to show that high perceptual load allows for reduced perception of irrelevant distractors, as indexed by reduced distractor effects of response competition, negative priming, motion aftereffects and distractor-related neural activity in sensory cortices. On the other hand, in conditions of low perceptual load, irrelevant distractors were clearly perceived and produced significant distractor effects on all these measures (e.g. significant effects of response competition, etc.). In the second part of this chapter, I provided evidence that control of behaviour by goal-relevant stimuli in such situations involves active inhibition of responses to the irrelevant distractors.

Acknowledgements

This research was supported by Medical Research Council (UK) grant G9805400.

References

Besner, D., Stolz, J. A., & Boutilier, C. (1997). The Stroop effect and the myth of automaticity. *Psychonomic Bulletin and Review, 4*, 221–225.

Chaudhuri, A. (1990). Modulation of the motion aftereffect by selective attention. *Nature, 344*, 60–62.

De Jong, R., Coles, M. G. H., & Logan, G. D. (1995). Strategies and mechanisms in nonselective and selective inhibitory motor control. *Journal of Experimental Psychology: Human Perception and Performance, 21*, 498–511.

Driver, J., & Tipper, S. P. (1989). On the nonselectivity of "selective" seeing: contrasts between interference and priming in selective attention. *Journal of Experimental Psychology: Human Perception and Performance, 15*, 304–314.

Eriksen, B. A., & Eriksen, C. W. (1974). Effects of noise letters upon the identifica-tion of a target letter in a non search task. *Perception and Psychophysics, 16*, 143–149.

Fox, E. (1995). Negative priming from ignored distractors in visual selection: a review. *Psychonomic Bulletin and Review, 2*, 145–173.

Fox, E., & DeFockert, J. W. (1998). Negative priming depends on prime–probe simi-larity: evidence for episodic retrieval. *Psychonomic Bulletin and Review, 5*, 107–113.

Henik, A., Ro, T., Merrill, D., Rafal, R., & Safadi, Z. (1999). Interactions between color and word processing in a flanker task. *Journal of Experimental Psychology: Human Perception and Performance, 25*, 198–209

Jennings, J. R., Van der Molen, M. W., Brock, K., & Somsen, R. J. (1992). On the synchrony of stopping motor responses and delaying heart beats. *Journal of Experimental Psychology: Human Perception and Performance, 18*, 422–436.

Lavie, N. (1995). Perceptual load as a necessary condition for selective attention. *Journal of Experimental Psychology: Human Perception and Performance, 21*, 451–468.

Lavie, N., & Cox, S. (1997). On the efficiency of attentional selection: efficient visual search results in inefficient rejection of distraction. *Psychological Science, 8*, 395–398.

Lavie, N., & DeFockert J. W. (2003). Contrasting effects of sensory limits and capacity limits in visual selective attention. *Perception and Psychophysics, 65*, 202–212.

Lavie, N., & Fox, E. (2000). The role of perceptual load in negative priming. *Journal of Experimental Psychology: Human Perception and Performance, 26*, 1038–1052.

Logan, G. D., & Zbrodoff, N. J. (1998). Stroop-type interference: congruity effects in color naming with typewritten responses. *Journal of Experimental Psychology: Human Perception and Performance, 24*, 978–992.

May, C. P., Kane, M. J., & Hasher, L. (1995). Determinants of negative priming. *Psychological Bulletin, 118*, 35–54.

McGarry, T., & Franks, I. M. (1997). A horse race between independent processes: evidence for a phantom point of no return in the preparation of a speeded motor response. *Journal of Experimental Psychology: Human Perception and Performance, 23*, 1533–1542.

Mizon, G., & Lavie, N. (2004). *Active inhibition of irrelevant distractors: evidence from a new paradigm*. Manuscript in preparation.

Neill, W. T. (1997). Episodic retrieval in negative priming and repetition priming. *Journal of Experimental Psychology: Learning, Memory and Cognition, 23*, 1291–1305.

Neill, W. T., & Valdes, L. A. (1996). Facilitatory and inhibitory aspects of attention. In A. F. Kramer, M. G. H. Coles, & G. D. Logan (Eds.), *Converging operations in the study of visual selective attention.* (pp. 77–106). Washington, DC: American Psychological Association.

Neisser, U. (1976). *Cognition and reality: Principles and implications of cognitive psychology.* San Francisco: Freeman & Company.

Norman, D. A., & Bobrow, D. G. (1975). On data-limited and resource-limited processes. *Cognitive Psychology, 7*, 44–64.

Pritchatt, D. (1968). An investigation into some of the underlying associative verbal processes of the Stroop colour effect. *Quarterly Journal of Experimental Psychology, 20*, 351–359.

Rees, G., Frith, C., & Lavie, N. (1997). Modulating irrelevant motion perception by varying attentional load in an unrelated task. *Science, 278*, 1616–1619.

Shiffrin, R. M., & Schneider, W. (1977). Controlled and automatic human informa-tion processing. II. Perceptual learning, automatic attending and a general learning theory. *Psychological Review, 84*, 127–190.

Shipp, S., & Zeki, S. (1985). Segregation of pathways leading from area V2 to areas V4 and V5 of macaque monkey visual cortex. *Nature, 315,* 322–325.

Sugg, M. J., & McDonald, J. E. (1994). Time course of inhibition in color-response and word-response versions of the Stroop task. *Journal of Experimental Psychology: Human Perception and Performance, 20,* 647–675.

Tipper, S. P. (1985). The negative priming effect: inhibitory priming by ignored objects. *Quarterly Journal of Experimental Psychology, 37A,* 571–590.

Tipper, S. P., & Milliken, B. (1996). Distinguishing between inhibition-based and episodic retrieval-based accounts of negative priming. In A. F. Kramer, M. G. H. Coles, & G. D. Logan (Eds.), *Converging operations in the study of visual selective attention* (pp. 77–106). Washington, DC: American Psychological Association.

Treisman, A. M. (1969). Strategies and models of selective attention. *Psychological Review, 76,* 282–299.

Ungerleider, L. G., Desimone, R., Galkin, T. W., & Mishkin, M. (1984). Subcortical projections of area MT in the macaque. *Journal of Comparative Neurology, 223,* 368–386.

Yantis, S., & Johnston, J. C. (1990). On the locus of visual selection: evidence from focused attention tasks. *Journal of Experimental Psychology: Human Perception and Performance, 16,* 135–149.

8 Object- and location-based inhibition in goal-directed action

Inhibition of return reveals behavioural and anatomical dissociations and interactions with memory processes

Sarah Grison, Klaus Kessler, Matthew A. Paul, Heather Jordan and Steven P. Tipper

Abstract

One way to increase understanding of the mechanisms that guide action towards relevant information is to examine processing of irrelevant information. In particular, our research suggests that goal-directed behaviour is aided by inhibition of irrelevant location- and object-based representations. Evidence from the inhibition of return (IOR) paradigm indicates that the nature of a task and the goals of action result in differing representational loci of inhibition, which elicit different behavioural effects and are mediated by distinct neural systems. Interestingly, our new research indicates that inhibition of object-based representations in particular can mediate response over longer periods. Support is provided here for IOR over six previously cued objects and delays of nearly 4 s, which suggests that action is aided by online maintenance of object inhibition in working memory. Importantly, we also provide the first evidence of long-term IOR effects over nearly 100 displays and 20 min, which indicate that inhibition of objects, but not object-less spatial locations, leaves a retrievable trace in episodic memory that affects behaviour over time. In summary, while inhibition of irrelevant objects and locations both aid correct transient response, goal-directed action over time may be mediated by retrieval of prior inhibitory processes.

Introduction

Goal-directed behaviour in our complex visual world depends on the detection and identification of relevant information while avoiding response to irrelevant items. For example, before we can write a note with a favourite pen, we must find the mislaid pen in an untidy office among all the other less-favoured pens. To achieve this goal of finding the target object, attention is applied to various candidate objects. However, a serious flaw in such a system would become evident without some mechanism to encourage examination of new items and prevent the return of attention to items already examined, because people would be continually trapped searching between the most recently attended items. Such perseveration would result in never finding the object of interest, and a failure of achieving one's behavioural goals. At worst, such a mechanism could clearly have fatal consequences as, for example, when humans and animals are foraging for food.

Posner and Cohen (1984) originally proposed a mechanism to prevent such perseveration in behaviour, where inhibitory processes are applied to internal representations of spatial locations just attended to force attention of novel information. They demonstrated this inhibition in a simple and elegant way. Participants were presented with boxes to the left and right of fixation within which cues and targets could be presented. A few hundred milliseconds before target onset, a box was cued with a bright flash. This cue was irrelevant to the task of target detection and did not predict subsequent target location. However, Posner and Cohen suggested that the sudden onset cue would capture attention, and when attention was re-oriented back to the centre of the display, it would be inhibited from returning to that recently attended location. Indeed, they found that response times to detect the target at the cued location were slowed, as attention was impaired in re-orienting to the inhibited location. This result has now been observed many times (for reviews, see Klein, 2000; Lupiáñez, Tudela, & Rueda, 1999) and has been termed "inhibition of return" (IOR).

It was originally proposed that IOR reveals suppression of a spatial location in the environment (e.g. Maylor, 1985). However, Tipper, Driver, and Weaver (1991a) argued that this is not the only mechanism guiding correct goal-directed behaviour, because the human visuomotor systems evolved to allow *behavioural interaction* with *objects* that occupy a certain spatial location. For example, if inhibition were only applied to locations, this would mean that humans could not efficiently search for moving objects because, as the object of interest moved into an uninhibited location, attention could waste time returning to previously examined objects in the scene. Instead, attention is applied to internal representations associated with candidate objects, or object files, in the environment when searching for a target, not to spatial locations devoid of objects. Accordingly, Tipper et al. (1991a) examined whether IOR could be associated with a moving object. After cueing in the usual manner (e.g. Posner & Cohen, 1984), both the cued and uncued objects moved to two new locations and a target was presented in one of the objects. Detection was significantly slower when the target was presented in the previously cued object, even though it occupied an uncued location, demonstrating for the first time the existence of object-based IOR without location-based IOR. This finding suggested that performance was achieved through suppression of objects without inhibition of locations.

Subsequent work (Tipper, Jordan, & Weaver, 1999; Tipper, Weaver, Jerreat, & Burak, 1994; Weaver, Lupiáñez, & Watson, 1998) went on to show that inhibition in IOR could be associated with either a location or an object (see Figure 8.1). After cueing one peripheral box (a), all the boxes moved 120° (b). This experiment replicated Tipper and colleagues' (1991a) finding of purely object-based inhibition, as reaction times were slower to detect the target in the cued box at an uncued location (c) compared with the control condition, in which the target was presented in an uncued object and location (e). However, it also allowed a test for inhibition remaining in the spatial location that was cued. Indeed, reaction times were slower to detect a target in one of the uncued objects that had moved to the location of the previous peripheral cue (d) compared with the control condition (e). This outcome indicated that inhibition could either remain in a cued spatial location or move with a cued object to facilitate examination of new information.

An important point worth stressing here is that this research not only replicated the existence of object-based IOR, it also provided one of the first demonstrations of a *purely spatial* IOR effect, which may be accounted for by inhibition of a location without inhibition of an object. That is, in virtually all other research arguing for location-based IOR, including the original work of Posner and Cohen (1984), there is a confound with object-based effects because the cue and target both appear in a static object at a specific peripheral location that is present throughout the trial. The IOR effects observed in such experiments are very robust and quite large (e.g. −40 ms), perhaps because they reveal the effects of inhibition of both object- and location-based representations. In the experiment described in Figure 8.1, where this confound is removed, location-based effects are often much smaller (−15 to −20 ms) than the traditional IOR effects. Furthermore, the effect of these separate location- and object-based effects (−15 and −25 ms, respectively) produces an overall object- plus location-based IOR effect of

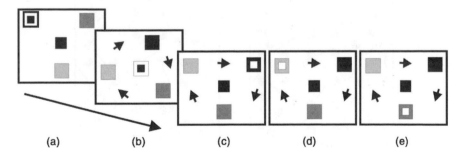

(a)   (b)   (c)   (d)   (e)

Figure 8.1 Dissociating inhibition of object- and location-based representations (adapted from Tipper et al., 1999). (a) Black box cued. (b) Boxes moved 120° clockwise and attention re-oriented with a central cue. (c) IOR examined for a target in the cued object. (d) IOR investigated for a target in the cued location. (e) Target shown in an uncued object and location.

approximately −40 ms (see Müller & von Mühlenen, 1996). These findings suggest that inhibition of object- and location-based representations can operate together or independently to guide response, depending on the nature of the task and the behavioural goals.

Jordan and Tipper (1998, 1999) examined directly whether the relatively large IOR effects observed when static boxes were cued was due to the combined effects of inhibition of location- and object-based information. This study simply compared IOR when an object was present versus absent at the cued location, while attempting to hold constant the physical features present in the two conditions. Figure 8.2a shows how Kanisza square figures were used to examine object-based IOR effects by having a cue and target appear in the horizontal apparent squares. It also shows how they could be used to examine location-based IOR by having cues and targets appear in the vertical object-less locations where the "pac-man" figures were re-oriented, so the contours were no longer aligned and objects were not apparent. Of course, IOR effects were also examined for the alternative layouts, shown in Figure 8.2b, where object-based IOR was examined when the Kanisza squares were in the vertical alignment and location-based IOR was examined when object-less locations were shown horizontally. The results showed that IOR was larger when apparent objects were cued (−42 ms) than when empty locations were cued (−18 ms). The former result revealed the effect of inhibition of both object- and location-based representations is similar in magnitude to that reported previously. In addition, the latter outcome revealed the much smaller effect of suppression of locations without object information, which is similar in magnitude to the location-based effect of the three-box experiment shown in Figure 8.1. These outcomes support the idea that inhibition of objects and locations can independently affect behaviour in IOR tasks. Furthermore, recent research suggests that the nature of the task and the salience of the objects will determine the relative engagement of these processes.

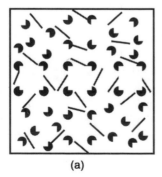 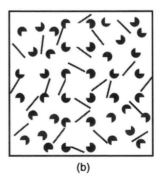

(a)   (b)

Figure 8.2 Kanisza figures used to reveal inhibition of object- or location-based representations (adapted from Jordan & Tipper, 1998). (a) IOR investigated in three apparent horizontal boxes and three vertical locations. (b) IOR explored in three apparent vertical boxes and three horizontal locations.

For example, McAuliffe, Pratt, and O'Donnell (2001, experiment 1) replicated the work of Jordan and Tipper (1998) by finding greater IOR when cueing one of four static object placeholders versus empty locations, but not when cueing one of two placeholders (McAuliffe et al., 2001, experiments 2 and 3). Although the authors suggested inhibition was not independently applied to object- and location-based representations, new research by Leek, Reppa, and Tipper (2003; see also Reppa & Leek, 2003) indicates that their results were primarily due to the fact that their two-object task reduced the salience of objects in the displays. Indeed, Leek et al. (2003) found evidence that when objects were salient (i.e. complex, varying in orientation and presented in a variety of spatial loci), an additive object- and location-based IOR effect was reliably obtained, indicating that inhibition was independently applied to these representations.

The importance of inhibition of object-based representations in mediating performance has also been revealed in several studies of visual search. For example, Wolfe and Pokorny (1990; see also Klein & Taylor, 1994) demonstrated that during search where attention was oriented to objects in a scene and then these objects were removed, performance to detect subsequent targets was not impaired. The lack of slowed processing was thought to reflect that inhibition did not prevent the return of attention to objects. However, it is possible that inhibition may become associated with irrelevant objects during search, but removal of objects when they were the goal of action also removed the inhibition and hence failed to reveal IOR effects. Subsequent studies have confirmed that when objects remain in view, IOR is demonstrated for previously attended objects (e.g. Klein & MacInnes, 1999; Müller & von Mühlenen, 2000; Takeda & Yagi, 2000).

In summary, the above studies have described how inhibitory processes can be independently applied to location- and/or object-based representations to mediate goal-directed action in IOR tasks. Although the existence of object-based IOR was originally questioned by Müller and von Mühlenen (1996), many researchers have now confirmed its presence in a range of experimental procedures (e.g. Abrams & Dobkin, 1994; Becker & Egeth, 2000; Gibson & Egeth, 1994; Jordan & Tipper, 1998, 1999; Leek et al., 2003; McCrae & Abrams, 2001; Müller & von Mühlenen, 2000; Ogawa, Takeda, & Yagi, 2002; Oonk & Abrams, 1998; Reppa & Leek, 2003; Ro & Rafal, 1999; Takeda & Yagi, 2000; Weaver et al., 1998; but see List & Robertson, 2001; Schendel, Robertson, & Treisman, 2001). In this chapter, we describe how engagement of location- and object-based inhibitory mechanisms reveals different behavioural effects that may be mediated by different neural structures. Accordingly, we suggest that inhibition of object-based representations may promote a unique view of how attention mediates goal-directed action over time. To that end, we provide evidence that inhibition of objects, especially object identity, allows suppression to be maintained online in working memory to impact behaviour over time. Additionally, we provide the first support for the idea that inhibition of objects can also be stored and retrieved with an episode in memory to affect action over the long term.

Behavioural properties of location- and object-based inhibition in IOR

There is now a large body of evidence showing that the behavioural properties of inhibition underlying location-based cueing effects are different from those that mediate object-based effects. For example, Tipper and Weaver (1998) reported that in the moving three-box task described above (Figure 8.1), location-based IOR persisted for at least 3 s, whereas object-based IOR was no longer observed after 3 s. They argued that dynamic, constantly changing objects should not be inhibited for long periods, as they may change their status relative to the viewer, such as when a predator suddenly approaches or a car veers into your path and suddenly requires a response. Maintaining object-based inhibition for longer durations in *dynamically changing* circumstances such as these could surely have grave behavioural consequences.

Second, Weaver et al. (1998) noted that the inhibitory processes underlying location-based IOR effects could be associated with an empty, featureless location. In contrast, Tipper et al. (1994) showed that object-based IOR only occurred when inhibition could be associated with a visible object at the time of cueing. If a different object that was relevant to the target detection task occluded it, no inhibition was associated with the occluded object.

Third, research suggests that younger and older adults inhibit these two representations differently. In particular, while both groups exhibit location-based IOR effects, only younger adults demonstrate object-based IOR, as older adults show facilitation of object-based representations (McCrae & Abrams, 2001). Interestingly, other research has indicated that older adults show greater object-based IOR effects in comparison with younger adults (McDowd, Filion, Tipper, & Weaver, 1995; Tipper et al., 1997b). Although these results are contradictory, in general they suggest that the process of inhibiting locations may remain invariant over age, while the ability to inhibit object-based representations changes as a person ages.

Finally, Abrams and Dobkin (1994) have shown that inhibition of locations in an IOR task could be observed when a target was to be detected, as well as when an eye movement, signalled via a central arrow, was made to the cued location. In contrast, inhibitory mechanisms mediating object-based IOR are only observed in the perceptual measure of target detection or discrimination, not in eye-movement measurements.[1] This latter observation

---

1   In tasks requiring detection of targets with a keypress, retinal location was not inhibited, as IOR survived an eye movement between cue and target onset. Such an eye movement ensured that the cue and target appeared at different locations on the retina. However, in tasks requiring saccades to loci determined by central arrows, IOR appears to occur in a retinotopic/oculocentric frame of reference (Abrams & Pratt, 2000).

will be relevant in a later section arguing that location-based effects could be mediated by the eye-movement controlling systems of the mid-brain superior colliculus, whereas object-based IOR may be mediated by the cortex (Tipper et al., 1997b).

Further dissociations in inhibition of object- and location-based information are found in two types of object representations (e.g. Costello & Warrington, 1987; Cubelli, Nichelli, Bonito, de Tanti, & Inzaghi, 1991; Humphreys & Riddoch, 1994, 1995; Riddoch, Humphreys, Lockhurst, Burroughs, & Bateman, 1995; Tipper & Behrmann, 1996): *within-object*, where the features of an object are represented with their specific locations in the entire object (e.g. Biederman, 1987; Marr, 1982), and *between-objects*, where the spatial relationship between separate objects is independent because they are not bound by any common object representation (e.g. Baylis & Driver, 1993; Kahneman, Treisman, & Gibbs, 1992). Specifically, Kessler and colleagues (Kessler, Pfennig, & Rickheit, 2001) have found that for within-object reference frames there is less accurate representation of spatial location of features within working memory than for between-objects reference frames, where there is more accurate representation of the environmental location of parts (see also Kessler & Rickheit, 1999, 2000). Interestingly, this contrast was also revealed in the inhibitory mechanisms underlying IOR when Tipper et al. (1999; see also Tipper & Behrmann, 1996) connected objects together in various ways (see Figure 8.3) to explore inhibition of locations in these representations. Three objects were connected to form a rotating triangle (a) or spokes (b), so that when the displays rotated they contained locations that were fixed and invariant relative to the other loci in the object. Accordingly, inhibition of within-object representations was investigated in these displays. By contrast, when the three objects were not connected by any lines (c), the spatial locations of the objects in relation to each other were arbitrary. Thus, inhibition of a between-objects frame of reference was examined in this display. Previous work was replicated by revealing object-based IOR in the two within-object displays, showing that inhibition moved with a cued box. Also replicated were findings that object-based IOR rotated with boxes when they were disconnected in a

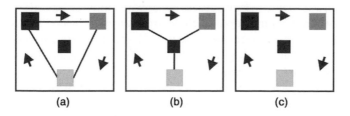

(a)   (b)   (c)

Figure 8.3 Examining object- and location-based inhibition in different reference frames (adapted from Tipper et al., 1999). (a, b) IOR examined for two different within-object conditions. (c) IOR investigated for a between-objects condition.

between-objects frame of reference. However, the most intriguing result was that inhibition of location-based representations was quite different in the within- and between-objects displays. In the between-objects display, location-based IOR was obtained as observed repeatedly in previous studies. In the two within-object displays, there was *no location-based IOR*; indeed, a small facilitation effect was found. It was suggested that across the two types of representations, the *locations* of objects varied in behavioural importance and hence engagement of inhibition. For example, when searching between separate objects, the locations of these objects are important, so that when looking in a kitchen for a knife, the places previously searched must be inhibited. In contrast, when moving attention within an object, for example attending to a knife blade to see if it is clean, the location of the blade in the environment is of little relevance to this task, thus it will not be associated with inhibition (see also Becker & Egeth, 2000).

Further experiments also demonstrated that inhibition of location information is not invariant, as location-based IOR effects are not always observed. In particular, previous studies of the inhibitory mechanisms underlying IOR used stimuli such as coloured pixels on a computer screen, and action requirements such as pressing a key, that were spatially dissociated from the stimuli on the monitor. However, our visuomotor systems have evolved to enable us to fluently directly interact with solid three-dimensional objects, by reaching-to-grasp items of interest (e.g. Tipper, Howard, & Jackson, 1997a; Tipper, Lortie, & Baylis, 1992). Therefore, Howard and Tipper (2001; see also Howard, Lupiáñez, & Tipper, 1999) examined the ecological validity of the inhibitory mechanisms underlying IOR in tasks in which participants responded by directly reaching to real objects. That is, after cueing by flashing a red key, on some trials the keys moved to a new location and participants were required to reach to and depress a target key. Interestingly, reaching responses to a previously cued key were slower even when it had moved to a new location. This IOR effect confirmed inhibition of object representations in a more naturalistic visuomotor task. However, somewhat surprisingly, reaching to a key in a previously cued location did not reveal any slowing. That is, there was no evidence for location-based IOR and therefore no suggestion that locations were inhibited in this task. Again, it would appear that in certain situations, as when moving attention within an object or when reaching to solid three-dimensional objects, the prior location occupied by the object is of little behavioural importance, such that it is not inhibited. That location- and object-based IOR can be dissociated has also been revealed by Schendel et al. (2001). In their study, however, the opposite pattern was observed, as location-based but not object-based IOR was obtained when objects became increasingly salient to participants.

It is also important to note that in some circumstances both object- and location-based IOR effects can be completely disrupted. Tipper and Weaver (1998) have argued previously that change in the environment signalling an important event, such as the sudden approach of a predator, would veto all prior inhibition, and set the system to a generally alert and responsive state. Indeed, they noted that sudden acceleration in the three moving box task disrupted all IOR effects. Similarly, unpublished studies of selective reaching showed that when an object moved, then stopped and returned to its starting position, no IOR was observed (see also Christ, McCrae, & Abrams, 2002). Accordingly, sudden stops, changes in motion direction, or sharp changes in direction such as a 90° turn, might signal important changes in the environment that require attention and response, not suppression.

In summary, the above studies have described how inhibition can be applied to object- and/or location-based representations, and that these can be dissociated to reveal different behavioural outcomes in IOR tasks. Additionally, it is clear that the demands of the task and the behavioural goals influence the relative engagement of inhibition to suppress these two types of representations. Specifically, certain different boundary conditions elicit object-based effects while location-based effects are absent, and other boundary conditions eliminate all IOR effects. Identifying what manipulations disrupt performance in IOR tasks helps to clarify the relationship between inhibitory mechanisms and different internal representations as well as how inhibition of locations and objects may be neurally implemented to guide action. Indeed, in the next section, evidence is provided that suggests inhibition of object- and location-based representations mediate behaviour in different ways because they are subserved by different neural structures.

Neural properties of location- and object-based inhibition in IOR

Posner and colleagues (Posner, Rafal, Choate, & Vaughan, 1985) have argued that the mechanisms underlying location-based IOR are mediated by processing in the retinotectal visual pathway, especially in the superior colliculus (SC). There are now several pieces of evidence that support this assumption. First, there are asymmetric pathways projecting to the SC from the retina, where greater inputs arise from the temporal hemifield than the nasal hemifield, that are not observed in retinal projections to the cortex (Lewis, Maurer, & Milewski, 1979; Posner & Cohen, 1980). In line with the asymmetrical projections to the SC, if stimuli are shown monocularly, IOR is larger when cues are presented to the temporal versus the nasal hemifield (Rafal, Calabresi, Brennan, & Sciolto, 1989; Rafal, Henik, & Smith, 1991; Sapir, Soroker, Berger, & Henik, 1999; Simion, Valenza, Umiltà, & Dalla Barba, 1995). Similarly, the endogenous allocation of attention reduces IOR in the nasal hemifield, but not in the temporal hemifield (Berger & Henik, 2000).

Second, Sapir et al. (1999) examined the role of the SC in the inhibitory mechanisms underlying IOR. One patient with unilateral right SC damage showed impaired IOR effects when stimuli were presented to hemifields processed by the damaged right SC, namely the temporal hemifield of the left eye and the nasal hemifield of the right eye. By contrast, IOR was normal when stimuli were presented to the hemifields processed by the intact left SC, specifically the temporal hemifield of the right eye and the nasal hemifield of the left eye. Accordingly, they concluded that the SC was responsible for generating inhibitory processes in IOR. More recently, Sapir, Rafal, and Henik (2002) further explored the role of the SC in IOR by investigating whether damage to a region further along the tectopulvinar pathway, such as to the pulvinar, would result in a failure to observe these effects. However, in three patients with unilateral pulvinar damage, they found IOR in both the contralesional and ipsilesional visual fields, thus confirming the role of the SC in IOR.

Third, patients with progressive supranuclear palsy have degeneration of the dorsal mid-brain, including the SC and the peritectal region, which results in deficient vertically oriented saccades (Rafal, Posner, Friedman, Inhoff, & Bernstein, 1988). Indeed, Posner et al. (1985) found that these patients did not reveal IOR effects in the vertical axis, while there was normal IOR in the horizontal axis.

Fourth, inhibitory effects in IOR are observed even when visual processing cannot be mediated by the geniculostriate processing system, but instead is subserved by the retinotectal visual pathways through the SC. For example, visual processing in the newborn human infant is mediated almost exclusively by subcortical structures such as the SC, and IOR has been observed in measures of eye movements in newborn infants when there were no hypometric saccades (e.g. Simion et al., 1995; Valenza, Simion, & Umiltà, 1994; but see Clohessy, Posner, Rothbart, & Vecera, 1991). Patients who are hemianopic due to damage to area V1 are also believed to process information in their blind, hemianopic field via subcortical systems such as the SC. Indeed, research has shown that presenting a cue and subsequent target in the blind field of a hemianopic patient activates saccades and elicits IOR effects (Danziger, Fendrich, & Rafal, 1997; see also Rafal, Smith, Krantz, Cohen, & Brennan, 1990). Therefore, evidence from both newborn infants and hemianopic patients suggests that the inhibitory mechanisms underlying IOR are processed through the retinotectal pathways, possibly through the SC.

Fifth, the gap effect, which is mediated by the SC (Dorris & Munoz, 1995; Munoz & Wurtz, 1993a, 1993b; Sparks & Mays, 1983), interacts with IOR effects. The gap effect occurs when a central fixation stimulus is offset at the same time as, or just before, the onset of a saccade, producing much faster saccades than when the fixation point remains visible. This effect is thought to be triggered by the offset of the fixated stimulus, which reduces the activity of cells in the rostral pole of the SC that are active during fixation and help keep the eyes from moving. When these fixation cells become less active, they disinhibit movement cells in the SC that help the eyes move to a new position. In this way, reaction time is speeded to move the eyes to a new peripheral target. Because the gap effect interacts with IOR, leading to a reduction in IOR effects when the two tasks are combined, this also implies that inhibition in IOR is mediated by processing in the SC (Abrams & Dobkin, 1995).

Finally, the close relationship between oculomotor processes and IOR also supports the idea that the SC mediates these effects (Abrams & Pratt, 2000; Kingstone & Pratt, 1999; Rafal et al., 1989; Taylor & Klein, 1998). For example, it is known that the SC is influenced by simple stimuli, such as sudden onsets and stimuli presented to fixation. Sudden-onset stimuli automatically evoke saccades that must be suppressed if ongoing goal-directed activity is to be maintained. These saccades can be encoded in retinotopic coordinates (e.g. Abrams & Jonides, 1988; Goldberg & Wurtz, 1972), as well as in environmental frames of reference (Van Opstal, Hepp, Suzuki, & Henn, 1995) in the SC. In addition, recall that location-based IOR, but not object-based IOR, is seen in measurements of eye movements (Abrams & Dobkin, 1994) that are mediated by the control systems of the SC. While this last piece of evidence suggests the importance of the SC in mediating inhibition of location-based representations underlying IOR, it also suggests this region is not solely responsible for generating all IOR effects.

Because the SC receives a variety of inputs from structures, including cortical areas such as the parietal lobe and frontal eye fields (FEF), this suggests that a network of brain structures probably mediate inhibition in IOR (Rafal, 1998). In particular, there is positive evidence that the underlying mechanisms are associated with processing in cortical regions. For example, Dorris, Taylor, Klein, and Munoz (1999) have proposed that IOR influences the latency of voluntary eye movements based on visuospatial and saccadic activity within the same cortical oculomotor structure. Indeed, there are several cortical regions that process both types of information (e.g. FEF: Bruce, 1990; supplementary eye fields: Schlag & Schlag-Rey, 1987; posterior parietal cortex: Andersen, 1989). Furthermore, recent single-cell recordings of neurons in the superficial and intermediate layers of the SC in rhesus monkeys suggested that while the SC plays a role in IOR, the inhibitory effects are actually due to inputs from neural regions upstream from the SC, possibly the posterior parietal cortex (Dorris, Klein, Everling, & Munoz, 2001). Indeed, a variety of new research also indicated that IOR effects may be associated with processing in cortical regions. For example, patients with left neglect (Bartolomeo, Chokron, & Siéroff, 1999) and with unilateral or bilateral inferior parietal damage (Vivas, Humphreys, & Fuentes, 2003) all fail to show IOR for stimuli presented in the ipsilesional visual field, which suggests that the inhibitory mechanisms are at least modulated by processing in the posterior parietal cortex (but see Posner et al., 1985). Furthermore, functional magnetic resonance imaging (fMRI) research has shown increased activation in cortical areas such as the FEF, dorsal premotor area and superior parietal cortex during trials where IOR was obtained (Rosen et al., 1999), while others have found supplementary and FEF activation (Lepsien & Pollman, 2002). New research using transcranial magnetic stimulation also suggests that the FEF could be the generator of inhibitory processes in IOR as stimulation over the right FEF after a cue and before a target impaired IOR effects for stimuli in the ipsilateral visual field (Ro, Farnè, & Chang, 2003). Finally, event-related brain potentials revealed reduced P1 and P2 components during trials in which IOR was observed (McDonald, Ward, & Kiehl, 1999), and P1 in particular is thought to be generated by extrastriate visual areas (Clark & Hillyard, 1996; Eimer, 1997; Mangun, Hillyard, & Luck, 1993).

Tipper et al. (1994) have further argued that object-based IOR is critically dependent on cortical processing and there are several lines of evidence to support this proposal. For example, they found that IOR is seen in object-based coordinates, but the SC cannot process this information, as it is primarily responsible for oculomotor coding of information for visuospatial orienting. Instead, object recognition computations are likely to be performed in cortical areas (e.g. lateroposterior occipital cortex: Kanwisher, Woods, Iacoboni, & Mazziotta, 1997; Malach et al., 1995; pre-motor and parietal cortex: Jeannerod, Arbib, Rizzolatti, & Sakata, 1995; inferotemporal cortex: Logothetis & Pauls, 1995; V4: Connor, Preddie, Gallant, & Van Essen, 1997; the supplementary eye fields: Olson & Gettner, 1995). Similarly, analysis of the Kanisza figures used to demonstrate object-based IOR (Jordan & Tipper, 1998, 1999) is known to take place in cortical areas of visual processing (see Lesher, 1995, for a review). Finally, regarding the moving objects used in previous studies (Tipper et al., 1991a, 1994, 1999), although neurons in the SC respond to moving stimuli, they are not efficient at encoding speed and direction of object motion, but depend on cortical systems such as the medial temporal lobes for analysis of moving stimuli (Gross, 1991; Schiller & Stryker, 1972; Wurtz & Goldberg, 1972). Indeed, it is primarily cortical lesions that destroy the ability to encode the motion of a moving object and to direct action towards it (e.g., Ingle, 1977; Ingle, Cheal, & Dizio, 1979).

Neuropsychological support for the idea that object-based IOR is mediated by processing in cortical regions comes from Tipper et al. (1997b). In two split-brain patients with a complete lesion of the corpus callosum, each cortical hemisphere was isolated from the other, in that there were no direct links between homologous regions of cortex. The authors predicted that if inhibition was associated with an object, and this inhibition was subserved by cortical structures requiring direct corpus callosum connections, it would continue to be associated with the object as long as it remained in the same visual field, and hence in the same cerebral hemisphere. On the other hand, if the cued object moved into the other visual field, and processing switched to the contralateral hemisphere, then object-based inhibition should not be able to cross the lesioned corpus callosum and no IOR should be observed. This result is precisely what was observed in two split-brain patients. By contrast, control participants demonstrated IOR regardless of whether the object remained within or moved between the visual fields.

A final piece of evidence to support the role of the cortex in inhibiting object-based representations in IOR is based on differences in the processing capacities of each cortical hemisphere (see Robertson & Ivry, 2000) that are not revealed by mid-brain structures such as the SC. For example, many studies have shown that IOR is larger after cueing objects presented to the left visual field versus the right visual field (e.g. Berlucchi, Aglioti, & Tassinari, 1997; Fenske, Kessler, Raymond, & Tipper, 2003; Handy, Jha, Kingstone, & Mangun, 1995; Kessler & Tipper, in press; McDonald et al., 1999; Nelson, Early, & Haller, 1993; White, Marks, & Wilkinson, 2001). Indeed, unpublished studies suggest that when the confound of objects appearing in a fixed location was removed, object-based IOR was significantly larger in the left than in the right visual field, while location-based IOR was equivalent in the two visual fields (Jordan & Tipper, 2001). These outcomes suggested that inhibition of object-based representations may be specialized to the right hemisphere, but that both hemispheres contribute equally to inhibitory processing of location-based representations. Indeed, additional evidence for hemisphere differences in IOR effects is reported later in this chapter.

In summary, the SC is critical in mediating IOR as thus far only lesions of this structure have been shown unequivocally to disrupt the effect (e.g. Posner et al., 1985; Sapir et al., 1999). This is especially true when the task requires processing of locations and an oculomotor response. However, when the task necessitates processing of objects and a manual response, inhibition within cortical regions may be responsible for IOR, although additional converging evidence must be sought in future studies of patients with specific, focal cortical lesions.

Relationship between object-based inhibitory processes and working memory

In the preceding sections, we have provided support for the idea that our visuomotor responses to the environment are primarily directed towards objects, so our attentional selection mechanisms have evolved to interact with object-based representations. Importantly, we suggest that inhibition of an object, rather than just with a location in space, can have a radical impact on theories of visuomotor processes.

A central assumption concerning inhibitory mechanisms of attention in IOR tasks is that they control ongoing behaviour in real-time to enable action towards a target by preventing attention from returning to information just examined. Accordingly, many researchers have argued that there is "no memory" in visual search (Horowitz & Wolfe, 1998) or that it is very limited (Pratt & Abrams, 1995). For example, Wolfe and Pokorny (1990; see also Klein & Taylor, 1994) investigated serial search through displays containing a number of objects, but failed to find any impairment for detection of a probe target at a location previously occupied by an object (but see

Klein, 1988). Similarly, when using more traditional cueing procedures, Pratt and Abrams (1995) demonstrated that IOR was only associated with the last place attended, thus suggesting that the underlying inhibitory mechanism served only a limited role in visual search over time.

By contrast, we suggest that while the spatial location of dynamically moving objects can change over time, revealing inhibition of locations, but not objects, for a few seconds (e.g. Tipper & Weaver, 1998), inhibition of *stable object representations* might be a foundation for successful action over long periods of time. Within such a framework, inhibitory processes mediating IOR may last between 3 and 5 s (e.g. Tassinari, Aglioti, Chelazzi, Marzi, & Berlucchi, 1987; Tassinari, Biscaldi, Marzi, & Berlucchi, 1989; Tipper & Weaver, 1998; for a review, see Lupiáñez et al., 1999) and be associated with a number of objects (e.g. Danziger, Kingstone, & Snyder, 1998; Snyder & Kingstone, 2000, 2001; Tipper, Weaver, & Watson, 1996). In this way, inhibitory mechanisms could enable successful action towards relevant information in the environment while avoiding repeatedly returning attention to previously examined items.

Accordingly, our recent interests have focused on investigating whether inhibition of objects can influence behaviour over time by being maintained online in working memory (e.g. Baddeley & Hitch, 1974). It is suggested that when IOR tasks are put into the realm of working memory by presenting intervening displays or increasing delays between the cue and target, inhibition should be engaged most robustly for object-based representations.

IOR reveals inhibition of objects maintained in working memory

Across several experiments, Paul and Tipper (2003) explored whether IOR effects could be associated with more than one object and/or location in working memory, which is assumed to maintain a limited amount of information (approximately four items; see Cowan, 2001, for a review) necessary for ongoing behaviour. The authors proposed that inhibition of eye movements to a spatial location are overwritten by intermediate trials and, therefore, is relatively transient. Thus, IOR effects based on inhibition of a location should decay quickly, after two or three intervening cues. By contrast, if inhibition can be associated with a stable object representation, this may allow suppression to be maintained online in working memory for longer and over the processing of many intervening trials.

Across three experiments there were eight spatial locations or objects in a display (see Figure 8.4): no objects (a), identical objects (i.e. grey squares) (b) or salient objects (i.e. different coloured shapes) (c). The procedures for all studies were the same (see Figure 8.5). Six consecutive cues were flashed in a location or object, then a target was presented in one of the previously cued items or in an uncued item. This resulted in six conditions, 1- through 6-back, where examination of the more temporally distant 2- through 6-back conditions should reveal inhibition over time. If inhibition can be associated

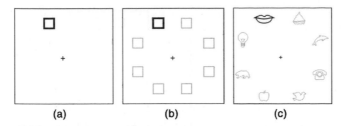

Figure 8.4 Exploring inhibition of locations and objects in working memory (adapted from Paul & Tipper, 2003). (a) IOR examined in no objects experiment. (b, c) IOR investigated in identical objects and salient objects experiments. A single cue is shown at the top left of each panel. Participants saw the stimuli in (c) in colour.

with objects, effects should be greater when identical and salient objects are cued versus when no objects are cued. Furthermore, if distinctiveness of cued objects maintains inhibition in working memory, IOR should be greatest when cueing salient objects.

The results for the 2- through 6-back conditions in all three experiments are shown in Figure 8.6. In the no objects experiment, there was a small overall IOR effect for the 2- through 6-back conditions (−3 ms), and IOR was significant for the locations cued 2-back (−9 ms) and 3-back (−7 ms). When identical objects were cued, IOR was found over the five conditions (−10 ms), which was significant for objects cued 2-, 3- and 4-back (−14, −17 and −7 ms, respectively). These results suggest that inhibition of non-distinct objects can be maintained in working memory for longer than objectless locations. Interestingly, when cueing salient objects, even though the identity of the object was not relevant to the task, an overall IOR effect was found for the five conditions (−13 ms), which was significantly different from that in the no objects experiment (−3 ms). Indeed, presenting coloured objects appeared to increase the stability of IOR in working memory, which was significant for the 2-, 3-, 4- and 6-back conditions (−17, −15, −17 and −9 ms, respectively). So, when examining the maintenance of IOR at the most distant point in time, for the sixth previously cued item (i.e. 3600 ms), the predictions concerning the role of inhibition of objects in working memory were supported. That is, IOR was most robust (−9 ms) when distinctive coloured-shapes were cued, less robust (−5 ms) when identical grey squares were cued, and non-existent (+3 ms of facilitation) when attention was drawn to empty loci.

In contrast to other views, these results indicated that inhibition could be maintained online in working memory to aid correct behaviour over time. Specifically, finding IOR over three successively cued objectless locations (i.e. 1800 ms) suggested that inhibition of locations could be maintained for a short time in working memory (see also Castel, Pratt, & Craik, 2002). However, that IOR was found for four cued objects (i.e. 2400 ms) suggested that inhibited object information could be maintained online for longer

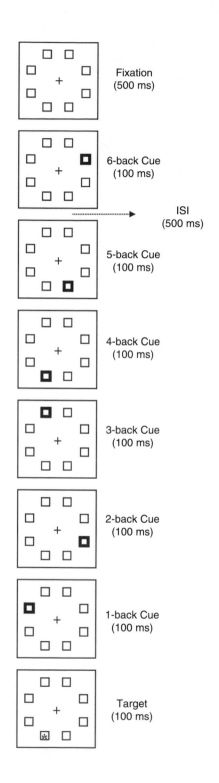

Figure 8.5 Procedure used to explore IOR in the identical objects experiment (adapted from Paul & Tipper, 2003). A cued trial is shown where the target appears in the 4-back cue condition. These procedures were also used for the no objects and salient objects experiments. ISI = inter-stimulus interval.

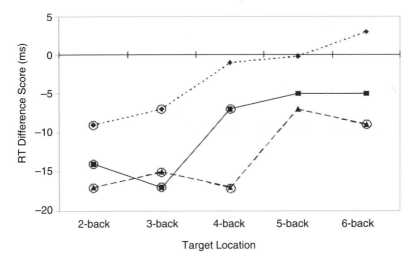

Figure 8.6 Effects for no objects (♦), identical objects (■) and salient objects (▲) cued 2- through 6-items back. Negative scores reveal IOR (circled data points indicate *p* < .05).

durations and over greater intervening delays. Importantly, finding IOR for up to six successively cued salient objects (i.e. 3600 ms) indicated that IOR effects were longer lasting and more stable for objects, especially depending on the distinctiveness of the inhibited object. That is, inhibition of salient objects seemed to be maintained online more robustly over time and across cueing of intervening items to aid correct behaviour.

IOR *reveals inhibition of object identity maintained in working memory*

Even if one accepts the existence of object-based IOR effects, it is generally assumed that inhibition suppresses low-level representations of objects encoded in parallel across a display such as candidate objects or object files (e.g. Driver, Davis, Russell, Turatto, & Freeman, 2001), not higher-level representations such as object identity. Accordingly, in another series of experiments, we investigated the possibility that inhibition can be associated with *object identity* by exploring whether IOR effects are more robust in a working memory task when identity can be computed versus when it cannot (Grison, Paul, Kessler, & Tipper, in press).

Naturalistic, colour, face stimuli were presented in these new working memory studies because humans are very efficient at processing faces (e.g. Bruce & Humphreys, 1994; Kanwisher, 1998) and they tend to be stored automatically in memory (Shah et al., 2001). Each face was only seen twice, once during initial encoding in the cue display and again in the target display. These faces were either shown in an upright position, such that the participants could easily recognize the faces, or in an inverted position, which should make recognition difficult (e.g. Kanwisher, Tong, & Nakayama, 1998; Yin, 1969). Specifically, in one experiment, two faces were presented upright (45° from vertical) in the cue and target displays (see Plate 8.1a), which allowed the faces to be easily recognized during initial encoding of the faces in the cue display and re-processing (i.e. retrieval) of the faces in the target display nearly 4 s later. In three other studies, however, the faces were shown inverted (90° from vertical) in the cue display and/or the target display, making them difficult to recognize during encoding only, retrieval only or during both encoding and retrieval (see Plate 8.1b, c and d, respectively). Importantly, note in Plate 8.1 that for all four experiments the change in physical orientation was controlled, as target positions were re-oriented 90° from the cue positions.

In all of the experiments, the procedures were the same (see Plate 8.2). In the cue display, a red signal appeared over one of the two faces and participants had to withhold response. In the target display, a green signal appeared over one of the two faces 3800 ms after cueing and participants made a localization response. The critical IOR condition occurred when the same face that became red during the cue display also became green during the target display. The sudden onset of the exogenous cue over a face should initiate orienting to that stimulus, but because the red cue signalled that the participant should withhold response, inhibition should be applied to representations associated with the cued face. Accordingly, if a green target appeared on the same face nearly 4000 ms later, participants' localization responses should be slower due to residual inhibition preventing attention from returning to that stimulus.[2] If the inhibitory mechanisms underlying IOR can be associated with object identities, even when no overt identification of faces is required, then IOR effects will differ across the four studies. Specifically, inhibition associated with a face will robustly affect performance when identity can be computed, such as when faces are easily recognized in the upright–upright experiment, due to the additive effects of inhibition of object identity, low-level object-based representations and location-based information (Jordan & Tipper, 1998). By contrast, when identity cannot be

---

2 Note that this procedure, and those used in experiments reported later in the chapter, is a simple variation on the classic IOR paradigm. Specifically, in both traditional IOR tasks and in those reported here, IOR is measured based on a response to one target signal following one cue signal, to which response should have been withheld. Furthermore, in both traditional and the current IOR tasks, only one imperative signal was present during a cue and target display, which is thought to engage attentional orienting mechanisms. Finally, in all IOR tasks there is, by necessity, a mismatch between the nature of the cue and target signal, which allows the participant to differentiate whether a signal does or does not require a response. Accordingly, the main difference between our experiments and previous IOR studies is that it is the *colour* of a signal that differentiates the cue and target (see also Lupiáñez & Solano, 1997).

processed, such as when a face is hard to recognize in the three inverted studies, inhibition of identity representations cannot contribute to performance and less IOR will be observed due to inhibition of only low-level object- and location-based information.

Figure 8.7 shows IOR in the upright–upright (–41 ms) (a), inverted–upright (–23 ms) (b), upright–inverted (–22 ms) (c) and inverted–inverted experiments (–15 ms) (d). Clearly, IOR was larger when faces were easy to recognize in both cue and target displays as opposed to when they were hard to recognize. Because low-level object and spatial location information remained constant across the studies, the results cannot be explained by inhibition of these representations. Instead, the only difference was the ability to compute object identity information, suggesting that inhibition of identity can be robustly maintained online in working memory to aid correct behaviour.

Importantly, these effects depended primarily on whether the objects could be easily recognized during encoding, during retrieval or during both processes. In the three inverted experiments, because the faces could not be easily recognized while encoding the stimuli in the cue display and/or retrieving the stimuli in the target display, inhibition could only be applied to low-level object- and location-based information, resulting in smaller IOR over the delay of nearly 4 s. Specifically, finding smaller IOR effects in the inverted–upright than in the upright–upright experiment suggests that initial *encoding of object identity* is critical to suppress that irrelevant information and elicit most robust IOR over time. Similarly, seeing less IOR in the upright–inverted than in the upright–upright experiment suggests that later

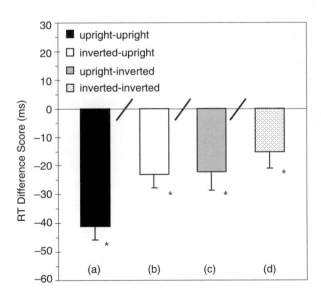

Figure 8.7 Effects for faces cued 3800 ms previously in the upright–upright (a), inverted–upright (b), upright–inverted (c) and inverted–inverted (d) experiments. Negative scores reveal IOR ($*p < .05$).

retrieval of object identity is also necessary to reveal suppression of that irrelevant information in IOR over time. Finally, smaller IOR was also seen in the inverted–inverted than in the upright–upright experiment, even though the physical orientation of the cue and target stimuli was matched so processing of low-level object and location information was similar. This effect further suggests that the ability to compute and inhibit object identity during *both* encoding and retrieval is critical to engage inhibition that aids behaviour over time.

Together, these four experiments revealed IOR effects over several seconds when inhibition was associated with object identity, which aids correct action over time by preventing attention and response to previously identified objects. Importantly, it appears that this effect depends upon encoding the identity of the irrelevant cued face with inhibition as well as later retrieving this information. Accordingly, these findings also suggest that inhibitory processes may mediate long-term behaviour when applied to stable objects.

Relationship between object-based inhibitory processes and long-term memory

Tipper (2001) has recently suggested that because inhibition can be associated with an object, this mechanism may guide correct behaviour over the long term. Indeed, there may be functional reasons for a relationship to evolve between long-term memory and inhibitory processes, because the goal of behaviour is not always met within one processing episode and may have to be completed later. Consider the following scenario in which you are searching the kitchen for a mislaid knife. After looking in a couple of places without success, the doorbell rings. At this point, you break off the search and exit the kitchen to answer the door. After you guide the guest into the living room, you have a long chat. Much later, you return to the kitchen. What mechanisms enable you to resume your search for the knife? It is proposed that there are at least two. The first is based on explicit recall, where you consciously remember looking for the knife. We also propose a second mechanism, which may be automatic and not available to recall, and this is retrieval of prior processing operations. That is, upon re-entering the kitchen, retrieval of previous inhibitory states could facilitate finding the knife by preventing the return of attention to previously attended objects. In this way, a link with the past could automatically facilitate response to novel information.

IOR *reveals inhibition of objects in long-term memory*

One short- and two long-term IOR tasks were initially conducted to test the radical idea that, in some circumstances, many items can be associated with inhibition and later retrieved to affect response (Tipper, Grison, & Kessler, 2003). The stimuli and procedures were similar to those used previously (see

Plate 8.2). In the short-term experiment, there was an interval of 1800 ms between the exogenous cue and the target, allowing examination of transient inhibition in IOR (see Plate 8.3). As suggested previously, the exogenous red cue should elicit initial orienting to a face followed by inhibition of irrelevant representations, causing slow response to a green target on the same face 1800 ms later. However, in the first long-term experiment there was an average of 3 min and 48 displays between the cue and its associated target, which allowed the first test of whether IOR effects can be found over long periods (see Plate 8.3). The second long-term task was conducted to confirm the presence of inhibition IOR over even longer delays of nearly 13 min and 192 displays (see Plate 8.3). In the two long-term tasks, it is suggested that inhibition can be associated with information stored in memory, then several minutes after originally viewing the event, that information could be retrieved, allowing reinstatement of inhibition to elicit IOR effects.

The data for the short-term task showed a standard IOR effect (−38 ms), although there was a trend towards a difference in IOR for the left (−41 ms) versus the right face (−35 ms) (see Figure 8.8a). The results of the first long-term task also showed IOR, although only for a previously cued left face (−16 ms), not right face (+6 ms) (Figure 8.8b). This result demonstrated the presence of inhibition when 3 min and 48 displays intervened between the cue and target, at least for stimuli presented in the left visual field (see also Kessler & Tipper, in press). Similarly, the data for the longer-term task also revealed IOR for the left (−11 ms) but not the right face (+4 ms) (Figure 8.8c), confirming that long-term IOR exists over delays of 13 min and 192 displays, but only for stimuli in the left visual field.

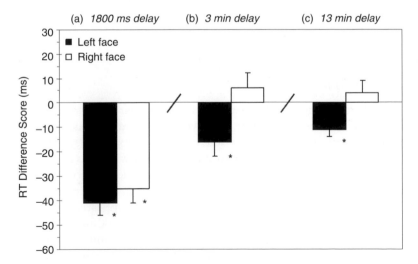

Figure 8.8 Effects associated with left and right faces for the short-term (a), long-term (b) and longer-term (c) tasks. Negative scores reveal IOR (*p < .05).

These experiments provided the first evidence that long-term IOR effects exist. Although the results in the short-term task could be explained by online inhibition, transient neural processing cannot be maintained for irrelevant information over several minutes and continued processing of other items. Instead, in the two long-term tasks, inhibition may have become associated with irrelevant information during initial encoding and then stored in episodic memory. When later encountering the same item, retrieval of the prior stimulus not only generated object recognition, but may have re-activated the network of inhibitory processes associated with correct selection and response to the previous configuration. Interestingly, this process also seemed to affect conscious recall of the cueing experience, as the results of another IOR task showed that participants erroneously reported that the uncued face had been cued 13 min and 192 displays previously (Tipper & Kessler, 2002).

Additionally, the discrepancy in IOR between the visual fields in these studies was intriguing. Indeed, IOR was greater for face stimuli appearing in the left visual field in all of these studies, although this effect was especially robust in the long-term experiments. Although this is an unusual finding, it is not unprecedented (e.g. Berlucchi et al., 1997; Handy et al., 1995; Jordan & Tipper, 2001; Kessler & Tipper, in press; McDonald et al., 1999; Nelson et al., 1993; White et al., 2001). For example, Fenske and his colleagues (2003) found that when participants withheld a response to an exogenously cued face, affective response to the same face 8–12 s later revealed greater inhibition for a face in the left than in the right visual field. However, because finding such large visual field differences in IOR effects is uncommon, we conducted two additional studies to confirm the existence of long-term object-based IOR, to explore whether inhibition of objects or locations could both elicit long-term effects, and to further examine visual field differences in IOR (Grison, Tipper, & Kramer, 2004).

IOR reveals inhibition of objects, but not locations, in long-term memory

The procedures of these two experiments were similar but two sets of stimuli were used. Naturalistic, colour faces were shown, where cues and targets were located within an eye to the left or right of fixation (see Plate 8.4). Additionally, naturalistic, colour scenes were shown, with cues and targets in a location above or below fixation, such that they did not conform to the boundaries of any object. For both sets of stimuli, participants did not respond if a red signal appeared, but if a blue signal appeared they made a localization response. In the short-term experiment, 1800 ms and zero displays intervened between the cue and target, allowing examination of transient inhibition of objects (i.e. face stimuli) and locations (i.e. scene stimuli) as well as visual field differences in these effects. The results of previous research suggest we might find short-term IOR regardless of whether objects or locations are cued, but that this effect may be greater in the left visual field. In the long-term task, there was an interval of almost 18 min and 96 displays between the cue and target. If inhibition can be associated with information stored in memory, the same information could be retrieved much later, reinstating inhibition to elicit IOR. Importantly, these effects may only be obtained for stable object-based information shown in the left visual field.

The results for the short-term task (Figure 8.9a) revealed that cueing an eye in a face elicited robust short-term IOR (−36 ms), which was greater for the left (−45 ms) than for the right eye (−26 ms). For scene stimuli, cueing an objectless location led to robust short-term IOR for both the top (−45 ms) and bottom locations (−37 ms), with no differences between these effects. Clearly, transient inhibition can suppress either objects or locations in short-term tasks; however, this effect is greater for an object cued in the left visual field. In the long-term task (Figure 8.9b) IOR was seen when cueing the left eye (−7 ms), while facilitation was seen for the right eye (+14 ms). Importantly, no long-term IOR was observed for a location cued at the top or bottom of a scene. These outcomes replicate the existence of long-term IOR when cueing objects while also confirming that long-term IOR differs across the visual fields. The results also indicate that the same long-term effects cannot be found when cueing locations that are not yoked to object properties.

To reiterate, in these tasks we suggest that it is possible for inhibition to have initially been associated with a variety of representations during the cue display, such as spatial location, low-level object information, object identity and response processes, and automatically encoded in memory. When the

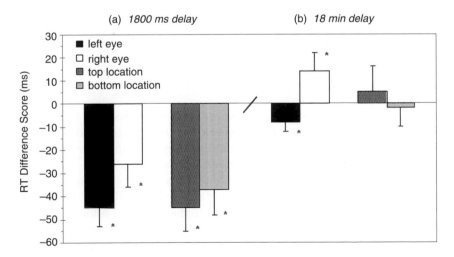

Figure 8.9 Effects associated with left and right eyes and top and bottom locations for the short-term (a) and long-term task (b). Negative scores reveal IOR (*$p < .05$).

target appeared a short time later (i.e. 1800 ms), robust object- and location-based IOR could have been a result of continued online suppression of one or more of these representations. However, when the target appeared a long time after the cue (i.e. 18 min), transient neural suppression could not have been maintained online, so retrieval of irrelevant information and associated inhibition may have elicited object- but not location-based IOR. This may be because inhibition of location information is not maintained in working memory as well as object information (Paul & Tipper, 2003) and because in these long-term tasks, when the target is finally presented, dozens of stimuli have been experienced in the same loci. Therefore, we suggest that only stable object-based representations may be easily retrieved to reinstate prior inhibition and affect behaviour over time. Interestingly, the fact that object-based IOR with face stimuli again differed between the visual fields in the short- and long-term tasks suggests that transient inhibition and long-term episodic retrieval of inhibition are preferentially engaged when these stimuli are shown in the left visual field. Indeed, it may be that the nature of the stimuli used in these tasks differentially engaged attentional processes to elicit different effects across the visual fields.

Specifically, there is ample evidence of right hemisphere specialization for processing of faces (Leehey, Carey, Diamond, & Cahn, 1978; McCarthy, Puce, Gore, & Allison, 1997; Rossion et al., 2000). For example, when viewing faces, imaging studies tend to show activity in the right hemisphere fusiform face area (e.g. Kanwisher, McDermott, & Chun, 1997), and lesions producing prosopagnosia (deficits in face processing) are most associated with the right hemisphere (e.g. De Renzi & Spinnler, 1966; Milner, 1968). Furthermore, research has shown preferential scanning and encoding of the side of a face, or an eye, presented to the left visual field (e.g. Gilbert & Bakan, 1973; Mertens, Siegmund, & Grüsser, 1993; Ricciardelli, Ro, & Driver, 2002), especially when the face is unfamiliar (see Althoff & Cohen, 1999). Previous research has also shown that faces lend themselves to be automatically stored in episodic memory (Shah et al., 2001), and episodic memory processing of faces may be localized to the right hemisphere as well (e.g. Zarate, Sanders, & Garza, 2000).

Therefore, it may be that in these experiments, a face presented to the left visual field, as well as the left eye of one face, received richer initial processing by the right hemisphere during encoding, resulting in greater transient suppression associated with that stimulus. An additional consequence of this greater transient inhibition might have been richer encoding of stable memory representations of the face and associated inhibition. Therefore, when the same face or eye was re-presented to the left visual field, retrieval of the stimulus and associated inhibition may have reactivated cortical systems to hamper orienting of attention, resulting in more robust long-term IOR in the left visual field. By contrast, a face or eye presented to the right visual field may have engaged relatively less initial processing by the right hemisphere during encoding, resulting in less robust inhibition of that stimulus.

As a result, the information might have been encoded with reduced inhibition, such that when the same face or eye was later re-presented to the right visual field, retrieval did not reinstate suppression, thus allowing faster orienting and long-term facilitation in that visual field.

An additional experiment tested this proposal by manipulating the efficiency of processing across the visual fields through the sudden onset of a stimulus, which may attract attention and cause preferential processing (Theeuwes, Kramer, Hahn, & Irwin, 1998). The previous long-term IOR task was used (see Plate 8.3; 3 min delay), but the two faces were not presented simultaneously. Instead, either the left face onset 150 ms after the right face or the right face onset 150 ms after the left face. Any biased processing elicited by the sudden late onset of the left or right face might modulate long-term IOR effects between the visual fields by "mimicking" right hemisphere biased processing of face stimuli in the left visual field. Indeed, long-term IOR was greatest when the naturally biased processing of a face in the left visual field by the right hemisphere combined with preferential processing of this stimulus, caused by its sudden, late onset. As mentioned, this may have been because the pattern of the face was more deeply encoded with associated inhibition such that, in the target display, the prior information was more likely to be retrieved, and inhibition reinstated, to elicit long-term IOR. Importantly, the sudden, late onset of a face in the right visual field did elicit some small long-term IOR, even though no effects have been seen with face stimuli in this visual field to this point. This may be because the preferential processing caused by sudden onset alone allowed greater encoding of the stimulus with inhibition into memory, and hence better retrieval and reinstatement of inhibition later on, than has previously been indicated in these long-term tasks.

Future research could further examine whether inhibition of face stimuli in short- and long-term IOR tasks is associated with processing in the right hemisphere fusiform gyrus. Interestingly, such research could also reveal whether cortical structures mediate processing of object-based representations in IOR. Alternatively, processing of the face itself may not be impaired, but retrieval of the stimulus may reactivate cortical systems controlling orienting of attention. Thus, attentional orienting to the face object could be impaired, while perceptual processing is unaffected by prior cueing. At the present time, this latter view is preferred.

General discussion

We have proposed that correct goal-directed behaviour in our complex visual world is aided by attentional selection of object-based representations. The evidence reviewed here from our research into IOR effects demonstrates that inhibitory mechanisms of attention can be applied to object-based representations to aid behaviour and that these behavioural effects and underlying neural mechanisms can be dissociated from those of inhibition of location-based information. Specifically, inhibition can be applied to empty locations and endures for more than 3 s, does not change over the course of human development, is revealed in measures of voluntary eye movements but not in reaches, and is seen in between-objects representations but not in within-object representations. Additionally, the mechanisms associated with inhibition of locations seem to depend on processing in the SC. By contrast, inhibition of objects seems to last for less than 3 s when they dynamically change position, requires the presence of visible objects, does change over the course of life, is not detected in eye movements but is in reaches, and is revealed in both between- and within-objects representations. Finally, inhibition of object-based representations may be mediated by processing in cortical regions.

This evidence for the existence of inhibition of object-based representations led to the unique proposal concerning interactions between attentional processes and memory in mediating goal-directed behaviour over time. We have suggested that inhibition of stable object-based representations could be the foundation for successful behaviour over time to avoid repeatedly attending and responding to previously examined information. Indeed, across a variety of experiments, evidence was provided to support this claim by showing IOR effects over several seconds and intervening displays when inhibition was associated with stable object-based representations, including identity information. These results imply that when inhibition is applied to objects, online processing can be maintained for longer durations and over processing of more items than inhibition of locations. Additionally, in these tasks, memory traces of the object and associated inhibition seem to be created because the magnitude of IOR depended on the ability to recognize an object during both initial encoding and later retrieval processes. To the extent that an object is recognized and encoded into memory, and to the extent that a later recognizable stimulus matches the stored episode, prior inhibitory states affect performance.

Accordingly, it was suggested that if inhibition can be associated with objects and affect behaviour over the time course of a few seconds and several intervening displays, then retrieval of that information during subsequent processing might also retrieve the inhibitory states originally acting on the object to impact long-term behaviour. The results from several unique experiments revealed the first evidence of IOR effects over many minutes and dozens of intervening displays when inhibition was associated with objects, but not with objectless locations. We suggest that these findings support the existence of a memory mechanism where encoding and retrieval of object-based inhibition in long-term memory aids correct behaviour even though it is unavailable to conscious recall. Cued objects may be automatically encoded into episodic memory along with associated inhibition, such that if the same stimulus is re-experienced, it automatically retrieves a prior matching episode and reinstates inhibitory processes that impede response. Finally, the discrepancy in effects across the two visual fields suggests that the effect is modulated by the degree of initial encoding of a stimulus, its association with inhibition and subsequent likelihood of retrieval, where face stimuli are more richly encoded when presented in the left visual field due to biased processing of these representations in the right hemisphere.

Counter to the standard view that attentional processes such as inhibition are transient, only influencing real-time interactions with perception and response, inhibition of stable objects may generally mediate goal-directed behaviour over time by affecting processing in working memory and episodic memory.[3] Indeed, future research must examine the relationships between these mechanisms in allowing correct behaviour (e.g. Tipper, 2001; Tipper, Weaver, Cameron, Brehaut, & Bastedo, 1991b). Such interactions between attention and memory processes could be considered within a neurally plausible model of inhibition originally proposed by Houghton and Tipper (1994; see also Houghton, Tipper, Weaver, & Shore, 1996). In brief, the model is based on the concept that activation-sensitive inhibition aids current behaviour by suppressing active representations that compete for response. The model states that external perceptual inputs are compared with an internal selection template based on task goals. For example, with respect to the IOR task described previously where a face was cued, the selection template might include information about "responding to the green face". Inputs that match the template (i.e. a green face) will receive excitatory feedback that facilitates response. However, inputs that mismatch the template (i.e. a red face) will receive inhibitory feedback that impedes response. Therefore, the selection of the green face is achieved by higher activation of the item due to its match with the task template and by backward-inhibition of the red face due to its mismatch with the template.

3   As support for the generality of episodic retrieval of inhibitory states, we have also found long-term negative priming effects (Grison, Tipper, & Hewitt, in press; see also DeSchepper & Treisman, 1996; Lowe, 1998; Neumann, Iwahara, & Tajika, 1999; Neumann & Russell, 2000; Treisman & DeSchepper, 1995). It should be noted that while the procedures of the negative priming and IOR paradigms differ (e.g. in IOR participants orient to a single cue signal, while in negative priming they must select between two concurrent signals), some researchers believe the underlying inhibitory mechanisms are similar (e.g. Buckolz, Boulougouris, O'Donnell, & Pratt, 2002; Houghton & Tipper, 1994; Milliken, Tipper, Houghton, & Lupiáñez, 2000). Accordingly, we suggest that in both of these paradigms inhibitory processes may be associated with irrelevant information and stored in memory in a similar manner, thus allowing later retrieval and reinstatement of suppression to elicit long-term IOR or negative priming effects. Furthermore, while the existence of long-term negative priming has sometimes been described as being due to episodic retrieval of 'do not respond' tags (for reviews, see Fox, 1995; May, Kane, & Hasher, 1995; Neill, Valdes, & Terry, 1995), we suggest that these tags may be operationalized in terms of neurally plausible inhibitory processes that are stored and retrieved with stimulus information to impact behaviour. Indeed, several proponents of episodic retrieval models have also suggested that episodes may retain some trace of the previous inhibition that affects performance later on (e.g. DeSchepper & Treisman, 1996; Neill, Valdes, Terry, & Gorfein, 1992; Tipper, 2001; Tipper et al., 1991b).

While the original form of Houghton and colleagues' (1996) model does not include a way for inhibition to affect performance over time, one can see how such a mechanism might be implemented. One notion, based on the work of Cohen, Braver, and O'Reilly (1998), is for transient inhibitory states to be encoded as part of an episode into a memory sub-network that represents hippocampal processes. In particular, if the neural substrate of inhibition is activated cells, as in the model of Houghton et al. (1996), that have an inhibitory influence on other cells, then it is essential for the system that they are only activated for a short time to avoid interference with on-going processes. However, the activation state of these cells associated with the processing of a certain object must also be stored in and recovered from episodic memory to affect long-term performance. Therefore, an episodic memory sub-network in the model of Houghton et al. (1996) could include a learning mechanism that "takes snapshots" of the activation patterns in the rest of the network and stores them as a part of an episode. Accordingly, the inhibition is part of the entire pattern of neural activity stored in episodic memory by adjusting synaptic links between neurons in sub-networks. The inhibition is implicitly encoded in the adjusted links, such that there is no inhibition active in the system after the transient IOR has decayed, thus preventing interference during on-going processing. However, when a sufficiently strong retrieval cue is supplied, the inhibitory processes are also recovered, resulting in reinstatement of the prior network state. In this way, retrieval of information and associated inhibition from episodic memory can mediate behaviour over time without interfering with on-going processes. More detailed analysis of the interaction between online inhibition and episodic retrieval of inhibitory states is currently underway.

The behavioural research described here has been successful in obtaining IOR effects over time, which provides indirect support for episodic retrieval of prior inhibitory states associated with stable object-based representations. These results provide the basis of a new neural network model of episodic retrieval of attention. However, behavioural measures alone will not fully reveal the nature of the processes and underlying representations that mediate performance over time in these tasks. Therefore, future research may employ converging techniques such as connectionist modelling, measures of eye movements and neuroimaging techniques, such as event-related potentials, fMRI and event-related optical signals (Gratton & Fabiani, 2001), to search for more direct evidence that object-based inhibition can aid goal-directed behaviour over time.

References

Abrams, R. A., & Dobkin, R. S. (1994). Inhibition of return: effects of attentional cuing on eye movement latencies. *Journal of Experimental Psychology: Human Perception and Performance, 20*, 467–477.

Abrams, R. A., & Dobkin, R. S. (1995). The gap effect and inhibition of return: interactive effects on eye movement latencies. *Experimental Brain Research*, 98, 483–487.

Abrams, R. A., & Jonides, J. (1988). Programming saccadic eye movements. *Journal of Experimental Psychology: Human Perception and Performance*, 14, 428–443.

Abrams, R. A., & Pratt, J. (2000). Oculocentric coding of inhibited eye movements to recently attended locations. *Journal of Experimental Psychology: Human Perception and Performance*, 26, 776–778.

Althoff, R. R., & Cohen, N. J. (1999). Eye-movement-based memory effect: a reprocessing effect in face perception. *Journal of Experimental Psychology: Learning, Memory and Cognition*, 25, 997–1010.

Anderson, R. A. (1989). Visual and eye movement functions of the posterior parietal cortex. *Annual Review of Neuroscience*, 12, 377–403.

Baddeley, A. D., & Hitch, G. (1974). Working memory. In G. H. Bower (Ed.), *The psychology of learning and motivation* (Vol. 8, pp. 47–89). New York: Academic Press.

Bartolomeo, P., Chokron, S., & Siéroff, E. (1999). Facilitation instead of inhibition for repeated right-sided events in left negalect. *Neuroreport*, 10, 3353–3357.

Baylis, G. C., & Driver, J. (1993). Visual attention and objects: evidence for hierarchical coding of location. *Journal of Experimental Psychology: Human Perception and Performance*, 19, 451–470.

Becker, L., & Egeth, H. (2000). Mixed reference frames for dynamic inhibition of return. *Journal of Experimental Psychology: Human Perception and Performance*, 26, 1167–1177.

Berger, A., & Henik, A. (2000). The endogenous modulation of IOR is nasal–temporal asymmetric. *Journal of Cognitive Neuroscience*, 12, 421–428.

Berlucchi, G., Aglioti, S., & Tassinari, G. (1997). Rightward attentional bias and left hemisphere dominance in a cue–target light detection task in a callosotomy patient. *Neuropsychologia*, 35, 941–952.

Biederman, I. (1987). Recognition by components: a theory of human image understanding. *Psychological Review*, 94, 115–145.

Bruce, C. J. (1990). Integration of sensory and motor signals for saccadic eye movements in the primate frontal eye fields. In G. M. Edelman, W. E. Gall, & W. M. Cowan (Eds.), *Signal and sense, local and global order in perceptual maps* (pp. 261–314). New York: Wiley-Liss.

Bruce, V., & Humphreys, G. W. (1994). Recognizing objects and faces. In V. Bruce & G. W. Humphreys (Eds.), Object and face recognition. Special issue of *Visual Cognition*, 1, pp. 141–180.

Buckolz, E., Boulougouris, A., O'Donnell, C., & Pratt, J. (2002). Disengaging the negative priming mechanism in location tasks. *European Journal of Cognitive Psychology*, 14, 207–225

Castel, A. D., Pratt, J., & Craik, F. I. M. (2002, November). *The role of working memory in inhibition of return*. Poster session presented at the 43rd Annual Meeting of the Psychonomic Society, Kansas City, MO.

Christ, S. E., McCrae, C. S., & Abrams, R. A. (2002). Inhibition of return in static and dynamic displays. *Psychonomic Bulletin and Review*, 9, 80–85.

Clark, V. P., & Hillyard, S. A. (1996). Spatial selective attention affects early extrastriate but not striate components of the visual evoked potential. *Journal of Cognitive Neuroscience*, 8, 387–402.

Clohessy, A. B., Posner, M. I., Rothbart, M. K., & Vecera, S. P. (1991). The development of inhibition of return in early infancy. *Journal of Cognitive Neuroscience, 3,* 345–350.

Cohen, J. D., Braver, T. S., & O'Reilly, R. C. (1998). A computational approach to prefrontal cortex, cognitive control, and schizophrenia: recent developments and current challenges. In A. C. Roberts & T. W. Robbins (Eds.), *The prefrontal cortex: executive and cognitive functions* (pp. 195–220). New York: Oxford University Press.

Connor, C. E., Preddie, D. C., Gallant, J. L., & Van Essen, D. C. (1997). Spatial attention effects in macaque area V4. *Journal of Neuroscience, 17,* 3201–3214.

Costello, A. D., & Warrington, E. K. (1987). The dissociation of visuospatial neglect and neglect dyslexia. *Journal of Neurology, Neurosurgery and Psychiatry, 50,* 1110–1116.

Cowan, N. (2001). The magical number 4 in short-term memory: a reconsideration of mental storage capacity. *Behavioral and Brain Sciences, 24,* 87–185.

Cubelli, R., Nichelli, P., Bonito, V., de Tanti, A., & Inzaghi, M. G. (1991). Different patterns of dissociation in unilateral spatial neglect. *Brain and Cognition, 15,* 139–159.

Danziger, S., Fendrich, R., & Rafal, R. D. (1997). Inhibitory tagging of locations in the blind field of hemianopic patients. *Consciousness and Cognition, 6,* 291–307.

Danziger, S., Kingstone, A., & Snyder, J. J. (1998). Inhibition of return to successively stimulated locations in a sequential visual search paradigm. *Journal of Experimental Psychology: Human Perception and Performance, 24,* 1467–1475.

De Renzi, E., & Spinnler, H. (1966). Visual recognition in patients with unilateral cerebral disease. *Journal of Nervous and Mental Disease, 142,* 515–525.

DeSchepper, B., & Treisman, A. (1996). Visual memory for novel shapes: implicit coding without attention. *Journal of Experimental Psychology: Learning, Memory and Cognition, 22,* 27–47.

Dorris, M. C., Klein, R. M., Everling, S., & Munoz, D. P. (2001). *Contribution of the primate superior colliculus to inhibition of return.* Manuscript submitted for publication.

Dorris, M. C., & Munoz, D. P. (1995). A neural correlate for the gap effect on saccadic reaction times in monkey. *Journal of Neurophysiology, 73,* 2558–2562.

Dorris, M. C., Taylor, T. L., Klein, R. M., & Munoz, D. P. (1999). Influence of previous visual stimulus or saccade on saccadic reaction times in monkey. *Journal of Neurophysiology, 81,* 2429–2436.

Driver, J., Davis, G., Russell, C., Turatto, M., & Freeman, E. (2001). Segmentation, attention, and phenomenal visual objects. *Cognition, 80,* 61–95.

Eimer, M. (1997). Attentional selection and attentional gradients: an alternative method for studying transient visual–spatial attention. *Psychophysiology, 34,* 365–376.

Fenske, M. J., Kessler, K., Raymond, J. E., & Tipper, S. P. (2003, May). *Attentional inhibition determines emotional responses to unfamiliar faces.* Poster presented at the 3rd Annual Meeting of the Vision Sciences Society, Sarasota, FL.

Fox, E. (1995). Negative priming from ignored distractors in visual selection: a review. *Psychonomic Bulletin and Review, 2,* 145–173.

Gibson, B. S., & Egeth, H. (1994). Inhibition of return to object-based and environment-based locations. *Perception and Psychophysics, 55,* 323–339.

Gilbert, C., & Bakan, P. (1973). Visual asymmetry in perception of faces. *Neuropsychologia, 11,* 355–362.

Goldberg, M. E., & Wurtz, R. H. (1972). Activity of superior colliculus in behaving monkey: I. Visual receptive fields of single neurons. *Journal of Neurophysiology, 35,* 542–559.

Gratton, G., & Fabiani, M. (2001). Shedding light on brain function: the event-related optical signal. *Trends in Cognitive Sciences, 5,* 357–363.

Grison, S., Paul, M. A., Kessler, K., & Tipper, S. P. (in press). Inhibition of object identity in inhibition of return of attention: Implications for encoding and retrieving inhibitory processes. *Psychonomic Bulletin and Review.*

Grison, S., Tipper, S. P., & Hewitt, O. (in press). Long-term negative priming: support for retrieval of prior attentional process. *Quarterly Journal of Experimental Psychology; Section A: Human Experimental Psychology.*

Grison, S., Tipper, S. P., & Kramer, A. F. (2004). *Long-term inhibition of return effects suggest episodic retrieval of attentional states.* Manuscript submitted for publication.

Gross, C. G. (1991). Contribution of striate cortex and the superior colliculus to visual function in area MT, the superior temporal polysensory area and inferior temporal cortex. Special issue in honor of Karl H. Pribram: Localization and distribution of cognitive function. *Neuropsychologia, 29,* 497–515.

Handy, T. C., Jha, A. P., Kingstone, A., & Mangun, G. R. (1995, November). Attentional hemispheric asymmetries in chronometric analysis of inhibition of return. Paper presented at the *25th Annual Meeting of the Society for Neuroscience,* San Diego, CA.

Horowitz, T. S., & Wolfe, J. M. (1998). Visual search has no memory. *Nature, 394,* 575–577.

Houghton, G., & Tipper, S. P. (1994). A model of inhibitory mechanisms in selective attention. In D. Dagenbach & T. H. Carr (Eds.), *Inhibitory processes in attention, memory, and language* (pp. 53–112). San Diego, CA: Academic Press.

Houghton, G., Tipper, S. P., Weaver, B., & Shore, D. I. (1996). Inhibition and interference in selective attention: some tests of a neural network model. *Visual Cognition, 3,* 119–164.

Howard, L. A., Lupiáñez, J., & Tipper, S. P. (1999). Inhibition of return in a selective reaching task: an investigation of reference frames. *Journal of General Psychology, 126,* 421–442.

Howard, L. A., & Tipper, S. P. (2001). *Frames-of-reference in inhibition of return: a selective reaching task.* Unpublished raw data.

Humphreys, G. W., & Riddoch, M. J. (1994). Attention to within-object and between-object spatial representations: multiple sites for visual selection. Special issue: The cognitive neuropsychology of attention. *Cognitive Neuropsychology, 11,* 207–241.

Humphreys, G. W., & Riddoch, M. J. (1995). Separate coding of space within and between perceptual objects: evidence from unilateral visual neglect. *Cognitive Neuropsychology, 1,* 283–311.

Ingle, D. (1977). Detection of stationary objects by frogs (*Rana pipiens*) after ablation of optic tectum. *Journal of Comparative and Physiological Psychology, 91,* 1359–1364.

Ingle, D., Cheal, M., & Dizio, P. (1979). Cine analysis of visual orientation and pursuit by the Mongolian gerbil. *Journal of Comparative and Physiological Psychology, 93,* 919–928.

Jeannerod, M., Arbib, M. A., Rizzolatti, G., & Sakata, H. (1995). Grasping objects: the cortical mechanisms of visuomotor transformation. *Trends in Neuroscience, 18,* 314–320.

Jordan, H., & Tipper, S. P. (1998). Object-based inhibition of return in static displays. *Psychonomic Bulletin and Review*, 5, 504–509.

Jordan, H., & Tipper, S. P. (1999). Spread of inhibition across an object's surface. *British Journal of Psychology*, 90, 495–507.

Jordan, H., & Tipper, S. P. (2001). *Evidence for object- and location-based inhibition of return in static displays: visual field asymmetries.* Unpublished raw data.

Kahneman, D., Treisman, A., & Gibbs, B. J. (1992). The reviewing of object files: object-specific integration of information. *Cognitive Psychology*, 24, 175–219.

Kanwisher, N. (1998). The modular structure of human visual recognition: evidence from functional imaging. In M. Sabourin, F. Craik, & M. Robert (Eds.), *Advances in psychological science, Vol. 2: Biological and cognitive aspects* (pp. 199–213). Hove: Psychology Press.

Kanwisher, N., McDermott, J., & Chun, M. M. (1997). The fusiform face area: a module in human extrastriate cortex specialized for face perception. *Journal of Neuroscience*, 17, 4302–4311.

Kanwisher, N., Tong, F., & Nakayama, K. (1998). The effect of face inversion on the human fusiform face area. *Cognition*, 68, 1–11.

Kanwisher, N., Woods, R. P., Iacoboni, M., & Mazziotta, J. C. (1997). A locus in human extrastriate cortex for visual shape analysis. *Journal of Cognitive Neuroscience*, 9, 133–142.

Kessler, K., Pfennig, H. E., & Rickheit, G. (2001, September). *Visual chunking in a connectionist model: behavioral data and eye-movements.* Poster presented at the Joint Meeting of the European Society for Cognitive Psychology and the British Psychological Society, Cognitive Psychology Section, Edinburgh, UK.

Kessler, K., & Rickheit, G. (1999). Dynamische Konzeptgenerierung in konnektionistischen Netzen: Begriffsklaerung, Modellvorstellungen zur Szenenrekonstruktion und experimentelle Ergebnisse. *Kognitionswissenschaft*, 8, 74–96.

Kessler, K., & Rickheit, G. (2000). Dynamic binding and context influences during scene perception: simulations and experimental results. In N. Taatgen & J. Aasman (Eds.), *Proceedings of the Third International Conference on Cognitive Modeling* (pp. 177–184). Veenendaal, Netherlands: Universal Press.

Kessler, K., & Tipper, S. P. (in press). Retrieval of implicit inhibitory attentional processes: the impact of visual field, object-identity, and memory dynamics. *Visual Cognition*.

Kingstone, A., & Pratt, J. (1999). Inhibition of return is composed of attentional and oculomotor processes. *Perception and Psychophysics*, 61, 1046–1054.

Klein, R. M. (1988). Inhibitory tagging system facilitates visual search. *Nature*, 334, 430–431.

Klein, R. M. (2000). Inhibition of return. *Trends in Cognitive Sciences*, 4, 138–147.

Klein, R. M., & MacInnes, W. J. (1999). Inhibition of return is a foraging facilitator in visual search. *Psychological Science*, 10, 346–352.

Klein, R. M., & Taylor, T. L. (1994). Categories of cognitive inhibition with reference to attention. In D. Dagenbach & T. H. Carr (Eds.), *Inhibitory processes in attention, memory, and language* (pp. 113–150). San Diego, CA: Academic Press.

Leehey, S., Carey, S., Diamond, R., & Cahn, A. (1978). Upright and inverted faces: the right hemisphere knows the difference. *Cortex*, 14, 411–419.

Leek, E. C., Reppa, I., & Tipper, S. P. (2003). Inhibition-of-return for objects and locations in static displays. *Perception and Psychophysics*, 65, 388–395.

Lepsien, J., & Pollman, S. (2002). Covert reorienting and inhibition of return: an event-related fMRI study. *Journal of Cognitive Neuroscience, 14,* 127–144.

Lesher, G. W. (1995). Illusory contours: towards a neurally based perceptual theory. *Psychonomic Bulletin and Review, 2,* 279–321.

Lewis, T. L., Maurer, D., & Milewski, A. (1979). The development of nasal detection in young infants. *Investigative Ophthalmology and Visual Science, 18,* 271.

List, A., & Robertson, L. C. (2001). *Inhibition of return and object-based attention.* Manuscript submitted for publication.

Logothetis, N. K., & Pauls, J. (1995). Psychophysical and physiological evidence for viewer-centered object representations in the primate. *Cerebral Cortex, 3,* 270–288.

Lowe, D. (1998). Long-term positive and negative identity priming: evidence for episodic retrieval. *Memory and Cognition, 26,* 435–443.

Lupiáñez, J., & Solano, C. (1997). Inhibition of return in a colour discrimination task: no interaction with the Simon effect. *Cognitiva, 9,* 195–205.

Lupiáñez, J., Tudela, P., & Rueda, C. (1999). Inhibitory control in attentional orientation: a review about inhibition of return. *Cognitiva, 11,* 23–44.

Malach, R., Reppas, J. B., Benson, R. R., Kwong, K. K., Jiang, H., Kennedy, W. A. et al. (1995). Object-related activity revealed by functional magnetic resonance imaging in human occipital cortex. *Proceedings of the National Academy of Sciences, USA, 92,* 8135–8139.

Mangun, G. R., Hillyard, S. A., & Luck, S. J. (1993). Electrocortical substrates of visual selective attention. In D. E. Meyers & S. Kornblum (Eds.), *Attention and performance XIV* (pp. 219–243). Cambridge, MA: MIT Press.

Marr, D. (1982). *Vision.* New York: W. H. Freeman.

May, C. P., Kane, M. J., & Hasher, L. (1995). Determinants of negative priming. *Psychological Bulletin, 118,* 35–54.

Maylor, E. A. (1985). Facilitatory and inhibitory components of orienting in visual space. In M. I. Posner & O. S. Marin (Eds.), *Attention and perfomance XI* (pp. 189–204). Hillsdale, NJ: Lawrence Erlbaum Associates Inc.

McAuliffe, J., Pratt, J., & O'Donnell, C. (2001). Examining location-based and object-based components of inhibition of return in static displays. *Perception and Psychophysics, 63,* 1072–1082.

McCarthy, G., Puce, A., Gore, J. C., & Allison, T. (1997). Face-specific processing in the human fusiform gyrus. *Journal of Cognitive Neuroscience, 9,* 605–610.

McCrae, C. S., & Abrams, R. A. (2001). Age-related differences in object- and location-based inhibition of return of attention. *Psychology and Aging, 16,* 437–449.

McDonald, J. W., Ward, L. M., & Kiehl, K. A. (1999). An event-related brain potential study of inhibition of return. *Perception and Psychophysics, 61,* 1411–1423.

McDowd, J. M., Filion, D. L., Tipper, S. P., & Weaver, B. (1995, November). *Object- and environment-based IOR in young and old adults.* Paper presented at the 36th Annual Meeting of the Psychonomic Society, Los Angeles, CA.

Mertens, I., Siegmund, H., & Grüsser, O. J. (1993). Gaze motor asymmetries in the perception of faces during a memory task. *Neuropsychologia, 31,* 989–998.

Milliken, B., Tipper, S. P., Houghton, G., & Lupiáñez, J. (2000). Attending, ignoring, and repetition: on the relation between negative priming and inhibition of return. *Perception and Psychophysics, 62,* 1280–1296.

Milner, B. (1968). Visual recognition and recall after right temporal-lobe excision in man. *Neuropsychologia, 6,* 191–209.

Müller, H. J., & von Mühlenen, A. (1996). Attentional tracking and inhibition of return in dynamic displays. *Perception and Psychophysics, 58,* 224–249.

Müller, H. J., & von Mühlenen, A. (2000). Probing distractor inhibition in visual search: Inhibition of return. *Journal of Experimental Psychology: Human Perception and Performance, 26,* 1591–1605.

Munoz, D. P., & Wurtz, R. H. (1993a). Fixation cells in monkey superior colliculus: I. Characteristics of cell discharge. *Journal of Neurophysiology, 70,* 559–575.

Munoz, D. P., & Wurtz, R. H. (1993b). Fixation cells in monkey superior colliculus: II. Reversible activation and deactivation. *Journal of Neurophysiology, 70,* 576–589.

Neill, W. T., Valdes, L. A., & Terry, K. M. (1995). Selective attention and the inhibitory control of cognition. In F. N. Dempster & C. J. Brainerd (Eds.), *Interference and inhibition in cognition* (pp. 207–261). San Diego, CA: Academic Press.

Neill, W. T., Valdes, L. A., Terry, K. M., & Gorfein, D. S. (1992). Persistence of negative priming: II. Evidence for episodic retrieval. *Journal of Experimental Psychology: Learning, Memory and Cognition, 18,* 993–1000.

Nelson, E., Early, T. S., & Haller, J. W. (1993). Visual attention in obsessive-compulsive disorder. *Psychiatry Research, 49,* 183–196.

Neumann, E., Iwahara, A., & Tajika, H. (1999, October). *Long-term negative priming for once ignored semantically meaningful shapes.* Poster session presented at the Annual Meeting of the Australian Psychological Society, Hobart, Tasmania.

Neumann, E., & Russell, P. N. (2000, November). *Persistence of token resistance: once-unattended words produce long-term negative priming.* Poster presented at the Annual Meeting of the Psychonomic Society, New Orleans, LA.

Ogawa, H., Takeda, Y., & Yagi, A. (2002). Inhibitory tagging on randomly moving objects. *Psychological Science, 13,* 125–129.

Olson, C. R., & Gettner, S. N. (1995). Object-centered direction selectivity in the macaque supplementary eye field. *Science, 269,* 985–988.

Oonk, H. M., & Abrams, R. A. (1998). New perceptual objects that capture attention produce inhibition of return. *Psychonomic Bulletin and Review, 5,* 510–515.

Paul, M., & Tipper, S. P. (2003). Object-based representations facilitate memory for inhibitory processes. *Experimental Brain Research, 148,* 283–289.

Posner, M. I., & Cohen, Y. (1980). Attention and the control of movements. In G. E. Stelmach & J. Requin (Eds.), *Tutorials in motor behavior* (pp. 243–258). New York: Elsevier.

Posner, M. I., & Cohen, Y. (1984). Components of visual orienting. In H. Bouma & D. Bouwhuis (Eds.), *Attention and performance* X (pp. 531–556). Hillsdale, NJ: Lawrence Erlbaum Associates Inc.

Posner, M. I., Rafal, R. D., Choate, L. S., & Vaughan, J. (1985). Inhibition of return: neural basis and function. *Journal of Cognitive Neuropsychology, 2,* 211–228.

Pratt, J., & Abrams, R. A. (1995). Inhibition of return to successively cued spatial locations. *Journal of Experimental Psychology: Human Perception and Performance, 21,* 1343–1353.

Rafal, R. D. (1998). The neurology of visual orienting: a pathological disintegration of development. In J. Richards (Ed.), *Cognitive neuroscience of attention: a developmental perspective* (pp. 181–219). Mahwah, NJ: Lawrence Erlbaum Associates Inc.

Rafal, R. D., Calabresi, P., Brennan, C., & Sciolto, T. (1989). Saccade preparation inhibits reorienting to recently attended locations. *Journal of Experimental Psychology: Human Perception and Performance, 15,* 673–685.

Rafal, R., Henik, A., & Smith, J. (1991). Extrageniculate contributions to reflex visual orienting in normal humans: a temporal hemifield advantage. *Journal of Cognitive Neuroscience, 3*, 322–328.

Rafal, R. D., Posner, M. I., Friedman, J. H., Inhoff, A. W., & Bernstein, E. (1988). Orienting of visual attention in progressive supranuclear palsy. *Brain, 111*, 267–280.

Rafal, R. D., Smith, J., Krantz, J., Cohen, A., & Brennan, C. (1990). Extrageniculate vision in hemianopic humans: saccade inhibition by signals in the blind field. *Science, 250*, 118–121.

Reppa, I., & Leek, E. C. (2003). The modulation of inhibition-of-return by object-internal structure: implications for theories of object-based attentional selection. *Psychonomic Bulletin and Review, 10*, 493–502.

Ricciardelli, P., Ro, T., & Driver, J. (2002). A left visual field advantage in perception of gaze direction. *Neuropsychologia, 40*, 769–777.

Riddoch, M. J., Humphreys, G. W., Lockhurst, L., Burroughs, E., & Bateman, A. (1995). "Paradoxical neglect": spatial representations, hemisphere-specific activation, and spatial cuing. *Cognitive Neuropsychology, 12*, 569–604.

Ro, T., Farnè, A., & Chang, E. (2003). Inhibition of return and the human frontal eye fields. *Experimental Brain Research*, DOI 10.1007/s00221-003-1470-0 http://link.springer.de/link/service/journals/00221/contents/03/01470/paper/s00221-003-1470-0ch000.html

Ro, T., & Rafal, R. D. (1999). Components of reflexive visual orienting to moving objects. *Perception and Psychophysics, 61*, 826–836.

Robertson, L. C., & Ivry, R. (2000). Hemispheric asymmetries: attention to visual and auditory primitives. *Current Directions in Psychological Science, 9*, 59–63.

Rosen, A. C., Rao, S. M., Caffarra, P., Scaglioni, A., Bobholz, J. A., Woodley, S. J. et al. (1999). Neural basis of endogenous and exogenous spatial orienting: a functional MRI study. *Journal of Cognitive Neuroscience, 11*, 135–152.

Rossion, B., Dricot, L., Devolder, A., Bodart, J., Crommelinck, M., de Gelder, B. et al. (2000). Hemispheric asymmetries for whole-based and part-based face processing in the human fusiform gyrus. *Journal of Cognitive Neuroscience, 12*, 793–802.

Sapir, A., Rafal, R., & Henik, A. (2002). Attending to the thalamus: inhibition of return and nasal–temporal asymmetry in the pulvinar. *NeuroReport, 13*, 1–5.

Sapir, A., Soroker, N., Berger, A., & Henik, A. (1999). Inhibition of return in spatial attention: direct evidence for collicular generation. *Nature Neuroscience, 2*, 1053–1054.

Schendel, K. L., Robertson, L. C., & Treisman, A. (2001). Objects and their locations in exogenous cuing. *Perception and Psychophysics, 63*, 577–594.

Schiller, P. H., & Stryker, M. (1972). Single-unit recording and stimulation in superior colliculus of the alert rhesus monkey. *Journal of Neurophysiology, 35*, 915–924.

Schlag, J., & Schlag-Rey, M. (1987). Evidence for a supplementary eye field. *Journal of Neurophysiology, 57*, 179–200.

Shah, N. J., Marshall, J. C., Zafiris, O., Schwab, A., Zilles, K., Markowitsch, H. J. et al. (2001). The neural correlates of person familiarity: a functional magnetic resonance imaging study with clinical implications. *Brain, 124*, 804–815 (special issue).

Simion, F., Valenza, E., Umiltà, C., & Dalla Barba, B. (1995). Inhibition of return in newborns is temporo-nasal asymmetrical. *Infant Behavior and Development, 18,* 189–194.

Snyder, J. J., & Kingstone, A. (2000). Inhibition of return and visual search: how many separate loci are inhibited? *Perception and Psychophysics, 62,* 452–458.

Snyder, J. J., & Kingstone, A. (2001). Inhibition of return at multiple locations: when you see it and when you don't. *Quarterly Journal of Experimental Psychology, 54A,* 1221–1237.

Sparks, D. L., & Mays, L. E. (1983). Spatial localization of saccade targets: I. Compensation for stimulation-induced perturbations in eye position. *Journal of Neurophysiology, 49,* 45–63.

Takeda, Y., & Yagi, A. (2000). Inhibitory tagging in visual search can be found if search stimuli remain visible. *Perception and Psychophysics, 62,* 927–934.

Tassinari, G., Aglioti, S., Chelazzi, L., Marzi, C. A., & Berlucchi, G. (1987). Distribution in the visual field of the costs of voluntarily allocated attention and of the inhibitory after-effects of covert orienting. *Neuropsychologia, 25,* 55–72.

Tassinari, G., Biscaldi, M., Marzi, C. A., & Berlucchi, G. (1989). Ipsilateral inhibition and contralateral facilitation of simple reaction time to non-foveal visual targets from non-informative visual cues. *Acta Psychologica, 70,* 267–291.

Taylor, T. L., & Klein, R. M. (1998). On the causes and effects of inhibition of return. *Psychonomic Bulletin and Review, 5,* 625–643.

Theeuwes, J., Kramer, A. F., Hahn, S., & Irwin, D. E. (1998). Our eyes do not always go where we want them to go: capture of the eyes by new objects. *Psychological Science, 9,* 379–385.

Tipper, S. P. (2001). Does negative priming reflect inhibitory mechanisms? A review and integration of conflicting views. *Quarterly Journal of Experimental Psychology: Human Experimental Psychology, 54A,* 321–343.

Tipper, S. P., & Behrmann, M. (1996). Object-centered not scene-based visual neglect. *Journal of Experimental Psychology: Human Perception and Performance, 22,* 1261–1278.

Tipper, S. P., Driver, J., & Weaver, B. (1991a). Object-centred inhibition of return of visual attention. *Quarterly Journal of Experimental Psychology: Human Experimental Psychology, 43A,* 289–298.

Tipper, S. P., Grison, S., & Kessler, K. (2003). Long-term inhibition of return of attention. *Psychological Science, 14,* 19–25.

Tipper, S. P., Howard, L., & Jackson, S. (1997a). Selective reaching to grasp: evidence for distractor interference effects. *Visual Cognition, 4,* 1–38.

Tipper, S. P., Jordan, H., & Weaver, B. (1999). Scene-based and object-centered inhibition of return: evidence for dual orienting mechanisms. *Perception and Psychophysics, 61,* 50–60.

Tipper, S. P., & Kessler, K. (2002). *Implicit retrieval of inhibitory states from memory.* Unpublished raw data.

Tipper, S. P., Lortie, C., & Baylis, G. C. (1992). Selective reaching: evidence for action centered attention. *Journal of Experimental Psychology: Human Perception and Performance, 18,* 891–905.

Tipper, S. P., & Weaver, B. (1998). The medium of attention: location-based, object-centered, or scene-based? In R. D. Wright (Ed.), *Visual attention: Vancouver studies in cognitive science* (Vol. 8, pp. 77–107). New York: Oxford University Press.

Tipper, S. P., Weaver, B., Cameron, S., Brehaut, J., & Bastedo, J. (1991b). Inhibitory mechanisms of attention in identification and localisation tasks: time course and disruption. *Journal of Experimental Psychology: Learning, Memory and Cognition, 17,* 681–692.

Tipper, S. P., Weaver, B., Jerreat, L. M., & Burak, A. L. (1994). Object-based and environment-based inhibition of return of visual attention. *Journal of Experimental Psychology: Human Perception and Performance, 20,* 478–499.

Tipper, S. P., Weaver, B., Rafal, R., Starrveldt, Y., Egly, R., Danziger, S. et al. (1997b). Object-based facilitation and inhibition from visual orienting in the human split brain. *Journal of Experimental Psychology: Human Perception and Performance, 23,* 1522–1532.

Tipper, S. P., Weaver, B., & Watson, F. L. (1996). Inhibition of return to successively cued spatial locations: commentary on Pratt and Abrams (1995). *Journal of Experimental Psychology: Human Perception and Performance, 22,* 1289–1293.

Treisman, A., & DeSchepper, B. (1995). Object tokens, attention, and visual memory. In T. Inui & J. McClelland (Eds.), *Attention and performance XVI* (pp. 16–46). Cambridge, MA: MIT Press.

Valenza, E., Simion, F., & Umiltà, C. (1994). Inhibition of return in newborn infants. *Infant Behavior and Development, 17,* 293–302.

Van Opstal, A. J., Hepp, K., Suzuki, Y., & Henn, V. (1995). Influence of eye position on activity in monkey superior colliculus. *Journal of Neurophysiology, 74,* 1593–1610.

Vivas, A. B., Humphreys, G. W., & Fuentes, L. J. (2003). Inhibitory processing following damage to the parietal lobe. *Neuropsychologia, 41,* 1531–1540.

Weaver, B., Lupiáñez, J., & Watson, F. L. (1998). The effects of practice on object-based, location-based, and static-display inhibition of return. *Perception and Psychophysics, 60,* 993–1003.

White, H., Marks, W., & Wilkinson, G. (2001, November). *Spatial and semantic inhibition of return: individual differences related to attention deficit hyperactivity disorder.* Poster session presented at the Annual Meeting of the Psychonomic Society, Orlando, FL.

Wolfe, J. M., & Pokorny, C. W. (1990). Inhibitory tagging in visual search: a failure to replicate. *Perception and Psychophysics, 48,* 357–362.

Wurtz, R. H., & Goldberg, M. E. (1972). Activity of superior colliculus in behaving monkeys. III. Cells discharging before movements. *Journal of Neurophysiology, 35,* 575–586.

Yin, R. K. (1969). Looking at upside down faces. *Journal of Experimental Psychology, 81,* 141.

Zarate, M. A., Sanders, J. D., & Garza, A. A. (2000). Neurological dissociations of social perception processes. *Social Cognition, 18,* 223–251.

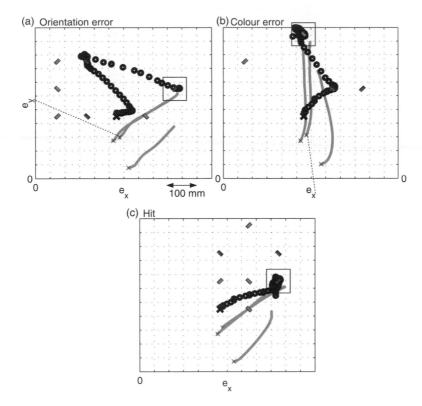

Plate 6.1 Grasping and looking to an object. The target in this example is an orange bar oriented at 45° among a green bar also oriented at 45°, a green bar oriented at −45°, and an orange bar oriented at −45°. Two possible erroneous saccades are drawn: an orientation error in (a) and a colour error in (b). A hit is depicted in (c). Also, the projection of the line thumb-index-finger on the table surface is drawn, which was used for the analysis of grasping dynamics.

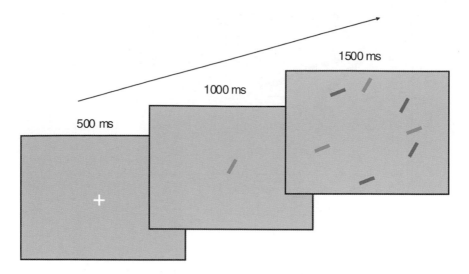

Plate 6.2 Experimental paradigm in Experiment 3 (two-dimensional display). A schematic overview of the stimuli. Objects were presented at 16 possible positions. Two distractors had the same colour as the target, two distractors had the same orientation as the target, and two distractors had both a different colour and a different orientation. The target in this example is a green bar oriented at 70° among red bars also oriented at 70°, green bars oriented at 20°, and red bars oriented at 20°.

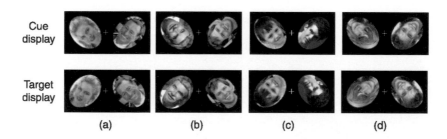

Plate 8.1 Exploring inhibition of object identity in working memory (adapted from Grison et al., 2004). IOR examined in (a) upright–upright condition, (b) inverted–upright condition, (c) upright–inverted condition, (d) inverted–inverted condition. Participants saw all stimuli in colour.

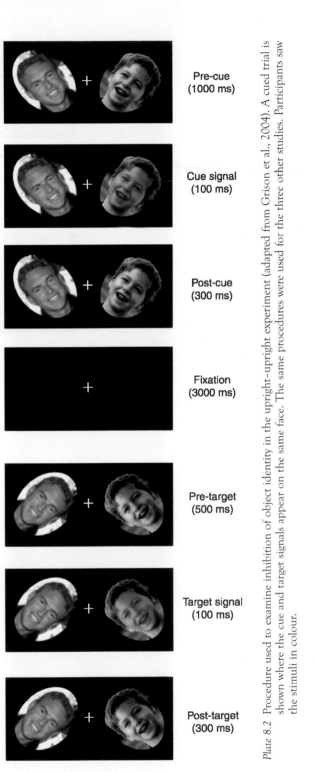

Plate 8.2 Procedure used to examine inhibition of object identity in the upright–upright experiment (adapted from Grison et al., 2004). A cued trial is shown where the cue and target signals appear on the same face. The same procedures were used for the three other studies. Participants saw the stimuli in colour.

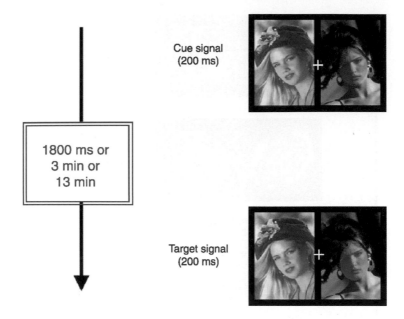

Cue signal
(200 ms)

1800 ms or
3 min or
13 min

Target signal
(200 ms)

Plate 8.3 An excerpt of the procedure used to examine IOR in short-, long- and longer-term tasks (adapted from Tipper et al., 2003). A cued trial is shown where the cue and target are on the same face. Participants saw the stimuli in colour.

(a)   (b)

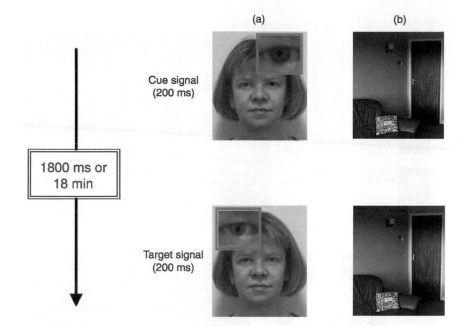

Cue signal
(200 ms)

1800 ms or
18 min

Target signal
(200 ms)

Plate 8.4 An excerpt of the procedure used to examine IOR in short- and long-term tasks (adapted from Grison & Tipper, 2003). The face stimuli show an uncued trial where the cue and target are in different eyes. The close-up views of the eyes are shown for clarity only. The scene stimuli show a cued trial where the cue and target are in the same location. Participants saw the stimuli in colour.

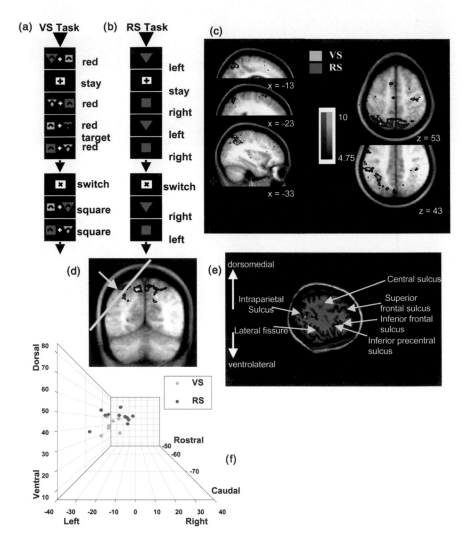

Plate 10.1 (a) VS paradigm. Participants saw pairs of stimuli (*items*) but attended to just one according to a rule based on either colour or shape. Every 9–11 trials a white *cue* instructed either *staying* with the current rule or *switching* to a rule based on the other stimulus dimension. The task was to detect a rare *target*, '∨' (*4th panel*) and respond with a key-press. Both the target and non-target, '∧', were only present for the final 15 ms of the total 70 ms of stimulus presentation. (b) RS paradigm. Participants were presented with a series of task *items* and responded with either left or right hands. Every 9–11 trials a white *cue* instructed either *staying* with the current response selection rule or *switching*. Brain activity related to attentional or intentional conflict is separated mediolaterally and dorsoventrally. Sagittal and axial sections are shown in (c) and a section orthogonal to the main axis of the IPS (d) is shown in (e). The separation is still clear when activations from the two tasks are plotted as if recorded in just the left hemisphere in (f).

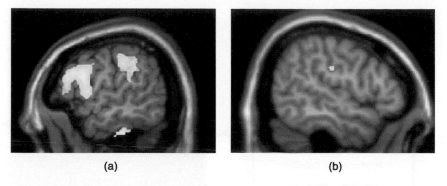

(a)   (b)

Plate 10.2 Activation recorded during a covert motor attention task in the left hemisphere
(a) and the right hemisphere (b). The parietal activation is in the supramarginal
gyrus anterior to the posterior IPS and superior temporal sulcal regions around
the angular gyrus that are activated during covert orienting. The accompanying
frontal activation is in the premotor cortex rather than the frontal eye fields, as
is the case in covert orienting paradigms. Parietal activation is almost exclusively
confined to the left hemisphere. Orienting attention, on the other hand, is
associated with a predominance of activity in the right hemisphere.

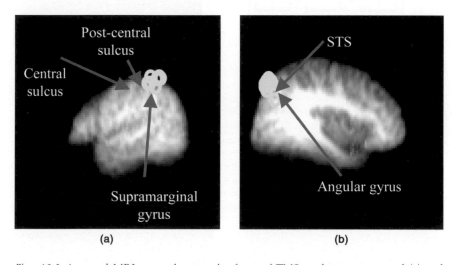

(a)   (b)

Plate 10.3 Averaged MRI scans showing the focus of TMS in the supramarginal (a) and
posterior parietal angular gyral (b) cortices in standard space.

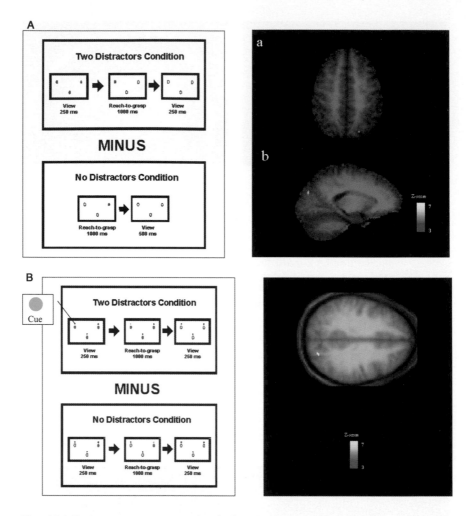

Plate 12.1 Brain activation associated with changing both a target's location and the number of visual stimuli presented before movement initiation. (A) Comparison between the three-stimuli condition (i.e. the two-distractor condition) and the one-stimulus, three possible locations condition (i.e. the no-distractor condition) in Experiment 1. The Talairach coordinates for the right IPS (a) and the left PO sulcus (b) are [x: 22, y: −70, z: 52 (BA7)] and [x: −16, y: −80, z: 36 (BA19)], respectively. (B) The activation found in the right occipital cortex [x: 28, y: −82, z: 22 (BA19)] for the comparison made during Experiment 2. Note that the red dots symbolize the stimuli, while the empty circles represent the locations where the stimuli that do not become targets (i.e. are not extended) are hidden. In (B) the small green dot represents the fibre optic cue.

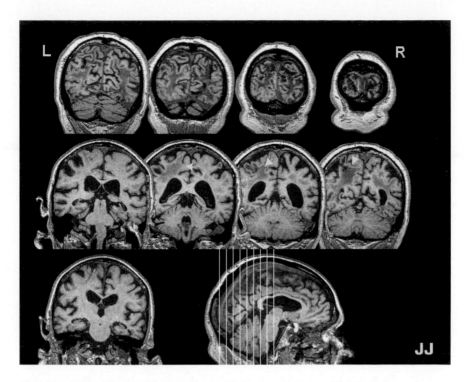

Plate 13.1 T1-weighted MRI scan of case JJ showing asymmetrical bilateral atrophy predominantly of the parietal lobes with the damage to the left parietal cortex extending further into the superior region than is the case within the right hemisphere.

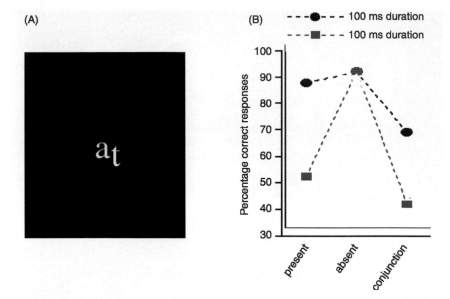

Plate 13.2 (A) Illustration of the visual display used to examine JJ's simultanagnosia. (B) Results of JJ's visual search. When presented with two coloured letters as shown in (A), JJ was required to make a manual response indicating the presence or absence of a target letter (e.g. a "red letter a"). Note JJ's ability to correctly identify target letters was very poor at short durations; he made almost no false-positives on target absent trials in which target colour or target form were not present. In contrast, he made a large number of conjunction errors, even when stimuli were presented for long durations, on target absent trials in which target colour and form were present on different stimuli.

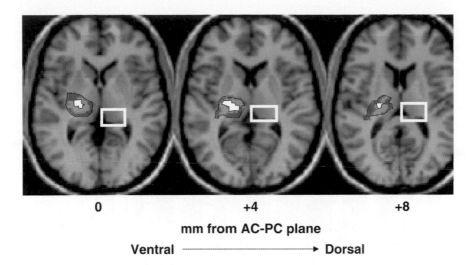

0   **+4**   **+8**

mm from AC-PC plane

Ventral ┈┈┈┈┈┈┈┈┈┈┈┈→ **Dorsal**

Plate 14.1 Normalization and reconstruction of the three cases reported here with unilateral damage to the pulvinar. Two of the cases (SM and CJ) had damage to the left hemisphere and one (TN) to the right, which has been mirror-reversed. The intact pulvinar is outlined in the white box. Colours show overlap of lesions: white = all patients; green = 2; purple = 1. (On grey-scale figure, white marks the site of lesion overlap for all patients, and the outer boundary marks the union of lesion sites for all patients.)

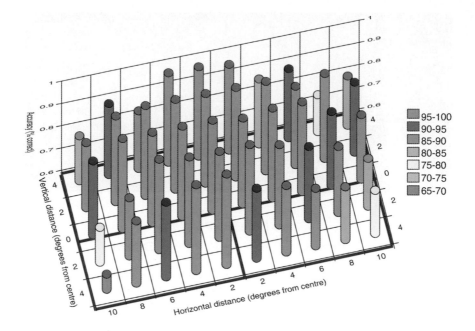

Plate 14.2 Localization accuracy for single targets. TN localized single briefly presented targets using a mouse. Location accuracy is best near the centre of the display and tapers off smoothly towards the periphery. The pattern of performance is roughly equivalent across quadrants.

Part II
Neural processes

9 A map of complex movements in motor cortex of primates

Michael S. A. Graziano,
Charlotte S. R. Taylor,
Dylan F. Cooke and Tirin Moore

Abstract

We used electrical microstimulation to study the organization of motor cortex in awake monkeys. Stimulation on a behaviourally relevant time scale (0.5–1 s) evoked coordinated, complex postures that involved many joints. For example, stimulation of one site caused the mouth to open and also caused the hand to shape into a grip posture and move to the mouth. Stimulation of this site always drove the joints towards this final posture, regardless of the initial posture. Stimulation of other cortical sites evoked different postures. Postures that involved the arm were arranged across cortex to form a map of hand positions around the body. This map encompassed both primary motor and lateral premotor cortex. Primary motor cortex appears to represent the central part of the workspace, where monkeys most often manipulate objects with their fingers. These findings suggest that primary motor and lateral premotor cortex might not be arranged in a hierarchy, but instead might operate in parallel, serving different parts of the workspace.

Introduction

How does the primate cerebral cortex control movement? Over the past century, three interrelated hypotheses have shaped the research. They are now thought to be at least partly incorrect. They are:

1   Primary motor cortex contains a detailed topographic map of the body. The foot is represented at the top of the hemisphere, the mouth is represented at the bottom, and other body parts are systematically arranged in between.
2   Each point in the map specifies the tension in a muscle or small group of related muscles. The pattern of activity across the map thus specifies a pattern of muscle tensions across the body.
3   The cortical motor areas are hierarchically organized. Premotor cortex projects to and controls primary motor cortex, which projects to and controls the spinal cord.

These three hypotheses were summarized as long ago as 1938 by Fulton. Since then a growing body of evidence has cast some doubt on them.

1   Investigators failed to find the hypothesized orderly map of the body in primary motor cortex (Sanes & Schieber, 2001). The somatotopy is fractured and intermingled (Donoghue, LeiBovic, & Sanes, 1992; Gould, Cusick, Pons, & Kaas, 1986; Nudo, Jenkins, Merzenich, Prejean, & Grenda, 1992; Penfield & Boldrey, 1937; Sanes, Donoghue, Thangaraj, Edelman, & Warach, 1995; Schieber & Hibbard, 1993; Woolsey, Settlage, Meyer, Sencer, Hamuy, & Travis, 1952). A broad organization exists, with a medial hind limb region, a lateral face region and a forelimb region in between. These regions partly overlap. The extent of somatotopy within each region is in debate. In the forelimb region, the fingers are represented in an intermingled fashion and overlap at least partly with a representation of the arm (Donoghue et al., 1992; Park, Belhaj-Saif, Gordon, & Cheney, 2001; Schieber & Hibbard, 1993).

2   It is now understood that each site in cortex does not control one muscle. The connectivity is more complex. Some investigators suggest that neurons in motor cortex influence high-level aspects of movement, such as direction or velocity of the hand through space (Caminiti, Johnson, & Urbano, 1990; Georgopoulos, Lurito, Petrides, Schwartz, & Massey, 1989; Georgopoulos, Schwartz, & Kettner, 1986; Reina, Moran, & Schwartz, 2001). Others suggest that joint angle is coded in motor cortex (Scott & Kalaska, 1995, 1997) or that muscle tension is coded, perhaps in a complex fashion in which each location in cortex influences many muscles (Cabel, Cisek, & Scott, 2001; Donoghue et al., 1992; Evarts, 1968; Kakei, Hoffman, & Strick, 1999; Todorov, 2000). Some suggest that several of these movement parameters are simultaneously encoded by motor cortex neurons (Kakei et al., 1999). The debate has not yet been resolved. Indeed, almost every movement parameter that has been tested has been found to be correlated with the activity of motor cortex neurons.

3   The hierarchical organization among the cortical motor areas is in question. Since Fulton (1938), many new motor areas have been described, including the supplementary and cingulate motor areas (He, Dum, & Strick, 1995; Penfield & Welch, 1949; Woolsey et al., 1952) and many subdivisions of premotor cortex (e.g. Rizzolatti & Luppino, 2001; Wise, Boussaoud, Johnson, & Caminiti, 1997). The hierarchical relationship among these areas is not certain, because many of them project to the spinal cord in complex, overlapping patterns (e.g. Dum & Strick, 1991, 1996; Maier, Armond, Kirkwood, Yang, Davis, & Lemon, 2002; Murray & Coulter, 1981). Lesions to the traditional "primary" motor cortex result in a specific deficit in complex finger coordination rather than a general deficit in movement

(e.g. DennyBrown & Botterell, 1947; Kermadi, Liu, Tempini, Wiesend-anger, & Rouiller, 1997; Rouiller, Yu, Moret, Tempini, Wiesendanger, & Liang, 1998; Travis, 1955).

To address some of these unresolved questions, we recently electrically microstimulated sites in motor cortex of monkeys (Graziano, Taylor, & Moore, 2002). Each site was stimulated for 500 ms, matching the time scale of a monkey's natural arm and hand movements (e.g. Georgopoulos et al., 1986; Reina et al., 2001). This stimulation caused the monkey to enact complex, coordinated movements such as reaching, grasping or pantomiming a flinch from a nearby object. The evoked movements were arranged across the cortical surface in a rough map of spatial locations to which the movements were directed. The map included parts of both primary motor and premotor cortex. Primary motor cortex emphasized hand locations in central space and manipulatory postures of the fingers and wrist. Premotor cortex emphasized other regions of space, such as grip postures near the mouth or reaching postures in lateral space.

Our stimulation results are consistent with previous findings; that is, we found a rough somatotopic organization of body parts though not muscles, and systematic differences between the traditional primary motor and premotor areas. However, our results suggest a modification of the traditional hypotheses described above. The results raise the possibility that motor cortex controls movement by means of a map of complex, behaviourally meaningful actions; and that primary and premotor cortex may be different because they encode different types of actions in different parts of space. Our aim here is to evaluate these possibilities in light of previous findings on motor cortex.

The use of electrical stimulation to study brain function

Electrical stimulation of motor cortex dates back to Fritsch and Hitzig (1870), who used stimulating electrodes on the surface of the dog brain to demonstrate a rough somatotopic organization. Over the next 80 years, many experiments obtained similar results in monkeys, apes and humans (e.g. Ferrier, 1873; Foerster, 1936; Fulton, 1938; Penfield & Boldrey, 1937; Sanes & Schieber, 2001; Woolsey et al., 1952).

Asanuma and colleagues pioneered the use of low currents delivered through a microelectrode (e.g. Asanuma, 1975; Asanuma & Arnold, 1975; Asanuma, Arnold, & Zarzecki, 1976; Stoney, Thompson, & Asanuma, 1968). This technique was subsequently used by many others (e.g. Huntley & Jones, 1991; Kurata, 1989; Sato & Tanji, 1989; Sessle & Wiesendanger, 1982; Stepniewska, Preuss, & Kaas, 1993; Strick & Preston, 1978; Weinrich & Wise, 1982; Wu, Bichot, & Kaas, 2000). Most of these experiments used brief trains of electrical pulses, each train typically less than 20 ms, to evoke a muscle twitch. The purpose of these previous studies was to map the location on the body affected by stimulation, rather than to study the evoked movement itself.

Microstimulation has now become widely used to study the function of many brain areas outside of motor cortex. When applied on a behaviourally relevant time scale, stimulation can evoke complex effects that appear to mimic the function of the directly stimulated tissue. For example, Newsome and colleagues (Salzman, Britten, & Newsome, 1990) stimulated monkey visual area MT and influenced the monkey's perceptual decisions about the motion of visual stimuli. Romo, Hernandez, Zainos, and Salinas (1998) stimulated primary somatosensory cortex and influenced the monkey's perceptual decisions about tactile stimuli. Electrical stimulation has been used to reveal functional maps of eye and head movement (e.g. Bruce, Goldberg, Bushnell, & Stanton, 1995; Freedman, Stanford, & Sparks, 1996; Gottlieb, Bruce, & MacAvoy, 1993; Robinson, 1972; Robinson & Fuchs, 1969; Schiller & Stryker, 1972; Tehovnik & Lee, 1993; Thier & Andersen, 1998). Complex sexual behaviour and feeding behaviour can be elicited by stimulation of portions of the hypothalamus (Caggiula & Hoebel, 1966; Hoebel, 1969; Okada, Aou, Takaki, Oomura, & Hori, 1991; Quaade, Vaernet, Larsson, 1974).

In these studies using electrical stimulation to probe the function of a brain area, stimulation activates not only the neuronal elements near the electrode tip, but also a network of neurons sharing connections with those directly stimulated. Thus, the effect of electrical stimulation is thought to depend on a spread of signal through physiologically relevant brain circuits.

It is important to note that electrical stimulation is non-physiological and thus should always be interpreted with caution. It can presumably activate neurons in unnatural patterns. The technique is most convincing when the evoked behaviours resemble naturally occurring behaviours, are organized in the brain in an orderly functional architecture, and match other known properties of the brain area such as single neuron properties and the effects of lesions.

As described in the next section, we stimulated motor and premotor cortex for 500 ms, on the same time scale as the reaching movements that monkeys typically make, and also on the same time scale as the elevated activity of motor cortex neurons during reaching (e.g. Georgopoulos et al., 1986; Reina et al., 2001). This duration of stimulation is within the range of the studies cited above, and the current intensities that we used are within the range used in the oculomotor studies.

A map of complex postures evoked by microstimulation in motor cortex

In this section, we first describe the results of stimulation on a behavioural time scale of several example sites in motor cortex. Then we summarize the two main findings.

On stimulation of one site (Figure 9.1a), the contralateral hand closed into a typical precision grip posture for a monkey, with the fingers together and slightly curled and the tip of the thumb against the side of the forefinger. The wrist and forearm rotated such that the point of the grip faced the mouth. The elbow and shoulder rotated such that the hand moved smoothly to the mouth, in a manner and with a velocity profile that matched the monkey's normal hand-to-mouth movements. The mouth opened. All of these movements occurred simultaneously. The hand moved to the mouth regardless of its starting position. Once the hand reached the space in front of the mouth, it stayed at that location; the hand, arm and mouth remained in this final posture until the end of the stimulation train. The movement was repeatable and consistent across hundreds of trials and occurred even after the monkey was anaesthetized.

Stimulation of another site (Figure 9.1b) caused the contralateral elbow and shoulder to rotate such that the hand moved to a position about 10 cm in front of the chest. The hand opened into a splayed posture with the fingers straight and separated from each other. The forearm supinated such that the open palm was aimed towards the monkey's face. For this site as for the last

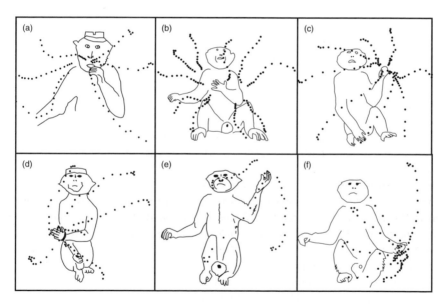

Figure 9.1 Six examples of complex postures evoked by stimulation of the precentral gyrus. Stimulation of each cortical site in the right hemisphere evoked a different final posture of the left hand and arm. Drawings were traced from video footage taped at 30 frames per second. The dotted lines show the frame-by-frame position of the hand during stimulation. Regardless of the starting position, stimulation caused the hand to move towards a specific final position. Adapted from Graziano et al. (2002).

site, stimulation evoked the same final posture regardless of the direction of motion required to reach the posture.

Stimulation of other cortical sites evoked other complex movements (e.g. Figure 9.2c–f). These movements had two basic properties:

1   Stimulation drove the relevant joints towards a final posture, regardless of the starting posture. The joints then remained in that final posture until the stimulation train ended. Thus we did not evoke sequences of movements or repetitive movements. We did not evoke a specific direction of movement; opposing directions could be obtained depending on the starting position.

2   Sites that involved movement of the arm were arranged across the precentral gyrus to form a rough map of evoked hand position (Figure 9.2). Hand position, however, was not the only variable specified by stimulation of this map. The posture of the entire arm and sometimes of the wrist and fingers was specified. The acceleration and speed of movement to the final posture also varied among sites. Because many muscles and joints contribute to such movement towards a complex posture, the map of postures may help to explain the long-standing puzzle that different muscles and joints are represented in an intermingled fashion in motor cortex (Sanes & Schieber, 2001).

Movement variables controlled by motor cortex

Georgopoulos et al. (1986) trained monkeys to reach in various directions from a central starting position and found that neurons in motor cortex responded during the reach. Each neuron generally responded most during one direction of reach and responded less well during neighbouring directions. That is, the neurons were tuned to the direction of reach. Although each neuron was broadly tuned, the authors pointed out that a population of such neurons could collectively provide precise spatial information about the direction of reach.

Other experiments suggested that the code for movement in motor cortex must be more complex than a simple direction code. Many groups have demonstrated that the firing of motor cortex neurons is correlated with parameters such as the angles of joints, the force applied by the arm muscles, and the velocity of the hand movement in space (Cabel et al., 2001; Caminiti et al., 1990; Georgopoulos, Ashe, Smyrnis, & Taira, 1992; Kakei et al., 1999; Kalaska, Cohen, Hyde, & Prud'homme, 1989; Reina et al., 2001; Scott & Kalaska, 1995, 1997).

Scott and Kalaska (1995, 1997) showed that the directional preference of most neurons changed when the monkey was required to maintain a different arm posture, with the elbow raised. Thus the neurons seemed sensitive to the posture of the entire arm and how that posture changed over time, rather than reflecting only the changing position of the hand in space. Scott and

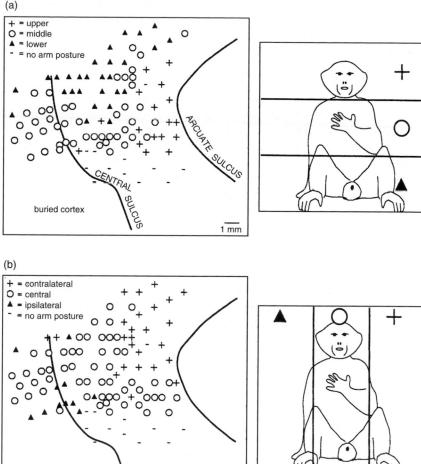

Figure 9.2 Topography of hand and arm postures in the precentral gyrus, based on 201 stimulation sites. Sites plotted to the left of the central sulcus were located in the anterior bank of the sulcus. (a) Distribution of hand positions along the vertical axis, in upper, middle and lower space. Each site was categorized based on the centre of the range of evoked final positions. Height categories were defined as follows: lower = 0–12 cm from bottom of monkey, middle = 12–24 cm, upper = 24–36 cm. Dashes show electrode penetrations where no arm postures were found; usually the postures from these locations involved the mouth or face. (b) Distribution of hand positions along the horizontal axis, in contralateral, central or ipsilateral space. Horizontal categories were defined as follows: contralateral = 6–18 cm contralateral to midline, central = within 6 cm of midline (central 12 cm of space), ipsilateral = 6–18 cm ipsilateral to midline. Adapted from Graziano et al. (2002).

colleagues speculated that motor cortex neurons may control so-called intrinsic variables, such as muscle force and joint angle, rather than extrinsic variables, such as the position or movement of the hand in external space. Other experiments (Kakei et al., 1999) suggest that, in the case of wrist movements, the firing of motor cortex neurons is correlated with both intrinsic and extrinsic variables.

These single-neuron experiments have the limitation that they test the correlation between neuronal activity and a restricted set of simple movements. Neurons that encode complex movements might produce a confusing and diverse pattern of results when filtered through these simpler tasks. Electrical stimulation can help to resolve this difficulty, because it is a causal technique rather than a correlational one. It is possible to measure the movement that is caused by activity at a location in motor cortex.

Does electrical stimulation of motor cortex specify hand location in space, individual joint angles, or the muscle forces involved in producing a particular velocity profile? Our results suggest that all of these aspects of movement may be specified. Stimulation of each site within the arm and hand representation evoked a movement to a specific, final posture. Because the arm posture was specified, the location to which the hand moved was also specified. However, each site did not appear to encode only hand location, independent of the joint angles that composed the arm posture. There are many postures of the arm that can correspond to the same hand location, and stimulation of one site specified only one arm posture. Thus our results agree closely with the findings of Scott and Kalaska (1995, 1997) in that the posture of the arm, not merely the position or movement of the hand, appears to be of critical importance.

Dynamic aspects of movement such as the acceleration of the hand also appeared to depend on the cortical site that was stimulated. For example, for a hand-to-mouth movement, the velocity profile of the hand was appropriate for putting food in the mouth without damaging the face (e.g. 20 cm/s at peak speed for one stimulation site). For a movement in which the hand moved to an upper lateral position and turned outward as if to block an impending threat to the head, the velocity was appropriately fast, consistent with a defensive gesture (230 cm/s at peak speed for one stimulation site).

These stimulation results suggest that movement control in motor cortex might be organized in terms of behaviourally useful actions aimed towards a goal posture. In this case, asking whether the control is extrinsic, intrinsic, kinematic or dynamic may be the wrong question, or at least a question with a complex answer. Movement control in motor cortex may involve all of these aspects of movement processing, perhaps to differing degrees for different types of movement.

Relationship between primary motor and premotor cortex

The map of stimulation-evoked arm postures that we obtained encompassed the forelimb representation in primary motor cortex, and also premotor cortex including ventral premotor (F4 and F5) and dorsal premotor (probably mainly PMDc). These areas appeared to be part of a complete, unitary map of the position of the hand in space. How can a single map be reconciled with the mosaic of separate areas described within this region of cortex?

The map of postures appeared to contain specialized subregions with different functions (Figure 9.3). One subregion corresponded to hand locations at the mouth (circles in Figure 9.3). Stimulation within this region always caused the hand to shape into a grip posture. At most hand-to-mouth sites, stimulation also caused the mouth to open. Rizzolatti and colleagues (Fogassi, Gallese, Buccino, Craighero, Fadiga, & Rizzolatti, 2001; Murata, Fadiga, Fogassi, Gallese, Raos, & Rizzolatti, 1997; Rizzolatti, Camarda, Fogassi, Gentilucci, Luppino, & Matelli, 1988) recorded from single neurons in this area, which they termed F5, and found that the neurons responded selectively during grip postures of the hand and movements of the mouth. Neurons in F5 were also active during movements of the arm, especially towards the mouth.

A second functionally distinct subregion of the map corresponded to hand locations in the space in front of the chest (triangles in Figure 9.3).

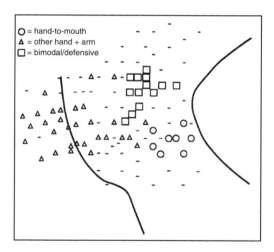

Figure 9.3 Specialized subregions within the map of stimulation-evoked postures. Circles show hand-to-mouth sites; these always involved a grip posture of the hand in addition to a movement of the arm that brought the hand to the mouth. Triangles show other sites where stimulation evoked both a hand and an arm posture; these sites often involved the hand moving into central space and the fingers shaping into a specific configuration. Squares show sites where bimodal, visual–tactile responses were found and stimulation evoked defensive movements. Adapted from Graziano et al. (2002).

Stimulation within this part of the map evoked a variety of hand postures, including a grip with the thumb against the forefinger, a fist, an open hand with all digits splayed, rotations of the wrist, and pronation or supination of the forearm, matching the natural behaviour of monkeys during manipulation of objects within central space. This part of cortex corresponded to the primary motor forelimb representation, an area that has long been known to emphasize the control of fine movements of the fingers. Lesions to it cause a deficit in manual dexterity (e.g. DennyBrown & Botterell, 1947; Kermadi et al., 1997; Rouiller et al., 1998; Travis, 1955). The direct projections from primary motor cortex to the spinal motor neurons tend to be related to the muscles of the hand and wrist (Bortoff & Strick, 1993; Lawrence, 1994; Lemon, Baker, Davis, Kirkwood, Maier, & Yang, 1998; Maier, Olivier, Baker, Kirkwood, Morris, & Lemon, 1997). The lowest electrical thresholds in motor cortex are correlated with movements of the hand and wrist (Asanuma et al., 1976; Gentilucci, Fogassi, Luppino, Matelli, Camarda, & Rizzolatti, 1988). Neurons in primary motor cortex, especially in the posterior part, respond during movements of the fingers, and have small tactile receptive fields on the fingers (Gentilucci et al., 1988; Lemon & Porter, 1976; Wong, Kwan, MacKay, & Murphy, 1978). On the basis of our data, we suggest that the emphasis on manual dexterity may be paired with an emphasis on hand locations in central space, the monkey's "manual fovea" in which manipulation is most commonly performed.

A third subregion of the map (squares in Figure 9.3) contained neurons that responded to tactile stimuli on the face and arms, and visual stimuli near the face and arms. Stimulation of these sites evoked apparent defensive movements. This multimodal subregion is described in greater detail in the next section. It matches a part of premotor cortex where bimodal, tactile–visual neurons have been reported previously (Fogassi, Gallese, Fadiga, Luppino, Matelli, & Rizzolatti, 1996; Graziano & Gandhi, 2000; Graziano, Hu, & Gross, 1997; Graziano, Reiss, & Gross, 1999; Rizzolatti, Scandolara, Matelli, & Gentilucci, 1981).

The single map that we obtained with electrical stimulation, therefore, may be consistent with previous findings of a mosaic of subregions. The single map also provides a possible organizing principle. The subregions may differ because they emphasize the types of actions that monkeys tend to make in different regions of space.

Multimodal neurons and the coding of a margin of safety

In addition to its motor output, the precentral gyrus also receives sensory input presumably for the guidance of movement. One class of precentral neuron has a distinctive type of response to tactile and visual stimuli. These bimodal neurons typically have a tactile receptive field on the face, arm or torso and a visual receptive field adjacent to the tactile receptive field, extending 5–30 cm into the space surrounding the body (Fogassi et al., 1996;

(a)

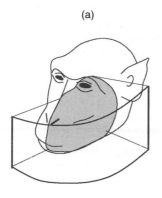

(b)

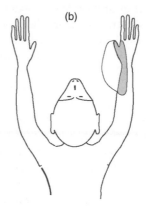

Figure 9.4 Receptive fields of two bimodal, visual–tactile cells in the polysensory zone. (a) The tactile receptive field (shaded) is on the snout and the visual receptive field (boxed) is confined to a region of space within about 10 cm of the tactile receptive field. Both receptive fields are mainly on the side of the face contralateral to the recording electrode. (b) The tactile receptive field for this neuron is on the contralateral hand and forearm and the visual receptive field surrounds the tactile receptive field.

Graziano et al, 1997; Rizzolatti et al., 1981) (see Figure 9.4). Recently, we found that a subset of these multimodal neurons are trimodal; they have spatially corresponding tactile, visual and auditory receptive fields (Graziano et al., 1999). We found that the multimodal neurons are clustered just posterior to the bend in the arcuate sulcus (Graziano & Gandhi, 2000; see also squares in Figure 9.3). They are concentrated in the dorsal part of F4, within ventral premotor cortex (PMv). Recently we termed this cluster of polysensory neurons the "polysensory zone" (PZ) (Graziano & Gandhi, 2000).

We found that for most of the multisensory neurons, the visual receptive field is anchored to the site of the tactile receptive field. For a cell with a tactile receptive field on the arm, when the arm is moved, the adjacent visual receptive field moves in tandem with the arm; when the eyes or the head move and the arm is stationary, the visual receptive field does not move and remains anchored to the arm (Graziano et al., 1997). For a cell with a tactile receptive field on the face, when the head is rotated, the visual receptive field moves in tandem with the head; when the eyes or the arm move and the head is stationary, the visual receptive field does not move and remains anchored to the head (Fogassi et al., 1996; Graziano et al, 1997). These cells therefore appear to encode the locations of nearby visual stimuli with respect to the body surface, in "body-part-centred" coordinates.

The visual and tactile modalities of these neurons match not only in spatial location but also in directional preference (Graziano et al., 1997;

Rizzolatti et al., 1981). For example, a cell that prefers a rightward moving stimulus in the tactile modality will also prefer a rightward moving stimulus in the visual modality. At least some cells respond preferentially to visual stimuli moving towards the animal on a collision course with the tactile receptive field.

Although the sensory properties of the multimodal neurons have been extensively characterized, their function was unknown. We speculated that they may play a general role in the sensory guidance of movement, contributing to reaching towards, pulling away from, nudging, reaching around and other movements in relation to nearby objects (Graziano et al., 1997; Graziano & Gross, 1998). However, we had no direct evidence for the motor functions of these neurons.

To address the question of function, we electrically stimulated sites within PZ (Graziano et al., 2002). Stimulation elicited movements that were consistent with defending the body against threatening objects. Different movements were evoked depending on the location of the sensory receptive fields. For example, at some sites the neurons had a tactile receptive field on the side of the head and a visual receptive field near the tactile receptive field. Stimulation of this type of site evoked movements consistent with defending the side of the head from an impending threat. These movements included a closure of the eye and facial grimace that was more pronounced on the side of the sensory receptive field; a turning of the head away from the side of the sensory receptive field; a rapid movement of the hand to an upper lateral location as if blocking an object in the sensory receptive field; and a turning outward of the palm (Figure 9.5a). At other sites, the neurons had a tactile receptive field on the arm and a visual receptive field near the arm. Stimulation of this type of site evoked a fast withdrawal of the arm behind the back. These movements resulted in the hand reaching a final position in lower space, generally beside the thigh or hip (Figure 9.5b). Defensive-like movements were obtained even when the monkey was anaesthetized, and thus appeared to be unrelated to the monkey's behavioural context. On the basis of these results, we now suggest that the multisensory neurons within PZ do not serve a general function in the sensory guidance of movement, but instead serve a highly specific function, locating nearby threatening stimuli and organizing the appropriate defensive movements.

Similar neuronal responses to tactile and visual stimuli have been described in area VIP in the parietal lobe. VIP neurons typically have a tactile receptive field on the contralateral side of the face and a visual receptive field that corresponds spatially. (Colby, Duhamel, & Goldberg, 1993; Duhamel, Bremmer, BenHamed, & Gref, 1997; Duhamel, Colby, & Goldberg, 1998; Schaafsma & Duysens, 1996). About half of the neurons respond best to nearby visual stimuli, within 30 cm of the tactile receptive field (Colby et al., 1993). The tactile and visual modalities generally share the same directional preference (Colby et al., 1993). For about half the neurons, the visual receptive field remains stationary in space when the eyes move, and is presumed to

TACTILE AND VISUAL
RECEPTIVE FIELDS

EVOKED POSTURE

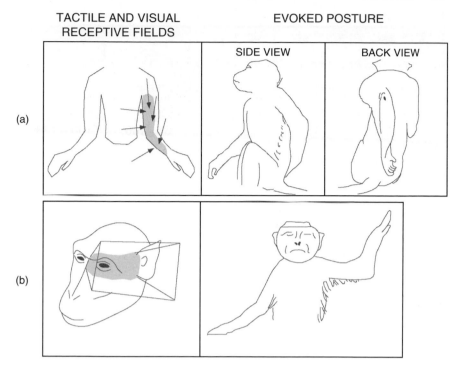

Figure 9.5 Defensive movements evoked from sites in area PZ. (a) Neurons at this site
responded to a touch on the arm (within the shaded area) and to
nearby visual stimuli moving towards the arm (indicated by arrows).
Microstimulation caused the arm to move to a posture behind the back.
(b) Multineuron activity at this site responded to a touch on the contralateral upper part of the face and to visual stimuli in the space near this
tactile receptive field. Microstimulation evoked a complex defensive posture involving a facial squint, a head turn, and the arm and hand moving to
a guarding position. Adapted from Graziano et al. (2002).

be anchored to the head (Duhamel et al., 1997, 1998). Thus almost identical
response properties have been found in VIP and PZ, although the propor-
tions of cell types are somewhat different. This similarity is especially interesting because VIP projects to the premotor cortex, and its main area of
projection appears to be PZ (Lewis & Van Essen, 2000; Luppino, Murata,
Govoni, & Matelli, 1999).

We recently found that stimulation of area VIP evoked defensive movements similar to those evoked by stimulation of area PZ (Cooke, Taylor,
Moore, & Graziano, 2002). Stimulation of cortex surrounding area VIP did
not evoke the same movements. Figure 9.6a shows video frames of a defensive movement evoked by electrical stimulation of a site in area VIP. The
figure shows a short latency closure of the eye and lifting of the upper lip on
the side of the face contralateral to the recording electrode. Figure 9.6b

(a)

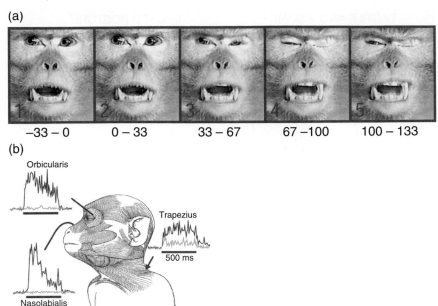

| −33 – 0 | 0 – 33 | 33 – 67 | 67 –100 | 100 – 133 |

(b)

Orbicularis

Trapezius

500 ms

Nasolabialis

Figure 9.6 Defensive movements evoked by stimulation of parietal area VIP. (a) An example of a facial flinch evoked by microstimulation of VIP. Images captured from video at 30 frames per second. Numbers beneath each frame indicate time in milliseconds relative to stimulation onset. By frame 3, the monkey's left eye (contralateral to stimulation) began to close and the left upper lip began to lift exposing the teeth. By frame 4, the lifting of the skin on the left snout was more pronounced, deforming the left nostril. The left eye was closed the right eye was partially closed and the left brow had lowered. Stimulation of this site also caused the ear to pull back and down and the left arm to move to the left. Stimulation at 200 μA for 500 ms. (b) EMG activity evoked by stimulation of an example site in VIP. EMG from orbicularis oculi muscle causing squint; nasolabialis muscle causing lifting of upper lip and facial skin; trapezius muscle causing shoulder shrug. Dark lines = EMG from muscles on the left side of body (contralateral to stimulation); light lines = EMG from muscles on the right side of body. Shoulder shrug was bilateral but stronger on the left side. Each EMG trace is the mean of 15 trials rectified and integrated in 10 ms bins. Horizontal line = stimulation period; y-axis in arbitrary units.

shows the EMG traces from three muscles during a stimulation-evoked flinching movement.

One hypothesis is that areas VIP and PZ form part of a pathway that is specialized for encoding nearby space and defending the body.

Postural coding as a general method of movement control

The idea of movement control by means of postural coding is not new. It has been particularly successful in the study of speech and of facial expressions. In speech, each phoneme may be defined by a posture of the vocal tract, including the mouth, tongue and larynx (Fowler, Rubin, Remez, & Turvey, 1980). To produce a phoneme, the speaking apparatus moves towards this final posture. It does not need to achieve the final posture, but only to move towards it. For example, in this view a given vowel "is an equivalence set of gestures that are equivalent because they all aim toward some particular limiting shape and length of the vocal tract" (Fowler et al., 1980). Speech is composed of a sequence of these gestures towards defined postures. Why should speech have evolved in this fashion? One possibility is that the mechanisms for speech were built on a pre-existing mechanism for motor control, one that emphasized the specification of complex, behaviourally useful postures. When we stimulated in the ventral part of the precentral gyrus, in the mouth and face representation, we often caused the lips and tongue to move towards specific postures (Graziano et al., 2002). For example, at one site, stimulation caused the mouth to open about 2 cm and the tongue to move to a particular location in the mouth. Regardless of the starting posture of the tongue or jaw, stimulation evoked a movement towards this final configuration. This type of posture may be useful to a monkey for eating, but could also be an evolutionary precursor to the phoneme.

Facial expressions appear to be controlled in a manner strikingly similar to the phonemes in spoken language. An emotional expression is conveyed by the movement of the facial musculature towards a particular posture (Ekman, 1993). A frown, a smile, an angry expression, a surprised expression, a disgust face, all these can be categorized by their archetypal final postures. However, even a subtle movement towards this postural endpoint will vividly convey an emotion to the viewer. Thus, again, the system appears to operate by means of a repertoire of complex postures towards which movements are made.

Could limb movements also be controlled at some level by means of a stored set of postures? Rosenbaum, Loukopoulos, Meulenbroek, Vaughan, and Engelbrecht (1995) proposed a model for limb control that uses linear combinations taken from a basis set of stored postures. The map of postures that we evoked by electrical stimulation in motor cortex could provide a basis for this method of limb control. The map in motor cortex is similar to a map of leg postures evoked by electrical stimulation of the spinal cord in frogs and rats (Giszter, Mussa-Ivaldi, & Bizzi, 1993; Tresch & Bizzi, 1999); thus the spinal cord might also control movement partly at the level of posture.

In motor control, there is a subtle but important distinction between specifying a final posture and specifying a trajectory that is aimed towards a final posture. An example of a control algorithm that specifies only the final posture is the equilibrium position hypothesis. According to this hypothesis, limb movement is controlled by specifying only a final set of muscle tensions (Bizzi, Accornero, Chapple, & Hogan 1984). If the muscles acquire that set of tensions and maintain them in a steady state, the limb will move to the desired final posture and remain there. The equilibrium position hypothesis is now known to be incorrect. During a limb movement to a specified posture, the muscles do not acquire a fixed set of tensions, but rather perform a complex dance of activity, resulting in a smooth path (Bizzi et al., 1984; Brown & Cooke, 1990; Hallett, Shahani, & Young, 1975; Morasso, 1981). This complex pattern of muscle activity depends on both the initial and final position of the arm. Thus the entire trajectory of the arm is specified, not only the desired final configuration.

The stimulation-evoked postures that we found in motor cortex follow the pattern of muscle activation observed during normal movement, rather than the pattern predicted by the equilibrium position hypothesis. Stimulation evokes a complex pattern of muscle activity in the upper arm that resembles the interplay between agonist and antagonist muscles observed during natural movement. This pattern of muscle activity depends on the starting position of the arm. Thus stimulation specifies more than just a final posture; it specifies the entire, coordinated trajectory that is aimed towards the final posture.

A final caveat

A final caveat is in order. Motor cortex is obviously highly complex, and may control movement by means of many overlapping strategies. This complexity is reflected in the diverse effects of stimulation, including movement of the hand to a location in space, movement of joints towards a final posture, movement at different speeds, and an emphasis on controlling the hand and fingers in certain regions of cortex. At the single neuron level, even more diversity has been found in coding schemes for movement. The coding scheme may even vary depending on the type of movement or the part of the map studied. For example, the manipulation of objects may employ a specialized anatomical and physiological machinery in which the cortex exerts an especially direct control over spinal motor neurons. It is probably incorrect to assign a single motor-control algorithm to motor cortex. Here we suggest that one of possibly many strategies used by motor cortex involves a topographic map of postures that are of behavioural relevance to the animal.

References

Asanuma, H. (1975). Recent developments in the study of the columnar arrangement of neurons within the motor cortex. *Physiological Review, 55,* 143–156.

Asanuma, H., & Arnold, A. P. (1975). Noxious effects of excessive currents used for intracortical microstimulation. *Brain Research, 96,* 103–107.

Asanuma, H., Arnold, A., & Zarzecki, P. (1976). Further study on the excitation of pyramidal tract cells by intracortical microstimulation. *Experimental Brain Research*, 26, 443–461.

Bizzi, E., Accornero, N., Chapple, W., & Hogan, N. (1984). Posture control and trajectory formation during arm movement. *Journal of Neuroscience*, 4, 2738–2744.

Bortoff, G. A., & Strick P. L. (1993). Corticospinal terminations in two new-world primates: further evidence that corticomotoneuronal connections provide part of the neural substrate for manual dexterity. *Journal of Neuroscience*, 13, 5105–5118.

Brown, S. H. and Cooke, J. D. (1990). Movement-related phasic muscle activation I. Relations with temporal profiles of movement. *Journal of Neurophysiology*, 63, 455–464.

Bruce, C. J., Goldberg, M. E., Bushnell, M. C., & Stanton, G. B. (1985). Primate frontal eye fields. II. Physiological and anatomical correlates of electrically evoked eye movements. *Journal of Neurophysiology*, 54, 714–734.

Cabel, D. W., Cisek, P., & Scott, S. H. (2001). Neural activity in primary motor cortex related to mechanical loads applied to the shoulder and elbow during a postural task. *Journal of Neurophysiology*, 86, 2102–2108.

Caggiula, A. R., & Hoebel, B. G. (1966). "Copulation-reward site" in the posterior hypothalamus. *Science*, 153, 1284–1285.

Caminiti, R., Johnson, P. B., & Urbano, A. (1990). Making arm movements within different parts of space: dynamic aspects in the primate motor cortex. *Journal of Neuroscience*, 10, 2039–2058.

Colby, C. L., Duhamel, J.-R., & Goldberg, M. E. (1993). Ventral intraparietal area of the macaque: anatomic location and visual response properties. *Journal of Neurophysiology*, 69, 902–914.

Cooke, D. F., Taylor, C. S. R., Moore, T., & Graziano, M. S. A. (2003). Complex movements evoked by microstimulation of Area VIP. *Proceedings of the National Academy of Sciences*, 100, 6163–6168.

DennyBrown, D., & Botterell, E. H. (1947). The motor function of the agranular frontal cortex. *Research Publications: Association for Research in Nervous and Mental Disease*, 27, 235–345.

Donoghue, J. P., LeiBovic, S., & Sanes, J. N. (1992). Organization of the forelimb area in squirrel monkey motor cortex: representation of digit, wrist, and elbow muscles. *Experimental Brain Research*, 89, 1–19.

Duhamel, J., Bremmer, F., BenHamed, S., & Gref, W. (1997). Spatial invariance of visual receptive fields in parietal cortex neurons. *Nature*, 389, 845–848.

Duhamel, J. R., Colby, C. L., & Goldberg, M. E. (1998). Ventral intraparietal area of the macaque: congruent visual and somatic response properties. *Journal of Neurophysiology*, 79, 126–136.

Dum, R. P., & Strick, P. L. (1991). The origin of corticospinal projections from the premotor areas in the frontal lobe. *Journal Neuroscience*, 11, 667–689.

Dum, R. P., & Strick, P. L. (1996). Spinal cord terminations of the medial wall motor areas in macaque monkeys. *Journal Neuroscience*, 16, 6513–6525.

Ekman, P. (1993). Facial expression and emotion. *American Psychologist*, 48, 384–392.

Evarts, E. V. (1968). Relation of pyramidal tract activity to force exerted during voluntary movement. *Journal Neurophysiology*, 31, 14–27.

Ferrier, D. (1873). Experimental researches in cerebral physiology and pathology. *West Riding Lunatic Asylum Medical Reports*, 3, 30–96.

Foerster, O. (1936). The motor cortex of man in the light of Hughlings Jackson's doctrines. *Brain, 59*, 135–159.

Fogassi, L., Gallese, V., Buccino, G., Craighero, L., Fadiga, L., & Rizzolatti, G. (2001). Cortical mechanism for the visual guidance of hand grasping movements in the monkey: a reversible inactivation study. *Brain, 124*, 571–586.

Fogassi, L., Gallese, V., Fadiga, L., Luppino, G., Matelli, M., & Rizzolatti, G. (1996). Coding of peripersonal space in inferior premotor cortex (area F4). *Journal of Neurophysiology, 76*, 141–157.

Fowler, C. A., Rubin, P., Remez, R. E., & Turvey, M. T. (1980). Implications for speech production of a general theory of action. In B. Buttersworth (Ed.), *Language production, Vol. 1: Speech and talk* (pp. 373–420). London: Academic Press.

Freedman, E. G., Stanford, T. R., & Sparks, D. L. (1996). Combined eye–head gaze shifts produced by electrical stimulation of the superior colliculus in rhesus monkeys. *Journal of Neurophysiology, 76*, 927–952.

Fritsch, G., & Hitzig, E. (1870). *Ueber die elektrishe Erregarkeit des Grosshirns.* Translated by G. von Bonin (1960), *The cerebral cortex* (W. W. Nowinski, ed.) (pp. 73–96). Springfield, IL: Thomas.

Fulton, J. F. (1938). *Physiology of the nervous system* (pp. 399–457). New York: Oxford University Press.

Gentilucci, M., Fogassi, L., Luppino, G., Matelli, M., Camarda, R., & Rizzolatti G. (1988). Functional organization of inferior area 6 in the macaque monkey. I. Somatotopy and the control of proximal movements. *Experimental Brain Research, 71*, 475–490.

Georgopoulos, A. P., Ashe, J., Smyrnis, N., & Taira, M. (1992). The motor cortex and the coding of force. *Science, 256*, 1692–1695.

Georgopoulos, A. P., Lurito, J. T., Petrides, M., Schwartz, A. B., & Massey, J. T. (1989). Mental rotation of the neuronal population vector. *Science, 243*, 234–236.

Georgopoulos, A. P., Schwartz, A. B., & Kettner, R. E. (1986). Neuronal population coding of movement direction. *Science, 233*, 1416–1419.

Giszter, S. F., Mussa-Ivaldi, F. A., & Bizzi, E. (1993). Convergent force fields organized in the frog's spinal cord. *Journal of Neuroscience, 13*, 467–491.

Gottlieb, J. P., Bruce, C. J., & MacAvoy, M. G. (1993). Smooth eye movements elicited by microstimulation in the primate frontal eye field. *Journal of Neurophysiology, 69*, 786–799.

Gould, H. J., III, Cusick, C. G., Pons, T. P., & Kaas, J. H. (1986). The relationship of corpus callosum connections to electrical stimulation maps of motor, supplementary motor, and the frontal eye fields in owl monkeys. *Journal of Comparative Neurology, 247*, 297–325.

Graziano, M. S. A., & Gandhi, S. (2000). Location of the polysensory zone in the precentral gyrus of anesthetized monkeys. *Experimental Brain Research, 135*, 259–266.

Graziano, M. S. A., & Gross, C. G. (1998). Spatial maps for the control of movement. *Current Opinion in Neurobiology, 8*, 195–201.

Graziano, M. S. A., Hu, X., & Gross, C. G. (1997). Visuospatial properties of ventral premotor cortex. *Journal of Neurophysiology, 77*, 2268–2292.

Graziano, M. S. A., Reiss, L. A. J., & Gross, C. G. (1999). A neuronal representation of the location of nearby sounds. *Nature, 397*, 428–430.

Graziano, M. S. A., Taylor, C. S. R., & Moore, T. (2002). Complex movements evoked by microstimulation of precentral cortex. *Neuron, 34,* 841–851.

Hallett, M., Shahani, B. T., & Young, R. R. (1975). EMG analysis of stereotyped voluntary movements in man. *Journal of Neurology, Neurosurgery and Psychiatry, 38,* 1154–1162.

He, S. Q., Dum, R. P., & Strick, P. L. (1995). Topographic organization of cortico-spinal projections from the frontal lobe: motor areas on the medial surface of the hemisphere. *Journal of Neuroscience, 15,* 3284–3306.

Hoebel, B. G. (1969). Feeding and self-stimulation. *Annals of the New York Academy of Sciences, 157,* 758–778.

Huntley, G. W., & Jones, E. G. (1991). Relationship of intrinsic connections to fore-limb movement representations in monkey motor cortex: a correlative anatomic and physiological study. *Journal of Neurophysiology, 66,* 390–413.

Kakei, S., Hoffman, D., & Strick, P. (1999). Muscle and movement representations in the primary motor cortex. *Science, 285,* 2136–2139.

Kalaska, J. F., Cohen, D. A., Hyde, M. L., & Prud'homme, M. A. (1989). Comparison of movement direction-related versus load direction-related activity in primate motor cortex, using a two-dimensional reaching task. *Journal of Neuroscience, 9,* 2080–2102.

Kermadi, I., Liu, A., Tempini, A., Wiesendanger, M., & Rouiller, E. M. (1997). Differential effects of reversible inactivation of the primary motor, supplementary motor, dorsal premotor, and posterior parietal cortices, on reaching, grasping, and bimanual movements. *Somatosensory and Motor Research, 14,* 268–280.

Kurata, K. (1989). Distribution of neurons with set- and movement-related activity before hand and foot movements in the premotor cortex of rhesus monkeys. *Experimental Brain Research, 77,* 245–256.

Lawrence, D. G. (1994). Central neural mechanisms of prehension. *Canadian Journal of Physiology and Pharmacology, 72,* 580–582.

Lemon, R. N., Baker, S. N., Davis, J. A., Kirkwood, P. A., Maier, M. A., & Yang, H. S. (1998). The importance of the cortico-motoneuronal system for control of grasp. *Novartis Foundation Symposium, 218,* 202–215.

Lemon, R. N., & Porter, R. (1976). Afferent input to movement-related precentral neurones in conscious monkeys. *Proceedings of the Royal Society of London, B, 194,* 313–339.

Lewis, J. W., & Van Essen, D. C. (2000). Corticocortical connections of visual, sensorimotor, and multimodal processing areas in the parietal lobe of the macaque monkey. *Journal of Comparative Neurology, 428,* 112–37.

Luppino, G., Murata, A., Govoni, P., & Matelli, M. (1999). Largely segregated parietofrontal connections linking rostral intraparietal cortex (areas AIP and VIP) and the ventral premotor cortex (areas F5 and F4). *Experimental Brain Research, 128,* 181–187.

Maier, M. A., Armond, J., Kirkwood, P. A., Yang, H.-W., Davis, J. N., & Lemon, R. N. (2002). Differences in the corticospinal projection from primary motor cortex and supplementary motor area to macaque upper limb motoneurons: an anatomical and electrophysiological study. *Cerebral Cortex, 12,* 281–296.

Maier, M. A., Olivier, E., Baker, S. N., Kirkwood, P. A., Morris, T., & Lemon, R. N. (1997). Direct and indirect corticospinal control of arm and hand motoneurons in the squirrel monkey (*Saimiri sciureus*). *Journal of Neurophysiology, 78,* 721–733.

Matelli, M., Luppino, G., & Rizzolatti, G. (1985). Patterns of cytochrome oxidase activity in the frontal agranular cortex of the macaque monkey. *Behavioral Brain Research*, *18*, 125–136.

Morasso, P. (1981). Spatial control of arm movements. *Experimental Brain Research*, *42*, 223–227.

Murata, A., Fadiga, L., Fogassi, L., Gallese, V., Raos, V., & Rizzolatti, G. (1997). Object representation in the ventral premotor cortex (area F5) of the monkey. *Journal of Neurophysiology*, *78*, 2226–2230.

Murray, E. A., & Coulter, J. D. (1981). Organization of corticospinal neurons in the monkey. *Journal of Comparative Neurology*, *195*, 339–365.

Nudo, R. J., Jenkins, W. M., Merzenich, M. M., Prejean, T., & Grenda, R. (1992). Neurophysiological correlates of hand preference in primary motor cortex of adult squirrel monkeys. *Journal of Neuroscience*, *12*, 2918–2947.

Okada, E., Aou, S., Takaki, A., Oomura, Y., & Hori, T. (1991). Electrical stimulation of male monkey's mid-brain elicits components of sexual behavior. *Physiology and Behavior*, *50*, 229–236.

Park, M. C., Belhaj-Saif, A., Gordon, M., & Cheney, P. D. (2001). Consistent features in the forelimb representation of primary motor cortex in rhesus macaques. *Journal of Neuroscience*, *21*, 2784–2792.

Penfield, W., & Boldrey, E. (1937). Somatic, motor and sensory representation in the cerebral cortex of man as studied by electrical stimulation. *Brain*, *60*, 389–443.

Penfield, W., & Welch, K. (1951). The supplementary motor area in the cerebral cortex: a clinical and experimental study. *American Medical Association Archives of Neurology and Psychiatry*, *66*, 289–317.

Preuss, T. M., Stepniewska, I., & Kaas, J. H. (1996). Movement representation in the dorsal and ventral premotor areas of owl monkeys: a microstimulation study. *Journal of Comparative Neurology*, *371*, 649–676.

Quaade, F., Vaernet, K., & Larsson, S. (1974). Sterotaxic stimulation and electro-coagulation of the lateral hypothalamus in obese humans. *Acta Neurochirurgica*, *30*, 111–117.

Reina, G. A., Moran, D. W., & Schwartz, A. B. (2001). On the relationship between joint angular velocity and motor cortical discharge during reaching. *Journal of Neurophysiology*, *85*, 2576–2589.

Rizzolatti, G., Camarda, R., Fogassi, L., Gentilucci, M., Luppino, G., & Matelli, M. (1988). Functional organization of inferior area 6 in the macaque monkey. II. Area F5 and the control of distal movements. *Experimental Brain Research*, *71*, 491–507.

Rizzolatti, G., & Luppino, G. (2001). The cortical motor system. *Neuron*, *31*, 889–901.

Rizzolatti, G., Scandolara, C., Matelli, M., & Gentilucci, M. (1981) Afferent properties of periarcuate neurons in macaque monkeys. II. Visual responses. *Behavioral Brain Research*, *2*, 147–163.

Robinson, D. A. (1972). Eye movements evoked by collicular stimulation in the alert monkey. *Vision Research*, *12*, 1795–1808.

Robinson, D. A., & Fuchs, A. F. (1969). Eye movements evoked by stimulation of the frontal eye fields. *Journal of Neurophysiology*, *32*, 637–648.

Romo, R., Hernandez, A., Zainos, A., & Salinas, E. (1998). Somatosensory discrimination based on cortical microstimulation. *Nature*, *392*, 387–390.

Rosenbaum, D. A., Loukopoulos, L. D., Meulenbroek, R. G., Vaughan, J., & Engelbrecht, S. E. (1995). Planning reaches by evaluating stored postures. *Psychological Review*, *102*, 28–67.

Rouiller, E. M., Yu, X. H., Moret, V., Tempini, A., Wiesendanger, M., & Liang, F. (1998). Dexterity in adult monkeys following early lesion of the motor cortical hand area: the role of cortex adjacent to the lesion. *European Journal of Neuroscience*, 10, 729–740.

Salzman, C. D., Britten, K. H., & Newsome, W. T. (1990). Cortical microstimulation influences perceptual judgements of motion direction. *Nature*, 346, 174–177.

Sanes, J. N., Donoghue, J. P., Thangaraj, V., Edelman, R. R., & Warach, S. (1995). Shared neural substrates controlling hand movements in human motor cortex. *Science*, 268, 1775–1777.

Sanes, J. N., & Schieber, M. H. (2001). Orderly somatotopy in primary motor cortex: does it exist? *Neuroimage*, 13, 968–974.

Sato, K. C., & Tanji, J. (1989). Digit-muscle responses evoked from multiple intracortical foci in monkey precentral motor cortex. *Journal of Neurophysiology*, 62, 959–970.

Schaafsma, S. J., & Duysens, J. (1996). Neurons in the ventral intraparietal area of awake macaque monkey closely resemble neurons in the dorsal part of the medial superior temporal area in their responses to optic flow patterns. *Journal of Neurophysiology*, 76, 4056–4068

Schieber, M. H., & Hibbard, L. S. (1993). How somatotopic is the motor cortex hand area? *Science*, 261, 489–492.

Schiller, P. H., & Stryker, M. (1972). Single-unit recording and stimulation in superior colliculus of the alert rhesus monkey. *Journal of Neurophysiology*, 35, 915–924.

Scott, S. H., & Kalaska, J. F. (1995). Changes in motor cortex activity during reaching movements with similar hand paths but different arm postures. *Journal of Neurophysiology*, 73, 2563–2567.

Scott, S. H., & Kalaska, J. F. (1997). Reaching movements with similar hand paths but different arm orientations. I. Activity of individual cells in motor cortex. *Journal of Neurophysiology*, 77, 826–852.

Sessle, B. J., & Wiesendanger, M. (1982). Structural and functional definition of the motor cortex in the monkey (*Macaca fascicularis*). *Journal of Physiology*, 323, 245–265.

Stepniewska, I., Preuss, T. M., & Kaas, J. H. (1993). Architectonics, somatotopic organization, and ipsilateral cortical connections of the primary motor area (M1) of owl monkeys. *Journal of Comparative Neurology*, 330, 238–271.

Stoney, S. D. Jr., Thompson, W. D., & Asanuma, H. (1968). Excitation of pyramidal tract cells by intracortical microstimulation: effective extent of stimulating current. *Journal of Neurophysiology*, 31, 659–669.

Strick, P. L., & Preston, J. B. (1978). Multiple representation in the primate motor cortex. *Brain Research*, 154, 366–370.

Tehovnik, E. J., & Lee, K. (1993). The dorsomedial frontal cortex of the rhesus monkey: topographic representation of saccades evoked by electrical stimulation. *Experimental Brain Research*, 96, 430–442.

Thier, P., & Andersen, R. A. (1998). Electrical microstimulation distinguishes distinct saccade-related areas in the posterior parietal cortex. *Journal of Neurophysiology*, 80, 1713–1735.

Todorov, E. (2000). Direct cortical control of muscle activation in voluntary arm movements: a model. *Nature Neuroscience*, 3, 391–398.

Travis, A. M. (1955). Neurological deficiencies after ablation of the precentral motor area in *Macaca mulatta*. *Brain*, 78, 155–173.

Tresch, M. C., & Bizzi, E. (1999). Responses to spinal microstimulation in the chronically spinalized rat and their relationship to spinal systems activated by low threshold cutaneous stimulation. *Experimental Brain Research, 129,* 401–416.

Weinrich, M., & Wise, S. P. (1982). The premotor cortex of the monkey. *Journal of Neuroscience, 2,* 1329–1345.

Wise, S. P. (1985). The primate premotor cortex: past, present, and preparatory. *Annual Review of Neuroscience, 8,* 1–19.

Wise, S. P., Boussaoud, D., Johnson, P. B., & Caminiti, R. (1997). Premotor and parietal cortex: corticocortical connectivity and combinatorial computations. *Annual Review of Neuroscience, 20,* 25–42.

Wong, Y. C., Kwan, H. C., MacKay, W. A., & Murphy, J. T. (1978). Spatial organization of precentral cortex in awake primates. I. Somatosensory inputs. *Journal of Neurophysiology, 41,* 1107–1119.

Woolsey, C. N., Settlage, P. H., Meyer, D. R., Sencer, W., Hamuy, T. P., & Travis, A. M. (1952). Pattern of localization in precentral and "supplementary" motor areas and their relation to the concept of a premotor area. *Association for Research in Nervous and Mental Desease, 30,* 238–264.

Wu, C. W., Bichot, N. P., & Kaas, J. H. (2000). Converging evidence from microstimulation, architecture, and connections for multiple motor areas in the frontal and cingulate cortex of prosimian primates. *Journal of Comparative Neurology, 423,* 140–177.

10 Spatial representations and attentional systems for action in the parietal cortex

Matthew F. S. Rushworth and
Amanda Ellison

Abstract

It is widely accepted that the human parietal cortex is concerned with visuospatial representation and attention. In the case of the macaque monkey, however, anatomical, neurophysiological and lesion data suggest that only limited regions of parietal cortex are involved in visuospatial representation and attention, while other areas are more concerned with the control of limb and hand movements. Recent imaging and transcranial magnetic stimulation data have suggested possible homologues of the different parietal regions in the human brain and have raised the possibility that there are different attentional systems within the parietal lobe. A posterior, possibly lateral, intraparietal area may be concerned with (1) visuospatial attentional selection and (2) orienting covert, preparatory visuospatial attention prior to an overt eye movement. Other parietal areas, one in the posterior, superior parietal lobule and adjacent medial intraparietal sulcus and one in the anterior inferior parietal cortex and adjacent anterior intraparietal sulcus, are concerned with (1) motor intentional selection and (2) directing covert, preparatory motor attention prior to an overt arm movement.

Attentional systems within the human parietal cortex

Visuospatial attention has been widely studied and there is a general consensus that it is associated with the parietal cortex. Lesions of the parietal cortex disrupt visuospatial representation (Mishkin & Ungerleider, 1981) and are associated with neglect syndromes (Mesulam, 1981). Neuron activity here is modulated in tandem with changes in the direction in which monkeys attend (Colby & Goldberg, 1999). Human neuroimaging studies confirm human parietal involvement in visuospatial attention (Corbetta & Shulman, 2002; Nobre, 2001). Although the visual nature of the parietal lobe attentional system is often emphasized, it is also important in the guidance of limb and hand movements (Jackson, Newport, Husain, Harvey, & Hindle, 2000). In turn, the parietal role in visual attentional selection is constrained by response selection contingencies (Humphreys & Riddoch, 2001; see also Humphreys et al., this volume).

Despite the agreement that the parietal cortex is an important substrate of attention, there has been less consensus as to which areas within the parietal cortex of the human brain are pre-eminent in visuospatial attention. The posterior parietal cortex can be divided into the superior and inferior parietal lobules (SPL and IPL) and different studies have emphasized the importance of one or other division, the intraparietal sulcus (IPS) that runs between them or even the parietal cortex tissue that extends onto the medial surface (Corbetta, Kincade, Ollinger, McAvoy, & Shulman, 2000; Corbetta, Miezin, Shulman, & Petersen, 1993; Corbetta & Shulman, 2002; Corbetta, Shulman, Miezin, & Petersen, 1995; Coull & Nobre, 1998; Fink, Dolan, Halligan, Marshall, & Frith, 1997; Fink et al., 1999; Gitelman et al., 1999; Hopfinger, Buonocore, & Mangun, 2000; Le, Pardo, & Hu, 1998; Macaluso, Frith, & Driver, 2000; Nobre, Sebestyen, Gitelman, Mesulam, Frackowiak, & Frith, 1997). Understanding such differences in activation patterns in the parietal cortex has been hampered by uncertainty about the relationship between parietal anatomy in the human and other primate brains (Figure 10.1). Divergent neuroimaging results can also be better reconciled if the parietal cortex is home to several distinct attentional systems that are tapped to varying degrees by different tasks. The rest of this chapter is, therefore, concerned with these two themes: comparing the anatomical organization of the human parietal cortex with that of other primates and the evidence for distinct attentional sub-systems. Some attentional systems are particularly closely related to the making of limb and hand movements. The next section reviews evidence that there are different types of spatial representation within the parietal cortex of the macaque monkey, which can

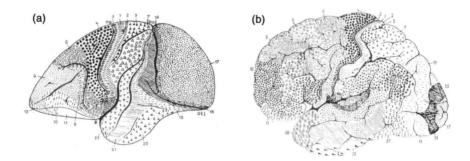

Figure 10.1 Brodmann's (1909) drawings of the cytoarchitectonic areas in (a) the monkey brain and (b) the human brain. The monkey parietal cortex is divided into the IPL and SPL by the IPS. The SPL and IPL are shown as mainly being occupied by areas 5 (black triangles), and 7 (open triangles), respectively. In the human brain, both areas 5 (black triangles) and 7 (white triangles) are shown in the SPL, while areas not shown for the monkey brain, areas 39 and 40, are indicated as occupying the IPL. Human brain imaging studies of visual attention have reported activations thoughout many parts of the parietal cortex.

influence movements in different ways. The argument will then be developed that separate attentional mechanisms operate in conjunction with different spatial representations.

Distinct spatial representations within the parietal cortex of the macaque monkey

Cytoarchitectonic and single unit recording studies suggest that the parietal cortex of the macaque monkey can be subdivided into a number of component regions (Figure 10.2). Only some of these regions are concerned with visuospatial representation and attention, but several of them are able to influence limb movement through a variety of direct and less direct routes. In terms of how they influence limb movements, a case can be made for categorizing the diverse areas into three groups.

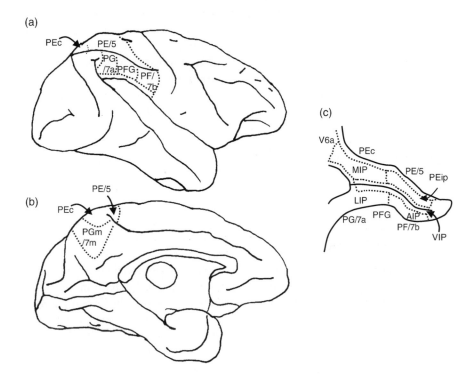

Figure 10.2 Subdivisions of the macaque monkey parietal cortex on the lateral surface (a) and medial surface (b). Subdivisions are shown using the terminologies that followed both Brodmann (1909) (for example areas 5 and 7) and Von Bonin and Bailey (1947) (PE, PF, PG). A large part of the parietal cortex is located in the IPS (c). The figure is based on previous figures (Geyer, Matelli, Luppino, & Zilles, 2000; Rushworth et al., 1997a). Reproduced with permission of Springer-Verlag. Copyright © 1997 Springer-Verlag.

The most posterior parts of the inferior parietal cortex, area PG (or 7a), and the adjacent lateral bank of the intraparietal sulcus, area LIP, receive projections (Figure 10.3a) from the dorsal visual stream (Andersen, Bracewell, Barash, Gnadt, & Fogassi, 1990b; Blatt, Andersen, & Stoner, 1990; Cavada & Goldman-Rakic, 1989a). There is good evidence that these areas are concerned with visuospatial representation and attention. Neurons in this area are visually responsive and their activity reflects the direction of attention (Costantinidis & Steinmetz, 2001, Gottlieb, Kusunoki, & Goldberg, 1998). The spatial representational and attentional roles of these neurons are intimately related to eye movements; neurons fire in advance of eye movements (Snyder, Batista, & Andersen, 1997) and responses to visual targets vary with eye position in a way that is consistent with a representation of space in an eye-centred reference frame (Andersen, Asanuma, Essick, & Siegel, 1990a; Cohen & Andersen, 2002).

Even though this visually dominated area is important for visual attention and the control of eye movements, it may also exert control over limb movements. The caudal IPL may influence hand movements through cortico-cortical connections with rostral IPL and ventral premotor cortex (Lewis & Van Essen, 2000, Nakamura et al., 2001, Tanne-Gariepy, Rouiller, & Boussaoud, 2002) and sub-cortically via the cerebellum (Classen et al., 1995; Glickstein, 1997; Glickstein, May, & Mercier, 1985; Stein, 1986). These connections are also summarized in Figure 10.3a. The integrity of the area is essential for accurate visually guided arm movements as well as eye movements. Lesions that include the caudal half of the IPL and adjacent IPS disrupt visually guided reaching movements (Faugier-Grimond, Frenois, & Peronnet, 1985; Rushworth, Nixon, & Passingham, 1997a; Stein, 1978) (Figure 10.4a). The disruption of visually guided reaching was only apparent when the lesion included the entire caudal half of the IPL; this meant that the lesions included PG and LIP, but also extended into the intermediate region sometimes referred to as PFG or 7ab (Figure 10.2) that lies in between PG and the more anterior area PF or 7b (Rushworth et al., 1997a).

Recently, there has been more interest in the possibility that tissue on the other side of the IPS, on the medial wall of the IPS and extending onto the caudal SPL as far as the mediodorsal parietal surface and the dorsal parieto-occipital sulcus (areas MIP, PEc, MDP and V6A), is concerned with the visual guidance of hand movements (Battaglia-Mayer et al., 2000; Battaglia-Mayer et al., 2001; Caminiti, Ferraina, & Johnson, 1996; Colby & Duhamel, 1991; Ferraina, Battaglia-Mayer, Genovesio Marconi, Onorati, & Caminiti, 2001; Galletti, Fattori, Kutz, & Battaglini, 1997). Whether these putative areas all make distinct contributions to visually guided arm movements remains to be clarified and a collective reference to the parietal reach region (PRR) is sometimes used instead (Snyder et al., 1997). Even though neurons here are concerned with arm movements, they still seem to represent space in an eye rather than an arm-centred coordinate system (Batista, Buneo, Snyder, & Andersen, 1999). This is consistent with the visual responsiveness of

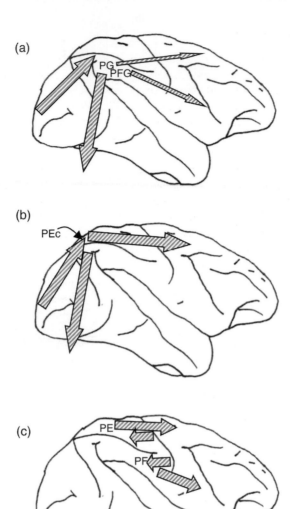

Figure 10.3 The macaque parietal cortex can be subdivided into three regions that influence limb movements in different ways. (a) The caudal IPL and adjacent lateral bank of the IPS is connected to the dorsal visual stream and the frontal and supplementary eye fields and is mainly concerned with visual attention and eye movements. Nevertheless, this region is in a position to exert some control over limb movements via the cerebellum. There are also some direct cortico-cortical connections to the premotor cortex, particularly from the intermediate PFG region to the ventral premotor cortex. (b) The caudal superior parietal lobule and adjacent medial bank of the IPS and dorsal parts of the parieto-occipital sulcus are interconnected both with the dorsal visual stream and with the premotor cortex. (c) The more anterior parts of both the SPL and the IPL receive fewer direct visual projections; instead, they have connections with primary and secondary somatosensory cortices. These areas also have substantial direct cortico-cortical connections to the premotor and motor cortices.

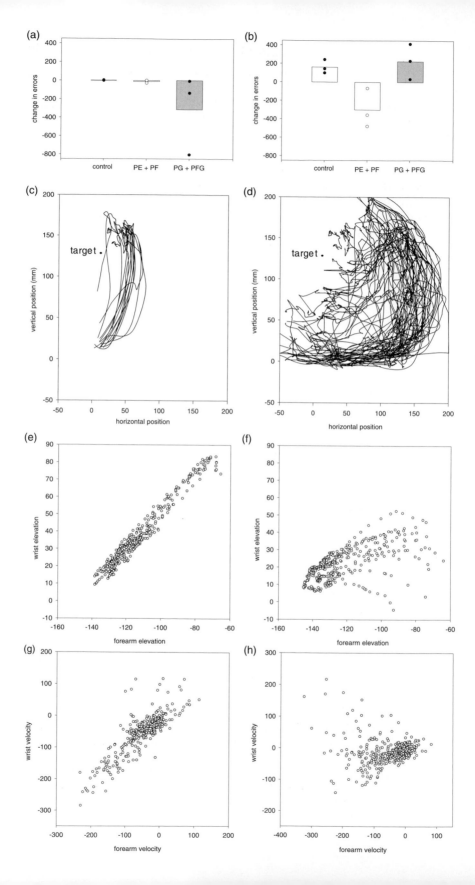

neurons in this region and their anatomical connections (Figure 10.3b) with both the dorsal visual stream and the premotor cortex (Caminiti et al., 1996; Colby, Gatass, Olson, & Gross, 1988; Shipp, Blanton, & Zeki, 1998). Whether this region is necessary for visually guided reaching (Battaglini, Muzur, Galletti, Skrap, Brovelli, & Fattori, 2002) or some other aspect of visuo-motor integration (Wise, Boussaoud, Johnson, & Caminiti, 1997) remains to be determined. Below, we suggest that these areas may be particularly important when there is "intentional conflict" and a choice must be made between different possible limb actions.

Other regions of the parietal cortex, such as area PE (or 5) in the anterior SPL and the adjacent, most dorsal part of the medial intraparietal sulcus (PEip), and area PF (or 7b) in the rostral inferior parietal cortex and the adjacent anterior lateral bank of the intraparietal sulcus (AIP), receive relatively few and less direct visual inputs. These regions, instead, are strongly interconnected with the somatosensory, motor, and premotor cortices (Cavada & Goldman-Rakic, 1989a, 1989b; Lewis & Van Essen, 2000; Pandya & Seltzer, 1982) and neural activity is dominated by somatic and active movement responses (Georgopoulos, Caminiti, & Kalaska, 1984; Robinson & Burton, 1980a, 1980b; Savaki, Kennedy, Sokoloff, & Mishkin, 1993; Seal Gross, & Biolac, 1982). Combined lesions of these areas have only a minimal effect on visually guided reaching (Figure 10.4a), but drastically impair kinaesthetically guided reaching (Rushworth et al., 1997a) (Figure 10.4b). The caudual IPL lesions of PG and PFG that impair visually guided reaching leave kinaesthetically guided reaching intact (Figure 10.4b). In the kinaesthetically guided reaching task, monkeys had to reach in the dark, without the aid of vision. On the first trial, monkeys found a food reward by trial and error and then had to return the hand to the same felt position for further rewards on subsequent trials. The impairment is worse when the starting position of each

---

Figure 10.4 The effect of parietal lesions on movement. (a) Visually guided reaching in the light is disrupted by PG+PFG lesions but unaffected by PE+PF lesions. (b) Kinaesthetically guided reaching in the dark is disrupted by PE+PF lesions but unaffected by PG+PFG lesions. (c) Repeated reaching movements made in the dark by an animal with PE+PF lesions. The figure shows every fourth movement made during a test session. (d) The PE+PF dark reaching deficit gets worse when animals make each movement from one of four different starting positions. The figure shows every fourth movement when movements were made from the same starting position as in (c), but now the other interleaved movements started from different starting positions. (e) On some reaching in the dark trials, control animals showed a steady relationship between the position of the wrist with respect to the shoulder and the elevation of the forearm, suggesting a repeated pattern of postural coordination during each movement. (f) Often this was disrupted in the animals with PE+PF lesions. (g) Not surprisingly, there was also a relationship between the velocity of the wrist and the forearm in the control animals. (h) The relationship between wrist and forearm velocities was disrupted by the PE+PF lesion.

movement is changed from trial to trial (Rushworth, Nixon, & Passingham 1997b) (Figure 10.4c,d). During some movements, there is a relationship between hand position in a shoulder-centred reference frame and the arm's postural configuration. The relationship is particularly simple when movements are made in the dark without visual guidance (Flanders, Helms Tillery, & Soechting, 1992; Helms Tillery, Ebner, & Soechting, 1995). Such relationships appear to break down after the removal of areas PE and PF (Rushworth, Johansen-Berg, & Young, 1998) (Figure 10.4e–h). A similar breakdown has been reported in patients with ideomotor apraxia who have sustained lesions affecting the left parietal cortex (Poizner, Clark, Merians, Macauley, Gonzalez Rothi, & Heilman, 1995). It is difficult to attribute the difficulties of apraxic patients to lesions of just one parietal subdivision; the parietal lesions in apraxic patients tend to extend over more than one cortical region and may also undercut the white matter connections of more than one region (Haaland, Harrington, & Knight, 2000).

In brief, there is a double dissociation between the roles of the two sets of parietal regions, areas PG and PGF (Figure 10.3a) and areas PE and PF (Figure 10.3c), in the spatial guidance of hand movements. One set of areas, PG and PGF, is critical for the correct spatial organization of a reaching movement in relation to visual information, while the other set, PE and PF, is crucial for the spatial coordination of the movement in relation to kinaesthetic information (Figure 10.4a,b). The latter areas are particularly important for representing not just the reach's target position, but also the hand's starting position at the beginning of the movement (Figure 10.4c,d).

By making lesions, it is possible to work out which parietal areas are the source of the various types of information that are essential for movements. During a normal reaching movement, however, different types of sensory information are combined. For example, the sense of the hand's position does not just depend on proprioceptive and somatosensory information, it is also influenced by vision. An individual's judgements about the felt position of the hands is biased towards the seen position of a realistic false arm (Botvinick & Cohen, 1998). Single neuron recording studies have demonstrated the neurophysiological basis of these interactions; Graziano, Cooke, and Taylor (2000) showed that the activity of 46% of neurons in area PE reflected the hand's position, but the activity of more than half of such cells was also influenced by the seen position of a fake arm. Area PE may be a source of proprioceptive and efference copy information about the arm's position (Seal et al., 1982), but the influence of visual information permeates even here. Just allowing individuals access to "non-informative" vision of the general workspace even while keeping the limb itself hidden changes the way they balance the importance of kinaesthetic and visual information when reaching a judgement about limb position (Newport, Hindle, & Jackson, 2001).

In addition to relying on different information, visual or kinaesthetic, separate parietal areas may underpin distinct representations of egocentric space. Several authors have put forward related arguments that different parietal regions are concerned either with the representation of external space or body-centred space (de Jong, van der Graaf, & Paans, 2001; Rizzolatti, Gentilluci, & Matelli, 1985). Rizzolatti et al. (1985) distinguished between an anterior parietal–premotor circuit and a posterior parietal–frontal eye field circuit that they argued were important when attending to peripersonal space, or more distant space, respectively. They argued that the attentional problems of monkeys with lesions within each of these circuits were best described by reference to different spatial representations. De Jong et al. (2001) asked human participants to perform two reaching tasks while they were in a PET scanner. A task requiring the accurate placement of the right hand index finger over one of an array of five dots emphasized the representation of external space and was associated with activity in the posterior intraparietal sulcus that spread into the parieto-occipital and dorsal extrastriate areas. The second task also required participants to place a finger over a dot, but the dot position stayed constant throughout and only the central one of the five dots was ever the target. However, between trials the finger used to make the response was changed. The second task therefore emphasized the representation of the body scheme rather than the representation of external space, and was associated with activity in the left anterior parietal cortex, the supramarginal gyrus and the intraparietal sulcus. Neuropsychological and neuroimaging evidence for different spatial representations can also be related to psychophysical evidence for two different egocentric spatial reference frames (Flanders et al., 1992; McIntyre, Stratta, Lacquaniti, 1998; Soechting & Flanders, 1989a,b).

Single cell recording studies also suggest that there are different spatial representations within the parietal cortex. Such studies have clearly indicated eye-centred representations of sensory stimuli appearing in external space in both lateral and medial posterior intraparietal areas (Batista et al., 1999; Cohen & Andersen, 2002). The evidence for body- or limb-centred representations in the parietal cortex is less clear. The activity of area 5/PE neurons, in the anterior SPL, is affected by eye position, but reaching targets are also represented with respect to the body and the hand (Buneo, Jarvis, Batista, & Andersen, 2002; Lacquaniti, Guigon, Bianchi, Ferraina, & Caminiti, 1995). Psychophysical experiments with humans indicate that it is easier to detect evidence for body- or limb-centred representations when visual information is removed (Flanders et al., 1992; McIntyre et al., 1998; Newport, Rabb, & Jackson, 2002); the evidence for limb- and body-centred representations in single cell recording studies may be clearer when animals are taught kinaesthetic reaching tasks that are to be performed in the absence of visual guidance.

In summary, the parietal cortex may not contain just a single representation of external space. Some parietal areas may be more closely associated with kinaesthetic representations of space, while others may be more closely associated with visual representations of space. Within the parietal lobe, areas may also be concerned with different egocentric representations of space: external space or body space. Although it is widely accepted that visuospatial attention must be understood in the context of parietal representations of external space, it is possible that there are analogous attentional mechanisms linked to body-centred representations of space. The case for different attentional systems within the parietal cortex is made below. Much of the evidence for different attentional systems within the parietal cortex is derived from studies of the human parietal cortex. The next section also attempts to identify the correspondences between anatomical regions in the human and macaque parietal lobes.

The organization of the human parietal cortex

There has been little consensus on the correspondence between the monkey and parietal cortex. On the basis of cytoarchitectonic considerations, Brodmann (1909) argued that the SPL and IPL in the monkey consisted predominantly of distinct regions he labelled areas 5 and 7, respectively (black and open triangles in Figure 10.1a). On investigating the human brain, however, Brodmann suggested that both areas 5 and 7 are limited to the SPL, but that newly differentiated areas 39 and 40 occupied the caudal and rostral IPL (Figure 10.1b). According to this analysis, the human parietal cortex is quite different from that of the monkey and it contains new areas that may not be found in other species. An attractive feature of this view is that it helps to explain the association between abilities that we have come to think of as uniquely human, such as number comprehension, and the parietal lobe; it is well established that restricted parietal lesions in the human brain are associated with acalculia and difficulty in processing numerical information (Butterworth, 1999; Mayer, Martory, Pegna, Landis, Delavelle, & Annoni, 1999).

Not all anatomists, however, have agreed with this parcellation of the parietal lobe. Von Bonin and Bailey (1947) and Eidelburg and Galaburda (1984) identified correspondences between human and macaque monkey IPL and between the human and macaque monkey SPL. According to this perspective, the IPL and SPL of both species are organized in a similar manner with an area PE in the SPL and areas PF and PG in the IPL.

In a recent experiment (Rushworth, Paus, & Sipila, 2001a), we used fMRI to determine whether the parietal cortex contains separate areas concerned with the resolution of attentional or intentional conflicts, and (2) whether the parietal cortex is organized in a similar way in macaques and humans. If the SPL and IPL are organized in a similar way in both species, then the IPS should divide the parietal cortex in a similar way in both species. The fMRI study looked for evidence of functional areas either side of the human intraparietal sulcus that resembled those found either side of the intraparietal sulcus in the macaque brain. In the previous section, we discussed how in the monkey the lateral and medial banks of the intraparietal sulcus (LIP and

MIP) contain cells concerned with visual attention/eye movements and with motor intention/hand movements, respectively (Calton, Dickinson, & Snyder, 2002; Colby & Duhamel, 1991; Eskandar & Assad, 1999; Snyder et al., 1997). The fMRI study used two task switching paradigms to look for these two types of parietal area. In the first visual switch (VS) paradigm, participants switched between attending to one or two stimuli on the basis of either colour or shape (Plate 10.1a). Attending to the shape or colour of a stimulus also means that participants must attend to its spatial location (Tsal & Lavie, 1988, 1993). On the other hand, the response switch (RS) paradigm required participants to select between responses made to visual stimuli but according to one of two changing rules (Plate 10.1b). Response switch, unlike visual switch, did not require participants to redirect visual attention; instead, it required a change of visuomotor-related intention. A "switching cue" was used to tell the participants when to switch in both paradigms. Event-related analyses compared the blood oxygen level dependent (BOLD) signal recorded on switching in both paradigms and compared it with the BOLD signal recorded at the time of a control "stay cue" that simply instructed the participants to carry on performing the task in the same way as previously. Participants performing the VS paradigm only had to respond with a keypress on some trials and these trials were normally presented some time after the switch and stay cues. In this way, it was hoped that the attentional switches manipulated by the VS paradigm would not be contaminated with intentional/hand response related changes.

Switching either attentional or intentional set in the VS or RS paradigms was associated with similar behavioural costs that could be measured in terms of reaction time but with distinct patterns of BOLD signal change in the parietal cortex (Plate 10.1, c–f). Intentional switching in the RS paradigm was associated with activity in a medial, superior and caudal region of the posterior parietal lobe adjacent to the intraparietal sulcus, while attentional switching in the VS paradigm was associated with activity in a lateral, inferior and more rostral region in the intraparietal sulcus of the posterior parietal lobe. In other words, activity related to attentional and intentional conflict was separated along all three standard brain axes. The separation is similar to that between macaque LIP and MIP (Calton et al., 2002; Colby & Duhamel, 1991; Eskander & Assad, 1999; Snyder et al., 1997). The attentional switch activity was interpreted as falling not just in the human LIP area, but also in a human homologue of the parieto-occipital area (PO) that contains visually responsive cells that encode the position of visual stimuli (Galletti, Battaglini, & Fattori, 1993, 1995). The intentional switch activity was interpreted as not just falling in a human equivalent of the medial intraparietal region (MIP), but extending into the adjacent posterior superior parietal lobule area PEp. The intentional switch activity might have extended into homologues of macaque areas sometimes known as MDP and V6A, which contain cells with activity that is modulated during visually guided hand movements (Battaglia-Mayer et al., 2000;

Caminiti et al., 1996; Ferraini et al., 2001; Galletti et al., 1997; Marconi et al., 2001).

The fMRI results suggest that the organizing principles for the human parietal cortex are similar to those for the macaque parietal cortex. Recently, other researchers have considered the same issue. Sereno, Pitzalis, and Martinez (2001) carefully mapped BOLD signal activity related to different directions of memory-guided saccades in individual humans to find the homologue of macaque LIP. The region they identified as LIP had a similar position in Talairach space to the one recorded by Rushworth et al. (2001a), but Sereno and colleagues located it on the medial rather than the lateral bank of the intraparietal sulcus. A strength of the approach used by Sereno and colleagues was that they were able to map the position of the activation in individual participants. It may still be difficult, however, to decide which side of the narrow intraparietal sulcus is activated in an fMRI experiment. The strength of the approach used by Rushworth and colleagues is that it simply identified the relative position of two sets of fMRI activations and compared them with the relative positions of the walls of the intraparietal sulcus. Marois, Larson, Chun, and Shima (2002) have used a similar approach and have similarly concluded that visual attention-related activations are lateral and ventral to activations related to selection between different possible hand movements. Chapman, Gavrilescu, Wang, Kean, Egan, and Castiello (2002) have also reported activity in a part of this region when participants must select between one of three possible targets for reaching. The results of another study also concur in suggesting that the IPS is organized in a similar way in the human and macaque brain. On the basis of PET data, Bremmer et al. (2001) concluded that the human homologue of parietal area VIP is at the bottom of the IPS as it is in the monkey (Colby & Duhamel, 1991).

In summary, although various authors have come to different conclusions about human parietal organization, several studies are consistent in suggesting that it is similar to that seen in other primates (Bremmer et al., 2001; Marois et al., 2002; Rushworth et al., 2001a). Preuss and Goldman-Rakic (1991) have concluded that the parietal cortex in the strepsirhine *Galago* has a similar organization to that of the anthropoid macaque. It is possible that the sensorimotor transformations and associated attentional processes that occur during eye and hand movements have remained relatively stable since the development of binocular vision and reaching and grasping hand movements (Sakata, Taira, Kusunoki, Murata, & Tanaka, 1997). In turn, parietal organization may have been relatively conserved during primate speciation.

This section has considered the anatomical organization of parietal areas concerned with different types of conflict: attentional conflict or intentional conflict. The next part of the chapter develops the argument for the existence of more than one capacity-limited attentional selection process and reviews the evidence that one of these is particularly concerned with the selection of limb movements.

Attentional selection and the psychological refractory period

Behavioural experiments also suggest separate mechanisms of intentional and attentional selection. Evidence for the limited and selective nature of a system for intentional selection comes from experiments on the psychological refractory period (PRP). Welford (1952) asked his participants to respond in two sets of two-alternative choice tasks, cued by two stimuli, S1 and S2, separated by a short stimulus onset asynchrony (SOA). Welford found that responses to S2 became slower as the SOA decreased and he argued that this was because a response selection "bottleneck" prevented the selection of the second response if the first response was still being chosen.

Intentional selection in the PRP is dissociable from visual attentional selection. Pashler and colleagues have shown that degrading the quality of the second visual stimulus in a PRP paradgim slowed the second reaction time but in an underadditive manner with respect to changes in the SOA (Pashler, 1984; Pashler & Johnston, 1989), suggesting that the extra difficulty imposed by the change in the visual stimulus could be dealt with while the first response was being selected. By the time the sensory analysis of the second stimulus was completed, the selection of the first response had also been completed and the selection of the second response could proceed. Pashler (1991) also showed that there was no interference between tasks when S1 and S2 cued a response selection and a visual orienting paradigm, respectively. The limiting bottleneck occurs during response selection rather than at the subsequent stage of response production (although see Cohen & Magen, this volume, for an alternative view). It is thought that when sequences of movements are to be made, all the component movements are to some degree selected before the first movement is made (Sternberg, Monsell, Knoll, & Wright, 1978). Pashler and Christian (1991) showed that the response to a second stimulus was only slowed to a limited extent when the first stimulus required a sequence of responses.

The behavioural dissociation between the PRP and visual attention may depend on the neuroanatomical distinction between the parietal areas concerned with attentional and intentional selection (Rushworth et al., 2001a). Marois et al. (2002) have shown that manipulation of PRP demands is associated with a change in activity in a parietal region medial to the IPS, while visual attentional selection is associated with the modulation of a parietal region lateral to the IPS.

Premotor theories and covert preparatory attention

In the previous section, we discussed the separation between visual attention and the PRP and reviewed similarities and analogies in the limited capacity and selective nature of both visual attention and the PRP. In this section, we briefly review the literature on covert preparatory attention paradigms to provide another line of evidence for the existence of separate visual and motor attentional systems.

The operation of preparatory orienting attention is indexed by a decrease in reaction time when participants respond to visual stimuli that appear in an expected location (Posner, 1980). Both behavioural and neuroimaging data indicate a close relation between covert attention and overt eye movements. Although covert orientation can be distinguished from overt eye movement (Posner, 1980), the two processes are usually coupled (Deubel & Schneider, 1996) and the direction of attention influences subsequent eye movements (Sheliga, Craighero, Riggio, & Rizzolatti, 1997; Sheliga, Riggio, & Rizzolatti, 1994). Neuroimaging studies indicate that there is a common area of acti-vation both when individuals covertly orient visuospatial attention and when they make overt eye movements (Corbetta et al., 1998; Nobre, Gitelman, Dias, & Mesulam, 2000).

If orienting attention is so closely related to overt eye movements, then it might be possible to identify other attentional systems that are related to other response modalities such as limb movements. Although this hypoth-esis has received relatively little attention, it is one with a long history. James (1890) reported an experiment, conducted by Lange who was working in Wundt's laboratory, in which individuals responded to a visual stimulus. Lange found that reaction times were slower either when participants pre-pared to see the stimulus or when they prepared to make a particular response. James invoked two distinct processes he referred to as *sensorial attention* and *muscular attention* to account for the two different ways in which responses had been facilitated. Other researchers have also contrasted pre-paratory attention-related processes concerned with stimulus or response selection (LaBerge, LeGrand, & Hobbie, 1969). Boussaoud and Wise (1993a, b) contrasted attentional and intentional activity in neurons' responses. They reported neurons with activity that was modulated either by the direction in which monkeys attended to stimuli or the direction in which the monkeys intended to make hand responses.

Even if the concept of motor attention is an old and established one, it is still the case that the term is not currently in widespread use. Instead, the ability to attend to an upcoming movement is often simply referred to as motor preparation. By using the term "motor attention", however, it is pos-sible to highlight how the operation of the two covert preparatory processes is similar. The operation of both processes is usually followed by an overt movement of either the eye or a limb, but in both cases it is possible to withhold the eye or limb movement or even to change to a different unprepared eye or hand movement. In the next section, we discuss the way in which parallel circuits within the parietal lobe appear to be concerned with the redirecting of each type of preparatory attentional process.

In summary, there are two important similarities between visual and motor attention. In the previous section, we described how limited capacity and selective processing are features of both visual and motor attention. In the current section, we argued that both orienting and motor attention may be linked to premotor processes that precede eye or limb movements.

Activation and disruption of covert attention systems

It has long been accepted that the parietal cortex is important for visuospatial analysis and attention and that the parietal cortex in the right hemisphere plays the dominant role (Mesulam, 1981). The right parietal cortex is also important in the particular case of covert orienting. Several well-controlled neuroimaging studies have identified activations in and around the angular gyrus and adjacent sulci, the IPS and the superior temporal sulcus, associated with covert orienting attention (Corbetta & Shulman, 2002; Corbetta et al., 2000; Gitelman et al., 1999; Nobre, 1997, 2001). The same studies also emphasized that the parietal cortex mediates orienting in conjunction with a frontal lobe area, the frontal eye fields.

The identification of the parietal cortex with covert orienting does not depend just on neuroimaging studies that have recorded activation in this region while participants orient. Other researchers have shown that parietal disruption, following a brain lesion, affects covert orienting (Posner, Walker, Friedrich, & Rafal, 1984). Parietal disruption most affects certain types of trials in covert orienting paradigms referred to as "invalid trials". On "valid trials", pre-cues instruct participants to attend to the position at which the stimulus for response will appear. On invalid trials, however, the warning precue is incorrect and the subsequent stimulus for response appears at a different location. Even healthy individuals tend to respond more slowly on invalid trials, but those with parietal lesions, especially right parietal lesions, are very slow (Posner, Inhoff, Friedrich, & Cohen, 1987; Posner et al., 1984). The results suggest that the parietal cortex has a particular role in the disengaging and redirecting of attention and not just in the continued maintenance of attention in a constant direction. A similar effect is also seen when repetitive transcranial magnetic stimulation (rTMS) is applied over the angular gyrus between the posterior IPS and superior temporal sulcus (Rushworth, Ellison, & Walsh, 2001b).

Both neuroimaging and disruption experiments attest to the existence of a separate region of the human parietal cortex concerned with spatial attention. In the same way that previous studies used positron emission tomography (PET) or fMRI to examine activation when participants were covertly orienting, it is possible to look for brain activation while participants covertly engage motor attention. In a PET study, Deiber, Ibanez, Sadato, and Hallett (1996) used various cue patterns to provide their participants with differing amounts of information about the movements they were to make at the end of short intervals. A reaction time analysis confirmed that the degree of covert movement preparation varied with the amount of information that participants had been given about the movements they would make and Deiber et al. found that this was related to activation in the supramarginal gyrus. The supramarginal gyrus, which is anterior to the parietal region, is most clearly concerned with visuospatial attention and it probably corresponds to area PF (or 7b) in the monkey brain. Other studies have also recorded activity in the supramarginal gyrus when participants covertly attend to imminent movements (Deiber et al., 1996; Krams, Rushworth, Deiber, Frackowiak, & Passingham, 1998). Krams et al. (1998) demonstrated that there was more activity in the supramarginal gyrus in a condition in which participants just prepared movements, but never subsequently executed them, than there was in a condition in which participants executed movements without prior preparation. Although little activation was reported in the more posterior parietal cortex and the frontal eye fields in these studies, activation is sometimes recorded in parts of the frontal lobe, such as the premotor cortices with which the supramarginal homologue, area PF, is known to be connected in the monkey (Cavada & Goldman-Rakic, 1989b; Pandya & Seltzer, 1982; Tanne-Gariepy et al., 2002).

Not only are orienting and motor attention associated with activation in different parts of the parietal lobe, but the two attentional processes exhibit a complementary lateralization. The right parietal cortex predominates in orienting visuospatial attention (Nobre, 2001; Posner et al., 1987), but the activation recorded during covert motor attention by Deiber et al. (1996) and Krams et al. (1998) was lateralized to the left hemisphere. Participants in those studies, however, responded with just the right hand so that the activation could have been in the left hemisphere simply because it was contralateral to the hand being moved. Rushworth, Krams, and Passingham (2001c) used PET to compare two conditions in which participants responded with just the left hand. In one condition, there was a delay of approximately 3 s between the presentation of an instruction cue telling the participants which movement to make and the "go" signal telling them when to make the movement. In another condition, the instruction and go cues were presented simultaneously and the participants executed the movement immediately without preparation. Covert motor attention was isolated by comparing the two conditions. Although the comparison was associated with some small areas of activity in the contralateral ventral premotor and secondary somatosensory cortex, other activation in the parietal lobe, in the supramarginal gyrus and the adjacent anterior intraparietal region was restricted to the left hemisphere (see Plate 10.2). Neuroimaging studies suggest that right, caudal and left, rostral IPL regions are activated when participants engage in two different types of covert preparatory attention, covert orienting and covert motor attention, respectively.

Several other recent neuroimaging studies have begun to consider attentional selection in relation to hand movements (Chapman et al., 2002; Indovina & Sanes, 2001; Marois et al., 2002). All of these studies concur in emphasizing the importance of the left rather than the right parietal cortex. An important caveat, however, is that these studies have tended to emphasize the role of the caudal SPL rather than the supramarginal gyrus in the rostral

IPL. Clearly, both the caudal SPL and the rostral IPL are concerned with aspects of attentional selection in relation to motor control (Rushworth et al., 2001a), but their different contributions remain unclear. It is noticeable, however, that the caudal SPL is activated when a need for selection between different possible visuomotor intentions is present (Chapman et al., 2002; Indovina & Sanes, 2001; Marois et al., 2002; Rushworth et al., 2001a). Activation of just the supramarginal gyrus seems to occur in situations that emphasize the covert preparation of an easily selected motor response (Deiber et al., 1996; Krams et al., 1998; Rushworth et al., 2001c). It is also possible that the supramarginal gyrus is involved when the task's different responses entail different hand and finger configurations; the supramarginal gyrus and adjacent anterior IPS region may be the human homologue of the AIP region of the monkey brain thought to play a particular role in the production of hand movements (Binkofski, Buccino, Stephan, Rizzolatti, Seitz, & Freund, 1999; Sakata et al., 1999; Toni, Rushworth, & Passingham, 2001).

Other studies have considered what happens when the left parietal cortex is disrupted during a motor attention task. In a TMS experiment on motor attention, participants made one of two responses depending on which visual stimulus had been presented on a monitor (Rushworth et al., 2001b). At the beginning of each trial, the participants rested their index and middle fingers on the middle of a row of four buttons. The row of buttons was oriented parallel to the mid-sagittal axis with the index finger on the button second nearest to the body. When a visual stimulus appeared in the lower position on the monitor, participants responded by moving the index finger to the next button down and keeping the middle finger in the same place as previously. When the visual stimulus appeared in the upper position, they responded by moving the middle finger to the next button up and keeping the index finger in the same place as previously. On 80% of trials, a precue correctly warned the participants where the stimulus would subsequently appear so that they could prepare the corresponding movement. On 20% of trials, the precue was invalid and the participants had to execute a different movement to the one that they had prepared. We attempted to decrease the task's visuospatial orienting load by using just two potential target positions, close above and below the central fixation position, and to increase the motor attention load by requiring participants to make a complicated motor response. A 500 ms train of 10 Hz rTMS was applied over either the angular or the supramarginal gyrus of either the left or the right parietal cortex 20 ms after the presentation of the imperative stimulus that instructed the response (see Plate 10.3). The rTMS led to a significant increase in reaction time when it was applied over the left supramarginal gyrus regardless of whether participants were responding with the left or the right hand (Figure 10.5b,c).

The use of rTMS is associated with a number of artefacts. When TMS is applied, participants also hear a sound and experience a tactile sensation (Walsh & Cowey, 2000; Walsh & Rushworth, 1999). Similar results,

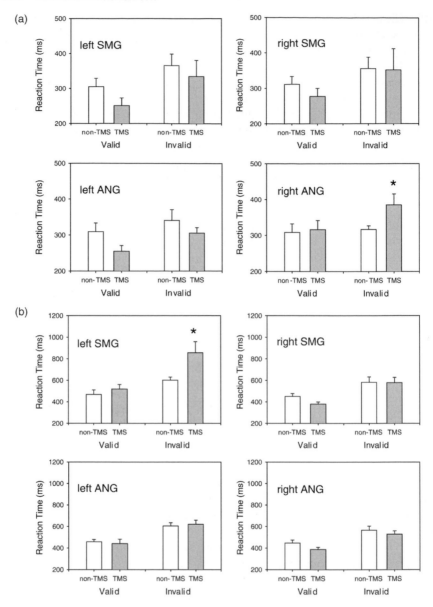

however, have also been observed in a simpler motor attention task designed for use by patients with lesions in either the left or the right parietal lobe (Rushworth, Nixon, Renowden, Wade, & Passingham 1997c). The lesions affected several subdivisions of the parietal cortex and it was not possible to disentangle the relative contributions of different areas. Nevertheless, the left parietal patients responded significantly more slowly than the controls or right parietal patients on invalid trials.

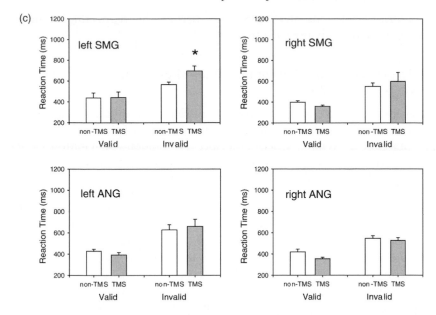

Figure 10.5 The effect of TMS over the left and right supramarginal (SMG) and angular gyri (ANG) on convert orienting (a) and on covert motor attention when subjects responded with either the right (b) or left (c) hands. Valid and invalid trial RTs are shown on the left and the right of each panel. Control and TMS trials are indicated by open and shaded bars respectively. Right angular gyrus TMS disrupted visuospatial orienting on invalid trails. (a, bottom right) but left supramarginal TMS disrupted motor attention on invalid trails (b, c, top left). Copyright © 2001 by the Journal of Neuroscience.

Once again the effects of disruption of the left hemisphere on motor attention seem to have been confirmed by other researchers. Castiello and Paine (2002) have recently reported the case of a patient with a left parietal lesion who performed well on a covert orienting paradigm. In a second task, the same patient made pointing movements to pre-cued targets. He exhibited a selective impairment in his slowness to respond when the location of the target had been invalidly pre-cued.

There is neuropsychological evidence for two systems of covert preparatory attention. Neuroimaging studies have shown that the region around the angular gyrus, the IPS and superior temporal sulcus are active when individuals covertly orient. Lesions and TMS in this area disrupt the redirecting of orienting attention from one location to another on invalidly pre-cued trials. The angular gyrus region in the right parietal cortex plays the dominant role. A parallel set of findings suggests that covert motor attention operates in a similar manner but depends on the supramarginal gyrus of the left hemisphere. This region is active when individuals covertly orient motor attention, and lesions and TMS here disrupt the redirecting of motor attention on invalidly pre-cued trials.

Updating representations of movement before the movement is completed

A separate tradition of research has considered the online correction of overt movements when reaching targets change position or orientation (Desmurget, Epstein, Turner, Prablanc, Alexander, & Grafton, 1999; Desmurget, Grea, Grethe, Prablanc, Alexander, & Grafton, 2001; Glover & Dixon, 2001, Grea et al. 2002; Pisella et al., 2000). Activation is recorded in the supramarginal gyrus when the directions of reaching movements are corrected in the PET scanner (Desmurget et al., 2001) and TMS in the same region disrupts the corrective movement (Desmurget et al., 1999). Interestingly, both the TMS and PET studies focused on the left supramarginal, although conditions that might have been more relevant for the right supramarginal gyrus were omitted. The same research group have also reported that a patient with a bilateral parietal lesion was unable to adjust the direction of reaching and grasping movements (Grea et al., 2002; Pisella et al., 2000). It is not yet clear whether it is appropriate to link on line correction of movement with the disengagement and redirection of covert motor attentional processes. Nevertheless, a common theme in both series of investigations is that the parietal cortex plays a critical role in redirection, whether it is the redirection of covert attention or the redirection of overt movements. Models of online correction of movement emphasize that control is based not simply on the sensory feedback that follows the overt movement, but on forward models of the *intended* movement (Desmurget & Grafton, 2000; Miall, 1998). Models of online control also emphasize the role of the cerebellum and it may be important that it is area PF (or 7b), the macaque homologue of the supramarginal gyrus, that it is the principal recipient within the parietal cortex of the cerebellum's output via the dentate nucleus (Clower, West, Lynch, & Strick, 2001).

Neurons in the LIP region of the parietal cortex update the representation of visual space when an eye movement is to be made (Duhamel, Colby, & Goldberg, 1992a). The updating of parietal neurons' receptive field positions actually occurs very rapidly when an eye movement is made. The visual field is re-mapped to its new location before the eye movement has been completed. It is possible that it was damage to such a mechanism that led to a patient with a parietal lesion having difficulties in making a two-step sequence of eye movements (Duhamel, Goldberg, Fitzgibbon, Sirigu, & Grafman, 1992b); the loss of such a mechanism would have impeded the patient's ability to update her visual representation after the first eye movement had been made.

Damage to a left parietal mechanism for redirecting motor attention may explain why apraxic patients, who may have left parietal lesions, find the sequencing of even ipsilesional movements difficult (Harrington & Haaland, 1991, 1992; Kimura, 1997; Kimura & Archibald, 1974; Rushworth et al., 1997c). The deficit could be explained by the requirement for repeated disengagement and redirection of the focus of motor attention during the course of a motor sequence.

Conclusion

This chapter has attempted to summarize the evidence for different attentional systems. It has proposed that different parietal areas are concerned with different attentional systems.

Visuospatial attention is often understood in the context of the parietal lobe's representations of visual space. There are, however, several spatial representations within the parietal lobe. Parietal spatial representations can be differentiated on a number of criteria. An important factor for any parietal spatial representation is the effector with which it is most closely linked, either the eye or the limb. Only some parietal areas appear to be concerned with the egocentric representation of external space, while others seem more concerned with the egocentric representation of body space. While visual information is important in some parietal spatial representations, kinaesthetic information is more important for others. Spatial representations in different areas are constructed in different reference frames. Attentional selection may occur not just in relation to the operation of the posterior parietal vision and eye-based representation of external space, but in relation to body-centred representations of body space more concerned with kinaesthetic information and limb movements.

The existence of attention in the limb motor system, sometimes called intention or motor attention, is indicated by the finding of different types of covert preparatory processes and different capacity-limited selective processes.

Several neuroimaging, TMS, and lesion studies converge in suggesting neural substrates for motor attention or intention. A critical region for covert motor attention may be the supramarginal gyrus, as opposed to the more posterior regions around the angular gyrus implicated in visuospatial orienting. A critical region for selecting between different motor intentions may be the caudal superior parietal lobule. In both cases, areas in the parietal lobe of the left hemisphere are dominant, in contrast to the well-known predominance of the right parietal cortex in visuospatial orienting and attention.

Acknowledgements

Supported by the Royal Society and the Medical Research Council.

References

Andersen, R. A., Asanuma, C., Essick, G., & Siegel, R. M. (1990a). Corticocortical connections of anatomically and physiologically defined subdivisions within the inferior parietal lobule. *Journal of Comparative Neurology, 296*, 65–113.

Andersen, R. A., Bracewell, R. M., Barash, S., Gnadt, J. W., & Fogassi, L. (1990b). Eye-position effects on visual, memory and saccade-related activity in areas LIP and 7a of macaque. *Journal of Neuroscience, 10*, 1176–1196.

Batista, A. P., Buneo, C. A., Snyder, L. H. & Andersen, R. A. (1999). Reach plans in eye-centred coordinates. *Science, 285*, 257–259.

Battaglia-Mayer, A., Ferraina, S., Genovesio, A., Marconi, B., Squatrito, S., Molinari, M., Lacquaniti, F., & Caminiti, R. (2001). Eye–hand coordination during reaching. II. An analysis of the relationships between visuomanual signals in parietal cortex and parieto-frontal association cortex. *Cerebral Cortex, 11*, 528–544.

Battaglia-Mayer, A., Ferraina, S., Mitsuda, T., Marconi, B., Genovesio, A., Onorati, P., Lacquaniti, F., & Caminiti, R. (2000). Early coding of reaching in the parieto-occipital cortex. *Journal of Neurophysiology, 83*, 2374–2391.

Battaglini, P. P., Muzur, A., Galletti, C., Skrap, M., Brovelli, A., & Fattori, P. (2002). Effects of lesions to area v6a in monkeys. *Experimental Brain Research, 144*, 419–422.

Binkofski, F., Buccino, G., Stephan, K. M., Rizzolatti, G., Seitz, R. J., & Freund, H.-J. (1999). A parieto-premotor network for object manipulation: evidence from neuroimaging. *Experimental Brain Research, 128*, 210–213.

Blatt, G. J., Andersen, R. A., & Stoner, G. R. (1990). Visual receptive field organization and cortico-cortical connections of the lateral intraparietal area (area LIP) in the macaque. *Journal of Comparative Neurology, 299*, 421–445.

Botvinick, M., & Cohen, J. (1998). Rubber hands "feel" touch that eyes see. *Nature, 19*, 756.

Boussaoud, D., & Wise, S. P. (1993a). Primate frontal cortex: neuronal activity following attentional versus intentional cues. *Experimental Brain Research, 95*, 15–27.

Boussaoud, D., & Wise, S. P. (1993b). Primate frontal cortex: effects of stimulus and movement. *Experimental Brain Research, 95*, 28–40.

Bremmer, F., Schlack, A., Shah, N. J., Zafiris, O., Kubischik, M., Hoffmann, K.-P. et al. (2001). Polymodal motion processing in posterior parietal and premotor cortex: a human fMRI study strongly implies equivalencies between monkeys and humans. *Neuron, 29*, 287–296.

Brodmann, K. (1909). *Vergleichende Lokalisationslehre der Grosshirnrinde in ihren Prinzipien dargestellt auf Grund des Zellenbaues.* Leipzing: Barth. Translated by L. J. Garey (1994). *Brodmann's "Localization in the Cerebral Cortex".* London: Smith-Gordon.

Buneo, C. A., Jarvis, M. R., Batista, A. P., & Andersen, R. A. (2002). Direct visuo-motor transformations for reaching. *Nature, 416*, 632–636.

Butterworth, B. (1999). *The mathematical brain.* London: Macmillan.

Calton, J. L., Dickinson, A. R., & Snyder, L. H. (2002). Non-spatial, motor-specific activation in posterior parietal cortex. *Nature Neuroscience, 5*, 580–588.

Caminiti, R., Ferraina, S., & Johnson, P. B. (1996). The sources of visual information to the primate frontal lobe: a novel role for the superior parietal lobule. *Cerebral Cortex, 6*, 319–328.

Castiello, U., & Paine, M. (2002). Effects of left parietal injury on covert orienting of attention. *Journal of Neurology, Neurosurgery and Psychiatry, 72*, 73–76.

Cavada, C., & Goldman-Rakic, P. S. (1989a). Posterior parietal cortex in rhesus monkey: I. Parcellation of areas based on distinctive limbic and sensory corticocortical connections. *Journal of Comparative Neurology, 287*, 393–421.

Cavada, C., & Goldman-Rakic, P. S. (1989b) Posterior parietal cortex in rhesus monkey: II. Evidence for segregated corticocortical networks linking sensory and limbic areas with the frontal lobe. *Journal of Comparative Neurology, 287*, 422–445.

Chapman, H., Gavrilescu, M., Wang, H., Kean, M., Egan, G., Castiello, U. (2002). Posterior parietal cortex control of reach-to-grasp movements in humans. *European Journal of Neuroscience, 15*, 2037–2042.

Classen, J., Kunesch, E., Binkofski, F., Hilperath, F., Schlaug, G., Seitz, R. J. et al. (1995). Subcortical origin of visuomotor apraxia. *Brain, 118*, 1365–1374.

Clower, D. M., West, R. A., Lynch, J. C., & Strick, P. L. (2001). The inferior parietal lobule is the target of output from the superior colliculus, hippocampus, and the cerebellum. *Journal of Neuroscience, 21*, 6283–6291.

Cohen, Y. E., & Andersen, R. A. (2002). Common reference frame for movement plans in the posterior parietal cortex. *Nature Reviews Neuroscience, 3*, 553–562.

Colby, C. L., & Duhamel, J.-R. (1991). Heterogeneity of extrastriate visual areas and multiple parietal areas in the macaque monkey. *Neuropsychologia, 29*, 517–537.

Colby, C. L., Gatass, R., Olson, C. R., & Gross, C. G. (1988). Topographic organization of cortical afferents to extrastriate visual area PO in the macaque: a dual tracer study. *Journal of Comparative Neurology, 238*, 1257–1299.

Colby, C. L., & Goldberg, M. E. (1999). Space and attention in parietal cortex. *Annual Review of Neuroscience, 22*, 319–349.

Corbetta, M., Akbudak, E., Conturo, T. E., Snyder, A. Z., Ollinger, J. M., Drury, H. A. et al. (1998). A common network of functional areas for attention and eye movements. *Neuron, 21*, 761–773.

Corbetta, M., Kincade, J. M., Ollinger, J. M., McAvoy, M. P., & Shulman, G. L. (2000). Voluntary orienting is dissociated from target detection in human posterior parietal cortex. *Nature Neuroscience, 3*, 292–297.

Corbetta, M., Miezin, F. M., Shulman, G. L., & Petersen, S. E. A. (1993). A PET study of visuospatial attention. *Journal of Neuroscience, 13*, 1202–1226.

Corbetta, M., & Shulman, G. L. (2002). Control of goal-directed and stimulus-driven attention in the brain. *Nature Reviews Neuroscience, 3*, 201–215.

Corbetta, M., Shulman, G. L., Miezin, F. M., & Petersen, S. E. (1995). Superior parietal cortex activation during spatial attention shifts and visual feature conjunction. *Science, 270*, 802–804.

Coull, J. T., & Nobre, A. C. (1998). Where and when to pay attention: the neural substrate for directing attention to spatial locations and to time intervals as revealed by both PET and fMRI. *Journal of Neuroscience, 18*, 7426–7435.

Deiber, M.-P., Ibanez, V., Sadato, N., & Hallet, M. (1996). Cerebral structures participating in motor preparation in humans: a positron emission tomography study. *Journal of Neurophysiology, 75*, 233–247.

de Jong, B. M., van der Graaf, F. H., & Paans, A. M. (2001). Brain activation related to the representations of external space and body scheme in visuomotor control. *NeuroImage, 14*, 1128–1135.

Desmurget, M., Epstein, C. M., Turner, R. S., Prablanc, C., Alexander, G. E., & Grafton, S. T. (1999). Role of the posterior parietal cortex in updating reaching movements to a visual target. *Nature Neuroscience, 2*, 563–567.

Desmurget, M., & Grafton, S. (2000). Forward modeling allows feedback control for fast reaching movements. *Trends in Cognitive Sciences, 4,* 423–431.

Desmurget, M., Grea, H., Grethe, J. S., Prablanc, C., Alexander, G. E., & Grafton, S. T. (2001). Functional anatomy of nonvisual feedback loops during reaching: a positron emission tomography study. *Journal of Neuroscience, 21,* 2919–2928.

Deubel, H., & Schneider, W. X. (1996). Saccade target selection and object recognition: evidence for a common attentional mechanism. *Vision Research, 36,* 1827–1837.

Duhamel, J.-R., Colby, C. L., & Goldberg, M. E. (1992a). The updating of the representation of visual space in parietal cortex by intended eye movements. *Science, 255,* 90–92.

Duhamel, J.-R., Goldberg, M. E., Fitzgibbon, E. J., Sirigu, A., & Grafman, J. (1992b). Saccadic dysmetria in a patient with a right frontoparietal lesion: the importance of corollary discharge for accurate spatial behaviour. *Brain, 115,* 1387–1402.

Eidelburg, D., & Galaburda, A. M. (1984). Inferior parietal lobule: Divergent architectonic asymmetries in the human brain. *Archives of Neurology, 41,* 843–852.

Eskandar, E. N., & Assad, J. A. (1999). Dissociation of visual, motor and predictive signals in parietal cortex during visual guidance. *Nature Neuroscience, 2,* 88–93.

Faugier-Grimond, S., Frenois, C., & Peronnet, F. (1985) Effects of posterior parietal lesions on visually guided movements in monkeys. *Experimental Brain Research, 59,* 125–138.

Ferraina, S., Battaglia-Meyer, A., Genovesio, A., Marconi, B., Onorati, P., & Caminiti, R. (2001). Early coding of visuomanual coordination during reaching in parietal area PEc. *Journal of Neurophysiology, 85,* 462–467.

Fink, G. R., Dolan, R. J., Halligan, P. W., Marshall, J. C., Frith, C. D. (1997). Space-based and object-based visual attention: shared and specific neural domains. *Brain, 120,* 2013–2028.

Fink, G. R., Marshall, J. C., Halligan, P. W., Frith, C. D., Driver, J., Frackowiak, R. S. et al. (1999). The neural consequences of conflict between intention and the senses. *Brain, 122,* 497–512.

Flanders, M., Helms Tillery, S. I., & Soechting, J. F. (1992). Early stages in a sensorimotor transformation. *Behavioural and Brain Sciences, 15,* 309–362.

Galletti, C., Battaglini, P. P., & Fattori, P. (1993). Parietal neurons encoding spatial locations in craniotopic coordinates. *Experimental Brain Research, 96,* 221–229.

Galletti, C., Battaglini, P. P., & Fattori, P. P. (1995). Eye position influence on the parieto-occipital PO (V6) of the macaque monkey. *European Journal of Neuroscience, 7,* 2486–2501.

Galletti, C., Fattori, P., Kutz, D. F., & Battaglini, P. P. (1997). Arm movement related neurons in the visual area V6 of the macaque superior parietal lobule. *European Journal of Neuroscience, 9,* 410–413.

Georgopoulos, A. P., Caminiti, R., & Kalaska, J. F. (1984). Static spatial effects in motor cortex and area 5: quantitative relations in two dimensional space. *Experimental Brain Research, 54,* 446–454.

Geyer, S., Matelli, M., Luppino, G., & Zilles, K. (2000). Functional neuroanatomy of the primate isocortical motor system. *Anatomy and Embryology, 202,* 443–474.

Gitelman, D. R., Nobre, A. C., Parrish, T. B., LaBar, K. S., Kim, Y. H., Meyer, J. R., et al. (1999). A large scale distributed network for covert spatial attention: further anatomical delineation based on stringent behavioural and cognitive controls. *Brain, 122,* 1093–1106.

Glickstein, M. (1997). Parietal lobe and the visual control of movement. In P. Thier & H. -O. Karnath (Eds.), *Parietal lobe contributions to orientation in 3D space* (pp. 23–33). Heidelberg: Springer-Verlag.

Glickstein, M. G., May, J., & Mercier, B. (1985). Corticopontine projection in the macaque: the distribution of labelled cortical cells after large injections of horse-radish peroxidase in the pontine nuclei. *Journal of Comparative Neurology, 235*, 343–359.

Glover, S., & Dixon, P. (2001). Dynamic illusion effects in a reaching task: evidence for separate visual representations in the planning and control of reaching. *Journal of Experimental Psychology: Human Perception and Performance, 27*, 560–572.

Gottlieb, J. P., Kusunoki, M., & Goldberg, M. E. (1998). The representation of visual salience in monkey parietal cortex. *Nature, 391*, 481–484.

Graziano, M. S. A., Cooke, D. F., & C. S. R. Taylor, (2000). Coding the location of the arm by sight. *Science, 290*, 1782–1786.

Grea, H., Pisella, L., Rossetti, Y., Desmurget, M., Tilikete, C., Grafton, S. et al. (2002). A lesion of the posterior parietal cortex disrupts on-line adjustments during aiming movements. *Neuropsychologia, 40*, 2471–2480.

Haaland, K. Y., Harrington, D. L., & Knight, R.T. (2000). Neural representations of skilled movement. *Brain, 123*, 2306–2313.

Harrington, D. L., & Haaland, K. Y. (1991). Hemispheric specialization for motor sequencing: abnormalities in levels of programming. *Neuropsychologia, 29*, 147–163.

Harrington, D. L., & Haaland, K. Y. (1992). Motor sequencing with left hemisphere damage: are some cognitive deficits specific to limb apraxia. *Brain, 115*, 857–890.

Helms Tillery, S. I., Ebner, T. J., & Soechting, J. F. (1995). Task dependence of primate arm posture. *Experimental Brain Research, 104*, 1–11.

Hopfinger, J. B., Buonocore, M. H., & Mangun, G. R. (2000). The neural mechanisms of top-down attentional control. *Nature Neuroscience, 3*, 284–291.

Humphreys, G. W., & Riddoch, M. J. (2001). Detection by action: neuropsychological evidence for action-defined templates in search. *Nature Neuroscience, 4*, 84–88.

Indovina, I., & Sanes, J. N. (2001). Combined visual attention and finger movement effects on human brain representations. *Experimental Brain Research, 140*, 265–279.

Jackson, S. R., Newport, R., Husain, M., Harvey, M., & Hindle, J. V. (2000). Reaching movements may reveal the distorted topography of spatial representations after neglect. *Neuropsychologia, 38*, 500–507.

James, W. (1890). *Principles of psychology*, (Vol. 1). New York. Hott.

Kimura, D. (1977). Acquisition of a motor skill after left hemipshere damage. *Brain, 100*, 527–542.

Kimura, D., & Archibald, Y. (1974). Motor functions of the left hemisphere. *Brain, 97*, 337–350.

Krams, M., Rushworth, M. F. S. Deiber, M. P., Frackowiak, R. S. J., & Passingham, R. E. (1998). The preparation, suppression, and execution of copied movements in the human brain. *Experimental Brain Research, 120*, 386–398.

LaBerge, D., LeGrand, R., & Hobbie, R. K. (1969). Functional identification of perceptual and response biases in choice reaction time. *Journal of Experimental Psychology, 79*, 295–299.

Lacquaniti, F., Guigon, E., Bianchi, L., Ferraina, S., & Caminiti, R. (1995). Represent-ing spatial information for limb movement: role of area 5 in the monkey. *Cerebral Cortex, 5*, 391–409.

Le, T. H., Pardo, J. V., & Hu, X. (1998). 4 T-fMRI study of nonspatial shifting of selective attention: cerebellar and parietal contributions. *Journal of Neurophysiology, 79,* 1535–1548.

Lewis, J. W., & Van Essen, D. C. (2000). Corticocortical connections of visual, senso-rimotor, and multimodal processing areas in the parietal lobe of the macaque monkey. *Journal of Comparative Neurology, 428,* 112–137.

Macaluso, E., Frith, C. D., & Driver, J. (2000) Modulation of human visual cortex by crossmodal spatial attention. *Science, 289,* 1206–1208.

Marconi, B., Genovesio, A., Battaglia-Mayer, A., Ferraina, S., Squatrito, S., Molinari, M. et al. (2001). Eye–hand coordination during reaching. I Anatomical relation-ships between parietal and frontal cortex. *Cerebral Cortex, 11,* 513–527.

Marois, R., Larson, J., Chun, M. M., & Shima, D. (2002). *The neural correlates of the response bottleneck.* Presentation to the 8th International Conference on Functional Mapping of the Human Brain, 2–6, 2002 June, Sendai, Japan. Available on CD-Rom in *NeuroImage, 16* (No. 2, 20583).

Mayer, E., Martory, M. D., Pegna, A. J., Landis, T., Delavelle, J., & Annoni, J. M. (1999). A pure case of Gerstmann syndrome with a subangular lesion. *Brain, 122,* 1107–1120.

McIntyre, J., Stratta, F., & Lacquaniti, F. (1998). Short-term memory for reaching to visual targets: psychophysical evidence for body-centered reference frames. *Journal of Neuroscience, 18,* 8423–8435.

Mesulam, M.-M. (1981). A cortical network for directed attention and unilateral neglect. *Annals of Neurology, 10,* 309–325.

Miall, R. C. (1998). The cerebellum, predictive control and motor coordination. *Novartis Foundation Symposium, 218,* 272–284.

Mishkin, M., Ungerleider, L. G., & Macko, K. A. (1983). Object vision and spatial vision: two cortical pathways. *Trends in Neurosciences, 6,* 414–417.

Nakamura, H., Kuroda, T., Wakita, M., Kusunoki, M., Kato, A., Mikami, A. et al. (2001). From three-dimensional space vision to prehensile hand movements: the lateral intraparietal area links the area V3A and the anterior intraparietal area in macaques. *Journal of Neuroscience, 21,* 8174–8187.

Newport, R., Hindle, J. V., & Jackson, S. R. (2001). Links between vision and soma-tosensation: vision can improve the felt position of the unseen hand. *Current Biology, 11,* 975–980.

Newport, R., Rabb, B., & Jackson, S. R. (2002). Noninformative vision improves haptic spatial perception. *Current Biology, 12,* 1661–1664.

Nobre, A. C. (2001). The attentive homunculus: now you see it, now you don't. *Neuroscience and Biobehavioural Reviews, 25,* 477–496.

Nobre, A. C., Gitelman, D. R., Dias, E. C., & Mesulam, M. M. (2000). Covert visual spatial orienting and saccades: overlapping neural systems. *NeuroImage, 11,* 210–216.

Nobre, A. C., Sebestyen, G. N., Gitelman, D. R., Mesulam, M. M., Frackowiak, R. S. J., & Frith, C. D. (1997). Functional localization of the system for visuospatial attention using positron emission tomography. *Brain, 120,* 515–533.

Pandya, D. P., & Seltzer, B. (1982). Intrinsic connections and architectonics of pos-terior parietal cortex in the rhesus monkey. *Journal of Comparative Neurology, 204,* 196–210.

Pashler, H. (1984). Processing stages in overlapping tasks: evidence for a central bottleneck. *Journal of Experimental Psychology: Human Perception and Performance, 10,* 358–377.

Pashler, H. (1989). Dissociations and dependencies between speed and accuracy: evidence for a two-component theory of divided attention in simple tasks. *Cognitive Psychology*, *21*, 469–514.

Pashler, H. (1991). Shifting visual attention and selecting motor responses: distinct attentional mechanisms. *Journal of Experimental Psychology: Human Perception and Performance*, *17*, 1023–1040.

Pashler, H., & Christian, C. (1991). Dual task interference and the production of motor responses. Quoted in Pashler, H. (1992). Attentional limitations in doing two tasks at the same time. *Current Directions in Psychological Science*, *1*, 44–48.

Pashler, H., & Johnstone, J. C. (1989). Interference between temporally overlapping tasks: chronometric evidence for central postponement with or without response grouping. *Quarterly Journal of Experimental Psychology*, *41A*, 19–45.

Pisella, L., Grea, H., Tilikete, C., Vighetto, A., Desmurget, M., Rode, G. et al. (2000). An "automatic pilot" for the hand in human posterior parietal cortex: toward reinterpreting optic ataxia. *Nature Neuroscience*, *3*, 729–736.

Poizner, H., Clark, M. A., Merians, A. S., Macauley, B., Gonzalez Rothi, L. J., & Heilman, K. M. (1995). Joint coordination deficits in limb apraxia. *Brain*, *118*, 227–242.

Posner, M. I. (1980). Orienting of attention: The VIIth Sir Frederic Bartlett Lecture. *Quarterly Journal of Experimental Psychology*, *32*, 3–25.

Posner, M. I., Inhoff, A. W., Friedrich, F. J., & Cohen, A. (1987). Isolating attentional systems: a cognitive-anatomical analysis. *Psychobiology*, *1*, 107–121.

Posner, M. I., Walker, J. A., Friedrich, F. J., & Rafal, R. D. (1984). Effects of parietal injury on covert orienting of attention. *Journal of Neuroscience*, *4*, 1863–1874.

Preuss, T. M., & Goldman-Rakic, P. S. (1991). Architectonics of the parietal and temporal association cortex in the strepsirhine *Galago* compared to the anthropoid primate *Macaca*. *Journal of Comparative Neurology*, *310*, 475–506.

Rizzolatti, G., Gentilluci, M., & Matelli, M. (1985). Selective spatial attention: one center, one circuit, or many circuits. In M. I. Posner & O. S. M. Marin (Eds.), *Attention and performance XI* (pp. 251–265). Hillsdale, NJ: Lawrence Erlbaum Associates Inc.

Robinson, C. J., & Burton, H. (1980a). Somatic submodality distribution within the second somatosensory (SII), 7b, retroinsular, postauditory, and granular insular cortical areas of m. *fascicularis*. *Journal of Comparative Neurology*, *192*, 93–108.

Robinson, C. J., & Burton, H. (1980b). Somatopographic organization in the second somatosensory area of m. *fascicularis*. *Journal of Comparative Neurology*, *192*, 43–67.

Rushworth, M. F. S., Ellison, A. E., & Walsh, V. (2001b). Complementary localization and lateralization of orienting and motor attention. *Nature Neuroscience*, *4*, 656–661.

Rushworth, M. F. S., Johansen-Berg, H., & Young, S. A. (1998). Parietal cortex and spatial-postural transformation during arm movements. *Journal of Neurophysiology*, *79*, 478–482.

Rushworth, M. F. S., Krams, M., & Passingham, R. E. (2001c). The attentional role of the left parietal cortex: the distinct lateralization and localization of motor attention in the human brain. *Journal of Cognitive Neuroscience*, *13*, 698–710.

Rushworth, M. F. S., Nixon, P. D., & Passingham, R. E. (1997a). The parietal cortex and movement. I. Movement selection and reaching. *Experimental Brain Research*, *117*, 292–310.

Rushworth, M. F. S., Nixon, P. D., & Passingham, R. E. (1997b). Parietal cortex and movement. II. Spatial representations. *Experimental Brain Research*, *117*, 311–323.

Rushworth, M. F. S., Nixon, P. D., Renowden, S., Wade, D. T., & Passingham, R. E. (1997c). The left parietal cortex and attention to action. *Neuropsychologia*, *35*, 1261–1273.

Rushworth, M. F. S., Paus, T., & Sipila, P. K. (2001a). Attention systems and the organization of the human parietal cortex. *Journal of Neuroscience*, *21*, 5262–5271.

Sakata, H., Taira, M., Kusunoki, M., Murata, A., & Tanaka, Y. (1997). The TINS lecture: The parietal association cortex in depth perception and visual control of hand action. *Trends in Neurosciences*, *20*, 350–357.

Sakata, H., Taira, M., Kusunoki, M., Murata, A., Tsutsui, K., Tanaka, Y. et al. (1999). Neural representation of three dimensional features of manipulation objects with stereopsis. *Experimental Brain Research*, *128*, 160–169.

Savaki, H. E., Kennedy, C., Sokoloff, L., & Mishkin, M. (1993). Visually guided reaching with the forelimb contralateral to a "blind" hemisphere: a metabolic mapping study in monkeys. *Journal of Neuroscience*, *13*, 2772–2789.

Seal, J., Gross, C., & Biolac, B. (1982). Activity of neurons in area 5 during a simple arm movement in monkeys before and after deafferentation of the trained limb. *Brain Research*, *220*, 229–243.

Sereno, M. I., Pitzalis, S., & Martinez, A. (2001). Mapping of contralateral space in retinotopic coordinates by a parietal cortical area in humans. *Science*, *294*, 1350–1354.

Sheliga, B. M., Craighero, L., Riggio, L., & Rizzolatti, G. (1997). Effects of spatial attention on directional manual and ocular responses. *Experimental Brain Research*, *114*, 339–351.

Sheliga, B. M., Riggio, L., & Rizzolatti, G. (1994). Orienting of attention and eye movements. *Experimental Brain Research*, *98*, 507–522.

Shipp, S., Blanton, M., & Zeki, S. (1998). A visuo-somatomotor pathway through the superior parietal cortex in the macaque monkey: cortical connections of areas V6 and V6A. *European Journal of Neuroscience*, *10*, 3171–3193.

Snyder, L. H., Batista, A. P., & Andersen, R. A. (1997). Coding of intention in the posterior parietal cortex. *Nature*, *386*, 167–170.

Soechting, J. F., & Flanders, M. (1989a). Errors in pointing are due to approximations in sensorimotor transformations. *Journal of Neurophysiology*, *62*, 595–608.

Soechting, J. F., & Flanders, M. (1989b). Sensorimotor representations for pointing to targets in three-dimensional space. *Journal of Neurophysiology*, *62*, 582–594.

Stein, J. F. (1978). Effects of parietal lobe cooling on manipulative behaviour in the conscious monkey. In G. Gordon (Ed.), *Active touch—the mechanism of recognition of objects by manipulation. A multidisciplinary approach* (pp. 79–80). Oxford: Pergamon Press.

Stein, J. F. (1986). Role of the cerebellum in the visual guidance of movement. *Nature*, *323*, 217–221.

Sternberg, S., Monsell, S., Knoll, R. L., & Wright, C. E. (1978). The latency and duration of rapid movement sequences: comparisons of speech and typewriting. In G. E. Stelmach (Ed.), *Information processing in motor control and learning* (pp. 117–152). New York: Academic Press.

Tanne-Gariepy, J., Rouiller, E. M., & Boussaoud, D. (2002). Parietal inputs to dorsal versus ventral premotor areas in the macaque monkey: evidence for largely segregated visuomotor pathways. *Experimental Brain Research*, *145*, 91–103.

Toni, I., Rushworth, M. F. S., & Passingham, R. E. (2001). Neural correlates of visuomotor associations: spatial rules compared with arbitrary rules. *Experimental Brain Research, 141*, 359–369.

Tsal, Y., & Lavie, N. (1988). Attending to colour and shape: the special role of location in selective visual processing. *Perception and Psychophysics, 44*, 15–21.

Tsal, Y., & Lavie, N. (1993). Location dominance in attending to colour and shape. *Journal of Experimental Psychology: Human Perception and Performance, 19*, 131–139.

Von Bonin, G., & Bailey, P. (1947). *The neocortex of Macaca mulatta.* Urbana: University of Illinois Press.

Walsh, V., & Cowey, A. (2000). Transcranial magnetic stimulation and cognitive neuroscience. *Nature Reviews Neuroscience, 1*, 73–77.

Walsh, V., & Rushworth, M. F. S. (1999). The use of transcranial magnetic stimulation in neuropsychological testing. *Neuropsychologia, 37*, 125–135.

Welford, A. T. (1952). The "psychological refractory period" and the timing of high speed performance: a review and a theory. *British Journal of Psychology, 43*, 2–19.

Wise, S. P., Boussaoud, D., Johnson, P. B., & Caminiti, R. (1997). Premotor and parietal cortex: corticocortical connectivity and combinatorial computations. *Annual Review of Neuroscience, 20*, 25–42.

11 Prefrontal cortex and attention to action

Richard E. Passingham, James B. Rowe and Katz Sakai

Abstract

We have used fMRI to study attention to action. When participants learn motor sequences, at first the dorsal prefrontal cortex is active, but as the task becomes automatic, so the activity reduces to baseline levels. It is then possible to reactivate the dorsal prefrontal cortex by asking the participants to attend again to their actions. Comparing performance with and without attention, there is an enhancement of activity in the prefrontal, premotor and parietal cortex. There is also a change in the covariance between activity in prefrontal cortex and premotor areas. The prefrontal cortex is in a position to exert a top-down influence because it has information about the external context and the participant's goals. These goals are set by the task instructions. We therefore scanned participants after they had received one of four instructions and before a sequence of spatial and verbal items was presented for them to remember. In the interval before the items were presented, there was sustained activity in dorsal spatial areas where the instruction was to remember the spatial items, and in ventral verbal and visual areas where the instruction was to remember the verbal items. Furthermore, there was a greater correlation between activity in frontal polar cortex and posterior areas when the task was to require a reordering of the items than when it was a simple memory task. In psychology experiments, the task instructions specify what the participants should attend to and what they should do. Our results indicate that these influences are exerted by top-down connections from the prefrontal to posterior areas.

Introduction

When pianists learn a new piece, they must attend to what they are doing. However, when they have learned the piece and practised it at length, they can play the notes automatically and without attention. Attention to action involves both the selection of and preparation for the actions to be performed and the monitoring of sensory feedback as the actions are performed. Our interest in this chapter is restricted to the attention paid to the selection of the action.

The evidence for the degree of attention that must be paid to the performance of a task comes from the amount of interference when the participants must simultaneously carry out a secondary task. Watkins and Passingham (in Passingham, 1998) trained participants on a manual sequence task. The participants first learned the task by trial and error until they made no errors. They were then given further practice trials. The secondary task was to generate a verb for each noun presented on the screen. In the dual-task condition, each time a noun appeared the participants made the next move in the motor sequence and simultaneously generated a noun. Dual-task trials were given early in practice (after 90 s of further practice) or late in practice (after 15 min of further practice).

Early in learning, performance of the verb generation task led to prolonged response times on the sequence task and caused participants to make many errors (Passingham, 1998). However, late in training, they made significantly fewer errors during dual-task performance. The response times were still elevated, though less so than during early practice. This suggests that the task had still not become fully automatic after 15 min of practice. This is not surprising.

The verb generation task was chosen because it is known that there are activations in the prefrontal cortex when participants perform this task compared with repeating the nouns (Petersen, Fox, Posner, Mintun, & Raichle, 1988; Raichle et al., 1994). We have also shown that there is activation of the prefrontal cortex early in the learning of a manual sequence task (Jenkins, Brooks, Nixon, Frackowiak, & Passingham, 1994). We have used fMRI to scan participants continuously for 45 min while they learned a sequence by trial and error (Toni, Krams, Turner, & Passingham, 1998). The dorsal prefrontal cortex was highly activated early in learning but, as learning progressed, the activation decreased until it reached baseline after 20–25 min. The implication is that for dual-task performance early in sequence learning, the prefrontal cortex is activated both for the generation of motor responses and for the generation of verbs, and is unable to carry out both processes concurrently. Thus there is interference between performance of the two tasks. However, late in sequence learning, the prefrontal cortex is no longer activated during the performance of the sequence, and thus the generation of verbs causes less interference.

If this is correct, then there should be no interference if the secondary task is not one that is associated with activation in the prefrontal cortex. We therefore chose noun repetition because it has been shown that the prefrontal cortex is not activated during repetition of words (Petersen et al., 1988; Warburton et al., 1996). There was no significant interference with the performance of the motor sequence early in practice, either in terms of response times or errors (Passingham, 1998). This supports the view that interference occurred when the participants generated verbs because verb generation was associated with activation of the prefrontal cortex. A fully convincing demonstration of this claim would require the use of a secondary task, which, though equal in difficulty to verb generation, was not associated with activation of the prefrontal cortex.

Attention to action

In the previous section, we showed that early in sequence learning participants must pay more attention to their actions than late in learning, and that prefrontal cortex is activated early but not late in learning. To further demonstrate a link between prefrontal activation and attention to action, we manipulated attention by setting up two conditions in which the same actions are performed, but in one condition the participants are required to attend to what they are doing. Jueptner, Stephan, Frith, Brooks, Frackowiak, and Passingham (1997) scanned participants using PET. In one condition, they performed a motor sequence that they had practised for 30 min before scanning. We found that the participants could perform it automatically because they were able to repeat a list of auditorily presented digits without loss of accuracy. In another condition, the participants again performed the automatic sequence but were now instructed to attend to what they were doing. The specific instruction was to "think about the next move". Whereas the dorsal prefrontal cortex was not activated when the sequence was performed automatically, it was reactivated when the sequence was performed under attentional control.

We have recently replicated this finding using fMRI (Rowe, Frackowiak, Friston, & Passingham, 2002a; Rowe, Stephan, Friston, Frackowiak, Lees, & Passingham, 2002b). This enabled us to examine interactions between the prefrontal cortex and the motor system. In both these fMRI studies, the participants performed the simple finger sequence 1, 2, 3, 4, 1, 2, 3, 4 and so on. They performed this sequence continuously for 10 min before scanning and at the end of this period were able to report back auditorily presented lists of digits accurately while simultaneously performing the sequence. During scanning, different conditions were interleaved in short blocks. At the beginning of each block, the participants were presented with an instruction. In the attentional condition, the same instruction was given on the screen as in the study by Jueptner et al. (1997): the participants were instructed to "think about the next move" between each move of the sequence. Evidence that the participants treated the task differently in this condition is provided by the fact that their inter-response times were significantly more variable than they were in the condition in which no instruction was given to attend (Rowe et al., 2002a, 2002b).

There was activity in the dorsal prefrontal cortex (area 46) when participants attended to their actions, but not when they performed the same actions without attention (Figure 11.1). It can be seen from Figure 11.1 that there was also enhanced activation in the premotor and parietal cortex when the actions were performed under attentional control compared with

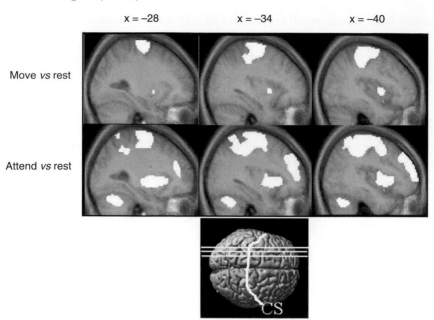

Figure 11.1 Activations for the comparison of movement without attention (Move *vs* rest) (upper) and movement with attention (Attend *vs* move) (lower). The parasagittal sections are taken from the levels shown on the brain at the bottom; the lateral coordinates (x) are shown at the top. Continuous line on bottom figure = central sulcus. Adapted from Rowe et al. (2002a).

when they were performed automatically. This difference was statistically significant when the two conditions were directly compared.

We then used structural equation modelling to investigate whether the enhanced activation in the premotor cortex was influenced by the activation in prefrontal cortex. In one study (Rowe et al., 2002b) we set up an anatomical model that included the prefrontal, premotor, supplementary and motor cortex. We know that the dorsal prefrontal cortex sends projections to the premotor and pre-supplementary motor cortex (Lu, Preston, & Strick, 1994; Luppino, Matelli, Camarda, & Rizzolatti, 1993; Wang, Shima, Osoda, Sawamura, & Tanji, 2002), and that there are projections to motor cortex from the premotor cortex and supplementary motor cortex (Lu et al., 1994; Muakkassa & Strick, 1979). When the task was performed under attentional control, there was a significant increase in the coupling between the prefrontal and premotor cortex and between the prefrontal and supplementary motor cortex. The effect was small, though statistically significant. We therefore repeated the study in another group of participants. We again found an increase in the coupling between the prefrontal and premotor cortex in the attention condition (Rowe et al., 2002a). Figure 11.2 presents both the path

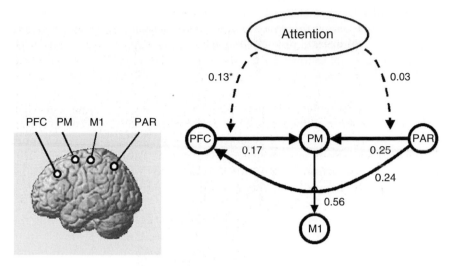

Figure 11.2 Anatomical model for structural equation modelling of the modulatory effect of attention. Brain on left shows areas included in the model. PFC = prefrontal cortex, PM = premotor cortex, M1 = motor cortex, PAR = parietal cortex. Arrows show connections between areas. The path strengths as assessed over all conditions are shown beside the arrows. The size of the modulatory changes in the strength of a path as the result of attention is shown by the dotted line. *Statistically significant. Data from Rowe et al. (2002a).

strength between these two areas as assessed over all conditions and the size of the modulatory influence of attention to action.

It might be thought that if there is covariance between activity in two areas, it is necessarily true that there will be a change in this covariance if both areas become more activated. However, this is not necessarily the case. For example, Rowe et al. (2002a) included in their anatomical model the pathway from the parietal to the premotor cortex. Both areas show enhanced activation under conditions of attentional control (Figure 11.1) and there was a significant coupling between activity in these two areas as assessed over all conditions (Figure 11.2). The numbers by the dotted line give the size of the modulatory change; an asterisk denotes statistical significance. Nonetheless, there was no significant change in the strength of the path between the parietal to premotor cortex under conditions of attentional control (Rowe et al., 2002a) (Figure 11.2). These results are consistent with the hypothesis that, when individuals are required to attend to their actions, the prefrontal cortex influences activity in the premotor areas. However, to prove the causal link it would be necessary to interfere with activity in the prefrontal cortex and show that the enhancement of activity in the premotor areas no longer occurs when participants attend to the selection of their actions.

The results leave unclear what the participants did when we instructed them to think about their next move. It is inelegant to manipulate the degree of attention by simple instruction; the participants could have used many strategies in following this instruction. They might have prepared the movement, imagined the movement or attended to the feedback from the movement. However, whatever they did, it led to a significant increase in the variability of inter-response times and we know that when individuals practise a motor task in the scanner there is a continuous decrease in the variability of response times as the task becomes more automatic (Toni, Ramnani, Josephs, Ashburner, & Passingham, 2001). This suggests the instruction to think of the next move succeeded in its aim, which was to ensure that the participants performed the task less automatically.

This could be either because the participants were thinking about the movement in advance or because they were attending to feedback from the movement as they performed it. While we cannot exclude the latter possibility, this would not easily explain the increase in inter-response times that we observed in the attention condition. It is more likely that this increase occurred because of variation in the selection of and preparation for the next move. We know that there is activation in the dorsal prefrontal cortex when individuals prepare moves (Pochon et al., 2001; Rushworth, Krams, & Passingham, 2001) or imaging performing movements (Deiber, Ibanez, Honda, Sadato, Raman, & Hallett, 1998; Gerardin et al., 2000). These activations can be shown to occur either in advance of movement (Pochon et al., 2001) or in the absence of movement (Gerardin et al., 2000).

Sustained activity in advance of actions can be found not only in the prefrontal cortex (Pochon et al., 2001), but also in the premotor (Simon, Meurnier, Piettre, Berardi, Segebarth, & Boussaoud, 2002; Toni, Shah, Fink, Thoenissen, Passingham, & Zilles, 2002) and parietal cortex (Deiber, Ibanez, Sadato, & Hallett, 1996). This raises the question as to whether the dorsal prefrontal cortex is necessarily activated when individuals prepare for action. This area was not activated during preparation in the study by Deiber et al. (1996) in which participants were given a visual cue and briefly prepared the appropriate action. On the other hand, activation related to preparation was reported in this area by Rushworth et al. (2001). One difference between the studies was that in the latter study the participants were specifically instructed to attend to the movement they were preparing during the delay. No such instruction was given in the study by Deiber et al. (1996). Thus, one possibility is that the crucial difference between the studies lay in the difference in the attentional demands of the tasks. However, it would be necessary to replicate both tasks within the same study to confirm that this is correct. If so, it would suggest that the activation in the dorsal prefrontal cortex is relating to attention—that is, not to preparation *per se*, but to attentive preparation of upcoming action.

Attentional selection

Attending to one representation is a selective process. Desimone and Duncan (1995) proposed a biased-competition model for selective attention in which a top-down signal biases one representation in posterior areas, and there is then competition in those areas between representations. Evidence in favour of this model comes from single unit studies in which the bias occurred as the result of a search task and competition was demonstrated in visual association cortex (Chelazzi, Duncan, Miller, & Desimone, 1998). The biased competition model can be generalized to the selection of action (Frith, 2000). In this case, it is proposed that a top-down signal biases the representations of action in the premotor areas. Cisek and Kalaska (2002) have reported evidence that when a macaque monkey is presented with two potential targets, but does not yet know which it is appropriate to select, there are subpopulations of cells in the premotor cortex that code for each of the potential movements. However, when a signal then tells the animal which one to select, the population activity codes for that movement. This evidence indicates that different potential actions can be represented in the premotor cortex.

To determine whether the biased competition model can be generalized to the motor system, we compared in the same fMRI study the selection of visual stimuli and the selection of actions (Rowe, Stephan, Friston, Frackowiak, & Passingham, in press). There were two conditions in which participants selected between fingers. In one, the participants decided themselves which of four fingers to move; on each trial they had to consider which finger to move. In the control condition, the appropriate finger was specified by a visual cue on the screen; the response was routine. There were also two conditions in which the participants selected between colours. In one condition, four colours appeared centrally on the screen on each trial and the participants had to decide themselves which one to choose. In the control condition, a single colour was presented in the centre of the screen and this specified the appropriate colour. In both conditions, the participants reported the colour by pressing the key that corresponded to that colour. At the bottom of the screen, symbols were presented for each key and these were coloured; the association between any key and a particular colour was randomized from trial to trial. In this way, we could arrange that the participants knew which key to press given either the colour that they had selected or the colour that was presented on that trial.

We first checked that there was activation in the dorsal prefrontal cortex both when participants selected between finger movements and when they selected between colours. As has been shown in several previous studies (Deiber, Passingham, Colebatch, Friston, Nixon, & Frackowiak, 1991; Frith, Friston, Liddle, & Frackowiak, 1991; Hyder, Phelps, Wiggins, LaBar, Blamire, & Shulman, 1997; Spence, Hirsch, Brooks, & Grasby, 1998), there was activation in this area when a comparison was made between the condition in which the participants chose between actions and the control condition in which the action was externally specified and routine. We also found activation in the same area when the corresponding comparison was made for the choice between colours. Furthermore, the peaks for the activity in these comparisons were very close anatomically.

We next used structural equation modelling to study changes in the path strengths between the dorsal prefrontal cortex and other areas when participants selected between movements or colours (Rowe et al., in press). We modelled the interactions between the prefrontal cortex, the motor cortex and the prestriate visual area V4. We chose to include motor cortex rather than premotor cortex because it is difficult to distinguish in the precentral sulcus between activity that is related to eye movements (frontal eye field) (Rosano et al., 2002) and activity that is related to finger movements (Fink, Frackowiak, Pietrzyk, & Passingham, 1997; Rintjes, Dettmers, Buchel, Kiebel, Frackowiak, & Weiller, 1999). Since individuals may make more eye movements when choosing between colours than when inspecting a single colour, we were concerned that there might be more activation in the precentral sulcus because of the difference in eye movements between the two conditions. This problem does not arise when considering motor cortex. We chose the ventral prestriate area V4 because around 50% of the cells in this area are known to be responsive to colour (DeYoe & Van Essen, 1988).

The results are shown in diagrammatic form in Figure 11.3. The model is simplified: there is no assumption that the paths shown are direct. For example, a projection is shown from prefrontal to motor cortex, although the connection is known to be indirect via connections through the premotor areas (Lu et al., 1994). The thick lines show paths where there was a significant difference in connectivity for the choice compared with the externally specified (routine) condition. The dashed lines show that the connectivity differed according to modality, where A shows that the connectivity was greater for action than colour and C for colour than action. Finally, the letters "i" indicates a significant interaction between task and modality, where the letters "ia" indicate that the connectivity was greater for choice of action and the letters "ic" for choice of colour.

It can be seen from Figure 11.3 that there were significant changes in connectivity of the path from prefrontal to motor cortex for action. Correspondingly, there were significant changes in connectivity of the paths from prefrontal to prestriate cortex for colour. Furthermore, for these latter paths there was a significant interaction, such that there was greater connectivity for the choice condition for colour. Finally, there were also differences in connectivity for the paths between the prefrontal and parietal cortex, and between the parietal cortex and motor cortex and prestriate cortex. Nonetheless, the difference in connectivity between the left prefrontal and left prestriate cortex could not be accounted for by the indirect pathway via parietal cortex.

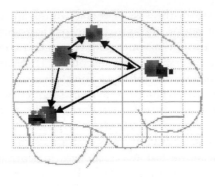

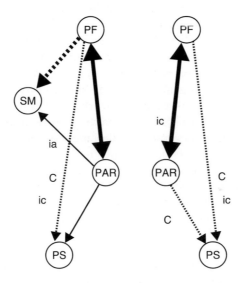

Figure 11.3 Anatomical model for structural equation modelling of the effect of selection of action or colours. Data from Rowe et al. (in press). PF = prefrontal, SM = sensorimotor, PAR = parietal, PS = prestriate cortex. Bold lines = connectivity differed for choice than routine. Dashed lines = connectivity differed according to modality (action/colour). A = connectivity greater for action than colour. C = connectivity greater for colour than action. i = interaction by task and modality. ia = connectivity greater for choice of action. ic = connectivity greater for choice of colour.

These results are consistent with the hypothesis that the dorsal prefrontal cortex influences selection by sending a bias signal to the relevant posterior regions. However, Frith (2000) has argued that it is unlikely that the activation in the dorsal prefrontal cortex represents a phasic signal involved in selecting the response. The reason is that Jahanshahi, Dinberger, Fuller, and Frith (2000) did not find, when participants generated numbers randomly, that there was an increase in the size of the activation in the dorsal prefrontal cortex as the rate of selection was increased by the pacing cue. Furthermore, at very fast rates of more than one response a second, there was a fall off in the activation of the dorsal prefrontal cortex. There are two points to be made. The first is that at very fast rates, the participants no longer generated numbers randomly but produced stereotyped sequences. Thus they were no longer selecting responses anew on every trial. Second, under the conditions in which the participants were required to generate numbers, they could prepare their responses between trials and assess the randomness of their responses by holding the last few responses in working memory. Yet we know that there is sustained activation in the dorsal prefrontal cortex when individuals can prepare their responses (Pochon et al., 2001) or perform working memory tasks that are attentionally demanding (Cohen et al. 1997; Courtney, Ungerleider, Keil, & Haxby, 1997; Leung, Gore, & Goldman-Rakic, 2002).

The consequence is that one would only expect a phasic signal in the dorsal prefrontal cortex if participants were required to select between responses under conditions in which there was no possibility of preparing the responses and there was a minimal working memory load. One of two paradigms could be used. The first is verb generation: we know that the dorsal prefrontal cortex is activated when individuals generate verbs from nouns (Warburton et al., 1996), even when new nouns are presented on each trial. The second is stem completion: there is activation in the dorsal pre-frontal cortex when individuals are presented with stems (the first three letters of a word) and choose which word to give as a completion. Further-more, the activation is greater when there are many possible alternatives available than when there are few (Desmond, Gabrieli, & Glover, 1998). Nathaniel-Jones and Frith (2002) have also reported activation in the dorsal prefrontal cortex when individuals complete sentences, and there are many possible completions. These results are compatible with the hypothesis that the activation in the dorsal prefrontal cortex reflects the process of selecting between alternative responses.

Generalizing from the biased competition model of attention (Desimone & Duncan, 1995), we propose that the selection of action involves a process of attentional selection. We interpret the increased coupling between the dorsal prefrontal cortex and the relevant posterior areas as reflecting a top-down bias signal that leads to the enhancement in posterior areas of one representation at the expense of the others. In the case of the selection of a colour, it is the goal of the action that is specified—that is, the colour. In the case of the selection of finger movements, it is almost certainly not the movements themselves that are selected but the goal of the action—that is, the position of the key. Even within the premotor cortex, most cells code for the spatial target of the action rather than the direction of movement (Shen & Alexander, 1997). The results reported here using imaging suggest that the biased competition model can be generalized to the attentional selection of action. As already mentioned, Cisek and Kalaska (2002) have provided electrophysiological evidence that there are subpopulations of cells in the premotor cortex that code for different potential actions. The studies of Rowe et al. (2002a, 2002b) are consistent with the hypothesis that signals from the prefrontal cortex influence the enhancement of activity in the premotor cortex. However, single unit studies are needed to demonstrate that the nature of the influence is to bias one representation of action at the expense of another.

Attentional sets

The experiments described in the previous sections have investigated attention to upcoming actions. But individuals can also prepare to perform even when they do not yet know the specific response that will be appropriate. Here they are not attending to a specific action, but rather to a specific task. The term "attentional sets" has been used by Corbetta and Shulman (2002) to refer to the direction of attention when no stimulus items have yet been presented and no specific response can yet be prepared. To investigate attentional sets, Sakai and Passingham (2003) have used fMRI to measure sustained activation when participants are given the task instruction but have not yet been presented with the task. The task was to remember a series of four locations or four letters, and to do so either in the order they were presented (forwards) or in the reverse order (backwards). Each trial started with one of four task instructions: "location forwards", "location backwards", "letter forward" or "letter backwards". There followed an unfilled interval that varied from 4 to 12 s. At the end of the delay, a list of four spatial locations and letters was presented on the screen; for each item in the sequence, a location and a letter were shown at the same time. By varying the delay before the items were presented, it was possible to distinguish activations that were sustained throughout the delay, whatever its length, from activations that were time-locked to the presentation of items at the end of the delay.

In anterior prefrontal cortex there were sustained activations after the instructions were given, irrespective of the nature of the instruction (Figure 11.4a). There were also sustained activations in posterior areas but these depended on the nature of the task instruction. When the instruction had been to remember locations, whether forwards or backwards, there were sustained activations during the instruction delay in the frontal area 8 and the intraparietal cortex; these occurred before the task items were presented (Figure 11.4b). These areas are interconnected with each other (Andersen, Asanuma, & Siegel, 1990; Cavada & Goldman-Rakic, 1989) and are also interconnected with the dorsal prefrontal cortex (Cavada & Goldman-Rakic, 1989; Petrides & Pandya, 1999). Both areas are involved in the processing of spatial material; for example, they are activated when individuals covertly direct attention to spatial locations (Corbetta et al., 1998; Nobre, Gitelman, Dias, & Mesulam, 2000).

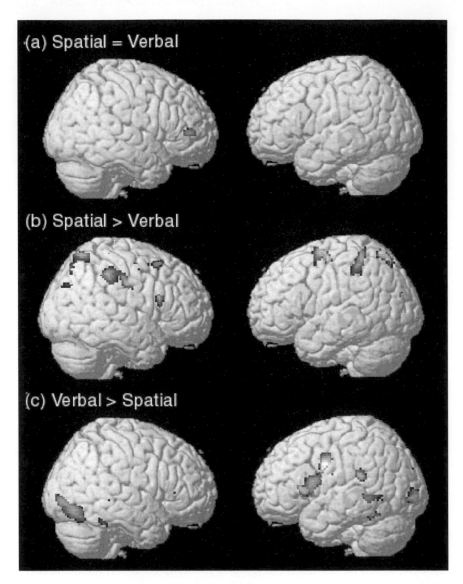

Figure 11.4 Areas in which there was sustained activity during the instruction delay before the task items were presented. Data from Sakai and Passingham (2003). (a) Activity irrespective of which of the four task instructions had been given. (b) Activity when the instruction had been to remember the spatial items. (c) Activity when the instruction had been to remember the verbal items.

When the instruction had been to remember letters, whether forwards or backwards, there was sustained activation during the instruction delay in Broca's area (area 44), Wernicke's area (area 22) and the visual temporal association cortex (Figure 11.4c). Again, these occurred before the items had been presented. It has been assumed that in the human brain, Wernicke's area and Broca's area are connected via the arcuate fasciculus (Geschwind, 1965), although direct evidence for this claim has not been provided because tracing methods for establishing connections cannot be used with humans. We do, however, know that in the human brain there are projections from the ventral temporal cortex to area 44 (Di Virgilio & Clarke, 1997). The connections of area 44 and the prefrontal cortex have to be inferred from anatomical studies of the macaque brain. There are some similarities in cytoarchitecture between Broca's area (area 44) and the posterior bank of the ventral limb of the arcuate sulcus in macaque brain (Galaburda & Pandya, 1982; Petrides & Pandya, 1995); and we know that there are connections between this premotor region and the dorsal prefrontal cortex (Lu et al., 1994; Wang et al., 2002). The fact that there were sustained activations in auditory language areas as well as in visual association area shows that the attentional set after the instructions to remember the letters occurred in both auditory and visual areas, even though the letters were later presented visually.

Others have previously shown that, if participants are warned about the location or nature of a target, there is activation in the areas that process that information even though no stimuli have been presented (Chawla, Rees, & Friston, 1999; Corbetta & Shulman, 2002; Kastner, Pinsk, De Weerd, Desimone, & Ungerleider, 1999). This activity reflects attentional sets. These are distinct from attentional effects that can be observed when the items are presented. They are also distinct from motor sets in that they can be observed even though no specific motor response can be prepared. For example, in the study by Sakai and Passingham (2003), the participants did not know the location of the spatial items or letters in advance of their presentation, and so could not plan either eye or hand movements during the instruction delay.

Although the data presented in Figure 11.4 provide evidence for attentional sets, they do not indicate whether the instruction simply directs attention to the relevant modalities or sets up the specific task operation. The sustained activations in posterior regions were the same whether the instruction was to remember the items forwards or backwards. To determine whether the prefrontal cortex sets up the specific task operations, we examined the covariance between the sustained activity in the anterior prefrontal cortex and the sustained activity in the modality-specific posterior areas. Figure 11.5 plots this relation during the period after each of the four instructions had been given. It will be seen that the regression slope for the relation between activity in the anterior prefrontal cortex and activity in area 8 was significantly steeper, and the correlation tighter, when the participants were waiting to remember the spatial locations and then reverse them in

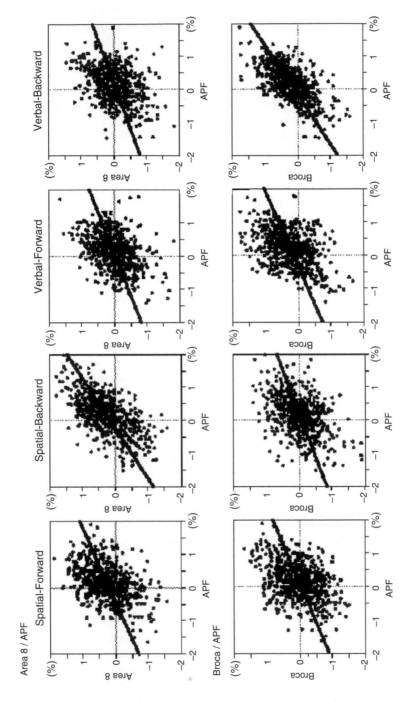

Figure 11.5 Regressions and correlations for the covariance between activity during the instruction delay in the anterior prefrontal cortex (APF) and either frontal area 8 (top row) or area 44 (Broca's) (bottom row). The data are given for the sustained activity after each of the instructions had been given as specified by the columns, but before the task items had been presented. From Sakai and Passingham (2003).

memory. We found the same pattern when we related activity in the anterior prefrontal cortex and activity in the intraparietal cortex; however, the data for this relation are not shown in Figure 11.5. Correspondingly, the regression slope for the relation between activity in the anterior prefrontal cortex and activity in Broca's area 44 was significantly steeper, and the correlation tighter, when the participants were waiting to remember the letters and then reverse them in memory. This was true even though at this point no items had been presented. Thus, these data suggest that the sustained activity reflects both attention to the modality of the stimuli that are relevant for the task, and preparation to carry out the specific task. We call this a "task set" to distinguish it from a simple motor set.

Since the instruction delay could be as long as 12 s, we were also able to plot the change in these correlations over time (Sakai & Passingham, 2003). The correlation between sustained activity in anterior prefrontal cortex and area 8 increased over time during the instruction delay when participants were waiting to remember the spatial items and then reverse them. This effect was significantly greater than when any of the other three task instructions had been given. The same was true for the corresponding correlation between anterior prefrontal cortex and Broca's area when participants were waiting to remember the verbal items and then reverse them. The high correlations for these conditions were maintained during the task epoch when the items were presented and the participants were tested for their memory. There was no significant correlation during the inter-trial interval.

One possible interpretation of the results of this experiment is that it is the anterior prefrontal cortex that sets up future task operations and that the "task set" is represented by top-down interactions between this area and the relevant posterior areas. This suggestion needs to be tested by studying the effect of interference with prefrontal activity on activity related to task sets in posterior areas. In psychological experiments, the task for the participants is defined by the instructions given before the experiment. The nature of the task determines what the participants will attend to during the experiment and what cognitive operations they will perform. If the instruction is to attend to finger movements, as in the experiments by Rowe et al. (2002a, 2002b), there are changes in the interaction between the prefrontal cortex and the premotor areas (Figure 11.2). If the instruction is to select a colour, there are changes in the interaction between the prefrontal cortex and prestriate area V4 (Figure 11.3). If the instruction is to remember letters in the reverse order, there are changes in the interaction between the prefrontal cortex and Broca's area and Wernicke's area (Figure 11.5).

These results are consistent with the hypothesis that when individuals attend to actions that they are going to perform, there is a top-down signal from the prefrontal cortex to the relevant modality-specific areas. In this case, attention is "goal directed" rather than "stimulus driven". The distinction is that in the first case the direction of attention is determined by the task instructions or the interest or goals of the individuals, whereas in the second it is determined by some property of the stimulus, such as its salience (Corbetta & Shulman, 2002). These authors have reviewed evidence from a series of imaging studies in which participants were instructed to attend to a peripheral location while fixating a central spot (Hopfinger, Buonocore, & Mangun, 2000; Kastner et al., 1999; Shulman et al., 1999). There is agreement between the studies that there is activation in the intraparietal cortex, but also in the frontal cortex in the region of frontal eye fields and area 8. Corbetta and Shulman (2002) argue that in goal-directed attention of this sort, there is a top-down signal from the frontal cortex.

In these studies, participants attended to a specific location, in expectation of visual stimuli at that location. The experiment by Sakai and Passingham (2003) differs in that, when instructed to remember locations, the participants did not know where the spatial stimuli would be presented. As in the experiments reviewed by Corbetta and Shulman (2002), we found sustained activity in frontal area 8, but we also found sustained activity in the anterior prefrontal cortex. We have argued that in this condition, the task set depended on interactions between the anterior prefrontal cortex and area 8, as well as between the anterior prefrontal cortex and the intraparietal cortex.

Attention and the prefrontal cortex

This raises the question as to why the anterior prefrontal cortex should be involved. We have provided evidence that each cortical area has a unique pattern of inputs and outputs, and have proposed that it is this that determines the operations that an area can perform (Passingham, Stephan, & Kotter, 2002). We have called the pattern of connections of an area its "connectional fingerprint" and related this to the "functional fingerprint" of the area—that is, the specific pattern of activity as assessed over a wide range of tasks. The question therefore becomes what it is about the unique pattern of connections of the prefrontal cortex that suggests a role for it in goal-directed attention.

The prefrontal cortex is unique in receiving projections from all five sense modalities (Barbas, 2000; Petrides & Pandya, 2001; Rolls, 1999). The prefrontal cortex is not, however, the only area to have inputs from more than one modality. For example, the perirhinal cortex of the temporal lobe receives both visual and tactile inputs (Murray & Bussey, 1999), and the lower bank of the intraparietal sulcus (LIP) receives both auditory and visual inputs (Andersen et al., 1990; Grunewald, Linden, & Andersen, 1999). However, these areas receive multimodal inputs for different reasons, the perirhinal sulcus for the identification of objects (Murray & Bussey, 1999) and area LIP for enhancing attention to spatial locations and the direction of eye and hand movements towards them (Gottlieb, Kusunoki, & Goldberg, 1998; Snyder, Batista, & Andersen, 1997). The prefrontal cortex differs in that it can use information from all five senses to specify the external context (Miller & Cohen, 2001).

What individuals attend to is determined not only by the external context but also by their goals. Electrophysiological studies in macaque monkeys have shown that there are many cells in the ventral and orbito-frontal cortex that fire selectively when the animals are expecting different rewards (Schultz, 2000; Schultz, Tremblay, & Hollerman, 2000; Watanabe, 1996; Watanabe, Hikosaka, Sakagami, & Shirakawa, 2002). In the case of animals, the rewards are food and drink. The animals attend to stimuli that are relevant to obtaining rewards and work so as to maximize their rewards.

In the case of humans, the goals are often less direct. In everyday life, humans work to obtain money, which can in turn be cashed in for the necessities of life. There are activations in the orbito-frontal cortex when humans work for monetary rewards (Elliott, Friston, & Dolan, 2000; O'Doherty, Kringelbach, Rolls, Hornak, & Andrews, 2001; Thut, Schultz, Nienhusmeier, Missimer, Maguire, & Leenders, 1997). In psychological experiments, the participants may be paid, but the immediate goals of the participants are set by the task instructions. It is these that define what stimuli it will be necessary to attend to and what actions are required. In the experiment by Sakai and Passingham (2003) described above, it is the instructions that tell the participants that they should attend either to the upcoming letters or to the locations.

The anterior prefrontal cortex is a candidate area for the interaction between information about task goals and action. Leon and Shadlen (1999) recorded in prefrontal area 46 while macaque monkeys performed a working memory task. They found many neurons that responded more when the animal expected high rather than low reward and were going to respond to a target in the neuron's response field. Using fMRI, Pochon et al. (2002) have demonstrated activation in the polar prefrontal cortex that is greater the more the executive demands of a working memory task; they also showed that in the same area there was activity that was related to the amount of monetary reward the participants expected for a correct response. The crucial question is whether it can be shown that there is an interaction in this area between action and reward value. Ramnani and Miall (2003) scanned individuals with fMRI and tested for areas in which there was an interaction between response preparation and the size of the expected reward. They demonstrated such an interaction in the frontal polar cortex.

The results of these studies are consistent with the proposal that the prefrontal cortex can integrate information about the current context and current goals so as to influence action. The orbito-frontal cortex is interconnected with the lateral prefrontal cortex (Barbas, 1988; Petrides & Pandya, 1999) and these regions are interconnected with the fronto-polar cortex (Cavada, Company, Tejedor, Cruz-Rizzolo, & Reinoso-Suarez, 2000; Petrides & Pandya, 1999). In turn, there are projections from the dorsal prefrontal cortex to the premotor cortex and supplementary motor cortex (Lu et al., 1994; Wang et al., 2002), as well as to the cerebellum via the pontine nuclei (Schmahmann & Pandya, 1997). Evidence that integration can occur within the prefrontal cortex can be obtained from single unit recording. There are cells in the orbito-frontal cortex that respond both to taste and to smell (Rolls, 1999), and cells in the lateral prefrontal cortex that code for the association between visual cues and sounds (Fuster, Bodner, & Kroger, 2000). Finally, there are cells in the lateral prefrontal cortex that respond both when macaques remember spatial cues and when they remember object cues (Rao, Rainer, & Miller, 1997). Thus information can be integrated both between senses and between different processing streams—for example, spatial information from the dorsal ventral systems and object information from the ventral visual system.

Conclusions

In this chapter, we have provided evidence that there are activations in the dorsal prefrontal cortex when individuals attend to their actions, and suggested that this area can influence the selection of action via top-down connections to the motor areas. This leaves the question as to why it is the dorsal rather than the ventral prefrontal cortex that is activated under these conditions. Rushworth (2000) has distinguished between the dorsal and ventral prefrontal cortex by contrasting the anatomical connections. The dorsal prefrontal cortex receives a heavy input from the parietal cortex (Cavada & Goldman-Rakic, 1989), whereas the ventral prefrontal cortex receives a heavy input from the temporal lobe (Petrides & Pandya, 2001; Webster et al., 1994). The dorsal prefrontal cortex (area 46) also receives an input from frontal area 8 as well as from the frontal eye fields (Petrides & Pandya, 1999). Goldman-Rakic (1998) has suggested that the dorsal prefrontal cortex is specialized for spatial working memory, since it receives inputs from the dorsal visual system. However, the parietal cortex is also crucially involved in spatial attention. There is enhancement of activation in parietal cortex and frontal area 8 when individuals covertly attend to spatial locations or shift the locus of attention (Corbetta et al., 2000) as well as when they actually move their eyes (Corbetta et al., 1998; Nobre et al., 2000). Furthermore, patients with right parietal lesions may suffer from a severe spatial neglect (Driver & Mattingley, 1998). Since the dorsal prefrontal cortex is closely interconnected with these areas, it may be part of a system that is specialized for spatial attention. Awh and Jonides (2001) have reviewed evidence linking the mechanisms of spatial attention and the rehearsal of spatial items in working memory. Everling, Tinsley, Gaffan, and Duncan (2002) have also demonstrated that cells in the prefrontal cortex are involved in the filtering out of non-attended stimuli on the basis of their spatial location. If actions are specified by their spatial target, and we know that this is the case for example in the premotor cortex (Shen & Alexander, 1997), there may be a link between the mechanisms of selection and the mechanisms for spatial attention.

As Rushworth (2000) has stressed, the cortico-cortical outputs to the motor system also come from the dorsal rather than the ventral prefrontal cortex (Lu et al., 1994; Wang et al., 2002). It has long been known that in macaque monkeys there is preparatory activity in all areas of the motor system (Evarts, Shinoda, & Wise, 1984; Shima & Tanji, 2000; Weinrich, Wise, & Mauritz, 1984) as well as in the parietal cortex (Crammond & Kalaska, 1989; Snyder et al., 1997). More recently, imaging has been used to demonstrate such activity both in premotor areas and in the parietal cortex in the human brain (Pochon et al., 2001; Toni et al., 2002). Since the prefrontal cortex is closely interconnected with these areas, it can also be seen as being part of an action system, including the preparation of action. The term "attention to action" has been used in this chapter to refer to attention in advance of action, and it is therefore inextricably bound up with preparation for action.

Acknowledgements

The research was supported by a grant to Dr Passingham from the Wellcome Trust. Dr Rowe was supported by the Wellcome Trust and Dr Sakai by the Human Frontier Science Program.

References

Andersen, R. A., Asanuma, C., & Siegel, R. M. (1990). Corticocortical connections of anatomically and physiologically defined subdivisions within the inferior parietal lobule. *Journal of Comparative Neurology, 296*, 65–113.

Awh, E., & Jonides, J. (2001). Overlapping mechanisms of attention and spatial working memory. *Trends in Cognitive Sciences, 5*, 119–126.

Barbas, H. (1988). Anatomical organization of basoventral and mediodorsal visual recipient prefrontal region in the rhesus monkey. *Journal of Comparative Neurology, 276*, 313–342.

Barbas, H. (2000). Connections underlying the synthesis of cognition, memory, and emotion in primate prefrontal cortices. *Brain Research Bulletin, 52*, 319–330.

Cavada, C., Company, T., Tejedor, J., Cruz-Rizzolo, R. J., & Reinoso-Suarez, F. (2000). The anatomical connections of the macaque monkey orbitofrontal cortex: a review. *Cerebral Cortex, 10*, 243–251.

Cavada, C., & Goldman-Rakic, P. S. (1989). Posterior parietal cortex in rhesus monkeys: II. Evidence for segregated corticocortical networks linking sensory and limbic areas with the frontal lobe. *Journal of Comparative Neurology, 28*, 422–445.

Chawla, D., Rees, G., & Friston, K. J. (1999). The physiological basis of attentional modulation in extrastriate visual areas. *Nature Neuroscience, 2*, 671–676.

Chelazzi, L., Duncan, J., Miller, E. K., & Desimone, R. (1998). Responses of neurons in inferior temporal cortex during memory-guided visual search. *Journal of Neurophysiology, 80*, 2918–2940.

Cisek, P., & Kalaska, J. F. (2002). Simultaneous encoding of multiple potential reach directions in dorsal premotor cortex. *Journal of Neurophysioly, 87*, 1149–1154.

Cohen, J. D., Perlstein, W. M., Braver, T. S., Nystrom, L. E., Noll, D. C., Jonides, J. et al. (1997). Temporal dynamics of brain activation during a working memory task. *Nature, 386*, 604–607.

Corbetta, M., Akbudak, E., Conturo, T. E., Drury, H. A., Linenweber, M. R., Petersen, S. et al. (1998). A common network of functional areas for attention and eye movements. *Neuron, 21,* 761–773.

Corbetta, M., Kincade, J. M., Ollinger, J. M., McAvoy, M. P., & Shulman, G. L. (2000). Voluntary orienting is dissociated from target detection in human posterior parietal cortex. *Nature Neuroscience, 3,* 292–297.

Corbetta, M., & Shulman, G. L. (2002). Control of goal-directed and stimulus-driven attention in the brain. *Nature Neuroscience Reviews, 3,* 201–215.

Courtney, S. M., Ungerleider, L. G., Keil, K., & Haxby, J. V. (1997). Transient and sustained activity in a distributed neural system for human working memory. *Nature, 386,* 608–611.

Crammond, D. J., & Kalaska, J. F. (1989). Neuronal activity in primate parietal cortex area 5 varies with intended movement direction during an instructed-delay period. *Experimental Brain Research, 76,* 458–462.

Deiber, M.-P., Ibanez, V., Honda, M., Sadato, N., Raman, R., & Hallett, M. (1998). Cerebral processes related to visuomotor imagery and generation of simple finger movements studied with positron emission tomography. *NeuroImage, 7,* 73–85.

Deiber, M.-P., Ibanez, V., Sadato, N., & Hallett, M. (1996). Cerebral structures participating in motor preparation in humans: a positron emission tomography study. *Journal of Neurophysiology, 75,* 233–247.

Deiber, M.-P., Passingham, R. E., Colebatch, J. G., Friston, K. J., Nixon, P. D., & Frackowiak, R. S. J. (1991). Cortical areas and the selection of movement: a study with positron emission tomography. *Experimental Brain Research, 84,* 393–402.

Desimone, R., & Duncan, J. (1995). Neural mechanisms of selective visual attention. *Annual Review of Neuroscience, 18,* 193–222.

Desmond, J. E., Gabrieli, J. D. E., & Glover, G. H. (1998). Dissociation of frontal and cerebellar activity in a cognitive task: evidence for a distinction between selection and search. *NeuroImage, 7,* 368–376.

DeYoe, E. A., & Van Essen, D. C. (1988). Concurrent processing streams in monkey visual cortex. *Trends in Cognitive Sciences, 11,* 219–226.

Di Virgilio, G., & Clarke, S. (1997). Direct interhemispheric visual inputs to human speech areas. *Human Brain Mapping, 5,* 347–354.

Driver, J., & Mattingley, J. B. (1998). Parietal neglect and visual awareness. *Nature Neuroscience, 1,* 17–22.

Elliott, R., Friston, K., & Dolan, R. J. (2000). Dissociable neural responses in human reward systems. *Journal of Neuroscience, 20,* 6159–6165.

Evarts, E., Shinoda, Y., & Wise, S. P. (1984). *Neurophysiological approaches to higher brain functions.* New York: Wiley.

Everling, S., Tinsley, C. J., Gaffan, D., & Duncan, J. (2002). Filtering of neural signals by focused attention in the monkey prefrontal cortex. *Nature Neuroscience, 5,* 671–676.

Fink, G. R., Frackowiak, R. S. J., Pietrzyk, U., & Passingham, R. E. (1997). Multiple non-primary motor areas in the human cortex. *Journal of Neurophysiology, 77,* 2164–2174.

Frith, C. D. (2000). The role of dorsolateral prefrontal cortex in the selection of action. In S. Monsell & J. Driver (Eds.), *Control of cognitive processes: attention and performance XVIII* (pp. 549–565). Cambridge, MA: MIT Press.

Frith, C. D., Friston, K., Liddle, P. F., & Frackowiak, R. S. J. (1991). Willed action and the prefrontal cortex in man: a study with PET. *Proceedings of the Royal Society of London, B, 244,* 241–246.

Fuster, J. M., Bodner, M., & Kroger, J. K. (2000). Cross-modal and cross-temporal association in neurons of frontal cortex. *Nature, 405*, 347–351.

Galaburda, A. M., & Pandya, D. N. (1982). Role of architectonics and connections in the study of primate brain evolution. In E. Armstrong & D. Falk (Eds.), *Primate brain evolution* (pp. 203–216). New York: Plenum Press.

Gerardin, A., Sirigu, A., Lehericy, S., Poline, J.-B., Gaymard, B., Marsault, C. et al. (2000). Partially overlapping neural networks for real and imagined hand movements. *Cerebral Cortex, 10*, 1093–1104.

Geschwind, N. (1965). Disconnection syndromes in animals and man. *Brain, 88*, 585–644.

Goldman-Rakic, P. S. (1998). The prefrontal landscape: implications of functional architecture for understanding human mentation and the central executive. In A. C. Roberts, T. W. Robbins, & L. Weiskrantz (Eds.), *The prefrontal cortex* (pp. 117–130). Oxford: Oxford University Press.

Gottlieb, J. P., Kusunoki, M., & Goldberg, M. E. (1998). The representation of visual salience in monkey parietal cortex. *Nature, 391*, 481–484.

Grunewald, A., Linden, J. F., & Andersen, R. A. (1999). Responses to auditory stimuli in macaque lateral intraparietal area. I. Effects of training. *Journal of Neurophysiology, 82*, 330–342.

Hopfinger, J. B., Buonocore, M. H., & Mangun, G. R. (2000). The neural mechanisms of top-down attentional control. *Nature Neuroscience, 3*, 284–291.

Hyder, F., Phelps, E. A., Wiggins, C. J., Labar, K. S., Blamire, A. M., & Shulman, R. G. (1997). Willed action: a functional MRI study of the human prefrontal cortex during a sensorimotor task. *Proceedings of the National Academy of Sciences, USA, 94*, 6989–6994.

Jahanshahi, M., Dinberger, G., Fuller, R., & Frith, C. D. (2000). The role of the dorsolateral prefrontal cortex in random number generation: a study with positron emission tomography. *NeuroImage, 12*, 713–725.

Jenkins, I. H., Brooks, D. J., Nixon, P. D., Frackowiak, R. S. J., & Passingham, R. E. (1994). Motor sequence learning: a study with positron emission tomography. *Journal of Neuroscience, 14*, 3775–3790.

Jueptner, M., Stephan, K. M., Frith, C. D., Brooks, D. J., Frackowiak, R. S. J., & Passingham, R. E. (1997). Anatomy of motor learning. I. Frontal cortex and attention to action. *Journal of Neurophysiology, 77*, 1313–1324.

Kastner, S., Pinsk, M. A., De Weerd, P., Desimone, R., & Ungerleider, L. G. (1999). Increased activity in human visual cortex during directed attention in the absence of visual stimulation. *Neuron, 22*, 751–761.

Leon, M. I., & Shadlen, M. N. (1999). Effect of expected reward magnitude on the response of neurons in the dorsolateral prefrontal cortex of the macaque. *Neuron, 24*, 415–425.

Leung, H.-C., Gore, J. C., & Goldman-Rakic, P. S. (2002). Sustained mnemonic response in the human middle frontal gyrus during on-line storage of spatial memoranda. *Journal of Cognitive Neuroscience, 14*, 659–671.

Lu, M.-T., Preston, J. B., & Strick, P. L. (1994). Interconnections between the prefrontal cortex and the premotor areas in the frontal lobe. *Journal of Comparative Neurology, 341*, 375–392.

Luppino, G., Matelli, M., Camarda, R., & Rizzolatti, G. (1993). Corticocortical connections of area F3 (SMA-proper) and area F6 (Pre-SMA) in the macaque monkey. *Journal of Comparative Neurology, 338*, 114–140.

Miller, E. K., & Cohen, J. D. (2001). An integrative theory of prefrontal cortex function. *Annual Review of Neuroscience, 24,* 167–202.

Muakkassa, K. F., & Strick, P. L. (1979). Frontal lobe inputs to primate motor cortex: evidence for four somatotopically organized "premotor areas". *Brain Research, 177,* 176–182.

Murray, E. A., & Bussey, T. J. (1999). Perceptual–mnemonic functions of the perirhinal cortex. *Trends in Cognitive Sciences, 3,* 142–150.

Nathaniel-Jones, D. A., & Frith, C. D. (2002). The role of the dorsolateral prefrotnal cortex: evidence from effects of contextual constraint in a sentence completion task. *NeuroImage, 16,* 1094–1102.

Nobre, A. C., Gitelman, D. R., Dias, E. C., & Mesulam, M. M. (2000). Covert spatial orienting and saccades: overlapping neural systems. *NeuroImage, 11,* 210–217.

O'Doherty, J., Kringelbach, M. L., Rolls, E. T., Hornak, J., & Andrews, C. (2001). Abstract reward and punishment representations in human orbitofrontal cortex. *Nature Neuroscience, 4,* 95–102.

Passingham, R. E. (1998). Attention to action. In A. C. Roberts, T. W. Robbins, & L. Weiskrantz (Eds.), *The prefrontal cortex* (pp. 131–143). Oxford: Oxford University Press.

Passingham, R. E., Stephan, K., & Kotter, R. (2002). The anatomical basis of functional localization in the cortex. *Nature Review Neuroscience, 3,* 606–616

Petersen, S. E., Fox, P. T., Posner, M. I., Mintun, M., & Raichle, M. E. (1988). Positron emission tomographic studies of the cortical anatomy of single-word processing. *Nature, 331,* 585–589.

Petrides, M., & Pandya, D. N. (1995). Comparative architectonic analysis of the human and macaque frontal cortex. In J. Grafman & F. Boller (Eds.), *Handbook of neuropsychology* (Vol. 9, pp. 17–58). Amsterdam: Elsevier.

Petrides, M., & Pandya, D. N. (1999). Dorsolateral prefrontal cortex: comparative cytoarchitectonic analysis in the human and the macaque brain and corticocortical connection patterns. *European Journal of Neuroscience, 11,* 1011–1036.

Petrides, M., & Pandya, D. N. (2001). Comparative cytoarchitectonic analysis of the human and macaque ventrolateral prefrontal cortex and corticocortical connection pattern in the monkey. *European Journal of Neuroscience, 16,* 291–310.

Pochon, J.-B., Levy, R., Fossati, P., Lehericy, S., Poline, J.-B., Pillon, B. et al. (2002). The neural system that bridges reward and cognition in humans: an fMRI study. *Proceedings of the National Academy Sciences, USA, 16,* 5669–5674.

Pochon, J.-B., Levy, R., Poline, J.-B., Crozier, S., Lehericy, S., Pillon, B. et al. (2001). The role of dorsolateral prefrontal cortex in the preparation of forthcoming actions: an fMRI study. *Cerebral Cortex, 11,* 260–266.

Raichle, M. E., Fiez, J. A., Videen, T. O., MacLeod, A. K., Pardo, J. V., Fox, P. T. et al. (1994). Practice-related changes in human brain functional anatomy during non-motor learning. *Cerebral Cortex, 4,* 8–26.

Rao, S. C., Rainer, G., & Miller, E. K. (1997). Integration of what and where in the primate prefrontal cortex. *Science, 276,* 821–824.

Ramnani, N., & Miall, R. C. (2003). Instructed delay activity in the human prefrontal cortex is modulated by monetary reward expectation. *Cerebral Cortex, 13,* 318–327.

Rintjes, M., Dettmers, C., Buchel, C., Kiebel, C., Frackowiak, R. S. J., & Weiller, C. (1999). A blueprint for movement: functional and antomical representations in the human motor system. *Journal of Neuroscience, 19,* 8043–8048.

Rolls, E. (1999). *The brain and emotion*. Oxford: Oxford University Press.

Rosano, C., Krisky, C. M., Welling, J. S., Eddy, W. F., Luna, B., Thulborn, K. R. et al. (2002). Pursuit and saccadic eye movement subregions in human frontal eye field: a high-resolution fMRI investigation. *Cerebral Cortex, 12*, 107–115.

Rowe, J., Frackowiak, R. S. J., Friston, K., & Passingham, R. E. (2002a). Attention to action: specific modulation of cortico-cortical interactions in humans. *NeuroImage, 17*, 988–998.

Rowe, J., Stephan. K. E., Friston, K., Frackowiak, R. S. J., Lees, A., & Passingham, R. E. (2002b). Attention to action in Parkinson's disease: impaired effective connectivity among frontal cortical regions. *Brain, 125*, 276–289.

Rowe, J. B., Stephan, K. E., Friston, K., Frackowiak, R. S. J., & Passingham, R. E. (in press). The prefrontal cortex: task specific effective connectivity to precentral and prestriate cortex during the selection of action and colour. *Cerebral Cortex*.

Rushworth, M. (2000). Anatomical and functional subdivision within the primate lateral frontal cortex. *Psychobiology, 28*, 187–196.

Rushworth, M., Krams, M., & Passingham, R. E. (2001). The attentional role of the left parietal cortex: the distinct lateralization and localization of motor attention in the human brain. *Journal of Cognitive Neuroscience, 13*, 698–710.

Sakai, K., & Passingham, R. E. (2003). Prefrontal interactions reflect future task operations. *Nature Neuroscience, 6*, 75–81.

Schmahmann, J. D., & Pandya, D. N. (1997). The cerebrocerebellar system. In J. D. Schmahmann (Ed.), *The cerebellum and cognition* (pp. 31–60). San Diego, CA: Academic Press.

Schultz, W. (2000). Multiple reward signals in the brain. *Nature Reviews Neuroscience, 1*, 199–207.

Schultz, W., Tremblay, L., & Hollerman, J. R. (2000). Reward processing in primate orbitofrontal cortex and basal ganglia. *Cerebral Cortex, 10*, 272–283.

Shen, L., & Alexander, G. E. (1997). Preferential representation of instructed target location versus limb trajectory in dorsal premotor cortex. *Journal of Neurophysiology, 77*, 1195–1212.

Shima, K., & Tanji, J. (2000). Neuronal activity in the supplementary and presupplementary motor areas for temporal organization of multiple movements. *Journal of Neurophysiology, 84*, 2148–2160.

Shulman, G. L., Ollinger, J. M., Akbudak, E., Conturo, T. E., Snyder, A. Z., Petersen, S. et al. (1999). Areas involved in encoding and applying directional expectations to moving objects. *Journal of Neuroscience, 19*, 9480–9496.

Simon, S., Meurnier, M., Piettre, L., Berardi, A. M., Segebarth, C. M., & Boussaoud, D. (2002). Spatial attention and memory versus motor preparation: premotor cortex involvement as revealed by fMRI. *Journal of Neurophysiology, 88*, 2047–2057.

Snyder, L. H., Batista, A. P., & Andersen, R. A. (1997). Coding of information in the posterior parietal cortex. *Nature, 386*, 167–170.

Spence, S. A., Hirsch, S. R., Brooks, D. J., & Grasby, P. M. (1998). Prefrontal cortex activity in people with schizophrenia and control subjects. *Journal of Psychiatry, 172*, 1–8.

Thut, G., Schultz, W., Nienhusmeier, M., Missimer, J., Maguire, R. P., & Leenders, K. L. (1997). Activation of the human brain by monetary reward. *NeuroReport, 8*, 1225–1228.

Toni, I., Krams, M., Turner, R., & Passingham, R. E. (1998). The time-course of changes during motor sequence learning: a whole-brain fMRI study. *NeuroImage*, 8, 50–61.

Toni, I., Ramnani, N., Josephs, O., Ashburner, J., & Passingham, R. E. (2001). Learning arbitrary visuo-motor associations: temporal dynamic of brain activity. *NeuroImage 14*, 1048–1057.

Toni, I., Shah, N. J., Fink, G. R., Thoenissen, D., Passingham, R. E., & Zilles, K. (2002). Multiple movement representations in the human brain: an event-related fMRI study. *Journal of Cognitive Neuroscience, 14*, 769–784

Wang, Y., Shima, K., Osoda, M., Sawamura, H., & Tanji, J. (2002). Spatial distribution and density of prefrontal cortical cells projecting to three sectors of the premotor cortex. *NeuroReport, 13*, 1341–1344.

Warburton, E., Wise, R. J. S., Price, C. J., Weiller, C., Hadar, U., Ramsay, S. et al. (1996). Noun and verb retrieval by normal subjects: studies with positron emission tomography. *Brain, 119*, 159–179.

Watanabe, M. (1996). Reward expectancy in primate prefrontal neurones. *Nature, 382*, 629–632.

Watanabe, M., Hikosaka, K., Sakagami, M., & Shirakawa, S.-I. (2002). Coding and monitoring of motivational context in the primate prefrontal cortex. *Journal of Neuroscience, 22*, 2391–2400.

Webster, M. J., Bachevalier, J., & Ungerleider, L. G. (1994). Connections of inferior temporal areas TEO and TE with parietal and frontal cortex in macaque monkeys. *Cerebral Cortex, 4*, 471–483.

Weinrich, M., Wise, S. P., & Mauritz, K.-H. (1984). A neurophysiological study of the premotor cortex in the rhesus monkey. *Brain, 107*, 385–414.

12 A neuroimaging study of selection-for-action

A reach-to-grasp study

Heidi Chapman, Maria Gavrilescu,
Michael Kean, Gary Egan and
Umberto Castiello

Abstract

In this chapter, we describe two experiments that used functional imaging techniques to identify the neural correlates underlying the selection mechanisms employed to reach and grasp a specific object in the visual field. We asked participants to perform a reach-to-grasp action towards three-dimensional stimuli presented either in isolation or flanked by physically identical distractor objects. In Experiment 1, three stimuli were presented simultaneously, two of which abruptly retracted into the apparatus leaving the remaining stimulus as the target to be grasped. In Experiment 2, the target and distractors remained visible at all times. From comparing the condition in Experiment 1 where a target object appeared at an unpredictable location with a condition where the target object appeared at a predictable location, activations in the left parieto-occipital sulcus and the right intraparietal sulcus were found. In Experiment 2, where the distractors were visible at all times, only the right occipital cortex was found to become activated. These results demonstrate functional modules within the parietal cortex, thus providing a starting point from which to address theoretically motivated questions related to the selection-for-action process.

Introduction

The identification of objects in the visual environment plays an important adaptive role in everyday life, in particular for acting in a goal-directed manner. A visual scene may (and frequently does) contain many objects that are potential targets for action, yet the visual system appears to be limited with respect to the number of objects that it can process at any one time. This limitation implies that at some stage (or stages) in the information stream, some objects are excluded from processing. The selection of only part of simultaneous sources of information is conventionally referred to as "selective visual attention".

One of the traditional issues in the study of selective visual attention concerns how perceptual information relevant to the performance of a task is separated from irrelevant information. In a "model" task commonly used to investigate the effects elicited by irrelevant information, a target appears in a known location, typically the centre of a computer screen alongside two (or more) stimuli called "flankers" or "distractors", and participants are required to make a rapid response (e.g. keypress) on the basis of the target's identity (Eriksen & Eriksen, 1974). When the distractors are associated with the same response as the target, they are referred to as "congruent"; when they are associated with a different response, they are called "incongruent". When the distractors are associated with any response, they are referred to as being "neutral". The measured response/reaction times are characteristically faster for targets with congruent distractors than those with incongruent distractors. Reaction times for neutral distractors are intermediate.

A common interpretation of these results is that all visual stimuli in the scene automatically activate their associated response codes (Eriksen & Schultz, 1979). Thus the longer reaction times recorded for incongruent distractors originate because multiple response codes are activated and the participant has to choose the appropriate response among these competing codes. In other words, at some point (or several points) between the visual input and motor response, objects in the visual field compete for representation, analysis and control on the basis of specific dimensions (e.g. location, colour, orientation).

Although selective visual attention in terms of the processing fate of unattended stimuli has been the target of extensive research, our understanding of some aspects of selective behaviour remains unclear. For instance, little is known about the limits governing the brain's ability to process information presented in parallel for the control of overt action towards three-dimensional stimuli (see also Cohen & Magen, this volume).

Selective attention: a call to "action"

Traditionally, selective visual attention research in cognitive psychology has been based on very brief presentations of two-dimensional stimuli (e.g. alphanumeric characters) on computer screens or tachistoscopes. This form of testing typically restricts attentional measurement to arbitrary and indirect responses such as keypresses or verbal naming (e.g. Eriksen & Eriksen, 1974). However, the emergence of more powerful methods (e.g. kinematic recordings) for investigating these mechanisms within three-dimensional environments has allowed a shift in focus of the theoretical discussion to a more integrative approach, which considers the selection of stimuli for the control of overt action (Allport, 1987). To this end, several recent experiments were designed specifically to look at changes in reach-to-grasp movement kinematics when non-target (i.e. distractor) objects were introduced into the workspace (Castiello, 1996; Chieffi, Gentilucci, Allport, Sasso, & Rizzolatti, 1993; Jackson, Jackson, & Rosicky, 1995; Tipper, Howard, & Jackson, 1997). The present work extends these previous studies on selective visual attention in two ways. First, simple keypress responses do not require the (visual) context in which the target appears to be processed. For example, in classic studies of selective visual attention, distractors are actually irrelevant to the task and, before the start of the experiment, participants are explicitly instructed to ignore them. In reach-to-grasp tasks, distractors might be relevant because they may constitute obstacles and thus have a direct influence on movement planning (Tresilian, 1998). Second, there is the need to confirm that distractor interference generalizes between tasks.

The reach-to-grasp movement is performed routinely within the familiar context of everyday life. It is also a movement that has been well characterized experimentally (for a review, see Bennett & Castiello, 1994). The everyday action of reaching-to-grasp an object is commonly described in terms of a proximal/distal distinction. The reaching and positioning actions, effected by upper arm and forearm musculature, are subserved by central nervous system visuomotor mechanisms that are largely independent of the mechanisms subserving the grasping action—that is, hand opening and subsequent closing on the object. Within this framework, the two neural channels—"reaching" and "grasping"—are said to be activated simultaneously, in parallel (the "channel" hypothesis of Jeannerod, 1981, 1984), and to be coupled functionally for goal-directed actions by a higher-order coordinative structure. The "reaching" channel is said to extract information about the spatial location of the object for transformation into motor patterns that bring the hand appropriately towards the object, whereas the "grasping" channel extracts information about the intrinsic properties of the object (such as its size and shape) for the determination of a suitable grasping pattern. This subdivision of the two component channels provides an ideal means by which to examine whether target objects and distractors compete at different levels. For example, they may compete at the level of either the reach or the grasp component depending on whether they differ from the target with respect to an extrinsic property (e.g. location) that affects reaching, or an intrinsic property (e.g. size) that affects grasping.

In support of this hypothesis, two series of studies in particular may be mentioned. In an attempt to target specifically the grasping component, Castiello and colleagues (for a review, see Castiello, 1999) asked participants to reach and grasp a target presented in conjunction with a distractor of a different size, but similar in colour and positioned roughly in the same position as the target. It was found that the participants' amplitude of peak grip aperture (i.e. the greatest distance between the thumb and index finger) while en-route to the target was influenced by the size of the distractor. If the target was small, the amplitude of peak grip aperture was greater when the distractor was large than when no distractor was present. Conversely, the amplitude of peak grip aperture for the grasp of a large target was less when the distractor was small than when there was no distractor. Little evidence for changes at the level of the reaching component was found. Importantly, interference effects emerged only when there was a requirement to direct visual attention to the distractor.

In the second series of studies, Tipper and colleagues (for a review, see Tipper et al., 1998) specifically targeted the reaching component. Participants were required to initiate the reach as quickly as possible after a visual cue (either blue or green in colour) had appeared followed by the presentation of two stimuli, a target (either a blue or green block) and a distractor (a red block), both similar in size but separately positioned at one of four different locations. Before the start of the experiment, the participants had been instructed only to move (i.e. reach and grasp the target) if the cue matched the target's colour. In such situations, distractors appear to compete for the control of action. These effects were evident from subsequent analyses of the spatial trajectory of the arm as it reached towards a target. Indeed, the hand was found to veer away from near distractors in reaches towards far targets and, conversely, to veer towards far distractors in reaches towards near targets. In general, it was suggested that both the target and distractor evoke competing parallel reaching actions that result in the modification of the reaching trajectory, thus revealing the inhibitory mechanisms that must of necessity resolve this competition.

Common to these studies is the suggestion that objects in a visual scene can evoke the parallel implementation of motor actions. If more than one motor pattern is simultaneously kept active, this parallel activation triggers mutual interference. In addition, both studies highlight the role of spatial visual attention in modulating the threshold levels for specific features within the mechanisms relevant for controlling the response process.

Both Castiello (1999) and Tipper et al. (1998) advanced speculations at the neurophysiological level to account for their results. Castiello (1999) proposed that competition arose from the different types of grasp required by different target and distractor objects. Thus parallel computations for different types of grasp, one for the target and one for the attended distractor, may have been at the origin of the changes found for the kinematics of the action directed towards the target. In support of this view, both Rizzolatti, Camarda, Fogassi, Gentilucci, Luppino, and Matelli (1988) and Sakata and Taira (1994) have reported neurophysiological evidence suggesting that different neural populations subserve different types of grasp or given types of action. In other words, conflicts can emerge when the distractor and target objects require different prehensile patterns in order to be grasped or manipulated. Neuronal populations located within the intraparietal sulcus (IPS) and premotor areas F4 and F5 activated for a planned-but-not-executed action towards an irrelevant distractor object might thus interfere with neuronal populations within similar areas activated by a planned-and-executed action towards a target object.

Tipper and colleagues (1999) also relied on neurophysiological findings to explain their reaching trajectory effects. In particular, they refer to the work of Georgopoulous (1990), who investigated the neural responses in both area

5 of the parietal cortex and the motor cortex of monkeys as they performed reaching actions, and concluded that a specific population of neurons represented the movement direction. These neurons responded to varying degrees when movements in a particular direction were programmed. In particular, it was assumed that the direction of a reaching movement was determined by the sum of the single neurons that contribute to the population vector. Critical for the possible adaptation of this model to Tipper and colleagues' observations is the finding that cells that do not respond to the direction of reach, respond in the opposite way and are inhibited relative to the (measured) baseline level. From this observation, Tipper et al. (1998) extrapolated that when the target is identified, the reach to the distractor becomes inhibited and it is the overlap between the neural activation for the target and the distractor that determines the interference effects.

Although these hypotheses are very speculative in nature, they may provide the starting point from which, using human brain mapping techniques, the areas concerned with the selection-for-action process in humans may be identified. The predictions are that human homologues of the monkey areas mentioned above should show differential activation dependent on whether a selective reach-to-grasp movement is performed towards a target presented alone or in the presence of a distractor(s).

Places to look for interference

In the selection-for-action imaging study described below, we expect activations to be present in regions of the parietal cortex that form a major component of the "dorsal" stream, which is thought to be fundamentally involved in spatial localization (Ungerleider & Mishkin, 1982), attention (Culham & Kanwisher, 2001) and the control of action (Goodale & Milner, 1992). Furthermore, although there is no current agreement on the subdivision within the premotor cortex in humans, areas F4 and F5 of the ventral premotor cortex in monkeys appear to contain a representation for reaching and specific grasping patterns (e.g. precision grip and whole hand prehension) that may be activated when selection occurs on the cumulative or individual basis of location and grasping codes (Gentilucci, Fogassi, Luppino, Matelli, Camarda, & Rizzolatti, 1988; Rizzolatti et al., 1988).

The role that the parietal lobes play in visual attention cannot be disputed. Most physiological research has focused on area 7 in the monkey inferior parietal lobule, which is believed to be homologous to area 7 in the human superior parietal lobule (SPL). In humans, endogenous and exogenous shifts of spatial attention-related activation have been found throughout the parietal lobe, and in particular within the SPL and IPS (Corbetta et al., 1998). We thus expect these areas to be more active in the condition where extra monitoring is required due to the presence of distractors.

The anterior IPS (AIP) of the macaque monkey contains neurons that respond to the visual and motor components of the grasp and are tuned to interpret specific corporal features of the shapes to be grasped (Sakata, Taira, Kusunoki, Murata, & Tanaka, 1997; Sakata et al., 1999). Similarly, Binkofksi et al. (1998) and Culham et al. (2000) demonstrated (grasping-induced) functional magnetic resonance imaging (fMRI) activation in the same brain area in human anterior IPS, although it appears that grasping activities overlap with reach-related movements (Culham et al., 2000). However, other neuro-imaging studies have reported reach-specific activation in the posterior IPS (Connolly, Goodale, DeSouza, Menon, & Vilis, 2000; Kertzman, Schwartz, Zeffiro, & Hallett, 1997) that may be the human homologue of the monkey parietal reach region (PRR; Andersen, Snyder, Bradley, & Xing, 1997). More recently, Fattori, Gamberini, Kutz, and Galletti (2001) discovered neurons in area V6A (i.e. within the anterior bank of the parieto-occipital (PO) sulcus) included within the PRR that discharged during the preparation of arm movements and were directionally selective. We expect the IPS and PO areas to show differential activation in our distractor condition where a reach-to-grasp movement towards three possible targets has to be planned and executed. Again, with respect to reaching behaviour, if the predictions made by Tipper and colleagues (Tipper et al., 1997; Tipper, Howard & Houghton, 1998) are correct, we should also expect activations in parietal area 5 (Brodmann's classification) on the basis of previous neurophysiological results (Georgopoulos, 1990).

A new investigation of selection-for-action in humans using fMRI

We began our search for a human selection-for-action neural network by developing a paradigm to study selective reach-to-grasp movements within a high-field (1.5T) magnetic environment using blood oxygenation level dependent (BOLD) activation. The participants ($n = 9$) lay supine within the magnet. We presented a diverse and unpredictable sequence of visual displays using custom-made equipment that allowed the experimenter to control for all stimuli visibility (see Figure 12.1).

The stimuli consisted of three red balls (each 15 mm in diameter) that were encased within three barrels (37 mm in diameter and 228 mm deep) situated behind a plastic mounting panel. The barrels were arranged in a triangular pattern, two up and one down. The distances between the barrels carrying the stimuli were as follows: 114 mm between the left and middle barrels; 114 mm between the middle and right barrels; and 200 mm between the left and right barrels. The middle barrel was vertically offset 52 mm below the left and right barrels. The face of the apparatus was mounted on a plastic arch and placed over the participant's body around the upper thigh region to minimize arm movement. Each barrel was attached to 8 m of pneumatic tubing with all three lengths of tubing connected to a computer-ized control system that regulated a compressed air supply (maximum pressure 137 kPa) to the apparatus. The delay between the control input

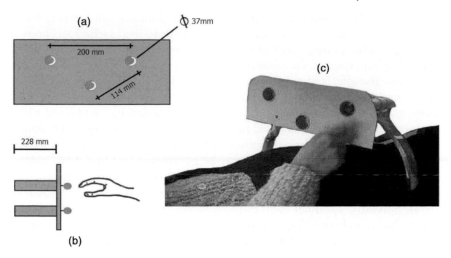

Figure 12.1 (a, b) Front and lateral views of the apparatus, respectively. (c) The position of the participant and how the apparatus was positioned within the fMRI scanner.

requesting each stimulus appearance and the actual appearance of the stimulus was 50 ms.

The apparatus worked as follows: The balls extended out of the barrels on the end of pneumatic pistons. The pistons extended to allow for the balls to be grasped using a precision grip consisting of the opposition between the index finger and the thumb of the right hand. The pistons were spring-loaded so that after such an action was performed, the stimuli automatically retracted back into the barrels. The participants viewed the apparatus through the head coil mirrors.

Great care was taken to minimize any confounding effects caused by motion of the participants' heads, which was estimated using the 6 degrees of freedom rigid body realignment algorithm implemented in SPM99. To test for any motion-induced activation, motion parameters were included as confounds during the analysis of the experimental data obtained for the participant who exhibited the largest head movements, but no changes were observed in the original activation map. Based on this finding, no correction for motion (using motion parameters as confounds) was included in the final statistical analyses.

Experiment 1: testing the effects of distractors on the reach-to-grasp movement

Rationale

We began by investigating whether any brain area showed significantly greater fMRI activation for reach-to-grasp movements performed in the presence or the absence of distractor objects. Initially, we restricted our investigation to selection-for-location, since (as described earlier) it is known that the reaching component is mainly concerned with the coding of the extrinsic properties of the objects (e.g. their location). Thus to specifically investigate the effects of target location, we made the intrinsic properties (i.e. colour and size) of the target and distractors identical and varied only their location. However, although the two components can be considered to be distinct, they seem to be coupled functionally, hence although arm reaching serves the function of bringing the hand to the immediate vicinity of the target object, and since therefore it may be postulated that its neural channel will be primarily affected by changing the object's spatial location, the object's size would also modify this component (Jakobson & Goodale, 1991). Similarly, although hand posture serves the function of grasping the target object, and since therefore it may be postulated that its neural channel will be primarily affected by changing the object's size, the object's spatial location would also modify this component (Jakobson & Goodale, 1991). Thus we cannot exclude the possibility that the neural areas concerned with grasping could not be activated by our "location" manipulation.

Methods

Experimental conditions

There were five conditions: (1) two-distractor condition; (2) one-distractor condition; (3) no distractor/one stimulus, three possible locations condition; (4) no distractor/one stimulus, one location condition; (5) view condition. Participants were instructed to reach-to-grasp (but not hold) the designated target stimulus using only their right-hand thumb and index finger (see Figure 12.1).

Each trial was repeated seven times over a 10.5 s condition period (1.5 s inter-stimulus interval) with the five conditions being presented randomly and without repetition within a scanning block. Two experimental blocks were presented per MR acquisition sequence with a total run time of 107 s. All participants were given a practice response period that included at least four blocks of trials, with each block containing all five conditions.

Here, we focus on the experimental comparison between the two-distractor condition compared with the no-distractor condition (conditions 1 and 3 above; for a comprehensive account of our results, see Chapman, Gavrilescu, Wang, Kean, Egan, & Castiello, 2002). This is because we wish here to focus both on the critical difference between the condition where the distractors were present with the condition where the distractors were absent.

Two-distractor condition

During this condition, three stimuli appeared for 250 ms, after which two of the stimuli retracted into the apparatus with the remaining stimulus thus becoming the target. Participants had 1 s to reach-to-grasp the target, which then retracted into the barrel. The final component of this condition was a 250 ms period during which no stimuli appeared (in preparation for the next trial).

No-distractor condition

During this condition, a single stimulus appeared at one of the three locations (i.e. either the left, middle or right) for 1 s. The location sequence was randomized *within* the condition period and the likelihood of the target appearing at any of the three locations was equal. Participants had 1 s to reach-to-grasp the target, which then retracted into the apparatus. Finally, a blank display (i.e. without any stimuli) appeared for 500 ms. As before, this period was included to clear the display in anticipation of the next trial.

Results and discussion

In support of the idea for the co-existence of visual attention and visuo-motor mechanisms within a single parietal region, we found that the right IPS (see Plate 12.1A) was differentially activated when comparing the two-distractor with the no-distractor conditions manipulating stimulus onset and offset when location uncertainty was held constant. Corbetta, Miezin, Shulman, and Petersen (1993) have shown in a PET study that cerebral flow selectively increases in this location in association with selective visuospatial attention. So it is thus possible that the increased IPS activation found when contrasting the "three-stimuli" with the "one-stimulus, three possible locations" conditions may reflect extra monitoring requirements. During the initialization of the "three stimuli" condition where all three stimuli are present, visual attention is diffused over the entire display to monitor all three stimuli. The abrupt offset of the distractors first drives the attentional focus onto them with the subsequent requirement that the focus of attention be reoriented towards the remaining stimulus (i.e. the target). The sum of these operations, which are present only in part (distribution/focusing) of this condition, given that the distractors are abruptly retracted, will contribute to the level of activation found in this area. However, in contrast with the findings of Corbetta et al. (1993), we found that the increase in IPS activation was not bilateral but confined to the right hemisphere, and we believe that it is the presence of the distractors that produced such a difference. Previous saccadic eye movement studies using distractors revealed IPS activation with a right-sided preponderance (Law, Svarer, Hom, & Paulson, 1997; Petit et al., 1999). They explained this as being related to the mechanisms required to inhibit a response to the distractors. The results of the present experiment may also be interpreted in this way.

An alternative view may be that it is harder to orient attention to offsets rather than onsets, though there is no strong evidence that offsets capture attention more than onsets (Watson & Humphreys, 1995). However, it is known that a potent feature for drawing attention to a stimulus is its sudden onset or offset (Atchley, Kramer, & Hillstrom, 2000; Pratt & McAuliffe, 2001; Watson & Humphreys, 1995; Yantis & Jonides, 1984). Furthermore, and relevant for this chapter, the kinematics of the reach-to-grasp action towards a target have been found to be significantly influenced by distractors when they were abruptly presented (Castiello, Badcock, & Bennett, 1999). By inference it could thus be advanced that distractor offsets may produce similar effects as distractor onsets. Along these lines, it can be advanced that in Experiment 1 the degree to which attention was drawn towards the distractors by their sudden offset might be one factor that may have determined the strength of brain activation within certain areas when comparing the two experimental conditions. This hypothesis will be tested in Experiment 2.

Whereas a contributing factor of at least part of the right IPS activation could be the greater visual attention requirement during the three-stimuli condition, a possible role for the IPS during action preparation cannot be discarded. Three pieces of evidence support this hypothesis. First, Sakata et al. (1997) have identified a concentration of cells in the lateral bank of the IPS that they determined to be of importance for the identification of the three-dimensional shape of objects. Second, the lateral intraparietal area of a monkey's brain contains cells that fire before either saccades and arm reaches (Snyder, Batista, & Andersen, 1997) or hand manipulation (Murata, Gallese, Kaseda, & Sakata, 1996). Third, it may be that the human homologue of the anterior intraparietal area mediates the processing of sensorimotor integration of grasp movements (Binkofski et al., 1998).

Thus, it might be proposed that the initial monitoring by the participant of the three stimuli (to be potentially acted on) places substantial requirements on the neural system concerned with the coding of object properties for the purpose of hand grasp. With respect to hand grasping, although we expected activation at the level of the ventral premotor cortex (as we highlighted in our predictions), no activation was found in Broca's area 44, the area in humans thought to correspond to the monkey F4–F5 ventral premotor cortex, the opercular cortex, or the frontal eye fields. On the other hand, we also predicted that given that the three stimuli required the same type of grasp (i.e. a precision grip), it is probable that competition would have not been enhanced.

Another area that activated differentially was the left PO sulcus (see Plate 12.1A). In connection with this, monkey studies have suggested that regions of the PO sulcus are well situated as an early "node" of a network mediating visually guided reaching (Caminiti et al., 1999). More recently, Fattori et al. (2001) discovered that neurons in monkey area V6A (found within the anterior bank of the PO sulcus) discharged during the preparation of arm movements and were direction selective. Although the human homologue for this set of areas is not clear, we suggest that in our experiment the simultaneous presentation of more than one potential target (at three separate locations) may have placed an increased demand on the reaching preparation processes.

Experiment 2: testing the effects of distractor offset

Rationale

The aim of Experiment 2 was to determine whether by manipulating the style of stimuli presentation differential levels of brain activation would be revealed. Our prediction is very clear. If the effects of distractors on the reach-to-grasp action towards a target are greater when the presence of the distractors is characterized by an abrupt event, then in a condition where there is no an abrupt event the effect of the distractors should be less evident. To test this prediction, we introduced a cue that indicated the stimulus (i.e. the target) to be grasped, while maintaining the visibility of the distractors at all times.

Methods

The method, task and procedures were the same as for Experiment 1, except that we tested more participants ($n = 15$) and introduced a cue that indicated the target stimulus (see Plate 12.1B). Additionally, in contrast to Experiment 1 where the distractor retracted into the apparatus, in Experiment 2 the distractors remained visible (i.e. extended). The sequence of events was as follows: The stimuli appeared for 250 ms, then the cue appeared and stayed on with the stimuli for 1000 ms.

Results and discussion

As we predicted, distractor effects were less evident in this experiment. Only the right occipital cortex was found to exhibit any significant neural activity (see Plate 12.1B). The crucial difference between Experiment 1 and Experiment 2 would appear to be the abrupt offset of the distractors. We found that the neural areas possibly concerned with the selection of target location and action planning were differentially activated depending on whether the distractors were abruptly retracted (Experiment 1) or remained present at all times, as in Experiment 2.

Why, therefore, do distractor objects produce a differential level of activation in the right IPS and left PO sulcus only when associated with an abrupt event? In Experiment 1, attention is initially diffused over the entire display when suddenly the abrupt offset momentarily draws the participant's attention towards the distractors, after which attention needs to be reoriented towards the target to complete the action. In Experiment 2, however, attention is (again) initially diffused over the entire display, the cue appears and attention is oriented towards the target. In principle, therefore, the reorienting phase was required in Experiment 1 and it was this that may have caused the difference in the measured right IPS activation.

It could also be advanced that any abrupt event could trigger these activations, but in Experiment 2 there was an abrupt event (i.e. the presentation of the cue) that did not give rise to differential activations in the right IPS and the left PO sulcus. This shows that there is a requirement for the presence of an object and suggests that we may have instead demonstrated a property of the attentional system concerned with selection-for-action. It is quite likely that these properties reflect processing in the higher levels of the dorsal stream where object-based representations and spatial visual attentional factors seem to be important (Goodale & Milner, 1992).

General discussion

The aim of the present study was to identify neural substrates for the processes involved in selection of reach-to-grasp responses in healthy adult humans on the basis of predictions drawn from selective reach-to-grasp behavioural studies (Castiello, 1999; Tipper et al., 1997, 1998). The hypothesis that parietal regions would be differentially activated according to the number of potential target locations was confirmed.

We found that when the disappearance of a distractor object was characterized by an abrupt offset and attention being directed to the remaining object for action, the result was an alteration to the level of activation. In contrast, when the distractor was present at all times, no significant level of activation in the specific parietal areas discussed was found. We thus hypothesize that not only a perceptual but also a motor representation of the "distracting" object was created. Our prediction is that at this point distractor objects can trigger competing reach-to-grasp programs, and the attentionally modulated resolution of this is played out within the brain areas concerned with visual attention and the control of action, namely the right IPS and the left PO sulcus, respectively. This may imply the existence of an active inhibitory process that suppresses the representation of distractor stimuli, and that the inhibitory mechanisms that resolve this competition are located within these two named areas.

Although we are inclined to suggest that our results reflect the processes involved in selection for reach-to-grasp responses, it cannot be excluded that the IPS and the PO sulcus activations are related to processes concerned with purely visual attention. However, if this were the case, it would have been reasonable to expect in Experiment 1, where attentional control was stimulus driven, activations lying outside the IPS network and housed in a more ventral cortical network (temporoparietal junction and ventral frontal cortex) strongly lateralized to the right hemisphere (Corbetta & Shulman, 2002) rather than a right IPS and a left PO activation. Furthermore, in Experiment 2, where advance information to signal the target and probably a top-down attentional control was elicited, it would have been reasonable to expect a largely bilateral IPS and frontal areas activation (Corbetta & Shulman, 2001), rather than a right occipital cortex activation.

In summary, we suggest that our results indicate that the activated areas are important for response or action selection. The activated regions are concerned with preparatory regions for impeding reaching (PO sulcus) and grasping (IPS). These regions may be proposed as the human homologue of the monkey areas V6A (Fattori et al., 2001) and AIP (Sakata & Taira, 1994) for reaching and grasping, respectively.

Finally, it is important to mention a possible limitation of the present study concerned with the experimental design. It is clear to us that a single-event design would have been more appropriate when attempting to make specific comparisons between the distractor and no-distractor conditions. Furthermore, the limitations of our data set do not allow a detailed exploration of the differential levels of brain area activation. Nevertheless, we believe that the results of the present study provide a good starting point for the future investigation of the selection-for-action process.

Acknowledgements

This research was supported by an Australian Research Council grant to Umberto Castiello and Gary Egan. We also thank Max Rademacher for his technical expertise and support. Some of the data reported here have been published as an abstract and a paper—Chapman, Gavrilescu, Wang, Kean, Egan, and Castiello (2001, 2002, respectively).

References

Allport, A. (1987). Selection-for-action: some behavioral and neurophysiological considerations of attention and action. In H. Heuer & A. F. Sanders (Eds.), *Perspectives on perception and action* (pp. 345–419). Hillsdale, NJ: Lawrence Erlbaum Associates Inc.

Andersen, R. A., Snyder, L. H., Bradley, D. C., & Xing, J. (1997). Multimodal representation of space in the posterior parietal cortex and its use in planning movements. *Annual Review of Neuroscience, 20*, 303–330.

Atchley, P., Kramer, A. F., & Hillstrom, A. P. (2000). Contingent capture for onsets and offsets: attentional set for perceptual transients. *Journal of Experimental Psychology: Human Perception and Performance, 26*, 594–606.

Bennett, K. M. B., & Castiello, U. (1994). *Insights into the reach-to-grasp movement.* Amsterdam: Elsevier.

Binkofski, F., Dohle, C., Posse, S., Stephan, K. M., Hefter, H., Seitz, R. J. et al. (1998). Human anterior intraparietal area subserves prehension. *Neurology, 50*, 1253–1259.

Caminiti, R., Genovesio, A., Marconi, B., Mayer, A. B., Onorati, P., Ferraina, S. et al. (1999). Early online coding of reaching: frontal and parietal association connections of parieto-occipital cortex. *European Journal of Neuroscience, 11,* 3339–3345.

Castiello, U. (1996). Grasping a fruit: selection for action. *Journal of Experimental Psychology: Human Perception and Performance, 22,* 582–603.

Castiello, U. (1999). Mechanisms of selection for the control of hand action. *Trends in Cognitive Science, 3,* 264–271.

Castiello, U., Badcock, D. R., & Bennett, K. M. B. (1999). Sudden and gradual presentation of distractor objects: differential interference effects. *Experimental Brain Research, 128,* 550–556.

Chapman, H., Gavrilescu, M., Wang, H., Kean, M., Egan, G., & Castiello, U. (2001). Selective attention for motor action: an fMRI study. *NeuroImage, 13,* S307.

Chapman, H., Gavrilescu, M., Wang, H., Kean, M., Egan, G., & Castiello, U. (2002). Posterior parietal cortex control of reach-to-grasp movements in humans. *European Journal of Neuroscience, 15,* 1–7.

Chieffi, S., Gentilucci, M., Allport, A., Sasso, E., & Rizzolatti, G. (1993). Study of selective reaching and grasping in a patient with unilateral parietal lesion: dissociated effects of residual spatial neglect. *Brain, 116,* 1119–1137.

Connolly, J. D., Goodale, M. A., DeSouza, J. F., Menon, R. S., & Vilis, T. (2000). A comparison of frontoparietal fMRI activation during anti-saccades and anti-pointing. *Journal of Neurophysiology, 84,* 1645–1655.

Corbetta, M., Akbudak, E., Conturo, T. E., Snyder, A. Z., Ollinger, J. M., Drury, H. A. et al. (1998). A common network of functional areas for attention and eye movements. *Neuron, 21,* 761–733.

Corbetta, M., Miezin, F. M., Shulman, G. L., & Petersen, S. E. (1993). A PET study of visuospatial attention. *Journal of Neuroscience, 13,* 1202–1226.

Corbetta, M., & Shulman, G. L. (2002). Control of goal-directed and stimulus driven attention in the brain. *Nature Neuroscience, 3,* 201–215.

Culham, J. C., DeSouza, J. F. X., Osu, R., Milner, A. D., Gati, J. F., Menon, R. S. et al. (2000, July). *Visually-guided grasping produces fMRI activation in human anterior intraparietal sulcus.* Paper presented to the Joint Meeting of the Experimental Psychology Society (UK)/Canadian Society for Brain, Behaviour and Cognitive Science, Cambridge, UK.

Culham, J. C., & Kanwisher, N. G. (2001). Neuroimaging of cognitive functions in human parietal cortex. *Current Opinion in Neurobiology, 11,* 157–163.

Eriksen, B. A., & Eriksen, C. W. (1974). Effect of noise letters upon the identification of a target letter in a non-search task. *Perception and Psychophysics, 16,* 143–149.

Eriksen, C. W., & Schultz, D. W. (1979). Information processing in visual search: a continuous flow conception and experimental results. *Perception and Psychophysics, 25,* 249–263.

Fattori, P., Gamberini, M., Kutz, D. F., & Galletti, C. (2001). Arm-reaching neurons in the parietal area V6A of the macaque monkey. *European Journal of Neuroscience, 13,* 2309–2313.

Gentilucci, M., Fogassi, L., Luppino, G., Matelli, M., Camarda, R., & Rizzolati, G. (1988). Functional organization of inferior area 6 in the macaque monkey: I. Somatotopy and the control of proximal movements. *Experimental Brain Research, 71,* 475–490.

Georgopoulous, A. P. (1990). Neurophysiology of reaching. In M. Jeannerod (Ed.), *Attention and performance XIII* (pp. 849–859). Hillsdale, NJ: Lawrence Erlbaum Associates Inc.

Goodale, M. A., & Milner, A. D. (1992). Separate visual pathways for perception and action. *Trends in Neuroscience, 15,* 20–25.

Jackson, S. R., Jackson, G. M., & Rosicky, J. (1995). Are non-relevant objects represented in working memory? The effect of non-target objects on reach and grasp kinematics. *Experimental Brain Research, 102,* 519–530.

Jakobson, L. S., & Goodale, M. A. (1991). Factors affecting higher-order movement planning: a kinematic analysis of human prehension. *Experimental Brain Research, 86,* 199–208.

Jeannerod, M. (1981). Intersegmental coordination during reaching at natural visual objects. In J. Long & A. Baddeley (Eds.), *Attention and performance IX* (pp. 153–168). Hillsdale, NJ: Lawrence Erlbaum Associates Inc.

Jeannerod, M. (1984). The timing of natural prehension movements. *Journal of Motor Behavior, 16,* 235–254.

Kertzman, C., Schwartz, U., Zeffiro, T. A., & Hallett, M. (1997). The role of posterior parietal cortex in visually guided reaching movements in humans. *Experimental Brain Research, 114,* 170–183.

Law, I., Svarer, C., Hom, S., & Paulson, O. B. (1997). The activation pattern in normal humans during suppression, imagination and performance of saccadic eye movements. *Acta Physiologica Scandinavica, 161,* 419–434.

Murata, A., Gallese, V., Kaseda, M., & Sakata, H. (1996). Parietal neurons related to memory-guided hand manipulation. *Journal of Neurophysiology, 75,* 2180–2186.

Petit, L., Dubois, S., Tzourio, N., Dejardin, S., Crivello, F., Michel, C. et al. (1999). PET study of the human foveal fixation system. *Human Brain Mapping, 8,* 28–43.

Pratt, J., & McAuliffe, J. (2001). The effects of onsets and offsets on visual attention. *Psycological Research, 65,* 185–191.

Rizzolatti, G., Camarda, R., Fogassi, L., Gentilucci, M., Luppino, G., & Matelli, M. (1988). Functional organization of inferior area 6 in the macaque monkey. II. Area F5 and the control of distal movements. *Experimental Brain Research, 71,* 491–507.

Sakata, H., & Taira, M. (1994). Parietal control of hand action. *Current Opinion in Neurobiology, 4,* 847–856.

Sakata, H., Taira, M., Kusunoki, M., Murata, A., & Tanaka, Y. (1997). The TINS lecture. The parietal association cortex in depth perception and visual control of hand action. *Trends in Neuroscience, 20,* 350–357.

Sakata, H., Taira, M., Kusunoki, M., Tsusui, K., Tanaka, Y., Shein, W. N. et al. (1999). Neural representation of three-dimensional features of manipulation objects with stereopsis. *Experimental Brain Research, 128,* 160–169.

Snyder, L. H., Batista, A. P., & Andersen, R. A. (1997). Coding of intention in the posterior parietal cortex. *Nature, 386,* 167–169.

Tipper, S. P., Howard, L. A., & Houghton, G. (1998). Action-based mechanisms of attention. *Philosophical Transactions of the Royal Society of London, B, 353,* 1385–1393.

Tipper, S. P., Howard, L. A., & Jackson, S. R. (1997). Selective reaching to grasp: evidence for distractor interference effects. *Visual Cognition, 4,* 1–38.

Todd, J. T., & Van Gelder, P. (1979). Implications of a transient-sustained dichotomy for the measurement of human performance. *Journal of Experimental Psychology: Human Perception and Performance, 5,* 625–638.

Tresilian, J. R. (1998). Attention in action or obstruction of movement? A kinematic analysis of avoidance behavior in prehension. *Experimental Brain Research, 120,* 352–368.

Ungerleider, L. G., & Mishkin, M. (1982). Two cortical visual systems. In D. J. Ingle, M. A. Goodale, & R. J. W. Mansfield (Eds.), *Analysis of visual behavior* (pp. 549–586). Cambridge, MA: MIT Press.

Watson, D. G., & Humphreys, G. W. (1995). Attention and capture by contour onsets and offsets: no special role for onsets. *Perception and Psychophysics, 57,* 583–597.

Yantis, S., & Jonides, J. (1984). Abrupt visual onsets and selective attention: evidence from visual search. *Journal of Experimental Psychology, 10,* 601–621.

13 Action binding and the parietal lobes

Some new perspectives on optic ataxia

Stephen R. Jackson, Roger Newport,
Dominic Mort, Masud Husain,
Georgina M. Jackson,
Rachel Swainson, Sally Pears
and Barbara Wilson

Abstract

To execute goal-directed movements, such as reaching to pick up an object, information specified in extrinsic (spatial) coordinates must be transformed into a motor plan that is expressed within intrinsic (motor) coordinates. For reaching movements directed to visually defined targets, this will involve translating visual information that is initially coded in retinotopic coordinates into a motor plan that specifies the sequence of postural changes required to bring the hand to the target. Several lines of evidence point to the important role played by the posterior parietal cortex (PPC) in carrying out the sensorimotor transformations that are associated with goal-directed action. In humans, damage to the PPC, particularly bilateral lesions, leads to impairments in the planning and control of reaching movements directed towards visual targets, known as optic ataxia. Recent theoretical accounts of this disorder propose that it arises as a result of a failure within successive stages of the sensorimotor transformation process. In this chapter, we present evidence from two patients presenting with the most commonly encountered form of misreaching deficit—non-foveal optic ataxia—in support of a novel account. Namely, that a key feature of this form of optic ataxia may be a failure to successfully de-couple the eye and limb visuomotor systems so that each might undertake simultaneously independent actions.

Introduction

To execute goal-directed movements, such as reaching to pick up an object, information specified in *extrinsic* (spatial) coordinates must be transformed into a motor plan that is expressed within *intrinsic* (motor) coordinates. For reaching movements directed to visually defined targets, this will involve translating visual information that is initially coded in retinotopic coordinates into a motor plan that specifies the sequence of *postural* changes required to bring the hand to the target. This is commonly referred to as the "sensorimotor transformation" problem and remains one of the most important and yet least understood issues within motor control research. Recent electrophysiological (e.g. Batista, Buneo, Snyder, & Andersen, 1999; Graziano, Yap, & Gross, 1994) and neuropsychological (e.g. Jackson, Newport, Husain, Harvey, & Hindle, 2000; Newport, Hindle, & Jackson, 2001) reports suggest that there is no single, supramodal map of space that is used to guide movements. Instead, movements appear to be capable of being planned and controlled within multiple coordinate systems, each one attached to a different body part. Several lines of evidence point to the important role played by the posterior parietal cortex (PPC) in carrying out the sensorimotor transformations that are associated with goal-directed action (see also Rushworth & Ellison, this volume).

In the monkey, electrophysiological studies have identified multiple representations of space in posterior parietal cortex (for reviews, see Andersen, Snyder, Bradley, & Xing, 1997; Rizzolatti, Fogassi, & Gallese, 1997), each associated with different types or combinations of action, such as saccadic eye movements and reaching or grasping movements of the upper limb. For example, recordings from parietal area LIP while monkeys make saccadic eye movements suggest that neurons in this area may be involved in dynamic re-mapping of space (Duhamel, Colby, & Goldberg, 1992), with representations of visual stimuli being re-mapped from a coordinate system with the initial fixation point as origin, to one centred upon the upcoming fixation point. Similarly, electrophysiological studies of the superior parietal lobe (SPL) have demonstrated the existence of a "parietal reach region" in which the targets of reaching movements appear to be represented within eye-centred rather than body-centred coordinates (Batista et al., 1999). In humans, lesions of the SPL lead to misreaching to visual targets, known as optic ataxia. While patients can correctly and accurately execute reaching movements directed to proprioceptively defined locations (i.e. targets defined by the position of body parts) they nevertheless mislocalize targets when pointing to visual stimuli, particularly when executing movements directed towards targets located in peripheral vision. Furthermore, when reaching to peripheral visual targets while fixating centrally, these patients tend to err in their reaches towards the direction of gaze (Buxbaum & Coslett, 1997; Carey, Coleman, & Della Sala, 1997; Ratcliff & Davies-Jones, 1972).

Some new perspectives on optic ataxia

As noted above, optic ataxia refers to a disorder of visually guided reaching movements that cannot be attributed to a basic motor or sensory deficit (Bálint, 1909; Rizzo & Vecera, 2002). The disorder was described initially by Reszö Bálint in connection with one of a triad of visuospatial symptoms that can result from bilateral damage to the occipital–parietal cortex in humans, and which has become known as Balint-Holmes or Balint's syndrome (Rizzo & Vecera, 2002). More recent studies have confirmed that optic ataxia can also occur in isolation from the other symptoms associated with Balint's syndrome, and may follow unilateral damage to the parietal cortex of either hemisphere, most frequently involving the intraparietal sulcus and the SPL (Perenin & Vighetto, 1988).

Optic ataxia has most often been described as arising from a "disconnection" between visual processing systems and motor regions. For example, Balint saw the disorder arising largely as a consequence of the transection of white matter tracts running beneath the parietal cortices and, consistent with this view, optic ataxia has been reported previously in a patient with a lesion involving the corpus callosum who presented without damage to parietal cortex (Gaymard, Rivauld, Rigolet, & Pierrot-Deseilligny, 1997). However, as pointed out by De Renzi (1996), the disconnection account oversimplifies the important role played by parietal cortex in processing spatial information and in guiding eye and limb movements towards extrapersonal targets. For this reason, recent theoretical accounts have attempted to reframe the disconnection account either as a failure within successive stages of the sensorimotor transformation process (Buxbaum & Coslett, 1997) or as a breakdown in the tuning fields of parietal neurons responsible for producing coordinated eye–hand movements (Battaglia-Mayer & Caminiti, 2002).

Case JJ: optic ataxia in a patient with bilateral parietal damage

We have been fortunate to study in some detail a patient presenting with optic ataxia following a series of strokes affecting the posterior parietal cortex bilaterally. Our patient (JJ) is a right-handed male who has suffered recurrent cerebral haemorrhages over a period of 6 years. At the time of testing he was 65 years old and a recent MRI scan (see Plate 13.1) revealed asymmetrical bilateral posterior atrophy predominantly of the parietal lobes, with the damage to the left parietal cortex extending further into the superior region than in the right hemisphere. Damage to the left hemisphere involved the SPL and IPS, and the angular gyrus. In addition, there was signal change consistent with degeneration of the white matter in the occipital lobe. Damage to the right hemisphere involved the IPS and the posterior aspect of the angular gyrus. Signal change was also observed within the white matter of the occipital lobe. In both hemispheres, there was evidence of damage to white matter tracts underlying the parietal cortex. Previous testing with finger presentation and Goldmann perimetry revealed an absolute visual field deficit in the left inferior quadrant. JJ showed no clinical signs of visuospatial neglect and his somatosensory detection was normal.

Simultanagnosia

JJ was quite unable, when assessed clinically, to name overlaid pairs of line drawings of familiar objects. When presented with a pair of objects, he would always report seeing only one item from the pair; however, on repeated testing he would vary which of the two objects he reported. Similarly, when presented with a complex line drawing containing many objects (e.g. the Boston Cookie Theft picture), JJ would report objects from the scene in a piecemeal fashion and would always fail to comprehend the meaning of the whole scene. We formally tested the extent of JJ's simultanagnosia using a wide range of experimental and psychophysical paradigms. Some example data are presented below (see also Plate 13.2).

We used a psychophysical staircase procedure (Leek, 2001) to assess JJ's threshold to report correctly a single coloured letter stimulus presented centrally on a CRT monitor, or a pair of coloured letters presented close together at fixation. JJ required a stimulus presentation of 150 ms to correctly report a single coloured letter. In contrast, JJ required a stimulus duration of 2600 ms to correctly report a pair of coloured letter stimuli. It is of interest to note that while JJ was unable to correctly report the identity of two letter stimuli presented at quite long durations (e.g. 1000 ms), he was nevertheless extremely accurate at reporting whether one or two stimuli had been presented. Thus, for stimulus durations of 100 ms, JJ was correct on 86% of trials in determining whether one or two letter stimuli had been presented. For stimulus durations of 1000 ms, his accuracy rose to 94% correct. We note that this finding raises some doubts with respect to the proposal that Balint-Holmes patients only "see" one item when a pair of stimuli are presented. Plate 13.2 shows data obtained in a conjunctive visual detection experiment in which JJ was required to indicate using a manual keypress response whether a target letter was present or absent in a display of two coloured letters. A key finding here is the high number of binding errors made on target-absent trials in which each non-target letter shares a feature in common with the target for that trial.

Motor function

JJ's spontaneous eye saccades, when he makes them, are full; however, he has difficulty in fixating targets voluntarily, and his gaze tends to fall 20° to the right of his midline. JJ also shows clear signs of optic ataxia. When reaching with his right limb towards extra-foveal targets presented in either hemifield, his movements exhibit large directional errors. These errors are always directed towards where he is looking. Reaching movements executed with his left limb towards non-foveated targets tend to be more accurate, as are unimanual reaching movements executed with either limb towards *foveated* targets. JJ is also extremely inaccurate when reaching bimanually to two objects spaced shoulder width apart. This is particularly so when he is required to foveate the left target object (Figure 13.1). This finding is consistent with previous reports of gaze-dependent misreaching following bilateral lesions (e.g., Buxbaum & Coslett, 1997; Carey et al., 1997).

Bimanual reaching task

To examine JJ's optic ataxia, we used a bimanual reaching task that we have used previously to examine upper limb coordination in neurologically intact individuals and in brain-injured patients (see Jackson, German, Peacock, 2002a; Jackson, Jackson, & Hindle, 2000a; Jackson, Jackson, Husain, Harvey, Kramer & Dow, 2000b; Jackson, Jackson, & Kritikos, 1999; Jackson, Jackson,

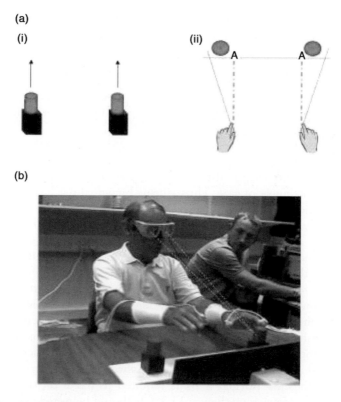

Figure 13.1 (a) Illustration of the bimanual reaching task. (i) JJ was instructed to reach bimanually to pick up two wooden dowels; painted red, which were placed upon two wooden pedestals presented shoulder width apart. (ii) During reaching movements, the spatiotemporal pattern of the movements of each of JJ's thumbs was tracked using an electromagnetic tracking device sampling at 81 Hz. (b) A still taken from video during a bimanual reaching movement executed by JJ in the "gaze left" condition. Note that as JJ's left hand approaches the left target object, his right hand is substantially leftward of the right target object.

Newport, & Harvey, 2002b). This task has two properties that make it particularly appropriate for use in investigating JJ's misreaching impairments. First, when neurologically intact individuals execute bimanual reaching movements, they show an extremely tight temporal coupling between the limbs. This is the case even if the individual is asked to make quite different movements with each hand (e.g. execute movements of different amplitudes or reach to grasp objects of quite different sizes). This can be seen in Figure 13.2.

Figure 13.2a shows the velocities of the right and left hand for a single bimanual reaching movement in which a neurologically normal individual is required to reach to objects at two different distances. Figure 13.2b shows the mean movement durations for bimanual reaches executed by a group of neurologically normal adults to targets at two different amplitudes where, on each trial, the right and left hands moved either the same distance (congruent reaches) or different distances (incongruent reaches). The data show that for unimanual and congruent bimanual trials, movement durations are scaled to movement amplitude. However, during incongruent bimanual reaches, the spatiotemporal pattern of each limb movement becomes tightly coupled and movement durations no longer scale for movement amplitude. Such coupling can be severely disrupted by damage to the anterior regions of the posterior parietal cortex (Jackson et al., 2000b, 2002b).

Second, unlike unimanual movements where there is usually a very tight coupling between direction of gaze and the direction of the reaching movement, bimanual movements directed to separate objects do not appear to depend upon the angle of gaze. Thus, during bimanual reach-to-grasp movements, movement durations do not differ between those objects that are viewed directly in foveal vision and those that are seen in peripheral vision (Jackson et al., 2002a).

As noted above, when executing unimanual reaches with either hand to target objects that he can foveate, JJ's movements are very accurate (Figure 13.3a). In contrast, JJ is unable to accurately execute bimanual reach-to-grasp movements towards two target objects. While his two limbs show the normal pattern of temporal coordination, he makes quite large directional errors with his right hand (Figure 13.3b). This is especially so if he is required to maintain fixation (gaze left) on the left-hand object while reaching (Figure 13.3d). Note that these directional errors are always leftward. In contrast, JJ's bimanual reaches are normal if he is required to fixate on the rightmost target object while reaching (Figure 13.3c). It should be noted that JJ is fully aware of these misreaching errors and tries to correct them over the course of a block of trials. However, if given a short break between blocks, the magnitude of his misreaching errors returns to initial levels. In summary, JJ can be seen to exhibit a limb-dependent form of misreaching that appears to be dependent upon the direction of his gaze (Figure 13.4).

It has been reported previously that in patients presenting with optic ataxia following unilateral lesions of the posterior parietal cortex, reaching

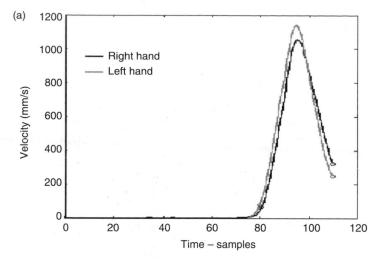

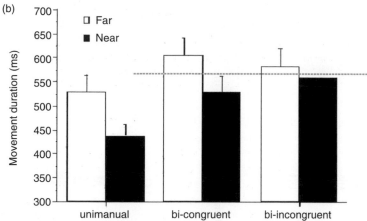

Figure 13.2 (a) Velocities for the right and left hands taken from a single bimanual reaching trial in which a neurologically intact adult participant was instructed to pick up two objects placed at different distances from the body. Note the tight temporal coupling for the movement onsets and peak velocities. (b) Mean movement durations for reaches executed by a group of neurologically normal individuals to targets at two different amplitudes. Movements were unimanual reaches, bimanual reaches where, on each trial, the right and left hands moved the same distance (congruent reaches), or bimanual reaches where, on each trial, the right and left hands moved different distances (incongruent reaches).

errors exhibit a constant directional bias towards ipsilesional space (Perenin & Vighetto, 1988). However, this proposal contrasts with earlier reports where is was stated that misreaching errors in optic ataxic patients are directed towards the point of fixation (e.g. Ratcliff & Davies-Jones, 1972). There are several important differences between these studies. Whereas the Perenin

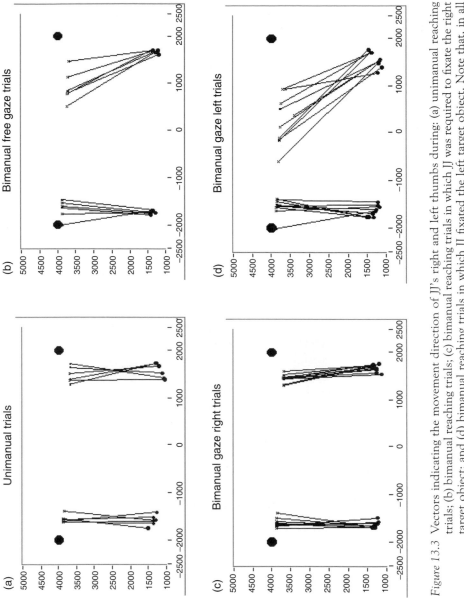

Figure 13.3 Vectors indicating the movement direction of JJ's right and left thumbs during: (a) unimanual reaching trials; (b) bimanual reaching trials; (c) bimanual reaching trials in which JJ was required to fixate the right target object; and (d) bimanual reaching trials in which JJ fixated the left target object. Note that, in all cases, accurate reaching movements will result in the thumb slightly to the left or right (depending upon the hand used) of the object's centre.

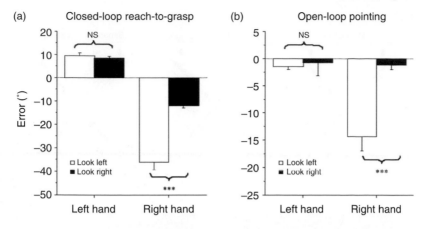

Figure 13.4 Mean direction errors for patient JJ while executing bimanual reaching movements to two targets while fixating the left or right target. Negative values indicate a leftward error. (a) Reach-to-grasp movements made with full visual feedback of the hand and target throughout the reach. (b) Pointing movements executed beneath an opaque surface in which JJ had no visual feedback of his limb but could see the target object throughout the reach. In both cases, JJ made large leftward direction errors with his right hand, but only when he was required to fixate the left target object. Gaze direction had no effect on reaching movements executed by JJ using his left hand. ***$p < .0001$.

and Vighetto (1998) investigated a relatively small number of patients presenting with unilateral damage primarily as a result of vascular damage (three patients had undergone surgery), Ratcliff and Daves-Jones (1972) reported a relatively large cohort ($n = 40$) who presented with brain injury primarily as a result of missile wounds, and who had mainly damage extending into both cerebral hemispheres. Currently, it remains an important question if the pattern of misreaching seen in *bilateral* cases of optic ataxia differs systematically from that seen following *unilateral* lesions; however, confirming evidence in favour of gaze-dependent misreaching following bilateral lesions has now been reported on a number of occasions (e.g. Buxbaum & Coslett, 1997; Carey et al., 1997).

We examined this issue with patient JJ by evaluating his ability to execute reaching movements into contralateral space (i.e. bimanual reaching movements that cross the body midline). Note that if optic ataxia presents as a constant direction error, then this manipulation should have no effect on the pattern of direction errors observed. However, if JJ's misreaching errors are linked to the direction of his gaze, then the direction of his misreaching errors should reverse when he executes reaches into contralateral space. The results of this study are presented in Figure 13.5, which shows quite clearly that JJ's misreaching errors do reverse direction when he executes reaches into contralateral space. When JJ was required to fixate the rightmost target and reach

(a)

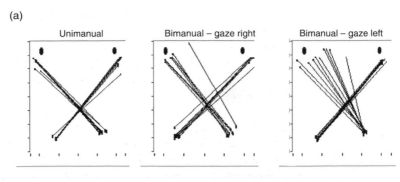

(b)

Figure 13.5 (a) Vectors indicating the movement direction of JJ's right and left thumbs during unimanual (left panel), bimanual gaze left (centre panel) and bimanual gaze right (right panel) trials. (b) A still taken from video during a bimanual reaching movement executed by JJ in the "gaze right" condition. Note that as JJ's left hand approaches the right target object, his right hand is substantially rightward of the left target object.

with his right hand to pick up the object presented within his left hemispace (and vice versa), his pattern of misreaching errors reversed direction. That is, he made rightward reaching errors with his right hand towards his point of gaze. These results confirm that JJ is not misreaching in a constant direction, but is instead misreaching in the direction of his angle of gaze. Furthermore, unlike previous reports (e.g. Carey et al., 1997), we show that this misreaching cannot be explained in terms of a simple perceptual deficit, or as a failure to understand the task, as during bimanual reaches JJ's left hand remains perfectly accurate and is unaffected by manipulations of gaze direction.

Furthermore, in several other experiments with JJ, we have established: (1) that his reaching errors are not a consequence of having been instructed to make an eye movement to one of the target objects. Thus, JJ's limb-dependent misreaching errors persist even when he maintains fixation centrally and on each trial the two objects are moved so that one or other is at his point of fixation. (b) That his reaching errors are not simply a result of his right hand "following" his left hand. When JJ executes unimanual reaching movements with his right hand to a single extrafoveal target, he continues to show misreaching errors in the direction of his gaze. Note also that this experiment also effectively rules out any simple explanation of his misreaching errors in terms of his simultanagnosic impairment (i.e. when faced with two visual targets he perceives only one). However, evidence from another patient (outlined below) suggests that simultanagnosia may contribute to some aspects of the visually guided misreaching problems observed in Balint's patients.

Gaze-dependent misreaching in case MU

We recently had the opportunity to study gaze-dependent misreaching in another Balint's syndrome patient (MU) who has been described previously as presenting with severe visuospatial impairment following a drugs overdose in 1981 (Wilson, Clare, Young, & Hodges, 1997). A computed tomography scan in 1995 revealed extensive bilateral damage to the occipito-parietal cortex, involving both grey and white matter, and extending from the level of the third ventricle to the upper parietal regions, with the left side being more severely affected. A full description of MU's neuropsychological assessment can be obtained by consulting Wilson et al. (1997). Formal testing of MU's visuospatial performance revealed that he exhibited a number of difficulties. For instance, he was at chance on a test involving the mental rotation of a manikin, and he achieved a score of 2/9 on the picture scanning subtest of the Behavioural Inattention Test (Wilson, Cockburn, & Halligan, 1988). His picture-matching performance was also poor (he achieved a score of 5/16 on the forced-choice version of the Benton Visual Retention Test) as was his visual short-term memory (3/24 correct items). Like patient JJ, MU also displayed clear visuomotor difficulties. Clinical observation revealed that while he frequently misreached for visually defined objects, he could nevertheless accurately point to parts of his body when instructed to do so. Formal testing of MU's visuomotor performance using the Corsi blocks task revealed a severe impairment. He was unable to touch a single block indicated by the tester (a span of zero). At the time that we tested MU, he had limited mobility and was seated within a wheelchair. He was unable to make use of his right arm and, therefore, could only be tested when executing unimanual reaches using his left arm. Nevertheless, he revealed two very interesting misreaching deficits that are worthy of report here.

When asked to reach towards single target objects that he was permitted to look at, MU was able to reach for them slowly, but accurately. However, when he was required to reach towards a target object presented in his peripheral vision while fixating a separate object, he was completely unable to initiate reaches without first looking towards the target object. We tested this observation formally by having MU reach for extrafoveal targets while we carefully monitored his eye movements. In all cases where he maintained fixation, he failed to initiate a reach. His hand would move about but would not make any forward motion until such time as we permitted MU to look away from the fixation object towards the target object, when he would then initiate a reaching movement towards the target. This was the case despite the fact that MU reported being able to clearly see the target object in his peripheral visual field on all trials.

To determine whether the simultaneous presence within the visual field of two separate objects was contributing to MU's difficulties, we first investigated the effect of placing the fixation and target objects on a continuous plinth so that they appeared, perceptually, more like two components of a single object than two separate objects. A similar manipulation has been shown previously to improve perceptual reporting in Balint's syndrome (Humphreys & Riddoch, 1993), and we have shown that this manipulation influences grip aperture programming in neurologically normal individuals executing bimanual reach-to-grasp movements (Jackson et al., 2002a). Note, that in this case the fixation and target objects are in identical spatial locations to previous trials, the only difference is that they now appear to be joined together as parts of a single object. When tested under these circumstances, patient MU was able to initiate a reaching movement on every trial while maintaining fixation on the fixated object (Figure 13.6a). However, his reaching was initially very inaccurate and his errors, like those of patient JJ, tended to be towards the point of fixation. Our finding that the perceptual grouping of the target and fixation objects influences MU's ability to initiate reaching movements, confirms previous reports that visual grouping can influence (bimanual) reaching movements in a patient presenting with Balint's syndrome (Edwards & Humphreys, 2002).

Patient MU has difficulty in initiating reaching movements towards extrafoveal target objects when he is required to fixate upon a second object. This is also the situation that gives rise to the "magnetic misreaching" phenomenon in the case of Mrs D reported by Carey et al. (1997). However, the data presented in Figure 13.6a show quite clearly that MU's difficulties in initiating reaching movements can be removed if the two objects presented within the visual field are made to appear as parts of a single object. As noted above, this manipulation has been shown previously to substantially improve perceptual report in Balint's syndrome patients. This finding is consistent with the integrated competition hypothesis (Duncan, Humphreys, & Ward, 1997), which proposes that visual information from different objects competes for processing resources. When processing resources are significantly reduced, as is the case for patients presenting with bilateral damage to the

(a)

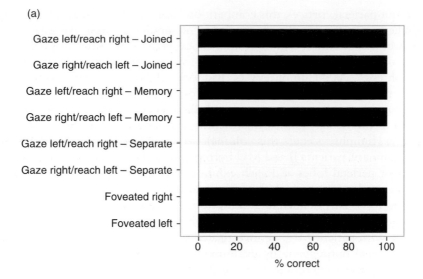

(b)

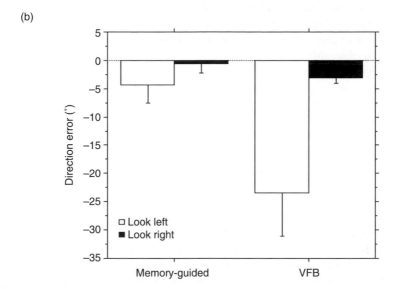

Figure 13.6 (a) Graph showing the percentage of trials on which patient MU correctly managed to initiate a reaching movement. (b) Graph illustrating that the large misreaching errors seen on visually guided trials are abolished for patient MU if vision is removed shortly before movement onset. VFB refers to trials conducted with full visual feedback of the target location and the moving limb.

posterior parietal cortices, this competition between objects may be particularly fierce, resulting in the phenomenon of simultanagnosia. Alternatively, it may be that attention is more readily allocated to the relationships between parts of a single object than to those of separate objects (Cooper & Humphreys, 2000; Humphreys & Riddoch, 1994, 1995). Irrespective of which theoretical model best accounts for these data, it is clear that the attentional impairments associated with Balint's syndrome might also contribute to the visually guided misreaching errors observed in those patients (see also Humphreys et al., this volume).

In summary, patients JJ and MU both present with bilateral damage to the posterior parietal lobes and each exhibits the classic signs associated with Balint's syndrome: particularly severe visuospatial disorientation and misreaching to visually defined targets (optic ataxia). Furthermore, both patients primarily exhibit a misreaching deficit when reaching to non-foveal visual targets. With patient MU, we investigated the contribution of online vision to non-foveal optic ataxia by examining how his misreaching errors were affected by removing online visual feedback at the moment he was required to initiate his movement. This was achieved using a pair of PLATO spectacles (which are seen being worn by patient JJ in Figures 13.1 & 13.5), which can be made to change from transparent to opaque very rapidly. With online vision available, MU executed reaching movements (to a target object "joined" to a fixation object) that were highly inaccurate and exhibited misreaching errors in the direction of fixation. In contrast, when vision was removed just before movement onset, MU's reaching became significantly more accurate (Figure 13.6b). One plausible explanation for these results is that the simultaneous presence of an object at fixation while reaching to an extrafoveal target object interferes with MU's ability to initiate reaching movements, and de-couples his reach direction from that of his gaze direction. This proposal is considered below.

Optic ataxia as impaired sensorimotor transformation

As noted earlier, recent theoretical accounts of optic ataxia have attempted to re-frame simple disconnection explanations of this disorder either as a failure within successive stages of the sensorimotor transformation process (e.g. Buxbaum & Coslett, 1997) or as a breakdown in the tuning fields of parietal neurons responsible for producing coordinated eye–hand movements (e.g. Battaglia-Mayer & Caminiti, 2002).

Buxbaum and Coslett (1997) have argued that a single disconnection model cannot account for all the symptoms of optic ataxia. They identify two main subtypes of optic ataxia: foveal optic ataxia in which the patient cannot reach accurately towards foveated targets, and non-foveal optic ataxia in which the patient is unable to reach accurately towards peripherally viewed visual targets. As noted above, our patient JJ can reach accurately to foveated targets, and his misreaching, as with many patients exhibiting optic ataxia, is most apparent when reaching towards extrafoveal visual targets. Thus JJ, like most optic ataxic patients reported in the literature, falls within the non-foveal subtype of optic ataxia.

Buxbaum and Coslett (1997) have suggested that non-foveal optic ataxia can be seen as a failure to encode the spatial location of the target relative to the hand within an extrinsic, limb-centred, coordinate system. This failure leaves the patient reliant upon spatial information encoded by undamaged oculocentric spatio-motor systems (i.e. eye-centred coordinates), resulting in misreaches directed more towards the direction of gaze than the target. While this proposal appears plausible, it is difficult to reconcile with the results of recent studies that have investigated the nature of the sensorimotor transformation that accompanies reaching movements. For instance, one problem with this view is that it assumes that there is a linear and hierarchical progression, via eye-, head- and trunk-based coordinate systems, from retinal input to a supramodal representation of target location specified in *extrinsic* coordinates relative to the shoulder or hand of the reaching limb (i.e. extrinsic limb-centred coordinates). By contrast, recent studies have indicated that the frames of reference used to plan and control reaching movements may be highly flexible and dynamically assembled using multiple coordinate systems to create a hybrid frame of reference that is suited to the specific demands of a particular task (Jackson, 2001). Most importantly, several psychophysical (e.g. Flanders, Helms-Tillery, & Soechting, 1992; Vetter, Goodbody, & Wolpert, 1999), electrophysiological (e.g. Batista et al., 1999) and neuropsychological (Jackson et al., 2000; Rushworth, Nixon, & Passingham, 1997) studies provide converging evidence to suggest that reaches to visually defined targets are planned and controlled in oculocentric coordinates in neurologically intact individuals, while reaches without vision (e.g. to posturally defined targets) may be planned and controlled largely using *intrinsic* (postural) limb-centred coordinates. Such a distinction may account for the finding that in non-foveal optic ataxics, misreaching errors are substantively reduced when reaching to target locations after a 5 s delay has been introduced (Milner, Paulignan, Dijkerman, Michel, & Jeannerod, 1999) or when reaching without vision to remembered target locations, as was demonstrated for patient MU above.

Battaglia-Mayer and Caminiti (2002) offer a different perspective on optic ataxia. Based largely upon the physiological properties of populations of neurons found within the superior parietal lobule, they argue that optic ataxia arises as a result of the breakdown in the combination of directional eye and hand information within the global tuning fields of parietal neurons. Within this view, the parietal lobe is seen as integrating *spatially congruent* retinal, eye and hand information within "global tuning fields" that provide the combinatorial basis for eye–hand coordination. Importantly, these authors explicitly propose that the role of these global tuning fields is to combine eye and hand signals that code for the same direction:

signals encoded and combined within the global tuning field of each individual cell share a common property: *they all point in the same direction*. In this context, it is worth stressing that combination of retinal, eye and hand signals is regarded as a necessary prerequisite of reaching to visual targets by virtually all coding hypotheses.

(Battaglia-Mayer & Camitini, 2002, p. 233)

Within this view, optic ataxia arises as a result of the breakdown in the ability to combine eye and hand movements that are spatially congruent.

Based upon our observations of non-foveal optic ataxia outlined above, we propose a rather different account. We suggest that non-foveal optic ataxia occurs not because individuals are unable to construct an *extrinsic* limb-based frame of reference and are forced to plan movements in an eye-based frame of reference, as suggested by Buxbaum and Coslett (1997), and not because of a breakdown in parietal mechanisms responsible for integrating spatially congruent eye and hand information and producing coordinated eye–hand movements, as proposed by Battaglia-Mayer and Caminiti (2002). Instead, we argue that misreaching in non-foveal optic ataxia may arise due to an inability to *simultaneously* represent two different visuomotor objects that must be specified in different frames of reference. We suggest that during non-foveal reaching executed by neurologically normal individuals, the object that is being fixated may be represented in oculocentric coordinates, while the extra-foveal target for the reaching movement may be represented within a different coordinate system [most likely in *intrinsic* (postural) limb-based coordinates]. Within this view, then, non-foveal optic ataxia may have some commonalities with the simultanagnosia phenomenon observed in patients with bilateral parietal lesions. Note that previously reported cases of "magnetic misreaching" [e.g. patients DP (Buxbaum & Coslett, 1997) and Mrs D (Carey et al., 1997)], together with patients JJ and MU reported here, all present with a very similar pattern of bilateral damage. While the spatial representation of multiple objects is not a necessary condition for accurate reaching to extrafoveal target locations, it may be that the "objects" to be represented in such cases need not correspond to real objects, but simply locations in space, possibly specified in separate motor coordinate systems. In the case of extrafoveal reaching, the point of gaze might represent one object or location and the target to be reached for the second object/location. In this manner, non-foveal optic ataxia could far less reflect a failure to bind eye and hand movements together (as suggested by Battaglia-Mayer & Caminiti, 2002), as it does a failure to successfully de-couple them so that the eye and limb visuomotor systems might undertake *simultaneously independent actions*.

Prism adaptation in patient JJ

We examined this idea further by investigating patient JJ's ability to adapt to the lateral visual displacement induced by his wearing optical prisms

(Newport, Brown, Husain, Mort, & Jackson, in press). It should be noted that prism adaptation provides an important test of our ideas in so far as successful adaptation to optical prisms necessitates that gaze direction and reach direction be dissociated from one another.

The ability of humans to adapt to optical prisms has been well documented (e.g. Harris, 1963). When neurologically healthy individuals are first exposed to displacing prisms, they typically misreach in the direction of the visual displacement when pointing towards a visual target. It takes only a few trials, however, before normal pointing accuracy is restored (see Harris, 1965; Welch, 1986). This phenomenon is known as the prism *adaptation effect*. Subsequent removal of the prisms causes participants to misreach once more, only this time in the direction opposite to that of the original visual displacement (known as the prism *after-effect*). Adaptation to optical prisms demonstrates the plasticity of the human brain as the body schema is rapidly and flexibly realigned with visuospatial input to maintain accurate goal-directed behaviour.

Patient JJ and six neurologically healthy adult controls completed three blocks of reaching trials in a set order: a pre-test phase in which baseline levels of end-point accuracy were assessed, a test phase during which the participants wore 25 dioptre rightward-deviating Fresnel prisms, and a post-test phase during which the prisms were removed. Each participant completed 48 reaching trials in each phase. Control participants executed movements with only their right hand. Patient JJ completed movements using both his right and left hands, which were tested on separate days.

This study is of some theoretical importance for several reasons. First, a great deal of interest has been generated by the demonstration that prism adaptation has been shown to ameliorate visuospatial disorders after parietal damage, and is now being employed as a means of rehabilitating patients presenting with unilateral visual neglect (Farnè, Rossetti, Toniolo, & Ladavas, 2002; McIntosh, Rossetti, & Milner, 2002; Rode, Rossetti, & Boisson, 2001; Rossetti et al., 1998; Tilikete, Rode, Rossetti, Pichon, Li, & Boisson, 2001). Second, the publication of a recent PET study indicating that the only area activated during prism adaptation (relative to a target perturbation control condition) is a region of posterior parietal cortex (PPC) contralateral to the adapting limb on the lateral bank of the intraparietal sulcus (IPS), has generated a great deal of controversy with respect to the precise role played by the posterior parietal cortex in prism adaptation. For example, failure to adapt to optically displacing prisms with either hand has only previously been reported in patients with cerebellar damage (e.g. Weiner, Hallett, & Funkenstein, 1983) and has not been reported in patients presenting with parietal damage. Finally, prism adaptation provides a clear example where it is absolutely necessary to de-couple gaze direction from reach direction.

The results of the prism adaptation study are presented in Figure 13.7. These results confirm: (a) that during the test phase, control participants initially misreach in the direction of the prismatically induced deviation, but

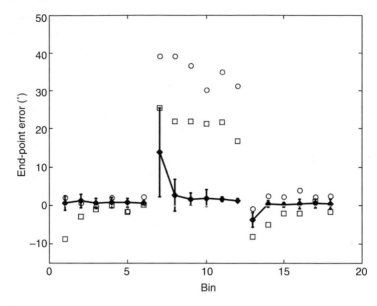

Figure 13.7 Plot showing the magnitude of JJ's end-point errors relative to control
participants (*n* = 6). Bins 1–6 represent performance during the pre-test
phase (before the optical prisms were worn), bins 7–12 the test phase
(during which the prism were worn throughout) and bins 13–18 the post-
test (after-effect) phase (when the prisms were removed). Errors for the
control group are shown as black diamonds and the error bars represent
the 95% confidence limits. The open squares represent mean errors for
each set of binned trials for patient JJ using his right hand. The open
circles represent mean errors for each set of binned trials for patient JJ
using his left hand.

this misreaching error is rapidly corrected (after about 6–12 trials); and (b)
that after adaptation has taken place and the prisms are removed (post-test
phase), controls misreach in the opposite direction to the prismatically
induced deviation (prism after-effect). Once again this misreaching error is
rapidly corrected. Both of these effects were statistically significant. In contrast, patient JJ showed no evidence of either a prism adaptation effect or a
prism after-effect. While his reaches were clearly affected when wearing the
Fresnel prisms (he showed clear evidence of misreaching in the direction of
the prisms), after 48 trials he showed no evidence of having adapted his
reaching movements to correct for the prism-induced optical deviation for
either hand. That is, at the end of 48 reaching trials with feedback, JJ's
reaches remain deviated by more than 15° to the right of the real position of
the target. Similarly, when the prisms were removed during the post-test
phase JJ, unlike the control participants, showed absolutely no evidence of
any prism after-effect for either hand. It should be noted that all six control
participants displayed normal prism adaptation effects when examined

individually. All controls had returned to pre-test levels of accuracy within 12 trials (most within 6 trials), and all showed very similar rates and magnitudes of both the prism adaptation effect and prism after-effect. Relative to control participants, JJ's performance fell well outside two standard deviations of the control group mean throughout the test phase (Figure 13.7). These results suggest that the brain structures that are damaged in JJ (bilateral parietal lesions, including white matter tracts underlying the posterior parietal cortex) may be crucial for the process of prism adaptation, but what function in this complex procedure do these brain structures perform?

During adaptation to optical prisms, despite there being only one target object, it is necessary to de-couple reach direction from gaze direction to produce spatially accurate movements. This is because the prisms induce a displacement in the seen position of the target object that affects the direction of gaze. Thus, individuals asked to look straight ahead through rightward displacing prisms will typically direct the angle of their gaze to the right of the midline (Paap & Ebenholtz, 1976), and the angle of gaze must therefore be directed to the right of a visual target to fixate it. Therefore, to execute an accurate reaching movement while wearing wedge prisms, it is necessary, at least initially, to reach in a different direction to that specified by vision of the target object. We have speculated that this initial spatial discrepancy between eye and hand may provide the necessary training signal required by the cerebellum to update the current internal model used to maintain spatial congruency between visual and proprioceptive maps of peripersonal space (Newport et al., in press). We have suggested that a key aspect of patient JJ's non-foveal optic ataxia, and maybe that of other optic ataxic patients, is a failure to successfully de-couple his reaching movements from his point of gaze, so that the eye and limb visuomotor systems might undertake simultaneously independent actions. We propose that this account of non-foveal optic ataxia may provide a plausible explanation of JJ's failure to adapt to optical prisms. That is, for JJ to correct his initial reach direction error (induced by the prisms), he must direct his limb to a target location other than that indicated by his direction of gaze. In other words, the motor program for guiding the limb must be de-coupled from the oculocentric coordinate system in which the target location/angle of gaze is specified. This crucial step, that of directing the limb away from the naturally programmed target location, may be what is required to bring about the process of perceptual recalibration. Without an induced discrepancy between the naturally occurring motor program (planned in extrinsic coordinates relative to the perceived target location) and the actually produced (incorrect) motor program (planned in intrinsic limb-based coordinates relative to the real target location), the body's sensorimotor system has nothing with which to realign.

These results suggest a role for the PPC in prism adaptation: that the reach direction to the *veridical* target location, specified in *intrinsic* limb-based coordinates, must be decoupled from the reach direction to the *perceived* target location, specified by *extrinsic* oculocentric coordinates, to produce spatially accurate movements. This spatial discrepancy between eye and hand may be the necessary training signal required by the cerebellum to update the current internal model used to maintain spatial congruency between visual and proprioceptive maps of peripersonal space.

Summary

Several lines of evidence point to the important role played by the posterior parietal cortex (PPC) in carrying out the sensorimotor transformations that are associated with goal-directed action. In humans, lesions of the PPC, particularly those involving the intraparietal sulcus, lead to misreaching to visual targets, known as optic ataxia. Recent theoretical accounts of this disorder propose that it arises either as a result of a failure within successive stages of the sensorimotor transformation process (Buxbaum & Coslett, 1997), or as a breakdown in the tuning fields of parietal neurons responsible for producing coordinated eye–hand movements (Battaglia-Mayer & Caminiti, 2002). In this chapter, we have presented evidence from two Balint's syndrome patients presenting with the most commonly encountered form of misreaching deficit—non-foveal optic ataxia—in support of a novel account. Specifically, that a key feature of this form of optic ataxia may be a failure to successfully de-couple the eye and limb visuomotor systems so that each might undertake simultaneously independent actions.

References

Andersen, R. A., Snyder, L. H., Bradley, D. C., & Xing, J. (1997). Multimodal representation of space in the posterior parietal cortex and its use in planning movements. *Annual Review of Neurosciences, 20*, 303–330.

Bálint, R. (1909). Seelenlähmung des "schauens", optische ataxie, räumliche störung der aufmerksamkeit. *Monattsschrifte für Psychiatrische Neurologie, 25*, 51–81.

Batista, A. P., Buneo, C. A., Snyder, L. H., & Andersen, R. A. (1999). Reach plans in eye-centred coordinates. *Science, 285*, 257–260.

Battaglia-Mayer, A., & Caminiti, R. (2002). Optic ataxia as a result of the breakdown of the global tuning fields of parietal neurones. *Brain, 125*, 225–237.

Buxbaum, L. J., & Coslett, H. B. (1997). Subtypes of optic ataxia: reframing the disconnection account. *Neurocase, 3*, 159–166.

Carey, D. P., Coleman, R. J., & Della Sala, S. (1997). Magnetic misreaching. *Cortex, 33*, 639–652.

Cooper, A. C. G., & Humphreys, G. W. (2000). Coding space within but not between objects: evidence from Balint's syndrome. *Neuropsychologia, 38*, 723–733.

De Renzi, E. (1996). Balint-Holmes' syndrome. In C. Code, C.-W. Wallesch, Y. Joanette, & A. Roch (Eds.), *Classic cases in neuropsychology* (pp. 123–143). Hove, UK: Psychology Press.

Duhamel, J.-R., Colby, C., & Goldberg, M. E. (1992). The updating of the representation of visual space in parietal cortex by intended eye movements. *Science, 255*, 90–92.

Duncan, J., Humphreys, G. W., & Ward, R. (1997). Competitive brain activity in visual attention. *Current Opinion in Neurobiology, 7,* 255–261.

Edwards, M. G., & Humphreys, G. W. (2002). Visual selection and action in Balint's syndrome. *Cognitive Neuropsychology, 19,* 445–462.

Farnè, A., Rossetti, Y., Toniolo, S. & Ladavas, E. (2002). Ameliorating neglect with prism adaptation: visuo-manual and visuo-verbal measures. *Neuropsychologia, 40,* 718–729.

Flanders, M., Helms-Tillery, S. I. H., & Soechting, J. F. (1992). Early stages in a sensorimotor transformation. *Behavioural Brain Sciences, 15,* 309–362.

Gaymard, B., Rivauld, S., Rigolet, M.-H., & Pierrot-Deseilligny, C. (1997). Bilateral crossed optic ataxia in a corpus callosum lesion. *Neurocase, 3,* 209–222.

Graziano, M. S. A., Yap, G. S., & Gross, C. G. (1994). Coding of visual space by premotor neurons. *Science, 266,* 1054–1057.

Harris, C. S. (1963). Adaptation to displaced vision: visual, motor or proprioceptive change? *Science, 140,* 812–813.

Harris, C. S. (1965). Perceptual adaptation to inverted, reversed and displaced vision. *Psychological Review, 72,* 419–444.

Humphreys, G. W., & Riddoch, M. J. (1993). Interactions between objects and space—vision revealed through neuropsychology. In D. E. Meyers & S. Kornblum (Eds.), *Attention and performance XIV* (pp. 143–162). Hillsdale, NJ: Lawrence Erlbaum Associates Inc.

Humphreys, G. W., & Riddoch, M. J. (1994). Attention to within-object and between-object spatial representations: multiple sites for visual selection. *Cognitive Neuropsychology, 11,* 207–241.

Humphreys, G. W., & Riddoch, M. J. (1995). Separate coding of space within and between perceptual objects: evidence from unilateral visual neglect. *Cognitive Neuropsychology, 12,* 283–311.

Jackson, G. M., German, K., & Peacock, K. (2002a). Functional coupling between the limbs during bimanual reach-to-grasp movements. *Human Movement Science, 21,* 317–333.

Jackson, G. M., Jackson, S. R., & Hindle, J. V. (2000a). The control of bimanual reach-to-grasp movements in hemiparkinsonian patients. *Experimental Brain Research, 132,* 390–398.

Jackson, G. M., Jackson, S. R., Husain, M., Harvey, M., Kramer, T., & Dow, L. (2000b). The coordination of bimanual prehension movements in a centrally deafferented patient. *Brain, 123,* 380–393.

Jackson, G. M., Jackson, S. R., & Kritikos, A. (1999). Attention for action: coordinating bimanual reach-to-grasp movements. *British Journal of Psychology, 90,* 247–270.

Jackson, G. M., Jackson, S. R., Newport, R., & Harvey, M. (2002b). Co-ordination of bimanual movements in a centrally deafferented patient executing open loop reach-to-grasp movements. *Acta Psychologica, 110,* 231–246.

Jackson, S. R. (2001). "Action binding": dynamic interactions between vision and touch. *Trends in Cognitive Science, 5,* 505–506.

Jackson, S. R., Newport, R., Husain, M., Harvey, M., & Hindle, J. V. (2000). Reaching movements may reveal the distorted topography of spatial representations after neglect. *Neuropsychologia, 38,* 500–507.

Leek, M. R. (2001). Adaptive procedures in psychophysical research. *Perception and Psychophysics, 63,* 1279–1292.

McIntosh, R. D., Rossetti, Y., & Milner, A. D. (2002). Prism adaptation improves chronic visual and haptic neglect: a single case study. *Cortex, 38,* 309–320.

Milner, A. D., Paulignan, Y., Dijkerman, H. C., Michel, F., & Jeannerod, M. (1999). A paradoxical improvement of misreaching in optic ataxia: new evidence for two separate neural systems for visual localization. *Proceedings of the Royal Society of London, B, 266,* 2225–2229.

Newport, R., Hindle, J. V., & Jackson, S. R. (2001). Vision can improve the felt position of the unseen hand: neurological evidence for links between vision and somatosensation in humans. *Current Biology, 11,* 975–980.

Newport, R., Brown, L., Husain, M., Mort, D., & Jackson, S. R. (in press). The role of the posterior parietal lobe in prism adaptation: failure to adapt to optical prisms in a patient with bilateral damage to posterior parietal cortex. *Cortex.*

Paap, K. R., & Ebenholtz, S. M. (1976). Perceptual consequences of potentiation in the extraocular muscles: an alternative explanation for adaptation to wedge prisms. *Journal of Experimental Psychology: Human Perception and Performance, 2,* 457–468.

Perenin, M. T., & Vighetto, A. (1988). Optic ataxia: a specific disruption in visuomotor mechanisms. Different aspects of the deficit in reaching for objects. *Brain, 111,* 643–674.

Ratcliff, G., & Davies-Jones, G. A. B. (1972). Defective visual localisation in focal brain wounds. *Brain, 95,* 49–60.

Rizzo, M., & Vecera, S. P. (2002). Psychoanatomical substrates of Bálint's syndrome. *Journal of Neurology, Neurosurgery and Psychiatry, 72,* 162–178.

Rizzolatti, G., Fogassi, L., & Gallese, V. (1997). Parietal cortex: from sight to action. *Current Opinion in Neurobiology, 7,* 562–567.

Rode, G., Rossetti, Y., & Boisson, D. (2001). Prism adaptation improves representational neglect. *Neuropsychologia, 39,* 1250–1254.

Rossetti, Y., Rode, G., Pisella, L., Farne, A., Li, L., Boisson, D., & Perenin, M. T. (1998). Prism adaptation to a rightward optical deviation rehabilitates left hemispatial neglect. *Nature, 395,* 166–169.

Rushworth, M. F. S., Nixon, P. D., & Passingham, R. E. (1997). Parietal cortex and movement 1. Movement selection and reaching. *Experimental Brain Research, 117,* 292–310.

Tilikete, C., Rode, G., Rossetti, Y., Pichon, J., Li, L., & Boisson, D. (2001). Prism adaptation to rightward optical deviation improves postural imbalance in left-hemiparetic patients. *Current Biology, 11,* 524–528.

Vetter, P., Goodbody, S. J., & Wolpert, D. M. (1999). Evidence for an eye-centred representation of the visuomotor map. *Journal of Neurophysiology, 81,* 935–939.

Weiner, M. J., Hallett, M., & Funkenstein, H. H. (1983). Adaptation to a lateral displacement of vision in patients with lesions of the central nervous system. *Neurology, 33,* 766–772.

Welch, R. B. (1986). Adaptation of space perception. In K. R. Boff, L. Kaufman, & J. P. Thomas (Eds.), *Handbook of perception and human performance, sensory processes and perception* (pp. 1:24.1–1:24.45). New York: Wiley.

Wilson, B. A., Clare, L., Young, A. W., & Hodges, J. R. (1997). Knowing where and knowing what: a double dissociation. *Cortex, 33,* 529–541.

Wilson, B. A., Cockburn, J., & Halligan, P. (1988). *Behavioural Inattention Test.* Windsor, UK: Thames Valley Test Company.

14 Selective attention and response control following damage to the human pulvinar

Robert Ward and Shai Danziger

Abstract

We report results from selective attention studies on a group of patients with focal lesion to the pulvinar. Our results do not seem compatible with some of the dominant characterizations of the pulvinar, including theories that the pulvinar is critical for contralateral filtering and that it plays an important role in allocating visual attention to the contralateral field. Instead, we find that the pulvinar is involved in contralateral response activation, especially under conditions of response competition, and contralateral spatial coding of visual features. The pulvinar appears to be involved both in binding a stimulus representation to a response, and in binding visual features to coherent representations of visual objects.

Introduction

The pulvinar and the lateral geniculate nuclei (LGN) make up the visual areas of the thalamus. These two nuclei have very different patterns of connections with the cortex. Retinal signals arrive at the striate cortex primarily through the LGN, so one important function of the LGN is to faithfully relay the crucial properties of these early visual signals. However, the pulvinar appears to play a very different role, and may be important in regulating communications between cortical areas. One reason to suspect this is based simply on its phylogenetics. The pulvinar has increased in size proportionally with increases in mammalian cortex (Armstrong, 1982). In the rat, for example, there is no observable pulvinar, while in humans the pulvinar reaches its largest dimensions (Browne & Simmons, 1984). Such development also suggests that it would be a mistake to dogmatically separate the functions of the "old" subcortex from the "new" cortex; these structures, in the human and other primates at least, appear to have developed together.

The connectivity of the pulvinar also hints at a role in regulating cortical communication. The pulvinar, via connections with the superior colliculus, is part of the "secondary" visual pathway. However, most inputs to and outputs from the pulvinar are cortical, so that the pulvinar is often characterized as a "higher-order" thalamic nucleus for associating areas within the cortex (Guillery, 1995). Connections between the pulvinar and cortex are widespread, bidirectional and organized. Cortical areas with strong spatial organization, such as striate and extrastriate cortices, are reciprocally connected to spatiotopic maps within the inferior (PI) and lateral (PL) subdivisions of the pulvinar (Bender, 1981). The PL spatial maps are also connected to parietal cortex (Yeterian & Pandya, 1997). The dorso-medial area (Pdm) and medial pulvinar (PM) are interconnected with many areas, including parietal (Yeterian & Pandya, 1985), temporal (Webster, Bachevalier, & Ungerleider, 1993), orbitofrontal, prefrontal (Romanski, Giguere, Bates, & Goldman-Rakic, 1997) and premotor (Darian-Smith, Darian-Smith, & Cheema, 1990) cortices. The so-called oral pulvinar region collects and sends signals to somatosensory cortex and parietal area 5 (Yeterian & Pandya, 1985), which, in turn, form principal inputs to primary motor cortex.

A long-standing and exciting theoretical proposal is that, given its extensive and bidirectional connections throughout much of the cortex, the pulvinar may be a well-placed nexus for selective attention (for a review, see LaBerge, 1995). Two factors are often noted. First, the pulvinar has reciprocal connections to other brain regions known to be important for the control of attention, including parietal and prefrontal cortex and the superior colliculus. Second, the pulvinar's extensive connections to visually responsive cortical areas afford the possibility of modulating activity in one cortical area on the basis of activity in another. This general hypothesis of cortical modulation has been instantiated in multiple forms, with the connectivity of the pulvinar used to achieve somewhat different computational goals. LaBerge and colleagues proposed that the pulvinar was crucial in the operation of visual attention, by allowing filtering of irrelevant objects on the basis of task-defined visual attributes (LaBerge, Carter, & Brown, 1992). For example, spatial filtering might be achieved if spatially specific activity in V1 cortex could sharpen the activity of target representations relative to non-targets in inferotemporal cortex. Robinson and colleagues proposed that the pulvinar was used in the computation of "visual salience", integrating over multiple visual characteristics and screening inputs into the cortex (Robinson & Cowie, 1997; Robinson & Petersen, 1992). Olshausen, Anderson, and Van Essen (1993) offered a proposal of a different sort, linking visual attention with the need to develop invariant object representations, suitable for recognition. In this case, the pulvinar allowed a windowed region of occipital activity to selectively activate inferotemporal processes.

However, despite the potential importance of the pulvinar as a hub for cortical messages, and despite active research in the neuroanatomy of the pulvinar, there are surprisingly few behavioural data to characterize selective attention functions for the pulvinar, particularly in humans. A few studies are commonly cited in support of the pulvinar's involvement in selective attention. First, Rafal and Posner (1987) investigated the effect of lesions to the pulvinar in human patients on a simple spatial cueing task. A brief onset cued attention to one of two stimulus positions. After a variable temporal interval (stimulus onset asynchrony, or SOA), the target appeared either in the cued (valid) or uncued (invalid) position. Targets in the contralesional field were detected more slowly than in the ipsilesional field. However, in both fields, valid cues produced very similar improvements in reaction time with increasing SOA. Finally, there was a relatively small effect such that, at short SOAs, invalid trials in the contralesional field were slower than in the ipsilesional field. Rafal and Posner (1987) explained these results by suggesting that there was an "engage" but not a "movement" deficit induced by the pulvinar lesion. That is, the lesion affected the time to detect and respond to the target with little effect on how quickly attention could be reallocated from one object to another.

Second, Petersen, Robinson, and Morris (1987) used a spatial cueing task with monkeys subjected to reversible chemical deactivation of the dorsomedial pulvinar. Similar to the lesion study of Rafal and Posner (1987), deactivation of the pulvinar slowed responses to contralesional targets on both valid and invalid trials, with roughly equal improvements in reaction time with increasing intervals between the cue and target.

A third behavioural study in support of the pulvinar as source of attentional modulation comes from Desimone and colleagues (Desimone Wessinger, Thomas, & Schneider, 1989). Monkeys were trained to make a lever press in response to the colour of a spatially cued target presented in either the left or right visual field. The target could either appear on its own or with a distractor object in the opposite field. The monkeys were tested in control conditions and following reversible chemical deactivation of the lateral pulvinar. When the target was presented alone, there was little effect of pulvinar deactivation, as measured by discrimination accuracy on target colour. However, under conditions of pulvinar deactivation, responses to a target in the contralesional field were significantly impaired by the presence of an ipsilesional distractor. Relative to single targets, accuracy was unaffected in the reverse condition, in which an ipsilesional target was presented with a contralesional distractor. This finding has been used to argue for a model in which the activities in multiple visual areas, including the pulvinar, compete to establish the focus of attention.

Activation studies of the pulvinar would most prominently include the PET study of LaBerge and Buchsbaum (1990), who examined the activation of the pulvinar in a filtering task. Lateralized letter targets were presented either alone or flanked by similar distractors presented within the same hemifield as the target. In flanker conditions, activity of the pulvinar contralateral to the stimulus display was greater than in the ipsilateral pulvinar. On single target presentations with no distractors, there was no difference between contralateral and ipsilateral pulvinar activity.

More recently, Morris, Friston, and Dolan (1997) measured brain activation changes following manipulation of the behavioural salience of stimuli
through adverse conditioning. During the initial conditioning phase of the
experiment, presentations of emotionally expressive faces were either paired
with an aversive white noise stimulus or with silence. During subsequent
attentive viewing of faces, the adversely conditioned faces were associated
with greater activation of the right pulvinar, as well as other right-hemisphere
structures, including the orbitofrontal cortex, the superior frontal gyrus and
other thalamic activation. Morris et al. (1997) claim that the observed
increase in pulvinar activity reflects increased attention to stimuli with
greater baseline salience for action.

A scattering of imaging studies has found activation of the pulvinar during visual selection tasks (e.g. Corbetta et al., 1990), but this is not always a
consistent finding. For example, Vandenberghe et al. (1997) did not find
significant pulvinar activation when attention was focused on one of two
objects, although they did find activation of the left pulvinar when single
targets were identified, regardless of target hemifield. That is, they did measure pulvinar activation under conditions of minimal selective attention
demand, and did not in an archetypical selective attention and filtering
task. The inconsistent nature of pulvinar activation may be explained by the
recent findings of Bender and Youakim (2001), who recorded variability in
firing rates from the pulvinar, the LGN and a variety of visual cortical areas
during periods of attention to a central target. Firing rates in the pulvinar,
unlike the LGN, were modulated as a function of selective attention, and to a
similar degree to those in visual cortex. However, approximately half the
cells recorded increased their firing rate under attention conditions, while
half decreased. Thus, it may be the case that overall activation within the
pulvinar (for example, as might be measured by blood flow) might not vary
greatly with attention, despite its involvement in selective attention
functions.

New behavioural studies of pulvinar function

The present literature on the pulvinar is striking in this sense: While there
is a substantial base of neuroanatomical and neurophysiological work
describing the connections and internal structure of the pulvinar, there is
relatively little on the behavioural significance of this structure. Compared
with the rich and established neuropsychological database on parietal cortex
and attention, the literature is absolutely impoverished. In collaboration
with Vanessa Owen and Bob Rafal, we have been studying some of the
behavioural implications of pulvinar lesions to human patients. Here we
review some of our recent case studies describing selective attention
function after focal unilateral lesion to the pulvinar.

These studies have been conducted on three patients who suffered hyper-
tensive haemorrhages centred in the pulvinar. Since their haematomas, all

patients have returned to independent living with residual motor and somatosensory deficits, but with no mental symptoms severely compromising
functions of daily life. The composite reconstruction of the three patients in
Plate 14.1 shows that in all patients, the residual lesion involves the posterior
lateral nucleus of the thalamus and extending to the pulvinar nucleus. The
entire pulvinar appeared to be destroyed in patient SM. Most of the lateral
pulvinar was destroyed in patient GJ. For patient TN, only the most anterior
and dorsal parts of the pulvinar were destroyed. (For detailed descriptions,
see Danziger, Ward, Owen, & Rafal, 2001; Ward, Danziger, Owen, &, Rafal,
2002.)

Below we describe the results of multiple experiments examining the
capabilities of these patients. However, perhaps the most striking aspect of
the group as a whole is that despite lesion to the pulvinar, and in the case of
SM loss of the entire pulvinar, these patients are very capable, visually and
otherwise. In all cases, extraocular movements were normal, the visual fields
were intact, and there was no visual or tactile extinction on double simultaneous stimulation, even using brief computerized visual presentations.
These patients have rarely complained of visual problems since testing has
begun, and their families or caretakers have not reported such problems
(although SM has reported that he dislikes the use of brief masked displays
in some of our experiments). The greatest challenges facing this group are
related to the restrictions on their mobility, which are likely to have resulted
from damage to the white matter tracts near the pulvinar, and spontaneous,
unpleasant somatosensation on the contralesional side of the body. This
makes one, admittedly speculative, hypothesis about pulvinar function
unlikely in our view, that the higher-order thalamic relays are the driving
signal for communication between cortical areas (Guillery & Sherman,
2002). Of course, the situation might be very different with bilateral pulvinar
lesions, or the effects of a single pulvinar lesion more severe with concomi-
tant cortical damage. However, at the most general level, the findings below
describe the pulvinar as a system for regulating cortical communication, not
as its primary signal.

Automatic response activation in the flanker paradigm

The flanker task, as developed by Eriksen and Eriksen (1974), is a method for
evaluating selective attention function in an environment in which there are
multiple objects that may be signalling conflicting responses. In a typical
flanker task, participants make speeded discrimination responses to a target
appearing at a known location. There are typically two response categories;
for example, if the target is red press the left key, if green the right. Presented
on either side of the target are two flanker stimuli that are to be ignored. The
flankers are drawn from the same stimulus set as the target. Congruent flankers signal the same response as the target; incongruent flankers signal an
opposing response. In most cases, reaction times to the target are faster and

more accurate in congruent than incongruent conditions. The difference between incongruent and congruent reaction times is called the flanker compatibility effect. The flanker compatibility effect demonstrates that flankers have been processed at least to the level of response activation: the greater the flanker compatibility effect, the greater the extent to which flanker response activation is influencing target responses.

In previous work, Rafal and colleagues (Cohen, Ivry, Rafal, & Kohn, 1995; Rafal et al., 1996) have adapted this paradigm for testing on patient groups with unilateral deficits, by using only a single flanker, presented contralesional or ipsilesional to the target. Patients respond either vocally or with the ipsilesional hand. The single flanker paradigm allows two measures of selective processing to be assessed independently. First, overall target latencies can be compared for flankers in contra- versus ipsilesional space. This provides a measure of selective attention bias against the contralesional field. That is, similar latencies in the two conditions suggest that flankers in the two fields are equally distracting; faster responses to targets with contralesional compared with ipsilesional flankers suggests that contralesional items are less able to compete for attention. Second, the flanker compatibility effect can be compared for contra- and ipsilesional flankers. A relatively large flanker compatibility effect for contralesional flankers would suggest that response activity from contralesional distractors is not being filtered efficiently—that is, a loss of control over selective attention. In contrast, a relatively small flanker compatibility effect for contralesional flankers would suggest a deficit in generating response activity for contralesional items.

We reasoned (Danziger, Ward, Owen, & Rafal, 2004) that if filtering theories of pulvinar function are correct, and the pulvinar is necessary for filtering contralateral distractors as suggested by LaBerge and Buchsbaum (1990), then in this paradigm we should expect to see larger flanker compatibility effects for contralesional flankers; ipsilesional flankers by contrast should be relatively efficiently filtered and produce less interference.

We have run several variants of the flanker task on this group of patients. However, we have never observed results in line with the filtering model. The consistent outcome has been that flanker interference is greater from ipsilesional than from contralesional distractors. Results from one typical experiment are illustrated in Figure 14.1. We have observed this same pattern both for arbitrary stimulus–response mappings (i.e. press a key depending upon the colour of the target) and for non-arbitrary mapping (i.e. name the colour).

In general, we do not see a selective attention bias against the contralesional field. A frequent result in the flanker task has been that the patients show equivalent overall latencies to targets with ipsilesional compared with contralesional flankers (as illustrated in Figure 14.2). The occasional exception is patient SM, who has the complete loss of the left pulvinar and who can show some contralesional slowing. We have also seen preserved selectivity in other domains. In a selective attention task requiring attention to one

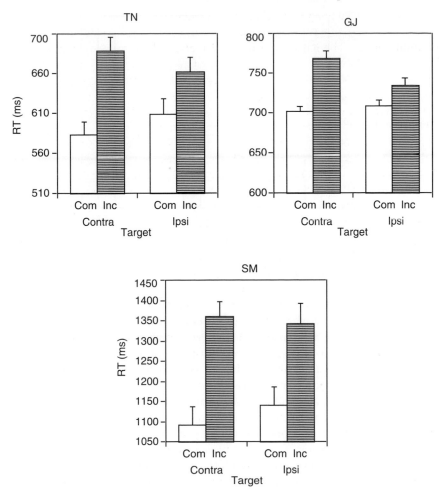

Figure 14.1 Results for each of the patients from a flanker task using peripheral targets with central flankers (central targets were also presented). Performance is shown for contralesional and ipsilesional targets when the flanker is either compatible (white bars) or incompatible (shaded bars) with the target response. Flanker compatibility effects are smaller when the target is in the ipsilesional field (i.e. when the flanker is relatively contralesional).

level of a single Navon figure, lateralized to one hemifield, we also found equivalent overall latencies in the contralesional and ipsilesional field (Danziger et al., 2001). Thus, at least in most of the circumstances we have tested, focal lesions of the pulvinar do not produce a strong bias against attending to the contralesional field. Equivalent reaction times to targets in both fields also argue against the possibility that contralesional processing is generally slowed.

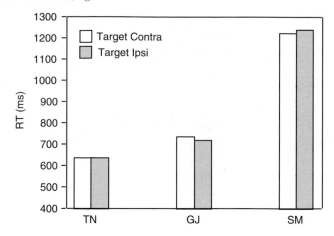

Figure 14.2 The results shown in Figure 14.1 averaged over compatibility, showing that overall reaction times to targets are equivalent, regardless of whether the target is in the contralesional or ipsilesional field.

We have also tested whether impaired contralesional performance is the result of competing responses between the relatively contralesional and ipsilesional items. In one variant of the flanker task, we have used only incongruent and neutral displays. In the neutral displays, the flanker was blue, which was not one of the possible target responses. As before, with incongruent flankers, all patients showed more interference when the flanker was relatively ipsilesional than contralesional. However, with neutral flankers and no response competition, two of the patients (GJ and TN) showed no difference between fields. The third patient (SM) did show some slowing, although this was small compared with the field difference with incongruent flankers. This outcome shows that deficits in contralesional response activation arise in circumstances of response competition, in particular when the response to a contralesional object must be activated in preference to a conflicting response from an ipsilesional object.

Finally, we have also investigated the effect of absolute versus relative target position in the flanker studies in three variants. In one, the target always appears centrally and the flanker is on one side or the other; in another, the flanker is always central and the target is peripheral; in a third, we present the two conditions above in mixed order, within-block. When target position is always central, we see very little effect of flanker position, so that the flanker compatibility effect for contralesional and ipsilesional flankers is essentially the same. We think this may simply be a form of floor effect. With the predictable, central target location, selection may be made efficient enough so that contralesional deficits are difficult to detect. However, if we remove the element of predictability, by mixing trials with central and peripheral targets, flanker compatibility effects are again reduced in the contralesional field, even with the central targets. Under conditions of target location uncertainty, we therefore see the same asymmetry in flanker compatibility effects whether the target is central and the flankers peripheral, or vice versa. That is, what predicts the deficit in response activation in most cases appears not to be the absolute position of target and flanker, but their relative position to each other.

In summary, all of the patients demonstrate impaired response activation with relatively contralesional targets under conditions of response competition. The reduced response activation we have measured in flanker tasks is not compatible with a filtering deficit. Instead, it appears that the pulvinar is involved in response activation and/or response selection processes for stimuli in the contralateral field, particularly under conditions of response competition.

A distributed network for selection and control

The unilateral flanker task has been used in other patient groups, to define components of a distributed network for selection and control. The parietal patients tested by Cohen et al. (1995) demonstrated essentially the reverse of our findings with pulvinar patients. Cohen et al. (1995) tested two parietal patients on a unilateral flanker task using exclusively central targets with peripheral flankers. They first found a selection bias against the contralesional field: overall latencies were significantly longer when flankers were in the ipsilesional than in the contralesional field. Second, however, they found equivalent flanker compatibility effects in the two fields. This result is in good agreement with the developing picture of attentional function in unilateral neglect following parietal damage. Many reports have demonstrated selection problems in the contralesional field, especially when the measure is explicit detection or report, as in the case of visual extinction. However, there is also a large literature demonstrating that even in the presence of selection deficits, semantic processing within the neglected field can still be preserved. Semantic processing in many cases would include implications for response.

The same flanker task was tested on a group of prefrontal patients by Rafal et al. (1996). Here the findings were similar to our results with pulvinar patients. Unlike the parietal patients, there was little evidence of selection bias against the contralesional field. And similar to our pulvinar patients, when the stimulus–response mapping is an arbitrary one (i.e. when participants are asked to press keys in response to the target colour), the same asymmetric flanker compatibility effect was observed, such that the flanker compatibility effect from a contralesional flanker was smaller than from an ipsilesional one. However, the prefrontal group is distinguished from the pulvinar patients on performance with non-arbitrary response mappings. When the prefrontal patients were asked to name the colour of the target rather than press a key, equivalent flanker compatibility effects were found for the two fields. In contrast, our pulvinar patients still demonstrate reduced flanker compatibility effect for flankers in the contralesional field in the naming task.

These findings reveal a distributed network for selection and control, including the pulvinar, parietal and prefrontal cortex. Damage to any part of this network will be likely to slow responses to contralesional space, but for different reasons. Most interesting perhaps is the distinction between the operation of prefrontal and pulvinar areas. It seems that prefrontal cortex may be needed when the relationship between stimulus and response is an arbitrary one, and maintenance of stimulus–response mappings is required. Given the complex and flexible behaviours associated with the development of prefrontal cortex, both in development within individuals and phylogenetically, the fact that the neocortex appears necessary for flexible and arbitrary stimulus–response mapping is perhaps expected, or at least plausible. Also perhaps expected might be that automatic response activation can arise normally even with damage to prefrontal areas. As an action becomes more automatic, the amount of brain tissue activated during the action appears to become more limited and more focused (Raichle et al., 1994). In contrast to prefrontal cortex, the pulvinar appears to be involved very generally in binding a stimulus to a response, even those "automatic" stimulus–response associations that may have developed over a great deal of experience and repetition.

Spatial coding and feature binding

The inferior (PI) and lateral (PL) subdivisions of the pulvinar, located towards the anterior of the structure, appear to contain multiple spatiotopic maps. These maps are organized such that the inferior field is represented dorsally, while the superior field is represented ventrally (Bender, 1981). In patient TN, we had a unique opportunity to investigate the possible function of these maps in the human (Ward et al., 2002). As shown in Figure 14.3, TN's lesion is at the anterior and most dorsal boundary of the pulvinar. In the monkey, the anterior position of such a lesion would be suspected to involve the PI and/or PL maps; its dorsal position would suggest damage to the representation of the inferior visual field within these maps. If the spatial organization of these areas applies in humans, then in patient TN we should expect to see performance deficits in her inferior (lower) contralesional (left) visual quadrant. We tested TN on a variety of tasks involving spatial coding and feature binding. As described below, in multiple experiments we have found that, despite intact recognition of visual features, TN shows a selective deficit in localizing and binding visual features in this quadrant.

The problem of integrating visual features is not always conceptualized clearly. Visual processing is distributed across specialized brain regions, yet the activity of these regions must be coordinated. Subjectively, this coordination is suggested by the integrated and cohesive nature of our visual

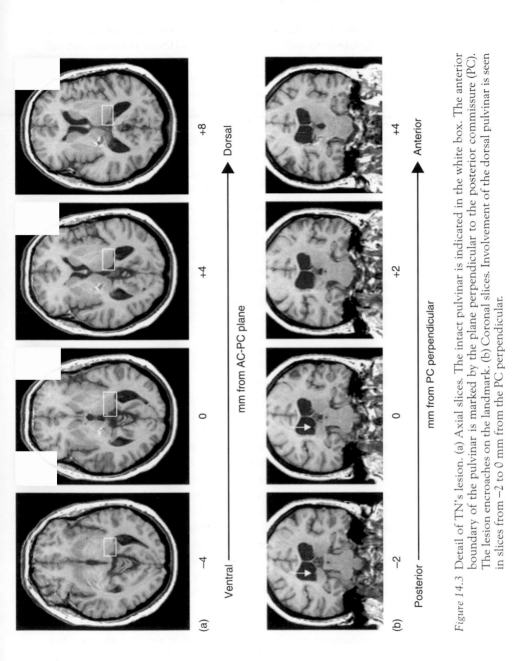

(a)

Ventral ←—————→ Dorsal

−4   0   +4   +8

mm from AC-PC plane

(b)

Posterior ←—————→ Anterior

−2   0   +2   +4

mm from PC perpendicular

Figure 14.3 Detail of TN's lesion. (a) Axial slices. The intact pulvinar is indicated in the white box. The anterior boundary of the pulvinar is marked by the plane perpendicular to the posterior commissure (PC). The lesion encroaches on the landmark. (b) Coronal slices. Involvement of the dorsal pulvinar is seen in slices from −2 to 0 mm from the PC perpendicular.

experience. But as some authors have pointed out, there is no need to have integration of features just so we can experience them as a whole (Dennett, 1991). Instead, the real value of coordination among multiple processors is in allowing efficient filtering and selection. Behaviourally, coordination is demonstrated by the object-based nature of visual selective attention: we can freely select one object from many on the basis of one visual attribute, and report that object's value on a range of other attributes (Duncan, 1993). For example, integration of visual form and motion is demonstrated when we identify our child's face from among many on a playground and accurately track his movement. Such a basic operation would not be possible unless processors identifying the child's face were linked to appropriate results from visual motion analysis.

Coordinating the activity of multiple visual processors to represent the features of a single object has been described as the "binding problem" (Treisman, 1996). Breakdowns in the process of feature binding can be observed in the form of *illusory conjunctions*, errors in which visual features are correctly perceived but incorrectly combined. For example, when shown a brief display containing a blue O and a pink X, observers might report the presence of a blue X (Treisman & Schmidt, 1982).

Behavioural studies have shown that space is one medium used to establish feature bindings. Features registered with overlapping or similar spatial codes are more likely to be conjoined than features with distinctive spatial codes, as shown by two lines of study. First, features that appear close together are more likely to be conjoined than more distant features (Cohen & Ivry, 1989; Wolford & Shum, 1980). Second, with long exposures (up to 1.5 s) and low attentional load, illusory conjunctions can be obtained in the periphery (Prinzmetal, Henderson, & Ivry, 1995), but not at the fovea where spatial coding is more precise (Treisman & Schmidt, 1982). It is also clear that focused attention can promote accurate feature binding, perhaps due to higher spatial resolution for attended features (Prinzmetal & Keysar, 1989).

The conclusion from the studies above is that spatial coding provides an important medium for determining feature binding. Here perhaps we should distinguish between a medium and a means of binding. One recent sugges- tion is that temporal firing synchrony of neurons may provide a flexible means for representing transient bindings of features (Singer & Gray, 1995). This would be one possible mechanism for coordinating the activity of remote multiple processors and for feature binding, but this mechanism can in principle be distinguished from the codes used to determine which features go together and which should be kept separate.

Our general method for measuring illusory conjunction rates largely follows previous studies (e.g. Cohen & Ivry, 1989; Treisman & Schmidt, 1982), and subjected to multiple rigorous analyses (Ashby, Prinzmetal, Ivry, & Maddox, 1996; Prinzmetal, Diedrichsen, & Ivry, 2001). On each trial, a target and a distractor are briefly presented, one above the other, and then masked. Presentations are brief to ensure that the stimuli are not foveated.

The target and distractor are manipulated along two feature dimensions: the defining and probe dimension. The defining dimension distinguishes the target from the distractor, and we use two possible values for the target on the defining dimension. We use four possible values on the probe dimension, and the target and distractor never share the same value. In most of our studies, letter identity has been the defining dimension: the target is either an F or X and the distractor an O. Colour is most frequently the probe dimension and can take the values of red, blue, green or yellow. Conjunction errors are indicated when the distractor colour was reported as that of the target.

The general method we use also includes a demanding central primary task. This is used both to encourage central fixation and to increase binding errors, by limiting attention to the periphery. We use a task in which two digits are presented, one physically larger than the other. On a typical trial, TN would report the identity of the physically larger of the two digits, the colour of the target, the identity of the target and, in some experiments, the relative position of the target (either upper or lower).

Two measures are of primary interest. The first is accuracy on the probe dimension. On a given trial, of the four possible values for the probe dimension, one will be held by the target, one by the distractor and two will not have been presented. A response is coded as a feature error when the target is reported with a value on the probe dimension that does not appear in the display. Feature errors indicate difficulties in feature perception rather than binding. Conjunction errors are responses in which a feature of the target (on the defining dimension) and a feature of the distractor (on the probe dimension) are reported together. For example, consider a task in which form is the defining feature, colour is the probe feature and a green X and red O are presented. A feature error would be the report of a blue X; a conjunction error would be the report of a red X.

Because there are four possible values on the probe dimension, random guessing would produce twice as many feature errors as conjunction errors. Traditionally, conjunction errors in excess of this ratio have been taken to indicate a systematic failure to bind the report and selection dimensions (Treisman & Schmidt, 1982), although we have also used more sophisticated models that have confirmed our findings with these data (Prinzmetal, Ivry, Beck, & Shimizu, 2002). Our approach also builds on that used in studies with normal populations in that we ensure that both feature error rates and misidentifications of the target defining feature are low and equivalent in the two fields, and compare the rates of conjunction errors between the good and bad fields.

The second measure of interest is localization accuracy. In addition to identifying the target on the defining and report dimensions, participants are asked to locate the target to the upper or lower position within its hemifield. As shown below, this explicit measure of spatial localization has proven to be very useful in conjunction with the implicit localization of probe and defining features required for correct responses in this task.

Spatiotopic maps in the pulvinar

Figure 14.4 illustrates results we have reported previously (Ward et al., 2002) in which TN selects the target on the basis of form and reports its colour. In this experiment, the target and distractor could be located 1.7° from each other in the Near condition or 5.1° apart in the Far condition. In both conditions, the stimuli were presented one above the other, symmetrically about the horizontal meridian. First we see that in the Near conditions, the rate of feature errors (i.e. reporting the target with a colour not appearing in the display) is low and equivalent between fields (2% in the contralesional field, 3% in the ipsilesional field). Not shown is accuracy on target identity (F or X), which was also very high in both fields (95% in the contralesional field, 99% in the ipsilesional field). Thus TN's feature perception in the contralesional field appears to be intact. However, despite the accurate perception of colour and form features, illusory conjunction errors are significantly greater in the contralesional than in the ipsilesional field.

The Far conditions show a very different pattern. The increased spatial separation produces two effects. First, the number of feature errors in both fields increases relative to the Near conditions. This outcome is expected because the stimuli are now further into the visual periphery and so are harder to identify. Second, however, the rate of illusory conjunction errors decreases in both fields. This result is not predicted by "confusion" accounts of illusory conjunctions in which the target is mistaken for the distractor. In

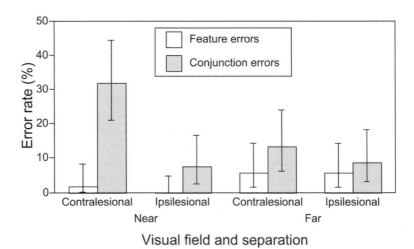

Figure 14.4 Illusory conjunction and feature errors for TN. In Near conditions, the target and distractor were 1.7° apart; in Far conditions, they were 5.1° apart. Feature error rates (white bars) are equivalent in the two fields. In the Near conditions, conjunction errors (shaded bars) are much more frequent in the contralesional field. In the Far conditions, this difference in conjunction errors is eliminated.

this case, putting the stimuli further into the periphery no doubt increases their confusability by making them harder to see. If confusability were the only basis for illusory conjunctions, this manipulation should then have increased rather than decreased conjunction errors. However, this result follows naturally if spatial coding is a factor that determines visual feature binding. By moving the target and distractor apart, the features of different objects are more likely to be represented by distinct spatial codes and, therefore, are less likely to be mistakenly combined. Finally, the increased spatial separation not only reduces errors in both fields, but also brings the number of contralesional conjunction errors to a similar level as that in the ipsilesional field. That is, the increased conjunction errors resulting from pulvinar damage in the Near conditions can be virtually eliminated by increasing the spatial separation of objects by 3–4°. This suggests the underlying deficit is one of spatial coding.

We should add that TN is asked to make accuracy on the digit task her primary goal, and has consistently been 95% or better on this four-alternative task. The requirement to first make a difficult discrimination at fixation combined with the brief exposure duration of the stimuli ensured that the peripheral target was reliably restricted to either the contralesional or ipsilesional field. Previous research has examined illusory conjunction rates conditional on correct target identification (Ashby et al., 1996), but given the small number of incorrect responses (several dozens of such errors out of thousands of responses), that was impractical here. Overall, we were impressed with TN's capacity to process these masked displays. We titrate exposure durations so that performance on the central digit task is high, but with significant numbers of errors on the measures of interest. Typically the duration of the masked presentations is around 100 ms.

Maps for localizing targets and feature binding

These results are a useful first pass at the role of the pulvinar in spatial coding and feature binding. However, we have further tested the spatial coding account of pulvinar function in TN. We reasoned that if TN's conjunction errors were due to degraded information about feature position, then her ability to explicitly localize the target might also be impaired. Figure 14.5 shows results in which TN makes four reports per trial: the central digit identity, target identity, target colour and relative target position (upper or lower). Plotted are her mislocalizations of the target as well as her feature and conjunction errors within each visual quadrant. Mislocalizations were much more frequent in her inferior contralesional visual quadrant than in any other. This deficit in localization was very specific, as localization in the superior contralesional quadrant was equivalent to the ipsilesional quadrants. Given TN's lesion to the most anterior and dorsal regions of the pulvinar, these behavioural data seem to reveal an organization to spatiotopic maps within the human pulvinar, such that the inferior field is represented

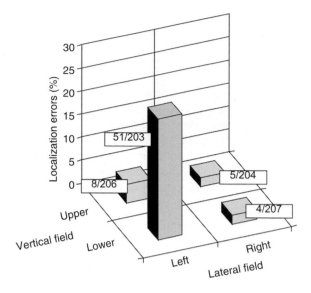

Figure 14.5 Mislocalizations of the target for TN, by visual quadrant. Here TN was asked to explicitly identify the relative target location. Errors are predominately in her inferior contralesional quadrant. Boxes show the number of errors from the number of available trials.

dorsally and the superior field ventrally, just as is found in the monkey through single cell recordings.

In addition to this evidence for impaired spatial coding in TN's lower contralesional quadrant, two other results link binding errors in TN to a spatial coding deficit. First, Figure 14.6 shows that the pattern of illusory conjunction errors by visual quadrant mirrors that for localization errors. Second, across quadrants, the conditional probability of an illusory conjunction given that the target is correctly localized was only 4%, while the probability of conjunction errors given that the target was mislocalized was 79%. This pattern held across all quadrants, suggesting that illusory conjunctions in this case are largely secondary to spatial coding errors.

Our experiments demonstrate that damage to the pulvinar can impair the ability to localize and conjoin features in contralesional space, even when feature perception is preserved. As shown both by the effects of spatial separation on binding errors, and the connection between localization accuracy and binding, it appears that spatial coding is degraded within TN's inferior contralesional quadrant. A straightforward interpretation is that, due to damage to the dorsal region of the right PI and/or PL maps, visual features in TN's lower left quadrant are registered with faulty or degraded location information. As a result of this degradation, target features in this quadrant are more likely to be mislocalized and, consequently, more likely to be incorrectly bound to features at nearby locations.

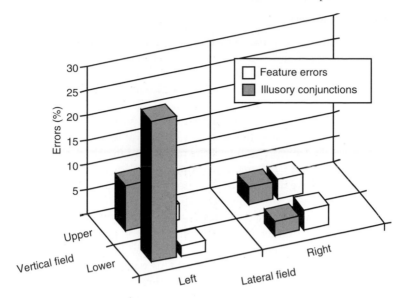

Figure 14.6 Feature errors and illusory conjunction errors by quadrant. This is from
the same data set represented in Figure 14.5. Feature errors are relatively
constant across quadrants; illusory conjunctions, like mislocalizations in
Figure 14.5, are predominately in the inferior contralesional quadrant.

To date, the neural basis for visual feature binding in humans has been
examined primarily in single-case studies with damage including parietal
cortex. Unilateral parietal damage can diminish the accuracy of feature
binding within the contralesional field (Arguin, Cavanagh, & Joanette, 1994;
Cohen & Rafal, 1991). Feature binding was also found to be severely
impaired in the case of a simultanagnosic with bilateral parietal damage. In
this case, even with exposures of several seconds, the patient RM made
frequent illusory conjunctions of colour and shape in displays with multiple
objects (Friedman-Hill, Robertson, & Treisman, 1995). These studies have
argued that damage to parietal cortex impairs a spatial feature representation
necessary for accurate feature binding. It appears, then, that spatial codes
generated in both parietal cortex and spatiotopic maps of the pulvinar are
used to define feature bindings. Both the parietal and pulvinar spatial coding
systems appear capable of operating independently, at least in the event of
damage to one system. However the resolution of either the cortical or
pulvinar system in isolation appears limited relative to the combined operation of both systems. This, and the extensive connectivity between parietal
cortex and the PI and PL maps, suggest that visual spatial coding and feature
binding is achieved by a distributed network of cortical and subcortical
codes.

Localizing single targets

Further investigations into the nature of spatial coding in the pulvinar have looked in more detail at TN's abilities to localize objects and features. We have recently seen that TN's ability to localize isolated, single objects is little affected by visual quadrant. We presented TN with single targets (either an L or T) flashed briefly for 15 ms, but not masked. The target could appear within a virtual 5 × 5 grid either in the left or right visual field. However, the visual display contained only the target and a central fixation point. In some blocks TN was asked simply to locate the target, and in others to both locate and identify the target. TN made her unspeeded location judgements by using a mouse to move a cursor to the spot where she perceived the target. Identification responses when required were made by unspeeded keypress. Location accuracy is illustrated in Plate 14.2, which plots the average accuracy for each possible target location. As expected, performance near the centre of the screen was better than at the periphery. However, there were no substantial differences between quadrants. This pattern was the same when concurrent identification of the target was required.

Preserved localization performance with single items suggests an interesting possibility—that we may be able to measure the resolution of a distributed coarse coding within the pulvinar. In coarse coding schemes, receptive fields of neurons overlap, so that a single object activates many receptive fields, but the pattern of activated fields differs for each distinguishable location (Hinton, McClelland, & Rumelhart, 1986). That is, the overlap inherent in coarse coding schemes improves the effective spatial resolution of receptive fields. However, there is a cost to coarse coding: if multiple objects are presented close together, the resulting crosstalk from the combined patterns of activity will produce ambiguous coding. The important point is that in coarse coding schemes, the effect of noisy or degraded signals may be minimal if only a single location is being coded, or when multiple objects are activating distinct groups of receptive fields. As objects are brought closer together, and their associated sets of activated receptive fields overlap more and more, interference and coding errors should increase. Parametric and modelling studies of localization errors in TN, showing how localization errors vary with the distance between multiple objects, might enable us in the future to estimate the degree of receptive field overlap within the spatiotopic maps of the human pulvinar.

Alternative coordinate frames in the pulvinar

Recently, we have found that the spatiotopic maps damaged in patient TN are not strictly retinotopic. Instead, the maps seem sensitive to the positions of objects in the visual display. In these experiments, the target appeared in an upper, middle or lower position in the display, flanked either above or below by the distractor. In this way, performance at the same absolute target

location could be compared for targets relatively above and below the distractor. TN reported target identity, colour and relative position. As usual,
she also performed a demanding identification task at fixation and the stimulus display was presented briefly to prevent foveation of the stimuli. In
addition, TN's eye movements were monitored with EOG, and the occasional trials in which she moved before the offset of the stimulus display
were discarded.

Mislocalization errors in the contralesional field are shown in Figure 14.7,
as a function of relative target position. The columns in the figure represent
the same absolute (retinotopic) positions. Conjunction errors followed localization errors, and were rare when the target was in the relatively upper
location, but were much more frequent with relatively low targets. Thus the
impaired quadrant for TN is not well described by an exclusively retina-
based coordinate frame. Instead, the origin of the reference frame that we are
measuring seems to be at a point in between the two items competing for
attention, at least such that the "superior" field would be defined by every-
thing above this midpoint and the "inferior" field below it. We would suggest
that this origin reflects an attention or salience-based frame. That is, the
spatial coding of objects we see here may be determined by the relative
positions of objects with respect to the centre of attention.

Another form of spatial coding within the pulvinar has been observed in
single cell recordings within the monkey pulvinar. The receptive fields of
some cells recorded are not defined retinotopically. Instead, the position of
the eye in orbit modulates the firing rates of some cells (Robinson,

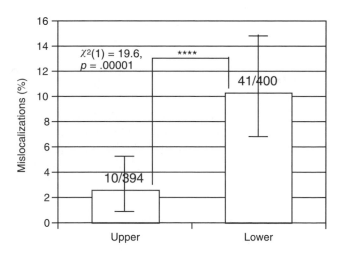

Figure 14.7 Mislocalizations as a function of relative target position. The absolute
retinal position of the target is the same. However, performance is
determined by the relative location of the target to the distractor.

McClurkin, & Kertzman, 1990). For example, the response to a given retinotopic stimulus may depend upon whether the eye is looking straight ahead
or upwards. However, a variety of other potential frames, such as head-
based, body-based and even action-based frames, have not yet been examined
in either the human or monkey. Taking these results together with our own,
we think it is likely that there are multiple spatial frames of reference
encoded within the pulvinar.

   Our results with TN have been especially informative, in that her lesion to
the pulvinar is very restricted, her deficits in binding are restricted to a single
quadrant, and she shows little or no signs of other visual deficits. However,
since our original report, we have now observed binding and spatial localization deficits in two other patients with focal pulvinar damage, although in
these cases the lesions are more extensive and affect binding within an entire
hemifield rather than a quadrant.

What pulvinar damage does not impair

For understanding the operation of a lesioned brain region, an understanding of preserved, as well as lost, performance is essential. As described
earlier, one function that seems generally preserved in our patients is the
ability to select items in the contralesional field. In other divided attention
tasks, we have also found equivalent latencies to contralesional and ipsilesional targets. We have already contrasted our results with parietal patients
demonstrating neglect and visual extinction, noting how parietal patients,
but not our pulvinar patients, are slowed in responses to the contralesional
field. However, a recent survey of subcortical patients demonstrating symptoms of neglect has suggested that damage to the pulvinar leads to spatial
neglect (Karnath, Himmelbach, & Rorden, 2002). The ultimate resolution to
this discrepancy awaits further research, but there are several important differences between the methods and results of Karnath et al. (2002) and our
own. First, the analysis of lesion overlap for thalamic patients used by
Karnath et al. (2002) results in a centre of overlap that appears to extend well
anterior to the posterior commissure marking the boundary of the pulvinar.
Thus it may be damage to the posterior thalamus anterior to the pulvinar
that results in signs of spatial neglect. Second, our patients have been tested
in their chronic state, many months after their haemorrhages. The patients
of Karnath et al. (2002) appear to have been tested while in hospital. As
Karnath et al. (2002) note, cognitive performance is not stable during this
period; for example, due to swelling, which may impinge upon undamaged
structures, or other forms of diaschisis. Third, the tests used by Karnath et al.
(2002) are readily applied bedside tests, which are clearly useful diagnostics,
but in themselves do not allow careful dissection of attentional processes.
For example, a line cancellation task may reflect impaired ability to orient
into contralesional space, impaired response activation from contralesional
objects, or even binding errors in contralesional space.

The study of Desimone et al. (1989) on pulvinar deactivation has also previously been described as evidence of a form of extinction (Duncan, Humphreys, & Ward, 1997). The idea being that in their task, with single contralesional targets, identification performance was unimpaired relative to controls; however, when there was a simultaneous distractor in the ipsilesional field, identification of the target became very difficult. There is certainly some analogy here with visual extinction, in which detection of contralesional targets is unimpaired when presented in isolation, but often shows a dramatic decline when presented with another ipsilesional target. However, our current findings suggest this analogy is mistaken, and that a better analogy is to the flanker task. The ipsilesional distractor in the study of Desimone et al. (1989) is acting like an incongruent, ipsilesional flanker in our flanker task. In both these situations, the presence of the non-target creates the potential for response conflict. It is in these situations of response conflict that we have observed deficits in contralesional response activation in the flanker task. The simplest account of all the data is that inactivation of the pulvinar in the study of Desimone et al. (1989) is slowing responses in the distractor condition, not due to a difficulty in contralesional orienting, but by preventing response activation and/or selection for contralesional objects, as in our flanker task.

However, the conclusion that contralesional slowing is not observed following pulvinar lesion needs to be qualified. In simple detection and left/right localization to isolated single targets tasks, we have observed contralesional slowing, as did Rafal and Posner (1987). Put another way, at present we find slowing to contralesional targets only under conditions in which selective attention demands are minimized, but not in tasks requiring selective attention and filtering. We have also noted circumstances in which patient SM can show some slowing in addition to response activation deficits in his contralesional field.

A second, related, preserved ability in our patients is the ability to filter distractor response activation. As emphasized in our studies with the flanker task, pulvinar damage does not mean that contralesional distractors "pass through" attentional filters, or that contralesional distractors activate their associate responses to produce greater interference. Instead, we see less contralesional response activation. Previous evidence, used to argue that the pulvinar was involved in filtering, can be easily interpreted to argue for a role in response activation. In particular, what LaBerge and Buchsbaum (1990) showed is that the contralateral pulvinar is active in a task that involves identifying and responding to a lateralized target letter with flanking distractor letters. Again, as in the study of Desimone et al. (1989), the target and the distractors are signalling conflicting responses, replicating the incongruent conditions of our flanker task. The result, showing activation of the contralateral pulvinar in conditions of response competition, is exactly what we would expect—not because the pulvinar is filtering the distractor, but because the pulvinar is active in contralateral response activation and selection. This interpretation of the data fits both the imaging results and the results from our flanker task.

We have also looked at the generation of inhibition of return (IOR) in the contralesional and ipsilesional field of the pulvinar group (Danziger et al., 2001). In the simple cueing task we used, a brief cue preceded a lateralized target by a variable temporal interval. The cue was either valid, appearing in the location of the subsequent target, or invalid, appearing on the other side. The well-established finding in this task with normal populations is an interaction of cue validity with temporal interval: at short intervals, there is typically facilitation for valid over invalid trials; at longer intervals, this pattern reverses, so that responses are actually faster at the invalid than the valid cue location. This pattern has been taken to indicate that shortly after the cue onset, attention is drawn automatically to the cue location; however, unless the target appears soon after that, attention is withdrawn and the location inhibited so that it does not return. This inhibition of return has been argued to support a primitive system for ensuring exploration of the environment and for avoiding errors in perseveration of search to the same targets.

In testing the patient group, we compared the generation of IOR for cues presented to the contralesional and ipsilesional field. The results were consistent with normal performance. Patients TN and GJ showed the standard interaction of cue validity with time: early facilitation followed by subsequent IOR. SM's mean latency was significantly slower than that of the other patients (in this task as in other speeded tasks), and he showed an advantage for invalid over valid trials at both the short and long SOAs. This lack of early facilitation, in the presence of later IOR, is not surprising: early facilitation is much less robust than the later IOR, especially when responses are slowed or difficult, as they apparently are in SM's case. What is crucial is that these patterns of performance were equivalent in the contralesional and ipsilesional fields—that is, inhibition of the cued location was generated in a similar way in both fields. This result with the pulvinar patients contrasts with an earlier case study of damage to the superior colliculus (Sapir, Soroker, Berger, & Henik, 1999). In this case, IOR was observed in the ipsilesional field only.

Summary

We are exploring selective attention and response control in a group of patients with focal lesions to the pulvinar. In particular, we have examined the notions that the pulvinar is involved in filtering and in orienting to the contralesional field. We have not found evidence to support these views. Instead, we see that the pulvinar is involved in a variety of binding operations. We have seen that, in cases of response conflict, the pulvinar is important for response activation and selection. We have also seen that the pulvinar is important for generating the spatial codes needed to bind together stimulus features. It may be possible that one type of binding can be subsumed by the other. That is, it may be possible to re-characterize response conflict in the flanker task, as we have used it, into a problem of feature binding. By such a characterization, conditions promoting response conflict are also promoting potential stimulus binding errors. Alternatively, our illusory conjunction tasks could be characterized as a situation for response competition, in which the target and distractor are signalling conflicting responses. We hope to explore these possibilities in future studies. In any case, the conclusion that the pulvinar is involved in binding of stimuli to responses and stimulus features to each other is appealing, because it suggests a value to the extensive connectivity of this region. However, it is unlikely that a single function, even one as broadly construed as "binding", will be an adequate characterization of such a complex brain region. Already we have seen that there may be a dissociable system, located within the medial pulvinar, for response to threat. The medial pulvinar is connected to the amygdala (Jones & Burton, 1976), as well as other structures important for reward conditioning (Romanski et al., 1997); and we are finding that damage to this area slows or prevents some forms of threat assessment.

References

Arguin, M., Cavanagh, P., & Joanette, Y. (1994). Visual feature integration with an attention deficit. *Brain and Cognition, 24*, 44–56.

Armstrong, E. (1982). Mosaic evolution in the primate brain: differences and similarities in the hominoid thalamus. In A. Armstrong & D. Falk (Eds.), *Primate brain evolution: methods and concepts* (pp. 131–161). New York: Plenum Press.

Ashby, F. G., Prinzmetal, W., Ivry, R., & Maddox, W. T. (1996). A formal theory of feature binding in object perception. *Psychological Review, 103*, 165–192.

Bender, D. B. (1981). Retinotopic organization of the macaque pulvinar. *Journal of Neurophysiology, 46*, 672–693.

Bender, D. B., & Youakim, M. (2001). Effect of attentive fixation in macaque thalamus and cortex. *Journal of Neurophysiology, 85*, 219–234.

Browne, B., & Simmons, R. M. (1984). Quantitative studies of the evolution of the thalamus in primates. *Journal für Hirnforschung, 25*, 261–274.

Cohen, A., & Ivry, R. (1989). Illusory conjunctions inside and outside the focus of attention. *Journal of Experimental Psychology: Human Perception and Performance, 15*, 650–663.

Cohen, A., Ivery, R., Rafal, R., & Kohn, C. (1995). Response code activation by stimuli in the neglected visual field. *Neuropsychology, 9*, 165–173.

Cohen, A., & Rafal, R. D. (1991). Attention and feature integration: illusory conjunctions in a patient with parietal lobe lesions. *Psychological Science, 2*, 106–110.

Corbetta, M., Miezin, F. M., Dobmeyer, S., Shulman, G. L., & Petersen, S. E. (1990). Attentional modulation of neural processing of shape, color, and velocity in humans. *Science, 248*, 1556–1559.

Danziger, S., Ward, R., Owen, V., & Rafal, R. (2001). The effects of unilateral pulvinar damage in humans on reflexive orienting and filtering of irrelevant information. *Behavioural Neurology, 13*, 95–104.

Danziger, S., Ward, R., Owen, V., & Rafal, R. (2004). Contributions of the human pulvinar to a distributed network for selective attention. *Journal of Cognitive, Affective, and Behavioral Neuroscience, 4,* 89–99.

Darian-Smith, C., Darian-Smith, I., & Cheema, S. S. (1990). Thalamic projects to sensorimotor cortex in the newborn macaque. *Journal of Comparative Neurology, 299,* 47–63.

Dennett, D. C. (1991). *Consciousness explained.* London: Penguin.

Desimone, R., Wessinger, M., Thomas, L., & Schneider, W. (1989). Effects of deactivation of the lateral pulvinar or superior colliculus on the ability to selectively attend to a visual stimulus. *Society for Neuroscience Abstracts, 15,* 162.

Duncan, J. (1993). Similarity between concurrent visual discriminations: dimensions and objects. *Perception and Psychophysics, 54,* 425–430.

Duncan, J., Humphreys, G. W., & Ward, R. (1997). Competitive brain activity in visual attention. *Current Opinion in Neurobiology, 7,* 255–261.

Eriksen, B. A., & Eriksen, C. W. (1974). Effects of noise letters upon the identification of a target letter in a non search task. *Perception and Psychophysics, 16,* 143–149.

Friedman-Hill, S. R., Robertson, L. C., & Treisman, A. (1995). Parietal contributions to visual feature binding: evidence from a patient with bilateral lesions. *Science, 269,* 853–855.

Guillery, R. W. (1995). Anatomical evidence concerning the role of the thalamus in corticocortical communications. *Journal of Anatomy, 187,* 583–592.

Guillery, R. W., & Sherman, S. M. (2002). Thalamic relay functions and their role in corticocortical communication: generalizations from the visual system. *Neuron, 33,* 163–175.

Hinton, G. E., McClelland, J. L., & Rumelhart, D. E. (1986). Distributed representations. In D. E. Rumelhart & J. L. McClelland (Eds.), *Parallel distributed processing: Vol. 1: Foundations* (pp. 77–109). Cambridge, MA: MIT Press.

Jones, E. G., & Burton, H. (1976). A projection from the medial pulvinar to the amygdala in primates. *Brain Research, 104,* 142–147.

Karnath, H. O., Himmelbach, M., & Rorden, C. (2002). The subcortical anatomy of human spatial neglect: putamen, caudate nucleus, and pulvinar. *Brain, 125,* 350–360.

LaBerge, D. (1995). Computational and anatomical models of selective attention in object identification. In M. S. Gazzaniga (Ed.), *The cognitive neurosciences* (pp. 649–663). Cambridge, MA: MIT Press.

LaBerge, D., & Buchsbaum, M. S. (1990). Positron emission tomographic measurements of pulvinar activity during an attention task. *Journal of Neuroscience, 10,* 613–619.

LaBerge, D., Carter, M., & Brown, V. (1992). A network simulation of thalamic circuit operations in selective attention. *Neural Computation, 4,* 318–331.

Morris, J. S., Friston, K. J., & Dolan, R. J. (1997). Neural responses to salient visual stimuli. *Proceedings of the Royal Society of London B, 264,* 769–775.

Olshausen, B. A., Anderson, C. H., & Van Essen, D. C. (1993). A neurobiological model of visual attention and invariant pattern recognition based on dynamic routing of information. *Journal of Neuroscience, 13,* 4700–4719.

Petersen, S. E., Robinson, D. L., & Morris, J. D. (1987). Contributions of the pulvinar to visual spatial attention. *Neuropsychologia, 25,* 97–105.

Prinzmetal, W., Diedrichsen, J., & Ivry, R. B. (2001). Illusory conjunctions are alive and well: a reply to Donk (1999). *Journal of Experimental Psychology: Human Perception and Performance, 27, 538–541.*

Prinzmetal, W., Henderson, D., & Ivry, R. (1995). Loosening the constraints on illusory conjunctions: assessing the role of exposure duration and attention. *Journal of Experimental Psychology: Human Perception and Performance, 21, 1362–1375.*

Prinzmetal, W., Ivry, R. B., Beck, D., & Shimizu, N. (2002). A measurement theory of illusory conjunctions. *Journal of Experimental Psychology: Human Perception and Performance, 28, 251–269.*

Prinzmetal, W., & Keysar, B. (1989). A functional theory of illusory conjunctions and neon colors. *Journal of Experimental Psychology: General, 118, 165–190.*

Rafal, R. D., & Posner, M. I. (1987). Deficits in human visual spatial attention following thalamic lesions. *Proceedings of the National Academy of Science, USA, 84, 7349–7353.*

Rafal, R. D., Gershberg, F., Egly, R., Ivry, R., Kingstone, A., & Ro, T. (1996). Response channel activation and the lateral prefrontal cortex. *Neuropsychologia, 34, 1197–1202.*

Raichle, M. E., Fiez, J. A., Videen, T. O., MacLeod, A. M. K., Pardo, J. V., Fox, P. T. et al. (1994). Practice-related changes in human brain functional anatomy during nonmotor learning. *Cerebral Cortex, 4, 8–26.*

Robinson, D. L., & Cowie, R. J. (1997). The primate pulvinar: structural, functional, and behavioral components of visual salience. In M. Steridade, E. G. Jones, & D. A. McCormick (Eds.), *The thalamus* (Vol. I, pp. 53–92). Amsterdam: Elsevier.

Robinson, D. L., McClurkin, J. W., & Kertzman, C. (1990). Orbital position and eye movement influences on visual responses in the pulvinar nuclei of the behaving macaque. *Experimental Brain Research, 82, 235–246.*

Robinson, D. L., & Petersen, S. E. (1992). The pulvinar and visual salience. *Trends in Neuroscience, 15, 127–132.*

Romanski, L. M., Giguere, M., Bates, J. F., & Goldman-Rakic, P. S. (1997). Topographic organization of medial pulvinar connections with the prefrontal cortex in the rhesus monkey. *Journal of Comparative Neurology, 379, 313–332.*

Sapir, A., Soroker, N., Berger, A., & Henik, A. (1999). Inhibition of return in spatial attention: direct evidence for collicular generation. *Nature Neuroscience, 2, 1053–1054.*

Singer, W., & Gray, C. M. (1995). Visual feature integration and the temporal correlation hypothesis. *Annual Review of Neuroscience, 18, 555–586.*

Treisman, A. (1996). The binding problem. *Current Opinion in Neurobiology, 6, 171–178.*

Treisman, A., & Schmidt, H. (1982). Illusory conjunctions in the perception of objects. *Cognitive Psychology, 14, 107–141.*

Vandenberghe, R., Duncan, J., Dupont, P., Ward, R., Poline, J., Bormans, G. et al. (1997). Attention to one or two features in left or right visual field: A positron emission tomography study. *Journal of Neuroscience, 17, 3739–3750.*

Ward, R., Danziger, S., Owen, V., & Rafal, R. (2002). Deficits in spatial coding and feature binding following damage to spatiotopic maps in the human pulvinar. *Nature Neuroscience, 5, 99–100.*

Webster, M. J., Bachevalier, J., & Ungerleider, L. G. (1993). Subcortical connections of inferior temporal areas TE and TEO in macaque monkeys. *Journal of Comparative Neurology, 335, 73–91.*

Wolford, E., & Shum, K. H. (1980). Evidence for feature perturbations. *Perception and Psychophysics, 55*, 350–358.

Yeterian, E. H., & Pandya, D. N. (1985). Corticothalamic connections of the posterior parietal cortex in the rhesus monkey. *Journal of Cognitive Neuroscience, 237*, 408–426.

Yeterian, E. H., & Pandya, D. N. (1997). Corticothalamic connections of extrastriate visual areas in rhesus monkeys. *Journal of Comparative Neurology, 378*, 562–585.

Author index

Subject index